PROVINCE, CITY & PEOPLE

The City Hall, Belfast

PROVINCE, CITY & PEOPLE

Belfast and its Region

Edited by R.H. Buchanan & B.M. Walker

Published by Greystone Books in association with the Northern Ireland Committee of the British Association for the Advancement of Science

First published in the United Kingdom 1987 by
Greystone Books, Greystone Road, Antrim
Northern Ireland

© Greystone Books Ltd, 1987

in association with
the British Association for the Advancement
of Science, Local Committee

The Queen's University of Belfast and the British Association, Northern Ireland
Committee, wish to acknowledge the generous financial contribution made by
Belfast City Council towards the cost of publishing this volume.

The views expressed in this volume are those of individual authors and are not
the responsibility of either the editors or the Local Committee of the British
Association.

Frontispiece: The City Hall, Belfast

Cover design: Rodney Miller Associates (with photographs by Chris Hill)

Printed in Northern Ireland by W&G Baird Ltd.

ISBN 1 870157 01

Contents

BLACK AND WHITE ILLUSTRATIONS

COLOUR ILLUSTRATIONS

Foreword

"In its natural history, its folk-history, even in the pattern of its society, Ulster still stands a little apart from Great Britain. Its scenery, its dialects, its farms, even some of the brands of merchandise it advertises, are refreshingly different, and to analyse the differences is a challenge to the scientifically trained observer."

These words, from my distinguished predecessor, Dr Eric Ashby, now Lord Ashby, were part of the foreword of the book *Belfast in its regional setting* which was published to mark the Meeting of the British Association for the Advancement of Science at Queen's University in September 1952. Thirty five years later, his words remain true. As a relative newcomer to this attractive Province I am too aware that Ulster remains refreshingly different. As we strive to maintain and, where possible, to surpass the high standards of our sister institutions and regions in other parts of the United Kingdom, we are highly appreciative of the positive and attractive quality of life in Ulster which is not always obvious to visitors who may have grown accustomed to the more familiar headlines which are associated with this part of the world. The educational system in Northern Ireland produces excellent results, the many facilities for outdoor recreation and entertainment are unsurpassed, and Ulster people are particularly warm and hospitable. I am confident that visitors to the BA Meeting in Belfast this year will find this out for themselves.

The purpose of this book is to record in some depth the character and setting of the historic city of Belfast within its scenically-attractive region. Fourteen of my colleagues from Queen's and other expert contributors, have outlined various aspects of the life of Belfast and the surrounding region, ranging from its resource base and built environment, to patterns of work and patterns of society. In the latter context, a member of the Arts Council of Northern Ireland has outlined the lively cultural and artistic life of the local community, in which we at the University play our full part. For example, the Belfast Festival at Queen's, which we present each November in association with the Arts Council, is one of the largest University-based Festivals in Europe, and second only to the Edinburgh Festival in its range and quality of performers.

Down the years, many citizens of this City and Province have made distinguished contributions to science and technology, and in some instances, the result of their work was presented at earlier meetings of the British Association. In this age of instant communication, though not necessarily of greater understanding, some people may wonder why such a large group of experts, participants and observers gather together each year in a major British city to present nationally, and to the world, some of the latest trends, discoveries, impacts and achievements in the world of science in its widest sense. The main objective is, of course, to use the advances in technology, the latest developments in radio, television and print technology, and the most modern techniques to broadcast this message from a central point to the widest audience possible.

There is the added advantage that a BA Meeting generates its own momentum and its very distinctive atmosphere and character each year. It is our privilege to welcome the BA back to Belfast and to add something of our own ethos, both in scientific and in human terms.

It is my firm belief that the world of science, of universities and of learning is not only about such matters as statistics, data, theories and information, but also about people. And what better way to get to know one another than to meet for several days in one place, and with a common purpose?

This is an important occasion for Belfast, for Northern Ireland and for Queen's University. It is my hope that it will prove also to be an important occasion for the British Association for the Advancement of Science. I commend to you this book, not only as setting the underlying scene for this meeting, but as providing a most fitting souvenir of this historic occasion in the life of a University, its Province and its people.

Gordon S.G. Beveridge
Vice-Chancellor
The Queen's University of Belfast

1 Province, City & People

R. H. BUCHANAN

Director, Institute of Irish Studies, The Queen's University of Belfast

This is my home and country. Later on
perhaps I'll find this nation is my own
but here and now it is enough to love
this faulted ledge, this map of cloud above,
and the great sea that beats against the west to swamp the sun.

from *Conacre* John Hewitt

Thirty-five years ago, when the British Association for the Advancement of Science last met in Belfast, Northern Ireland was a largely unknown territory to most of the delegates who travelled by cross-channel steamer from the Irish Sea ports of mainland Britain. A few had visited the Province previously as tourists; some had been stationed on its airfields and army camps during the war; but the majority knew little about this detached and distant part of the United Kingdom. Some visiting academics would have been familiar with sites of major scientific interest such as the Giant's Causeway in County Antrim, but on the whole, research papers relating to Ireland did not figure prominently in the national journals published in Britain. Even the general reader, seeking information on the Province's history or topography, would have found few books on the shelves of his local library: Hugh Shearman's *Ulster*, published by Robert Hale in 1949, or Estyn Evans' short but perceptive booklet *Northern Ireland*, published by Collins for the festival of Britain in 1951, might well have been the only works available.

Today the situation is very different. For nearly twenty years Northern Ireland has figured almost daily in the headlines of the world's press, its shattered buildings and grieving families visible testimony to the political violence and civil unrest which now seem almost endemic. Television, which thrives on such visual drama, has made the people of this once little known Province an all-too-familiar topic to their fellow citizens on the British mainland. Topicality however does not necessarily lead to

Belfast, 1979. This view looks west over the city centre to the Antrim hills on the skyline. The original site of the seventeenth century town was immediately inland of the twin bridges spanning the River Lagan. (C.F.S. Newman)

understanding, for the political problems are complex and difficult to interpret for the professional much less the layman. Not that endeavour has been lacking: on the contrary, as violence increased journalists and scholars converged on the Province from all corners of the world, and the output of learned work has been prodigious. Between 1968 and 1983, John Whyte estimates some two hundred books and nearly three thousand academic articles and papers were published on "The Northern Ireland Problem" (Whyte, 1983, 5). Given this volume of material, visitors to Northern Ireland today are much better informed than their predecessors, although they may be less aware of other aspects of life in the Province, or the way these too have changed during the period of the present "Troubles".

The book, *Belfast in its regional setting*, published to mark the 1952 visit of the British Association, may be taken as the base-line from which to judge the extent of change in the environment and in economic and social life. Planned by a committee chaired by the Queen's University geographer, Estyn Evans, and edited by his younger colleague, Emrys Jones, the book aimed to provide a wide ranging compendium of scientific information about the Province. It outlined the basic elements of its geology, climate and soils, flora and fauna, dealt with the human background from prehistoric to modern times, and provided a statement on the contemporary economy, education and social services, settlement and population. There were ommissions: for example, there is no systematic account of the Province's social or political structure, and, with the exception of the chapter on Belfast, few references to the sectarian differences which were to erupt in political violence late in the following decade. But the book itself was a notable achievement, as a synthesis of work in many disciplines, and a perceptive portrait of regional character.

The publication of *Belfast in its regional setting* marks the beginning of a new era of academic work within the Province, for its individual chapters raised many questions which stimulated the interest of the new generation of young scholars who came to work in Northern Ireland following the expansion of the university system in the 1960s and 1970s. Major developments ensued in the earth sciences, for example in archaeology, geology and geography; and publications followed, such as Emrys Jones' *A social geography of Belfast* (1960), *Land use in Northern Ireland* (1963), edited by Leslie Symons; and *Irish geographical studies* (1970) edited by Nicholas Stephens and Robin Glasscock. New academic disciplines were established at Queen's University, including sociology, social anthropology and town and country planning, and two new institutions were founded, the New University of Ulster and the Northern Ireland Polytechnic – both now combined in the University of Ulster. Academics in these and other disciplines have contributed to an information explosion in publications relating to the Province which must equal that in the field of political science, to which reference has already been made.

The present book concentrates on some of the major changes which have occurred in Northern Ireland since 1952. It does not attempt to provide a new synthesis, but instead is selective, examining areas in which change has been greatest and topics which may have been under-represented in the earlier volume. Each chapter has been contributed by a specialist in the area concerned, the authors being drawn mainly from the academic staffs of the Province's two universities. The present chapter is intended to provide an introduction rather than a summary of what follows, and, where possible, it links the contents of the present work with material presented in the earlier volume.

Natural resources and environment

Few parts of Ireland or Great Britain can equal the variety of landscape and scenery to be found within the Province, with its diversity of compact mountains and extensive uplands, its lake-filled lowlands and broad valleys. A glance at the map (Figure 1) shows that Lough Neagh is the hub of the eastern lowlands, fed by the River Bann which neatly bisects the Province on its long journey from the Mournes in south Down to the

Whitepark Bay, Co. Antrim. One of the finest stretches of the north Antrim coast, with the Island of Rathlin in the distance. (N.I. Tourist Board)

Atlantic coast of north Antrim. East of the Bann, the Antrim plateau tilts gently upward to meet the North Channel in a spectacular coastline of cliff and deep-cut glen, and fronts the Lagan Valley above Belfast in the finely etched profile of the Cave Hill. Further south the lowlands of County Down stretch inland, interrupted along the low eastern coast by the inward curve of the sea lough of Strangford. The Mourne Mountains, rearing upward from the sandy shores of Dundrum Bay, dominate southern County Down, and together with the Carlingford Mountains of County Louth and Slieve Gullion in south Armagh they provide the Province with its most dramatic mountain group. The Sperrin Mountains, which lie to the west of the Bann in Counties Londonderry and Tyrone, have a more gentle profile, and merge almost imperceptibly with the bog-strewn uplands of the west, drained by the river systems of the Foyle and the Erne. The latter is perhaps the most scenic of the Province's lowland areas, with its intricate system of lakes, drumlin islands and slow-moving rivers backed by the bare ridges of millstone grit and limestone, Pennine-like in character, which here form the boundary between Fermanagh and the Counties of Cavan and Leitrim in the Republic of Ireland.

Northern Ireland's varied scenery is largely explained by its geological structure, which includes rocks of virtually every age, from the most ancient Pre-Cambrian rocks to the most recent. The Dalradian schists which form the Sperrins and the slatey rocks of Lower Palaeozoic age which underlie Armagh and Down are among the oldest in the Province, and are linked structurally with the Highlands of Scotland and the Southern Uplands respectively. Younger rocks of Devonian and Carboniferous age found in Fermanagh and south Tyrone, are northern extensions of those which form the Central Lowlands of Ireland; but the most widespread rocks are the basalts, intruded through the older rocks in Tertiary times and which now cover some 4,000 km^2 in the north-east of the Province. These have been weathered to form some of the better soils, as J.G. Cruickshank shows in Chapter 2. None of these rock outcrops contains minerals capable of economic exploitation, although structural similarities with the Central Lowlands of Scotland have long suggested that coal deposits, similar to those of Lanarkshire and Sterling, may lie buried deep beneath the basalts of south Antrim. Exploration through the basalt was not possible until the 1960s, when the search for oil provided both the incentive and the finance for the deep boring made necessary by the thickness of the overlying deposits. Hydrocarbons have not been found in economic quantities, either along the north coast, or inland; but as A.E. Griffith and his associates show in Chapter 3, extensive deposits of lignite have been discovered at Bally-money in north Antrim, and to the west and east of Lough Neagh, at Coagh and Crumlin respectively. The finds are of considerable importance, for hitherto the Province has been entirely dependent on imported raw materials for fuel and for industry. The rising cost of electric power during the oil crises of the 1970s was a major problem for local industry and for the domestic consumer, and government subsidies were required to keep prices at a competitive level. Experiments with wind and wave power as alternative sources of energy, and the proposal for a tidal barrage across the mouth of Strangford Lough, have not proved economically feasible at present; and with no prospect of a direct link to the electricity or natural gas grids in Britain, lignite is highly attractive as a new local fuel source for generating electricity. Trial open-cast mining has already been undertaken at Crumlin, and proposals are currently under consideration for a new lignite-based power station located nearby.

Demand for electric power in modern society is matched only by that for water, and here too new sources have had to be found, as more domestic users were connected to mains supply in rural areas and new industries were established. Until the early 1970s, local authorities had this responsibility, and demand was largely met from local sources, the exception being Belfast which drew its main supplies from two large reservoirs in the Mourne Mountains. Following the reorganisation of local government, the Department of the Environment's newly established Water Service began to look for additional sources, large enough to cater for the Province's

Border Country: a typical lowland landscape of scattered farmsteads and small fields near the land border with the Republic of Ireland. Aughnacloy, County Tyrone. (N.C. Mitchell)

anticipated needs to the end of the century. Demand is heaviest in the Belfast urban area and in the eastern counties, and initial plans favoured an increase in supply from the Mournes and the development of Lough Neagh as a major source. Conservation groups were strongly opposed to further water abstraction from the Mournes, and the original plans were substantially altered following a public enquiry; but fuller use of Lough Neagh involves problems of water treatment and increased costs in pumping supplies to the main centres of population. The Lough represents the Province's largest source of fresh water and one of its most important natural resources: as Brian Wood shows in Chapter 4, commercial fishing of eels alone provides considerable local employment and exports worth several million pounds. But like all the Province's water systems, Lough Neagh is vulnerable to pollution; from sewage, accidental discharge or seepage from slurry and silage, and run-off from fields spread with artificial fertiliser.

Demand for increased productivity from agriculture has led to modifications in many of the Province's rivers through the implementation of major schemes for arterial drainage during the past decade. With a relatively high rainfall and often impermeable soils, field drainage is essential for agriculture, and the gentle gradients of river systems like the Bann and the Erne have required extensive engineering treatment to increase flow. Adverse comment from angling and amenity groups led to modifications in the schemes proposed for the Rivers Main and Blackwater, both of which drain into Lough Neagh, in recognition of the importance of fish stocks for recreation and tourism. Lough Erne for example, is outstanding for coarse fishing, and its amenities have been greatly improved both by the local council and the Department of Agriculture. It now ranks as an important centre for tourism within the Province, with a large fleet of hire cruisers and an established reputation among visitors, including many from central Europe. Game fishing also attracts visitors to the upland areas of the west, and although stocks of salmon have declined severely in recent years the Foyle system is still one of the major salmon fisheries in Europe (Wilcock, 1982, 63). Both Lough Foyle in County Londonderry and Strangford Lough in County Down are of international significance for another form of wildlife, the geese and duck which come in winter to these food-rich and sheltered sealoughs. Strangford also attracts large numbers of breeding seabirds in summer, and with its rich marine life it is a prime area for conservation and for outdoor recreation, especially yachting and other water-sports.

In the 1950s there was little public recognition that areas like Strangford might need special legislation to protect their wildlife and natural environment. Such legislation was enacted in Britain in 1949, but despite pressure from voluntary bodies such as the Ulster Society for the Preservation of the Countryside, no similar legislation was passed in Northern Ireland until 1965 (Buchanan, 1982). Since then, as Professor Newbould shows in Chapter 5, protection of wildlife habitats has proceeded along lines similar to that in Britain, except that statutory designation for purposes both of nature conservation and countryside amenity is here the responsibility of the Department of the Environment. In effect, the Department exercises the functions which in Britain are undertaken mainly by two independent bodies, the Nature Conservancy and the Countryside Commission, and although the system works effectively in many respects it is not without critics (Chapter 6). Failure to designate National Parks for example, is seen by many conservationists as a major defect in current policy, since as yet there are no alternative structures for providing effective resource management over extensive tracts of the Province's most scenic areas. Opposition by farming interests has been a major political obstacle to designation in the past, but these same areas have been adversely affected by current changes in the agricultural policies of the European Community. The Community now recognises that new forms of land use and employment are urgently needed, and there is every possibility that new policies for conservation and outdoor recreation could generate new additional sources of income, alongside farming and forestry. This will require a much higher degree of policy co-ordination and management than has existed in the past, not least because these areas are the responsibility of a bewildering number of statutory boards and authorities, of funding agencies and different branches and tiers of government. Experiments with the administrative concept of Integrated Rural Development (Chapter 6) would seem highly appropriate for these areas at the present time.

The increase in government bureaucracy during the past thirty years is well exemplified by the development of a Planning Service, formerly a function of local government, but since 1972, one of the many responsibilities of the Department of the Environment. In the early 1950s, physical planning was in its infancy: Northern Ireland had no equivalent of the 1947 Town and Country Planning Act in Britain, and the Provincial government, conservative in its attitude and in its politics, was not convinced of the need for such legislation. A Planning Advisory Board, chaired by the then Vice-Chancellor of Queen's University, warned of the problems of continued suburban expansion and ribbon development around Belfast, but its 1947 Report was ignored by the government of the day. By 1960 however, land use and housing problems in the Belfast urban area had become so acute that the government was moved to act: Professor Robert Matthew of the University of Edinburgh was appointed as a consultant to prepare a plan for the Belfast region, and his 1962 Report laid the foundations for subsequent policy and legislation. Matthew followed the planning orthodoxy of his time, advocating a policy of constraints to the continued expansion of Belfast City, and encouragement to growth in several of its satellite towns as well as in a new city, later named Craigavon, created by linking the towns of Lurgan and Portadown. Matthew's brief was limited to the eastern counties, but his growth centre strategy was accepted by the government's economic consultant, Professor Tom Wilson, and extended to the rest of the Province. As J.V. Greer and P.M. Jess show in Chapter 6, these policies remained in vogue throughout the growth decade of the 1960s, until their revision was made necessary by the economic recession of the 1970s.

The combination of recession and civil unrest had a particularly serious effect upon the Province's two major cities, Belfast and Londonderry. Employment was severely affected as government's attempts to attract new industry began to falter, and even the vigorous man-made fibres sector established during the 1960s, faced increasing difficulties as the price of oil continued to rise. Housing problems in both cities were exacerbated by the "Troubles", especially in Belfast, where the destruction of property and flight to safer residential areas resulted in a major redistribution of population, especially in the western areas of the city. The sectarian boundaries between Roman Catholic and Protestant, first mapped by Estyn Evans in 1944 and revised by Emrys Jones for the British Association volume of 1952, were redefined once more through street violence and paramilitary activity as F.W. Boal has shown (Chapter 7). But the urban dereliction caused by the recession and terrorist bombs have also provided an opportunity for reconstruction, and an unprecedented level of public investment and rebuilding has been undertaken during the past decades. In Belfast for example, the shipyard has been re-equipped with building and dry-dock facilities second to none in Europe; the harbour has invested in major new facilities for both bulk and unit loading; the city is now bisected by a through-way linking the Province's two motorways, with greatly improved access and parking in the city centre; and massive schemes are underway for a new, centre-city shopping area.

Perhaps the greatest change has been in housing, a constant source of friction between City Council and government throughout the post-war period which was finally resolved in 1972, when the Northern Ireland Housing Executive became the Province's sole public housing authority. The background to the city's housing problem and its resolution is examined by D.A. Singleton in Chapter 8, but it should be stressed that inadequate housing was not only an urban phenomenon. A survey undertaken forty years ago by John Mogey in County Fermanagh noted: "There are more houses inhabited which are classified as unfit for human life than there are satisfactory dwellings ...." Only 8 per cent of rural houses had a w.c. and piped water supply. He added: "The rural problem is more serious than in other areas of the United Kingdom, because it affects 40 per cent of the population of Ulster" (Mogey, 1947, 207). Today mains water is available throughout the Province; virtually all houses in rural areas are connected to the electricity grid; and housing provision and standards in both the public and private sectors are the equal of those in the city.

Economy, work and politics

Most of the infrastructure, together with the road network described in Chapter 9, was planned and executed before the worst effects of the recession were felt in the mid-1970s. As C.W. Jefferson shows in Chapter 10, this has had a disastrous effect on the Province's economy, with major job losses in manufacturing and agriculture; only the service sector has grown during the past decade, and Northern Ireland has become increas-

Belfast: the city hall dominates the city centre which has still remarkably few high-rise buildings. (N.I. Tourist Board)

ingly dependent on public expenditure to maintain employment. The "Troubles", he notes, have resulted in some loss of jobs, but to a great extent these have been offset by new opportunities in the security services and in the construction industry. Nonetheless, unemployment has continued to grow during the past decade: it now stands at 20 per cent of the labour force, and as Jefferson remarks, the present levels seem set to continue at least into the next decade. Not that the Province's employment record is unique: the pattern in the Belfast urban area is similar to that of Glasgow, Liverpool and Newcastle. Where it differs from the other peripheral regions of Britain is the high unemployment in rural areas and country towns, like Strabane with its appalling level of 52 per cent male unemployment. This reflects the lack of alternative employment in rural areas, made all the worse by farm amalgamation which has more than halved the number of holdings in the Province since 1951: 20,000 holdings alone have gone during the past decade. Even so, many thousands of farms are still too small to provide an adequate standard of living, a point of major concern since agriculture still employs 10 per cent of the work force in Northern Ireland, compared with 2 per cent in England and Wales. Farming in the Province is likely to become more precarious in the coming decade, following major changes in the Common Agricultural Policy announced in December 1986. These aim to reduce the current surplus in beef and dairy products within the Community, thus affecting the two major products of Ulster farms. Since average farm income is estimated to have fallen by 48 per cent in 1985 alone, the prospect for agriculture is not encouraging. As W.I. Hunter indicates in Chapter 11, there is now an urgent need to diversify, to seek new land uses and alternative employment.

Already many country people have moved to urban areas; nearly 75 per cent of the Province's population live in towns compared with 56 per cent in 1951, and almost half are to be found within 25 to 30 kms radius of Belfast. Most of this movement occurred during the 1950s and 1960s, for as P.A. Compton shows the proportion of total population living west of the Bann actually increased slightly during the decade 1971-1981; only the most remote rural areas continued to lose population. Meantime in Belfast, people continued to leave the older residential districts. The area administered by the City Council lost some 25 per cent of its population during the same decade, as population rose in the outer suburbs and in neighbouring towns like Antrim, Bangor, Lisburn and Newtownards. Many city people it seems are seeking safer locations and better housing away from the inner city, and the rural unemployed are simply staying where they are. Dr Compton's analysis of the 1981 Census in Chapter 12 also reveals increasing denominational segregation, a demographic response, as he remarks, to eighteen years of political tensions and uncertainty. Most aspects of life in Northern Ireland have been affected by these tensions; many families have suffered great personal tragedy through the deaths of relatives and the loss of houses and possessions, and an entire generation of young people have come to accept bomb scares and security searches as part of "normal" life.

The reasons behind the present civil unrest in Northern Ireland are complex, but the ingredients are to be found in many modern states, where there is a mixture of ethnic, cultural, social, religious and political groups. Diversity is common, and although animosities may occasionally erupt into outright violence very rarely is this on a scale sufficient to undermine the integrity of the state and its institutions. Usually issues are resolved and compromise achieved through the established political and legislative processes. The reasons why this has not been the case in Northern Ireland are explained in the penultimate chapters of this book which look at the political issues and events of the last eighteen years. The political analysis, by B.M. Walker and P. Arthur, is preceded by an account of the administrative changes that have occurred during this same period, as successsive British governments have experimented with different froms of legislature and government in an attempt to achieve political accommodation between the opposing Nationalist and Unionist parties (Chapter 14). Institutional reforms initiated in the 1970s are described by S. Elliott and R.A. Wilford; these include several designed specifically to deal with discrimination in employment, long a contentious issue and one of even greater moment now when new jobs are few and great efforts are being made to attract foreign investment. In Chapter 13, R.D. Osborne examines the basis for the

Ulster people, personified by Michael Murphy, a folklorist, broadcaster and short-story writer who has spent most of his life in the countryside around Slieve Gullion in County Armagh. (Arts Council)

allegations concerning discrimination, noting the effect of geographical location and education on the occupational structure and employment of both religious groups. He concludes that present policies are effective as long as employers and government co-operate in their implementation.

Community divisions and identities

The innumerable personal tragedies of families caught up in the "Troubles" provide much material for the Province's artists and writers, many of whom have won international acclaim for their work during this time. Dramatists such as John Boyd, Brian Friel, Martin Lynch, Stewart Parker and Graham Reid have explored this rich vein in both historical and contemporary settings, while novelists like Brian Moore and Bernard MacLaverty have turned to broader themes. Most outstanding of all perhaps has been the writing of a group of contemporary poets, whose number includes Seamus Heaney, John Hewitt, Michael Longley, Maebh McGuckian, Paul Muldoon and James Simmons. Artists and musicians have also contributed to the extraordinarily vigorous cultural life of the Province during the 1970s and 1980s, a development in which the Arts Council has played a prominent role as the major public patron. Brian Ferran discusses its contribution in the concluding chapter, and also draws attention to the annual Belfast Arts Festival, organised by Queen's University. This has become one of the major arts festivals in the United Kingdom, providing a direct link between artists, musicians, poets and authors and the public at large.

Another feature of intellectual life in the Province during the past decade has been the growth of interest in local history, a movement which has resulted in the foundation of more than forty societies in different areas throughout Ulster. This growth of interest may arise in part from a search for communal identity and territorial affinity which is one of the broader questions raised by the "Troubles"; but it also owes much to the work of a generation of teachers, many of them former students of Estyn Evans, who taught Geography at Queen's University for more than forty years. Much of Evans' work related to Ireland, and both in his lectures and in his writing he laid emphasis on the role of field work and local study in the development of broader theories relating to the environment and to human history. He had a special interest in folk culture and tradition, believing that it provided a common bond which transcended community and sectarian divisions in Northern Ireland. Careful advocacy of his beliefs led ultimately to the establishment of the Ulster Folk Museum at Cultra near Belfast in 1961. Charged with illustrating "the way of life, past and present, of the people of Northern Ireland", the Museum has acted as a powerful stimulus in kindling interest in the Province's rural past, just as the Ulster Museum in Belfast provides a rich source of material for archaeology and local history. Regional museums, supported by their respective district councils,

have also been established at Downpatrick and Enniskillen during the past
decade, joining the former County Museum at Armagh to provide an
important regional service. Both the Public Record Office and the Archaeological Survey of the Department of the Environment take considerable
pride in making their archives and material accessible to the public, and
both make a major contribution to increasing public awareness and maintaining interest in local history. Through these institutions, the state
preserves the documents and monuments of the past, while the care of the
finest country houses is in the hands of the National Trust, whose regional
committee looks after its properties in Northern Ireland. Public interest in
this heritage is reflected in articles in the local press and programmes on
radio and television; and in public reaction when an important prehistoric
site like Navan was recently threatened by quarrying. Archaeological
excavation shows that this legendary capital of early Ulster was a ritual
site of great complexity, and public concern about the quarry extension led
to a lengthy Planning Enquiry in 1985. The Planning Commission's
recommendation that the development be allowed was rejected by the
Minister, who cited as a primary reason for his decision, the expression of
increased public awareness in the importance of the site. One of the more
surprising features of the enquiry, is that opponents of the development
included both Nationalist and Unionist politicians; their joint action was a
rare display of public accord and a perhaps unwitting acknowledgement of
a sense of shared cultural identity (Mallory, 1987).

The question of identity lies at the root of the Northern Ireland problem,
for each community has a strongly-held perception of its origins. The
Roman Catholic sees himself as Irish, descended from the indigenous
population of Ireland and anxious to advance the political re-unification of
the country; the Protestant sees himself as British, settled in Northern
Ireland since the Plantations of the seventeenth century, and determined
to retain the constitutional link with Britain. For more than sixty years the
Province has been an integral part of the United Kingdom of Great Britain
and Northern Ireland, its status confirmed at countless elections, by the
vote of Unionists who are a majority in the community and guaranteed by
successive governments at Westminster. Protestant confidence in the
permanency of the union has been shaken however, by Britain's attempts
to accommodate the Nationalist viewpoint of the minority in the light of the
continuing violence of the past decades. This crisis of confidence reached its
peak with the signing of the Anglo-Irish Agreement in November 1985, for
to the Unionist community, this gave a foreign government, the Republic of
Ireland, an unprecedented right to interfere in the internal affairs of part of
the United Kingdom. For the Protestant, the old Unionist slogans "No
Surrender" and "Not an Inch" have once more become the rallying call of a
beleaguered garrison, rather than the triumphant proclamation of a powerful and secure elite.

In these circumstances it is not surprising that unionists have begun to
reassess their cultural origins, to look beyond the plantations for evidence
which might help to refute the nationalist gibe that they are colonists and

usurpers of Irish land. This search goes back to the legendary history which links Scotland with the north of Ireland in early times, from which the suggestion can be made that the Plantation was really a homecoming, the repossession of ancestral land rather than a colonial enterprise. There is a factual case for the Scottish connection, in archaeology and folk tradition as well as in legend; but there is always a danger that myth may be substituted for historical fact, especially when it enters the repertoire of the politician. Nevertheless, this search for a new identity does signal a break with the straight jacket of the recent past, and it could be developed in constructive ways if there is an honest desire for dialogue. Ian Adamson expresses this point of view in his book *The identity of Ulster* (1981, xi):

> The complete expression of the native Ulster tradition, broader than Irish Protestantism and Catholicism, and populist in sentiment, could prepare for the political development of a new Ulster based on co-operative democracy.

The need for a new beginning will become very evident to those who read this book, for the main resource of Northern Ireland is its people. The divisions of the past have not only squandered precious lives in futile violence; they have also diverted energy and talent which should have been concentrated on the economic and social development which the Province so greatly needs.

References

Adamson, Ian, 1981. *The Identity of Ulster*. Belfast.
Buchanan, R.H., 1982. Landscape, *in* Cruickshank, J.G. and Wilcock, D.N., (eds) *Northern Ireland: environment and natural resources*. Belfast.
Evans, E.E., 1944. Belfast: the site of the city *in Ulster J. Archaeol.*, 7, 25-29.
Mallory, J., 1987. The saving of Navan *in Antiquity*, 61, 64-6.
Mogey, J.M., 1947. *Rural life in Northern Ireland*. Oxford.
Warner, Alan (ed.), 1981. *The selected John Hewitt*. Belfast.
Whyte, J.H., 1983. *Is research on the Northern Ireland problem worth while?* Belfast.
Wilcock, D.N., 1982. Rivers, *in* Cruickshank, J.G. and Wilcock, D.N., (eds) *Northern Ireland: environment and natural resources*. Belfast. 43-71.

LAND & RESOURCES

Land & Land Use

J. G. CRUICKSHANK

Senior Lecturer, Department of Geography, The Queen's University of Belfast

The area of Northern Ireland is 13,580 km^2 or 5,242 square miles, and while this is about the same size as Yorkshire and only one sixth of the area of the Island of Ireland, it contains a variety of relief and structure possibly unequalled in any other region of these islands. Relief reflects closely the underlying geology, and is explained partly by differential denudation between hard and soft rocks, and partly by faulting of the main geological blocks (Chapter 3).

The land surface of the Province is predominantly lowland, approximately 75 per cent of its total area being below 150 m or 500 ft, with most of it forming an extensive saucer-shaped lowland around Lough Neagh (Figure 2.1). From there, a coastal lowland extends along the north coast westward into the Foyle estuary; in the south, there are corridors of lowland connecting into the basin of the Upper and Lower Lough Erne in County Fermanagh and also eastwards into the Lagan Valley, through Belfast and ultimately to the Ards peninsula beyond Strangford Lough. Much of the lowland is underlain by clay-rich glacial deposits of low permeability, and with stream gradients often being very gentle in lower courses, it is inevitable that poor land drainage restricts land use potential, unless artificial improvements have been made.

In Northern Ireland there are few mountains but often they have a striking appearance in the landscape by virtue of their isolated position. Only 6 per cent of the total land area is above 300 m or 1,000 ft, but the mountains are distributed in isolated blocks peripheral to the central lowland, giving them a dominance over the surrounding landscape that belies their areal extent. The location of the Mountains of Mourne and the Antrim plateau cliffs adjacent to the coastline allows these mountains to rise high above the shore, and to provide a lasting impression in the mind of the traveller arriving by sea.

There are four main uplands in Northern Ireland (Figure 2.1). Two are visible from Belfast, from where both near and distant skylines are made

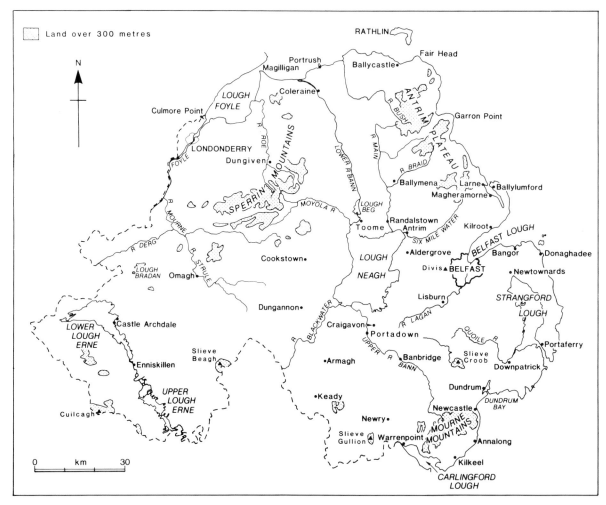

Figure 2.1 Places and land over 300 metres in Northern Ireland.

from young and tough volcanic rocks. To the north of the city, the near skyline of three summits (Divis at 477 m, Black Mountain 375 m, and Cave Hill 358 m) is part of the Tertiary basalt plateau of County Antrim and beyond. From above Belfast, the extruded sheets of basalt lava extend some 80 km to the cliff coastline of the spectacular "Giant's Causeway" in north Antrim, with the main plateau surface being between 300 and 400 m above sea level. From a vantage point above Belfast and looking south across 50 km, the distant skyline of the Mourne Mountains is built up of hard, Tertiary granites; in between, the lower upland of Slieve Croob in mid-Down was formed of much older "Newry" granite. Towering above the coastal town of Newcastle, Slieve Donard at 847 m is the highest summit in the Mournes, indeed in the whole of Northern Ireland, and literally "sweeps down to the sea". The Mournes are small in area (only 187 km²), but have fifteen summits above 600 m, and a further thirty above 300 m. To the west of the Lough Neagh basin, the more extensive Sperrin Mountains, running about 30 km east to west, are formed from metamorphosed sediments, the relatively resistant micha-schist rock. Among the oldest rocks found in Northern Ireland, the Dalradian mica-schist of the Sperrins also seems to be in a more advanced stage of denudation than its counterparts in west highland Scotland. The main summits of the Sperrins are about 600 m, the highest being Sawel at 683 m, and only just stand out above rounded ridges and gentle slopes. Ice sheets of the Pleistocene swept over and smoothed the outlines of the Sperrins, while valley glaciers cut deep into the Mournes producing many more summits in a smaller area. The fourth upland forms the western border of the Province; a table-land of hard Carboniferous limestone capped with grits, its cliff-line edge just over 300 m, makes a striking feature west of the Lough Erne basin in County Fermanagh. The highest plateau block of these sedimentary stacks is Cuilcagh at 670 m, rising above the area of the Marble Arch caves – which have been opened recently for public viewing.

There are other mountains over 300 m in Northern Ireland, but these are even more restricted in area. There is the isolated peak of Slieve Gullion at 574 m, with a few other hills in ring formation close by, in South Armagh. Again, these are formed from a mixture of hard volcanic rocks, produced from multiple volcanic activity. In County Tyrone, there are rolling uplands of Old Red Sandstone where a few summits just break through the 300 m level. The upland structure of the Province is also controlled by major fault lines, the most important of which is the Southern Uplands of Scotland fault which enters by Belfast Lough and fashions the hill slopes on the south of the city. The Scottish Highland Boundary fault plays a less obvious role in the landscape, being buried below the Antrim basalts, but it does delimit the south-eastern slopes of the Sperrins. Of greatest scale is the internal, and relatively- recent Tertiary down-faulting of the basalts which takes those lava sheets down 800 m below sea level below Lough Neagh. The down-faulting of the central lowlands contributes in some measure to the relative prominence of the surrounding uplands, and has much affected the drainage pattern.

Drainage

The most notable feature of the drainage pattern in the Province (Figure 2.2 below) is that so much appears to feed inward and pass through Lough Neagh. This inward, or centripetal, drainage is now represented by the catchment of the River Bann and its tributaries, which drains 39 per cent of the land area of the Province, and which may have been more extensive in the past, when the basalt was more extensive. The system began to develop quite early in the Tertiary (about 55 million years ago in the Eocene period), and just after the main period of basaltic vulcanicity. First, the Lough Neagh depression started to be formed by downwarping and faulting while the rivers of the time carried down debris that was deposited, in places surviving to thicknesses of around 300 m, as the Lough Neagh clays and lignite beds. Secondly, the drainage system of the central depression gradually extended outward for a time, before finally losing its

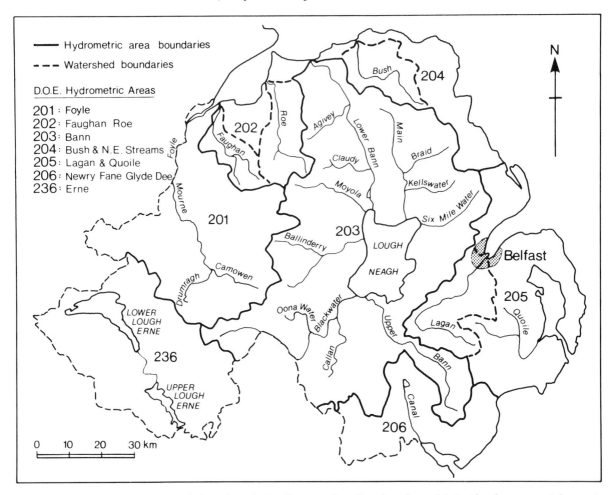

Legend:
— Hydrometric area boundaries
- - - Watershed boundaries

D.O.E. Hydrometric Areas
201 : Foyle
202 : Faughan Roe
203 : Bann
204 : Bush & N.E. Streams
205 : Lagan & Quoile
206 : Newry Fane Glyde Dee
236 : Erne

Figure 2.2   Rivers and river catchments in Northern Ireland.

peripheral parts to rivers extending headward into the former catchment. The rivers of the Antrim glens and the Lagan, working though soft Triassic sandstone, are the best examples of this river capture, and the Lower Bann carrying the main drainage northward and outward is the drainage reversal that is most difficult to explain. Glacial diversion of pre-existing drainage is well-demonstrated in the now westward flowing course followed by the River Bush in north Antrim, after the deposition of the moraine through Armoy.

The main catchments, with tributary and main rivers, are shown in Figure 2.2. Within the boundaries of Northern Ireland, the following catchments are of size indicated and percentage proportion of the Northern Ireland territory.

Bann   is 5,300 km^2 or 39.0%   Lagan is   562 km^2 or   4.1%
Foyle is 2,090 km^2 or 15.3%   Bush is   344 km^2 or   2.5%
Erne   is 1,901 km^2 of 14.0%

Some of these catchments have extensions outwith the boundaries of Northern Ireland, and these are excluded from figures above. The

Drainage: on the River Blackwater at Benburb, County Tyrone: a major arterial drainage scheme undertaken by the Department of Agriculture for Northern Ireland. (N.C. Mitchel)

remaining 25 per cent of the area of the Province is contained in the catchments of the Roe and Faughan in the northwest, and a number of small catchments in the southeast from the Quoile, around the Mournes and into south Armagh. Sixty one per cent of the drainage of the Province flows north, 25 per cent to the east coast, and only 14 per cent through the Erne system to the Atlantic west coast of the Republic of Ireland.

Wilcock (1979 and 1982) has reviewed the problems of land drainage in Northern Ireland and has discussed some of the drainage improvement schemes. He has pointed to the fact that most of the Province is lowland underlain in many parts by clay-rich deposits of low permeability, and where the lower courses of rivers have very little fall in gradient to the sea. The Lower Bann, for example, falls only 15 m in the 64 km from Toome Bridge at Lough Neagh to the north coast.

The problems of land and field drainage had to be tackled initially by improving the rate of flow of the arterial drainage of the main rivers, and the first comprehensive arterial drainage scheme implemented was on the Lower Bann during the 1930s. Made possible by the 1929 Drainage Act (NI), the strategy was to increase stream flow capacity at Toome, and to lower the level of Lough Neagh to 16.32 m, thus lowering the outfall of all rivers draining into the Lough. The scheme was highly successful, with the capacity increased by 29 per cent from 330 m^3/sec to 425 m^3/sec, and the level of the Lough lowered further than planned to between 15.24 m and 15.39 m. The Government of Northern Ireland provided finance for 80 per cent of the cost, and drainage benefit was given to 57,500 ha around Lough Neagh. Only three other smaller arterial drainage schemes were implemented in the 1930s.

However, after the Second World War, further Drainage Acts allowed arterial drainage schemes to receive 75 per cent State grant. In the period

Land drainage on a farm at Knockninny, County Fermanagh. (N.C. Mitchel)

since 1950, discharge capacity has been improved along 1,250 km of main rivers, and along 3,250 km of minor rivers. The total land area to benefit from these schemes is over 100,000 ha, and the work is continuing with the current cross-border scheme of the Monaghan-Tyrone Blackwater. Arterial drainage is the necessary forerunner of all attempts to drain agricultural land by field underdrainage or by open ditches, and it has been estimated (Green, 1979) that almost half of all agricultural land in the Province, or about 550,000 ha, benefits from some type of artificial drainage. In the decade of the 1950s, about 100,000 ha came under improved field drainage, in the 1960s about 185,000 ha, and since 1970 about a further 125,000 ha. Wilcock (1982) has calculated from these figures that about 75 per cent of the agricultural area now benefitting from efficient field drainage has been improved since 1950, and that there is a direct connection with the extension of arterial drainage in the same period. The proportion of 75 per cent refers to about half the agricultural land, so it may be about 36-38 per cent of the total agricultural area. It does include benefit from open ditch drainage, and the author (Cruickshank, 1982) has calculated that the benefit of field underdrainage alone installed since 1950, affects about 20 per cent of all agricultural land. Some of the recent drainage work was replacement of earlier installations, often dating back to the nineteenth century. There is little doubt that in Northern Ireland, the achievement of the physical potential for land use lies in the control of land drainage.

Superficial deposits

In Northern Ireland, the "parent materials" from which soils are developed are mainly glacial deposits left by successive glaciations during the

past million years (the Pleistocene period). We are not concerned here with
the problem of reconstructing a sequence of probable glaciations that may
have left their mark on the land surface of the Province, and even though
the geomorphologists (Stephens et al. 1975; Herries, Davies and Stephens,
1978) have described two major glaciations of Ireland, most glacial landforms and deposits are associated with the last or later glaciation, the
Midlandian. Almost contemporary with the Devensian glaciation in England, the Midlandian ice was most active between 40,000 and 13,000 years
ago, and unlike the more extensive earlier glaciations, had its southern
limit through the midlands of Ireland. It was a weaker glaciation than the
previous Munsterian General glaciation, and because of that, underlying
topography exerted more control on the ice movement, producing moraines
around uplands and inland of the present shoreline. Scottish ice was able to
penetrate into north Antrim and produced the extensive moraine running
through Armoy. Stagnant melting ice around the Sperrins fed meltwater
from which the sand and gravel "kame" formations of most of County

Figure 2.3 Simplified
subdivision of the landscape
of Northern Ireland,
showing the main landform
types and glacial deposits.

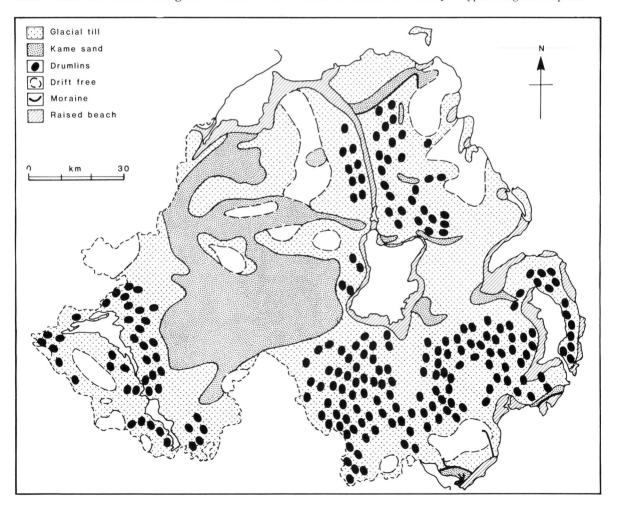

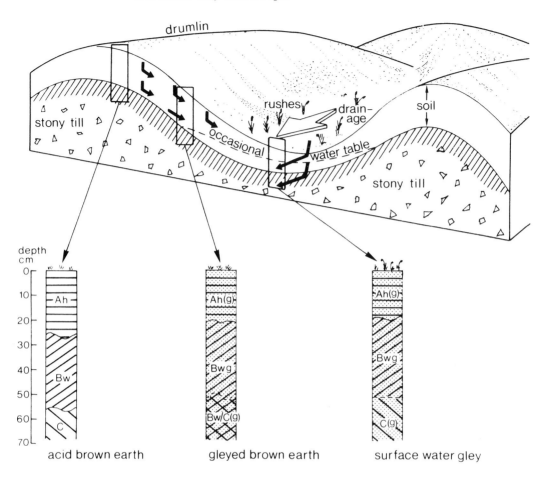

Figure 2.4 The pattern of soil profiles in a drumlin landscape.

Tyrone were made. Perhaps most important of all the landscape features of the last glaciation is the swarm of drumlins, one of the greatest drumlin fields known anywhere, that stretches from north Down through the southern part of the Province into County Fermanagh. The drumlin (or "little hill") even derived its name from its Irish origin, and in its home area, was formed by the ice sheets of the Late-Midlandian cold stage, moving outward and mainly southward from an ice source in the Lough Neagh depression between 25,000 and 18,000 years ago (Dardis, 1985).

The main areal units of glacial landforms can be seen in Figure 2.3. From the distribution of drumlins, it is clear that most of the lowlands of the Bann valley and the southern part of the Province have been modified by "drumlinisation", where ice sheets have moulded locally-derived till over cores of rock or older till. The drumlin landform is a dominant feature of the lowlands, restricted to areas below 150 m, but variable in shape and density (Hill, 1971 and 1973). It may be almost circular in shape as in the open lowlands of north Down, affected by ice movement in two directions, or elongated to four times their width as in the areas around the upland of Slieve Croob in mid-Down. Hill (1973) has observed that drumlin density declines towards the margins of the "drumlin field" in the north of Ireland, and that there are alternating zones of low and high density perpendicular to the direction of ice movement. Drumlin shape, size and steepness of slope, exert a strong influence on the size and arrangement of farms and fields, and sometimes on the siting of farm dwellings. Where drumlins appear above the waters of Strangford Lough and above the peat south of Lough Neagh, the associated pattern of farms and fields is most striking.

Soil drainage varies greatly within the drumlin area, and even on individual drumlins. Even a landform with sloping sides may have drainage problems if the glacial till matrix has a high clay content, as is the case with the drumlins around Lough Erne and with drumlins, at least partly derived from Lough Neagh clays, in south Antrim and into the Lower Bann valley. There is much less drainage difficulty in the loam-textured soils of the drumlins in much of County Down and County Armagh. Individual drumlins may have perched watertables supported by lenses of impermeable material, which leads to drainage problems over the drumlin top in otherwise well-drained soils. The possible relationships between soil profile types and drumlin topography is shown in Figure 2.4.

Most drumlins are surrounded by wet and poorly drained inter-drumlin hollows, which create management and access problems for the land user. Despite such physical limitations, the drumlin landscapes of the Province are among its most intensively managed agricultural grasslands.

While drumlins are part of the glacial till plains, there are other areas of till such as in north Londonderry, north Antrim inside the Armoy moraine, and in South Antrim east of Lough Neagh, where drumlins are absent or weakly developed. The character of the glacial till closely reflects the mineral composition of the underlying rocks, as the glacial movement of till (in contrast to the fate of erratic stones and boulders) is rarely possible more than 1 or 2 km away from a geological boundary in the direction of ice movement. More detail on the nature and composition of the main till types, which are also the main soil parent materials, is provided in the soil section.

The sand deposits of the last glaciation are found in extensive fluvio-glacial ice-contact sandy "kame" formations around the Sperrin Mountains, particularly on the south side, in the stony deposits of the moraines of local ice around the Mournes and of Scottish ice at Armoy, and lastly in limited areas of post-glacial raised beaches – the last feature being even more restricted elsewhere in Ireland. The land use limitation of these sand and gravel deposits is partly in the steepness and highly variable nature of slopes, partly with stoniness and related cultivation difficulty, and lastly, the risk of drought in dry growing seasons. Such physical problems can be difficult and expensive to modify. Surface sprinkler irrigation is used in the drier eastern lowlands where sandy deposits occur (such as around Comber in County Down) but fortunately most of the sandy soils are in the kame formations of the wetter west in County Tyrone. The level and lime-rich raised beach deposits provide top quality agricultural land, which is best seen in the Myroe area of north Londonderry.

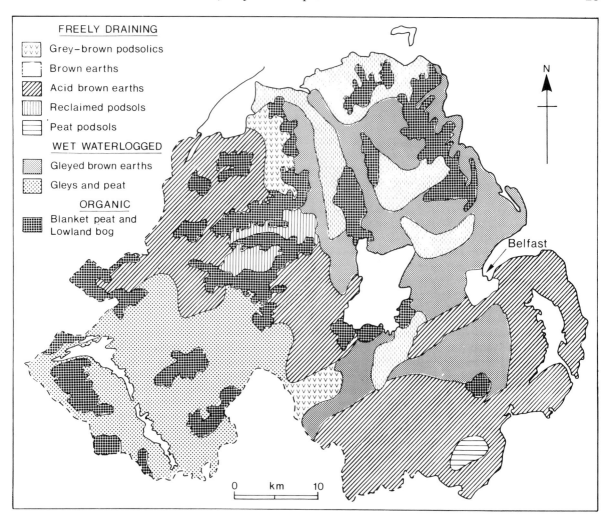

FREELY DRAINING

▨ Grey–brown podsolics

▢ Brown earths

▨ Acid brown earths

▥ Reclaimed podsols

▤ Peat podsols

WET WATERLOGGED

▨ Gleyed brown earths

⠿ Gleys and peat

ORGANIC

▩ Blanket peat and Lowland bog

N

Belfast

0   km   10

Figure 2.5   Simplified soil map of Northern Ireland.

Soils

From vegetation history based on pollen records, it is known that the north of Ireland has had a mild, humid climate, promoting soil-forming processes like gleying and leaching, for most of the post-glacial period or the last 10,000 years. In the Atlantic phase starting around 7,000 years ago, and again in the Sub-Atlantic from about 2,500 years ago (Smith et al., 1971), the climate became wetter than before, leading to more gleying or waterlogging and to faster rates of leaching. Peat had started to infill lowland basins soon after deglaciation (Smith, 1961), but blanket peat build-up over the hills began during the Sub-Atlantic wet phase, in some places covering earlier man-made monuments of the Neolithic period (Smith, 1970). Mineral soils profiles developed in glacial drift material, that was in part weathered before the glaciations, and apparently did not reach the advanced stages of leaching in upland areas until the Sub-Atlantic (Cruickshank and Cruickshank, 1981). The pattern of the main soil profile types in Northern Ireland (as shown in Figure 2.4) did not become established until the past two or three thousand years in the uplands, while for the past four thousand years, man has been modifying lowland soils by cultivation and drainage.

The wetness of climate means that precipitation exceeds evapotranspiration in almost every month of the year everywhere in Northern Ireland (with only a few exceptions in the eastern lowlands between May and July), and that consequently there is almost always an excess of moisture available to enter soil as a weak organic acid and behave as a "leachate" solution, dissolving and carrying chemical compounds from surface into subsoil horizons.

This process of leaching is found wherever soils are freely draining in the north of Ireland, and the end product is to make such soils increasingly acid in surface horizons. Under alkaline conditions in soils derived from base-rich parent materials like basalt and limestone, acidity can be resisted, but leaching takes a physical form, carrying fine clay particles in suspension from surface into subsoil horizons (creating texturally altered Bt horizons, rich in clay, which are part of grey-brown podsolic profiles). The acid sequence of leached soils starts with acid brown earths, and moves on through brown podsolic profiles, to podsols and even to podsols with iron pans or humic layers in their B horizons. Only about 40-45 per cent of our local soils are in the leached class, because the majority of our soils are imperfectly or poorly drained. Of the wet site soils, about 40 per cent of all soils are gleyed or poorly drained mineral soils and between 13 and 18 per cent (depending on thickness definition) are poorly drained organic soils.

The distribution of the main soil profile types in the Province is shown in Figure 2.5, but as profile development is still in its early stages, soil parent materials exert a strong influence on the range of profile types and on the character of soil as a growth medium for plants. Accordingly, the following review of soils is arranged by rock or soil parent material, and summarised in the same way in Table 1.

Basalt: Tertiary basalt lavas still cover 4,009 km^2 or 1,548 square miles, and provide parent material for almost one-third (30 per cent) of the soils in the Province, covering a wide altitudinal range from sea level to over 500 m. About three-quarters of this area lies below 300 m in County Antrim, and to a large degree, is improved soil used in agriculture. Generally highly valued for grassland-cattle systems (McAllister and McConaghy, 1968), "basalt soils" have some very distinctive properties such as chocolate-brown colour, strong and stable structure, large and usually base-saturated cation exchange capacities, and an active iron-aluminium complex with phosphate fixing implications (McAleese and McConaghy, 1957 and 1958). Basalt soils can be subdivided into three geographical divisions as shown on Table 2.1, and in the agricultural area, most are gleyed to some degree due to high clay content in basalt-derived glacial till.

Shale and greywacke: The second largest soil parent material unit is that derived from Ordovician and Silurian shale, slate and greywacke in County Down and County Armagh, covering 26 per cent of Northern Ireland's

Table 2.1

Northern Ireland soils arranged by rock type parent materials

Soil Parent Rock	Soil Profile Type	Approx. Area hectares	% Area of N.I.	
Basalt	Peat and peaty soils over 300 m	100,000	7.4	
	Gleys on middle slopes	180,000	13.3	
	Brown earths and some gleys on loam till in lowlands	130,000	9.6	30.3
Silurian Shale and greywacke	Gleys and acid brown earths on drumlins	140,000	10.4	
	Acid brown earths and gleys on sloping ground above drumlins	160,000	11.8	26.0
	Acid brown earths in east coastal	50,000	3.8	
Mica-Schist	Peat and peaty gleys of high land	90,000	6.6	
	Acid brown earths and brown podsolics of valleys	110,000	8.0	17.6
	Podsols and peat podsols of kame sands in County Tyrone	40,000	3.0	
Carboniferous	Gleys and peat gleys of Fermanagh and Tyrone lowlands	170,000	12.6	
	Grey-brown podsolics in Armagh and Londonderry	20,000	1.5	14.1
Granites and Triassic Sandstone	Acid brown earths and brown podsolics, mainly in County Down	140,000	10.4	
Old Red Sandstone	Gleys and gleyed acid brown earths in Tyrone–Fermanagh	20,000	1.5	

soils. Soil textures are normally loam or silt loam, characteristic of weathered shale, and drainage conditions are highly variable due to the association with the drumlin landscape in the south-east (Figure 2.4). Possibly about half the area of the shale soils is gleyed, and the remaining part is composed of acid brown earths. Shale parent material is not of high base status, without reserves of exchangeable base ions, and consequently becomes acid rapidly where loam textures and site conditions allow leaching. Generous liming and fertiliser application is desirable to maintain fertility levels, and the high standard of farm management in Down and Armagh guarantees that this is found almost everywhere. Usually, there is little need for artificial underdrainage in these soils (Cruickshank, 1975).

Mica-Shist: Ancient and altered sediments of Pre-Cambrian times, the Dalradian mich-schist of the north-west in County Londonderry and County Tyrone, and in north-east Antrim, provide soil parent material for 18 per cent of the area of the Province, if the associated kame sands are included. Most of the soils are in the Sperrin Mountains and hill margins between 100 m and 600 m and divide almost equally between peaty gleys and blanket peat of the wetter sites in the uplands and the sequence of leached soils in the valleys and kame sands of County Tyrone. Schist-derived soils are sandy in texture, and naturally acid. Leached, they become very acid and require frequent and heavy applications of lime and other fertiliser. They are deficient in iron and potash, but respond well to potash application. Farm size tends to be small in the Sperrins and management poor, after years of declining returns and the struggle against the effects of leaching and extremes of weather (Cruickshank, 1978). In the hill areas, net farm incomes are derived mainly from grants and subsidies, but well-managed profitable farms can be found in lowland areas like the Roe Valley (Limavady to Dungiven) in County Londonderry. In such areas, schist soils have a good reputation as potato soils.

Carboniferous Limestone: Sedimentary series of the Carboniferous provide a variety of parent materials for about 14 per cent of the soil area, mostly calcareous sediments and limestones. The majority of the soils are gleys, especially in the drumlins around the Lough Ernes where they have developed as a highly tenacious and poorly draining clay loam from the "Calp" series of the Middle Carboniferous. In these soils, the clay content can be 40 per cent of the Fine Earth, and combined with a high silt fraction, makes underdrainage necessary but difficult to maintain. Mole drains have been used, and more recently, gravel-filled mole drains are proving more effective (O'Neill, 1980). Severe drainage problems may require stone-filled ditches at close spacing. However, there are parts of west Armagh, between Armagh city and Monaghan town, and also on the east side of the Roe valley in County Londonderry, where soil drainage is good and base-rich, grey-brown podsolics are found (Figure 2.5).

Old Red Sandstone: Apart from a small unit in north-east Antrim, there is only one extensive area of Old Red Sandstone soils, comprising 1.5 per cent of the total, from west Tyrone into Fermanagh. This unit joins and extends the gleyed soils of the Carboniferous Limestones, but has the additional problem of soils being deficient in phosphate, low in potash, and requiring frequent liming. Under intensive management, grass production can be good, but access remains a problem.

Granite and Triassic Sandstone: Soils developed on different parent materials but showing a common property of sandy textures, comprise 10 per cent of the total and are found in the granite uplands of Slieve Croob and the Mournes in County Down, as well as lowland Triassic Sandstone of the Lagan Valley and in east Tyrone. On the granite, soils are gravelly and very sandy, freely draining and leached often to the podsol stage. Climatic conditions are often limiting for agriculture, and fields have to be small because of stone clearance. In the sandstone lowlands, freely draining soils are acid brown earths, requiring extra liming.

Organic soils: Soil profiles with a high content of organic matter to thicknesses of over 40 cm, are classed in a separate category as organic soils or peat. They occur on all the geological groups of soils, but should also be considered as a distinctive group of soils. About 13 per cent of the land surface is covered with deep peat in Northern Ireland, but the area could be greater if soils with peat surface horizons are included. Hammond (1979) has measured that 35,940 ha is in lowland basin peat, and about 130,800 ha is in upland blanket peat or blanket mire. The distribution of the blanket peat is controlled by climate, level or slightly sloping topography, and a wet and acid ground surface. The lower altitudinal limit is about 300 m in the east (in Antrim encouraged by the level plateau surface at that height), and may be down to 200 m in the west in Fermanagh. Blanket peat is associated with the uplands of Antrim, Londonderry, Tyrone and Fermanagh, there being very little in Down and Armagh. Land use is in rough grazing, heath and recently planted forest. The mainly alkaline basin peat is mainly in patches around Lough Neagh, the Lower Bann valley and in north Antrim, enclosed behind the Armoy moraine.

Quality of land for agriculture and forestry

When assessing the value of land for agriculture or forestry, soil is only one of a range of physical factors to be considered, and the whole physical environment has an influence that has to be placed in a particular socio-economic context of a particular time and place. In Ireland, Sir Richard Griffith twice directed a General Valuation of land, first in the 1830s and later in the 1850s, but detailed and comprehensive as these surveys were, they are now a historical curiosity. In 1963, an agricultural land classification was part of the publication *Land use in Northern Ireland* (Symons, 1963), and was based on physical criteria relevant to contemporary land use. The main quality classes of land reflect altitude and aspect, expressions of climate, slope, depth of free drainage in soil, soil depth, stoniness and texture. In some classes, types of landscape are the bases of classification such as class B3 for the highly variable drumlin landscapes, and B4 for uneven rocky and peaty hill margins. A simplified version of the classification is shown in Figure 2.6, and a key to the main classes, their percentage areas and soils in Northern Ireland is in Table 2.

The influence of soil or soil properties is not isolated in the classification, partly because of the experimental problems in doing so and also because the influence is specific to particular crops. However, it is clear that soil conditions are influential in a general way on land use and productivity through leaching and gleying, the two main processes of soil formation. The freely draining soils are inclined to be acid naturally, and can become very acid after a period of crop production without liming, because climatic conditions encourage leaching almost everywhere. In the 1940s, it was realised that the whole of the agricultural area was lime-deficient, and an Agricultural Lime Scheme was introduced. Farmers received a 60 per cent grant towards costs, and liming reached a peak between 1958 and 1962. It was estimated that, after the original lime deficiency had been restored, losses of lime from the soil due to plant growth and leaching could be replaced by an annual application of about 250,000 tonnes per year (Wilcock, 1979), and this has been approximately the rate of application since 1970.

Table 2.2

Land quality for agriculture in Northern Ireland (Symons, 1963)

Class	% Area of N.I.	Soils and main locations
A	4	Acid brown earths and brown earths on basalt drift, around Limavady, Coleraine, Ballyclare. Also Lagan Valley and Omagh area
B1	14	Brown earths of basalt loam drift. Acid brown earths on sandy drift in lowlands of County Londonderry and County Down
B2	10	Gleys of clay-rich till of lowlands around Lough Neagh
B3	17	Drumlin landscapes, variable soils but most gleyed. Some brown earths and grey-brown podsolics in County Down
B4	24	Hill margins and middle sloped, variable soils often gleyed and variable topography
C1	17	Peaty soils of higher hill margins around 240–300m, mostly in the Sperrins
D1	9	Blanket peat and mountain land over 300m
C2+D2	5	Gleys and basin peat, lowland bog

The lime subsidy scheme was terminated in 1984, but possibly may have to be re-introduced in the future should soils become markedly lime-deficient again. Improvement of land and field drainage has been discussed in an earlier section, and the benefit to agriculture cannot be underestimated. Drainage work dates back to the early nineteenth century, and although most of the effective schemes are from the 1950s and 1960s, drainage improvement is an inheritance of man's modifying activities from the past, and forms an extension to land that is naturally well-drained. Agricultural land value is based on the state of soil drainage more than any other single physical factor.

In an attempt to measure the influence of soil series (the same soil profile on the same parent material) on agricultural profit margins, soil series were investigated in the Roe Valley of County Londonderry (Cruickshank and Armstrong, 1971). There, it was possible to find seven soil series, distinctively different from each other, in a lowland area where the agricultural enterprises and farm management were similar, if not uniform. It was found that the gross margin profit per unit area for the least profitable soil series (acid and gleyed schist-derived soil) was 65 per cent of the best (well-drained, slightly acid sandy soil) for mixed farming enterprises based on grass. Some of the difference might be overcome by greater management efficiency, but this study was limited to a restricted range of soils within the Roe Valley. It is almost certain that Province-wide an even greater difference could be found between the worst and best in terms of soil series influence on gross margin profit per unit area for the

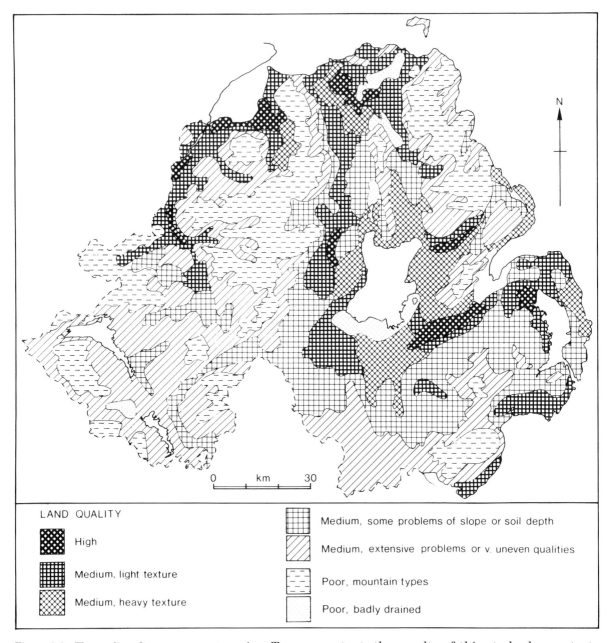

Figure 2.6 The quality of
land classified for
agricultural land use,
adapted from Cruickshank
and Symons (1963) in *Land
use in Northern Ireland.*

same enterprise. To some extent, the results of this study demonstrate
some influence of soil series on agricultural land value, if other variables
are controlled.

Agricultural land use

Just as the availability of a lime subsidy and grants for field drainage
have determined change in related soil properties, so government policy

has influenced change in land use through the availability of grants and control of market prices at provincial, national and EEC levels. The agricultural industry is examined in a later chapter, and the changing character of the industry has to be understood in some detail before changes in land use can be explained.

There have been dramatic changes in land use in the Province, the scale of which depends on the period under review. In the mid-nineteenth century, the area of "improved land" was considerably greater than now, and about then also, the "cultivation maximum" of land under tillage was reached. The tillage area comprised the majority of the improved agricultural land, and was devoted to cereal crops, flax and potatoes. The contrast with the present land use pattern could not be greater, but even within the past 50 years since 1936-38, there have been major changes in agricultural land use, as can be seen in Figure 2.7. It is with this recent sequence of changes that this discussion will be concerned.

The first point of change is that the area devoted to crops and grass, the improved land, decreased rapidly from 1936 through to 1960, from when it has settled to about 80 per cent of the original area. Since then it has been just above 800,000 ha to which about 200,000 ha of rough grazing should be added to give the total agriculturally used area. Within the area of crops and grass, there has been a notable decrease of the tillage area and proportion since 1936. The area has fallen to about 72,000 ha, which is only about one-third of the tillage area in 1936. As a proportion of the area in crops and grass, tillage has decreased from 19 per cent to just over 8 per cent, and consequently the combined grassland has increased from 81 per cent to over 91 per cent. Within the tillage, barley has almost completely replaced oats, but still the cereal area is less than half the 1936 amount, and the area of the potato crop has fallen to one quarter of its former area. The actual areas devoted to rotation/temporary grass and permanent grass have remained steady over the past fifty years, and stand out as the most constant elements of the land use pattern, but the production from temporary grass has been increased by intensive management practices. Looking at the distribution of grassland by county, Armagh, Tyrone and Fermanagh have proportions above the provincial average, and lead in the order stated. Antrim, Down and Londonderry are below average, and the last mentioned is markedly below. The best tillage soils, sandy and freely drained, found in large and level management units, are in north Down and north Londonderry. These are the main areas of market gardening, cereal and potato production and arable agriculture.

Another major change is the trend towards larger farms, as shown in Figure 2.8. The diagram shows the number of farms or holdings in each size range of the key, which is size by amount of land in crops and grass (excluding rough grazing). The number of farms in Northern Ireland has fallen to half the 1939 figure, 88,951 to 44,050, and of this last number only 24,000 farms are considered to be "working" farms, large enough to support a family. The average size "working" farm in 1983 had just 30 ha in crops and grass, and as shown in Figure 2.8, only 32 per cent of all farms in the

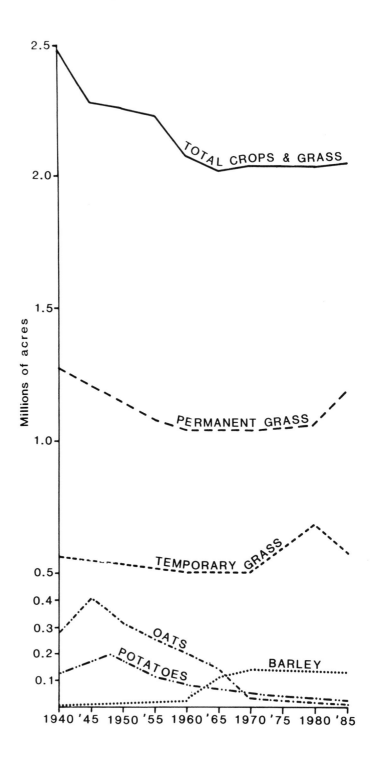

Figure 2.7 Changing
agricultural land-use in
Northern Ireland.

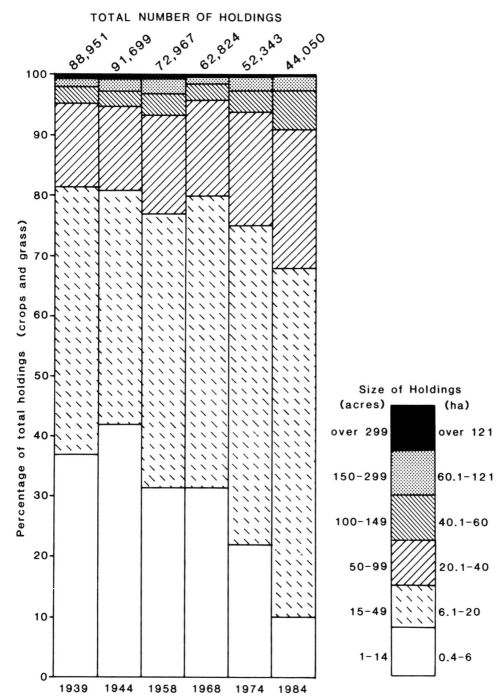

Figure 2.8   Changing
number of holdings in
Northern Ireland.

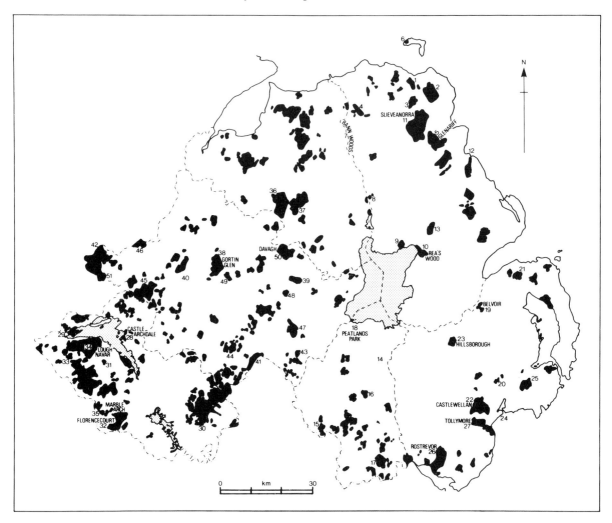

Figure 2.9 Distribution of State Forests and Forest Parks in Northern Ireland.

Province have more than 20 ha in crops and grass. About half the number of all farms, the lower half of the size range, are too small to make a living for the farmer, and are the source of only part-income, probably let out in annual conacre (i.e. for eleven months at a time). These small farms comprise the majority of all farms in marginal hill areas, where they are frequently neglected or even abandoned if the living becomes too difficult to win. Even the desired objectives for farm amalgamation are too large, and would involve the amalgamation of too many small farms, to be possible in these areas.

Woodlands

There are about 13,000 ha of private woodlands, and about 73,000 ha of potential woodland owned by the State, through the Forest Service of the Department of Agriculture in Northern Ireland (Figure 2.9). The amount of State-owned land planted in forest was 55,845 ha in 1984, so the overall total of woodland in the Province is about 69,000 ha, or 5.3 per cent of the land surface. The total woodland is close to the area of tillage, but is in no way related. Five per cent is not a large proportion, but represents a ten-fold increase from only 5,230 ha in State forest in 1940. Annual planting in State forests was at its highest rate of about 2,000 ha per year in the decade of the 1960s, and has now fallen to about 700 ha per year in the 1980s. For a variety of reasons it seems unlikely that the planted target of 120,000 ha by the year 2000 can be achieved.

Table 2.3 shows that Sitka spruce is the most commonly planted tree in State forests (in 62 per cent of the planted area), and also shows that three quarters of forest land is poorly drained. The distribution of State forests in Figure 2.9 shows a preference for upland and western parts where poor drainage and wet climate usually combine to produce wet and acid peat soils. This is the type of land usually made available for sale to the Forest Service, or is cheap enough to be bought within the price limitation of the Forest Service budget. In these environments, windthrow of growing trees becomes a problem of forest management, and the part played by soil is difficult to isolate from climate, slope, altitude and aspect. MacKenzie (1974) did find a significant relationship between windthrow and soil, mainly with soil rooting depth. In brown earths and podsols, where rooting depth could be up to 1 m, the windthrow risk was negligible, becoming a moderate risk in blanket peat, and a high risk on peaty gleys and gleys with

Table 2.3 Class data for planted tree species

Soil profile types	% forest land	Average yield class for:		
		Sitka spruce	Lodgepole pine	Norway spruce
1. Leached soils, brown earths and podsols	17	16.8 (90.3)	9.2 (100)	17.0 (99.4)
2. Leached soils with surface peat (mor)	10	14.9 (80.1)	7.4 (80.4)	12.9 (75.4)
3. Surface water gleys	18	18.6 (100)	7.7 (83.6)	17.1 (1000)
4. Peaty gleys	16	15.2 (81.7)	6.3 (68.5)	14.7 (85.9)
5. Shallow peat (1 m)	12	13.2 (70.9)	8.4 (91.3)	13.8 (80.7)
6. Deep peat	27	12.9 (63.3)	7.3 (79.3)	11.6 (67.8)
Area planted in hectares		19,913	3,068	2,629
% of total area planted		62	10	8

These figures were provided by the Forest Service, Department of Agriculture for Northern Ireland and are based on the area planted up to end of 1969 (32,170 ha) and not the area planted by end of 1984 (55,845 ha).

less than 35 cm rooting depth. Table 2.3 gives quantitative yield class data for the three main planted tree species on various soils, and shows that for Sitka and Norway Spruce, highest yields are found on surface water gleys, that is mineral gleys in lowland areas. Lowest productivity is on deep peat, where climate is a limitation as well, and where the yield class values for the spruce group is only about 63-68 per cent of yield on the better soils.

Conclusion

The land of the Province is mainly lowland surrounded by a ring of upland, and because of the extensive area of fairly level lowland, wet climatic conditions and low permeability of soil, land use and production are adversely affected by drainage problems. There has been a long history of human effort to improve land drainage, starting in a co-ordinated fashion in the early nineteenth century and being greatly extended in the 1950s and 1960s. Greater efficiency of arterial drainage of the main rivers has led to widespread improvement of underdrainage in fields, and to new techniques of field drainage in the most intractable clays. Poor land drainage is the expression of the total physical environment in Northern Ireland, and despite massive improvement schemes, drainage remains the main constraint to land quality, land use and access for agriculture and forestry.

References

Cruickshank, J.G., 1970. Soils and pedogenesis in the north of Ireland, *in* N. Stephens & R.E. Glasscock (eds), *Irish geographical studies*. Belfast. 89-104.

Cruickshank, J.G., 1972. Soils and changing agricultural land values in part of County Londonderry, *in Irish Geography*, 6 (4), 462-79.

Cruickshank, J.G., 1975. Soils of the northern and central parts of County Armagh, *in Irish Geography*, 8, 63-71.

Cruickshank, J.G., 1978. Soil properties and management levels of marginal hill land in the Sperrin Mountains, Co. Tyrone and Co. Londonderry. *Irish Journal of Agricultural Research*, 17, 303-14.

Cruickshank, J.G., and Armstrong, W.J., 1971. Soil and agricultural land classification in County Londonderry, *in Transactions of the Institute of British Geographers*, 53, 79-94.

Cruickshank, J.G. and Cruickshank, M.M., 1977. A survey of neglected agricultural land in the Sperrin Mountains, Northern Ireland, *in Irish Geography*, 10, 36-44.

Cruickshank, J.G., 1982. Soil, *in* J.G. Cruickshank and D.N. Wilcock (eds), *Northern Ireland, environment and natural resources*, 165-84.

Dardis, G.F., 1985. Till facies associations of drumlins and some implications for their mode of formation, *in Geografisker Annaler*, 67A, 13-22.

Green, F.H.W., 1979. *Field-drainage in Europe: a quantitative survey.* (Institute of Hydrology, Report No. 57), Oxon.

Griffith Valuation. See valuation books and valuation maps (e.g. for 1834 and 1858), Public Record Office of Northern Ireland, Belfast.

Hammond, R.F., 1979. *The peatlands of Ireland.* Dublin.

Herries Davies, G.L. and Stephens, N., 1978. *Ireland.* London.

Hill, A.R., 1971. The formation and spatial distribution of drumlins in a portion of north-east Ireland, in relation to hypotheses of drumlin origin, *in Geografisker Annaler*, 53A, 14-31.

Hill, A.R., 1973. The distribution of drumlins in County Down, *in Annals of the Association of American Geographers*, 63, 226-240.

McAleese, D.M. and McConaghy, S., 1957-1958. Studies on the basaltic soils of Northern Ireland, *in Journal of Soil Science*, 8, 127-34, 135-40; 9, 66-75, 176-80, 81-8, 289-97.

McAllister, J.S.V. and McConaghy, S., 1968. Soils of Northern Ireland and their influence upon agriculture, *in Record of Agricultural Research*, Ministry of Agriculture, Northern Ireland, 17, 101-8.

MacKenzie, R.F., 1974. Some factors influencing the stability of Sitka spruce in Northern Ireland, *in Irish Forestry*, 31 (2), 110-29.

O'Neill, D.G., 1980. An investigation of the gravel tunnel drainage system. *Annual Report on Research and Technical Work for 1980: Enniskillen Agricultural College*, 10-13. Enniskillen.

Savill, P.S. and Dickson, D.A., 1975. Early growth of Sitka spruce on gleyed soils in Northern Ireland, *in Irish Forestry*, 32 (1), 34-49.

Smith, A.G., 1961. Cannons Lough, Kilrea, Co. Derry: stratigraphy and pollen analysis, *in Proceedings of the Royal Irish Academy*, 61B, 369-83.

Smith, A.G., 1970. Late- and post-glacial vegetation and climatic history of Ireland: a review. N. Stephens and R.E. Glasscock (eds.), *Irish geographical studies*. Belfast, 65-88.

Smith, A.G., Pearson, G.W. and Pilcher, J.R., 1971. Belfast radiocarbon dates III, *in Radiocarbon*, 13 (1), 103-25.

Stephens, N., Creighton, J.R. and Hannon, M.A., 1975. The late-Pleistocene period in north-eastern Ireland: an assessment 1975, *in Irish Geography*, 8, 1-23.

Symons, L.J., ed., 1963. *Land use in Northern Ireland*, London.

Wilcock, D.N., 1979. Post-war land drainage, fertiliser use and environmental impact in Northern Ireland, *Journal of Environmental Management*, 8, 137-49.

Wilcock, D.N., 1982. Rivers, J.G. Cruickshank and D.N. Wilcock (eds.), *Northern Ireland, environment and natural resources*. Belfast, 43-71.

3 Mineral Resources

A. E. GRIFFITH, I. C. LEGG AND W. I. MITCHELL*

Geological Survey of Northern Ireland

The recent discovery of thick seams of lignite in Counties Antrim and Tyrone and of gold bearing rocks in the Sperrin Mountains in County Londonderry highlights the potential of Northern Ireland to become a substantial mineral producer and represents the culmination of years of systematic geological work by many people. Before it is known whether commercial production of either mineral is possible, more exploration is needed and is now underway. While all the information currently available indicates that lignite mining in particular may be established within a few years, it must be borne in mind that mining feasibility studies may highlight unexpected difficulties and that a previously optimistic forecast may suddenly fail to live up to expectations. Furthermore, even when mining is in progress a fall in the price of the mineral or the availability of a competing product can result in mining becoming uneconomic.

Irrespective of the outcome of the present favourable prospects for establishing gold and lignite mining, Northern Ireland is endowed with a great diversity of rock types – a diversity which has been long recognised and which led our ancestors to search for lead, copper, iron, salt, coal, lignite, aluminium, silver and gold and indeed to mine some of these minerals.

Geological framework to the mineral deposits

A great variety of rock types exists in Northern Ireland but the geology of the north-east of the Province is dominated by the occurrence of Tertiary lavas which cover some 4,000 km^2. The basalts are known to be up to at least 769 m thick (Ballymacilroy Borehole) and although their existence poses major problems for exploration, the hard basalt layers have protected from erosion not only the underlying Cretaceous chalk, Jurassic mudstones and limestones and Triassic mudstones and sandstones, which now

---

* Published with the permission of the Director of the Geological Survey of Northern Ireland and the Department of Economic Development Northern Ireland.

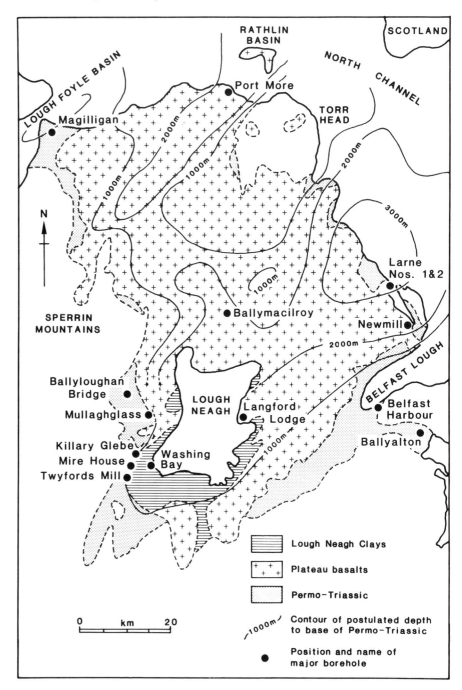

Figure 3.1 Permo-Triassic basins in Northern Ireland.

outcrop intermittently around the edge of the basalt-covered ground, but also, possibly, Carboniferous and Permian rocks. If these Carboniferous rocks contain certain lithologies, in particular coal, and have been subjected to the appropriate temperatures and pressures, then it is possible that hydrocarbons may have been generated and trapped in the overlying Triassic sandstones. Indeed, it is the recognition that such a geological situation could exist that led to the recent issue of two licences to explore for oil and gas in east Antrim and also to earlier, but so far unsuccessful, exploration in the on- and off-shore areas between Fair Head and Magilligan Point and in the south-east Antrim area in the 1970's.

Apart from the extensive outcrop of basalts in the north-east of the Province the geological framework of Northern Ireland is remarkably similar to that of Scotland with Devonian, Carboniferous and Permian rocks occupying the south-westward extension of the Midland Valley of Scotland and flanked to the north-west by Dalradian metamorphic rocks and to the south-east by Lower Palaeozoic strata, which are intruded by the granitic rocks of the Mourne Mountains and the Newry area. Although largely masked by the basalts, the "Midland Valley" structure (Figure 3.1) is known to be separated from the Rathlin and Lough Foyle basins, with their fill of Triassic and Carboniferous rocks, by Dalradian schists which outcrop at Torr Head in the north-east and in the Sperrin Mountains in the south-west.

The occurrence of thick deposits of clay in places around the shore of Lough Neagh has been known since early times but the first scientific account is provided by Barton in 1757 who described the succession exposed by digging at the foot of a boulder clay cliff near the mouth of the Glenavy River:-

> The upper stratum of matter is red clay, three feet deep; the second stratum is stiff blue clay, four feet deep; the third stratum is a black wood lying in flakes, four feet deep; the next stratum is clay ... this stratum of wood ... is one uniform mass capable of being cut any way with a spade.

The potential significance of the "black wood lying in flakes" was obviously recognised and Stewart (1800) recorded that in 1799 the Marquis of Hartford drilled for coal at "the sandy bay on Portmore" – now identified as Sandy Bay (Irish Grid J11 71) on the east shore of Lough Neagh. Presumably it was the record of this borehole which Griffith cited in the Second Report of the Railway Commissioners (1837-8) where he observed that three seams of lignite 7.6, 6.1 and 4.6 m thick were encountered in blue clay to a depth of 23.2 m. Griffith also noted that deeper boreholes at Annaghmore, 3 km south-east of Coalisland, presumably drilled in the hope of locating Carboniferous coal, penetrated 89 m of "Tertiary clay". He concluded that the basin in which these clays accumulated must have been both deeper and more extensive than the present day Lough Neagh, a view confirmed by the numerous boreholes which have since been drilled. Deposits of similar lithology and age were also recently (1983) discovered by the Geological Survey in the vicinity of Ballymoney. The Tertiary clays have been referred to as Lough Neagh Clays. More recently this term has been superseded by that of Lough Neagh Group as, in addition to clay, the sequence comprises a wide variety of lithologies.

Lough Neagh Group

The Group consists mostly of pale-coloured clays with thin bands and irregular nodules of ironstone (siderite) but it also contains subordinate horizons of sand and conglomerate and, most importantly, thick beds of lignite in places. As has already been mentioned, the Group was previously thought to occur only in areas beneath and around the shores of Lough Neagh (Figure 3.2) in Counties Antrim, Armagh, Londonderry and Tyrone with an extent of about 500 km^2 of which some 300 km^2 underlie the Lough. It is now known that there is also a substantial outcrop in an area extending from near Garvagh, County Londonderry, through Ballymoney to Stranocum, County Antrim, a distance of about 25 km.

Whether or not the Lough Neagh Group sediments in north Antrim and around Lough Neagh were deposited in a single lake or in a system of smaller, disparate lakes is not clear. It is known, however, that the sediments accumulated in shallow, freshwater conditions during the Oligocene Stage of the Tertiary Period, some 30-38 million years ago, and that the substantial variations in thickness of the Group resulted largely from the development of localised centres of subsidence whose inception and development was controlled by penecontemporaneous, intra-basin faults. Around the edge of the outcrop of the Lough Neagh Group the rocks, with the exception of part of north Armagh where sandstone of Triassic age occurs, invariably consist of Tertiary lavas (about 60 million years old) of the Antrim Lava Group or their weathered products.

The basalts can be observed in the field but the existence of their weathered products was only recognised during the extensive exploratory drilling programme by the Geological Survey in 1983-4. In the majority of the boreholes which penetrated the full sequence of the Lough Neagh Group, the underlying rocks were not fresh basalt lavas; rather they consisted of up to 296 m of lithomarge which is a multicoloured, clay-based weathering product of the lavas; or an interbedded sequence of lithomarge, volcanic acid tuffs, ashes, agglomerates and lacustrine sediments. The latter sediments comprise clays with ironstone bands, occasional conglomerate and palaeosol horizons and also beds of lignite and lignitic clays, which rarely exceed 1 m in thickness. This sequence of deposits probably accumulated during the late-Eocene while vulcanism, although still a potent force in moulding the Tertiary landscape, was waning in importance and was interspersed with quiescent periods when rivers and temporary lakes developed and the land surface was cloaked in vegetation. In places, this vegetation accumulated to form *in situ* peat beds, which are now preserved as thin lignite seams. Elsewhere in Northern Ireland beyond the limits of the Lough Neagh Group, there is no evidence of the final stages in the decline of Tertiary vulcanism as any rocks of this age have been removed, presumably by a combination of post-Tertiary denudation and, particularly, by the erosive power of the succeeding Quaternary ice sheets.

History of exploration for lignite in the Lough Neagh Group

The discovery of thick seams of lignite in the Crumlin, Coagh and Ballymoney areas resulted from the analysis by the Geological Survey of Northern Ireland of information carefully recorded by succeeding generations of geologists since Barton's 1757 account. Boreholes were drilled specifically to investigate the lignite potential of the Crumlin area in 1964; this work was followed in 1968 by drilling by English China Clays Lovering Pochin and Company Ltd primarily intended to investigate the ceramic clay characteristics of the Lough Neagh Group. Further, relatively shallow, drilling in the Crumlin area by the Geological Survey followed in 1975 and 1976 (Bazley, 1978). The real importance, however, of the lignite beds at Crumlin was first established by a drilling programme carried out by Mossbrook Colliery Ltd and Shirland Fireclay Ltd in 1978. Their original intention was to explore for shallow Carboniferous coal at Bally-castle and in east Tyrone. During early discussions with the Geological Survey in October 1975 about the Carboniferous coal prospects the available information on lignite at Crumlin was drawn to the company's attention. Subsequently, the company obtained a prospecting licence, from the Department of Commerce (since renamed the Department of Economic Development) which enabled exploration to take place both in the Carbo-niferous coalfield areas and at Crumlin. When the company concluded that there was little prospect of locating substantial deposits of Carboniferous coal at shallow depths attention was concentrated on the Crumlin area.

After 1978 the Geological Survey planned to investigate by drilling the

Table 3.1

Fuel Technology (partial proximate analyses) of lignite from Northern Ireland

	BALLYMONEY *	COAGH *	CRUMLIN (Lower seam as mined)
			(Planning Application – 1985 submitted by Northern Strip Mining Ltd)
Ash content Range (average) %	11.4–76.4% (47%)	4.4–69.4% (39.23%)	(6.9%)
Moisture content Range (average) %	30.7–59.5% (36.2%)	30.9–53.1% (39.9%)	(51%)
Calorific value	690–9330Btu/lb (2674Btu/lb) 383–5183 Kcal/kg (1486 Kcal/kg)	1680–10180Btu/lb (5704Btu/lb) 933–5655 Kcal/kg (3169 Kcal/kg)	(5101 Btu/lb) (2834 Kcal/kg)
Sulphur (Dry basis) %	0.51%	0.17%	0.2%

* All lignite samples were subject to atmospheric drying prior to analysis.

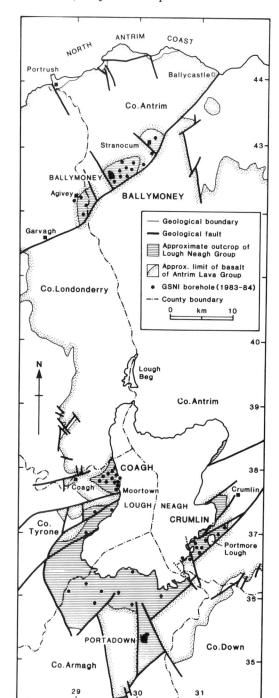

Figure 3.2 Distribution of
the Lough Neagh Group in
Northern Ireland.

lignite and ceramic clay potential of the Lough Neagh Group outcrop outside the Crumlin area but the work was deferred due to priority being given to other exploration projects including experimental seismic surveys. In 1981-2 and 1983 the Department of Economic Development, acting on the advice of the Geological Survey, commissioned seismic surveys in east Tyrone, primarily to provide information on the hydrocarbon prospects but also to give an indication of the extent and thickness of the Lough Neagh Group outcrop which had been postulated on the basis of both gravity and limited geological evidence, in the area to the east of Coagh.

Later in 1983 the Geological Survey commenced drilling the first of 49 boreholes (Figure 3.2) in the Ballymoney and Coagh areas and around the southern shore of Lough Neagh. In the first of these boreholes at Greenville near Ballymoney some 70 m of lignite was encountered while later in 1984 the first hole in the Coagh area penetrated 34 m of lignite in two seams thus establishing the basis on which subsequent drilling was founded. No thick lignite beds were encountered in the other areas explored.

The results of qualitative assessments of lignite from Ballymoney, Coagh and Crumlin are presented in Table 3.1.

On the basis of these findings the Department of Economic Development in 1986 awarded prospecting licences to BP Coal Ltd for the Coagh area, the Meekatharra Minerals for the Ballymoney area and to Anglo United Development Corporation/Grenmore Holdings Ltd for the area at Lough Beg adjacent to the Crumlin deposit.

Ballymoney deposit

Prior to 1983 there was no evidence that rocks other than basalts of the Antrim Lava Group occurred on the north-west side of the Tow Valley Fault Zone in the Garvagh-Ballymoney-Stranocum area of Counties Antrim and Londonderry. In fact, the geological map of Northern Ireland published in 1977 indicates that the Upper Basalt Formation occurs to the north-west of the fault and that to the south-east only Lower Basalts occur.

On the gravity map of Northern Ireland (originally published in 1967) the existence of a major north-east to south-west trending zone of steep gravity gradient running from Ballycastle, through Ballymoney and on further to the south-west, is conspicuous (Figure 3.3). This zone is correlated with the Tow Valley Fault, a major deep-seated crustal fracture of probable Caledonoid origin which has undergone reactivation, mainly comprising downthrow to the north-west, at least in the Mesozoic and also in the early and late Tertiary. Between the trace of the Tow Valley Fault Zone and the North Antrim coast, the observed Bouguer anomalies are dominated by a low gravity field.

In 1965-6 a borehole at Port More confirmed the existence of a thick succession (1,197 m) of Permo-Trias rocks in the North Antrim Basin, without reaching the base of the sequence. Interpretation of the regional gravity anomalies therefore attributed the low gravity field of this area to the thick "basin" of Mesozoic and Carboniferous strata underlying the

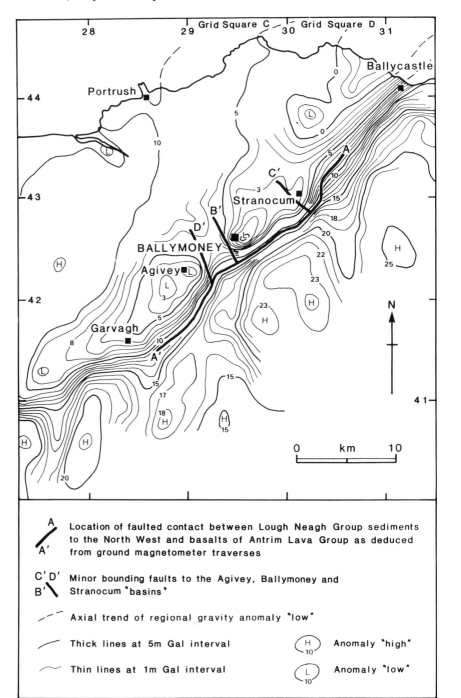

Figure 3.3 Simplified
Bouguer anomaly map of
parts of Counties Antrim
and Londonderry.

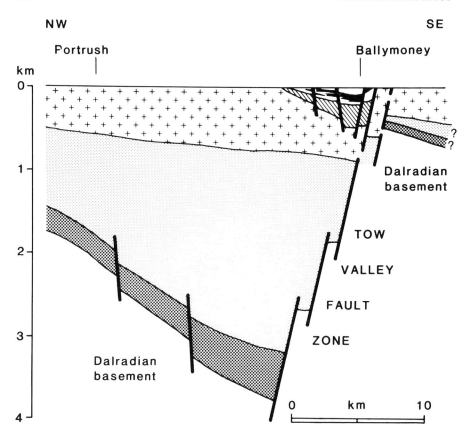

NW   SE

Portrush   Ballymoney

Dalradian
basement

TOW

VALLEY

FAULT

ZONE

Dalradian
basement

0   km   10

Figure 3.4   Schematic
section of the north Antrim
Basin.

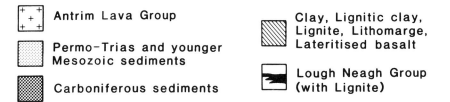

Antrim Lava Group

Permo-Trias and younger
Mesozoic sediments

Carboniferous sediments

Clay, Lignitic clay,
Lignite, Lithomarge,
Lateritised basalt

Lough Neagh Group
(with Lignite)

lavas (Bennett, 1978). It was surprising then that rock samples from a water borehole located on the south-west fringe of Ballymoney in the autumn of 1983 on the assumed trace of the Tow Valley Fault Zone did not consist of basalt, as expected by the Geological Survey, but yielded grey clay with wood and lignite fragments to a depth of 151 m. Fortunately this information became available while the plans for the Geological Survey's lignite exploration programme were being finalised and a borehole (13/598) drilled in December 1983 was sited to check on the inconclusive evidence from the water borewell.

A subsequent review of gravity data (JRP Bennett, personal communication) for the Ballymoney area reaffirmed the existence of the zone of steep gravity gradient which is correlated with the Tow Valley Fault Zone

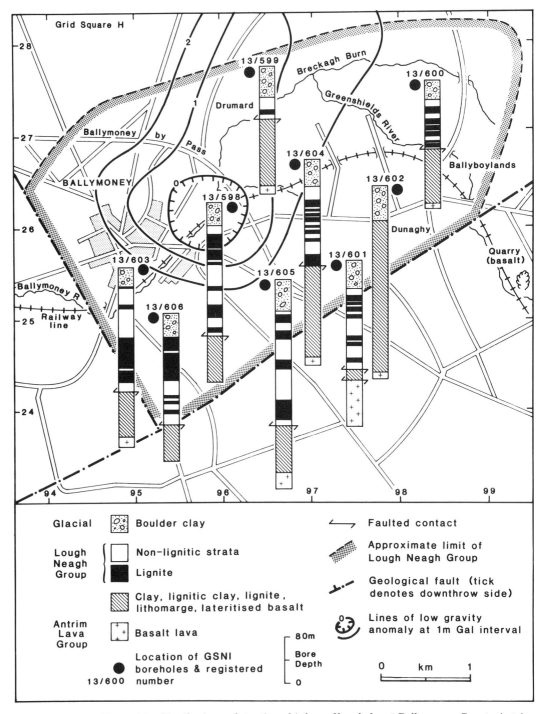

Figure 3.5   Distribution and stratigraphic logs of boreholes at Ballymoney, County Antrim

and also noted the existence of two separate closures around areas of low Bouguer anomalies at Agivey, County Londonderry and Ballymoney-Stranocum, County Antrim. It was also apparent that the south-eastward deflection of the isogals representing the Tow Valley Fault Zone, particularly at Ballymoney and Stranocum, was probably caused by the superimposition of the south-easterly-thickening wedge of Tertiary sediments consisting mainly of clay, with subordinate lignite, on top of the Tow Valley Fault Zone (Figure 3.4).

The first borehole (13/598) drilled at Ballymoney by the Geological Survey was sited more or less in the axis of the local gravity low (Figure 3.5). This borehole, which reached a final depth of 318.7 m, penetrated almost 200 m of Lough Neagh Group sediments including a gross thickness of 70 m of lignite in a multiple seam deposit.

To try and establish the extent of the Lough Neagh Group outcrop groundbased magnetometer surveys were subsequently undertaken in the Agivey-Ballymoney-Stranocum areas. These indicate that the southern edge of the sedimentary basin lies about 1.5 km south of Ballymoney Railway Station. Both the southern and western margins of the Ballymoney basin may be faulted (Figure 3.5). Elsewhere the Lough Neagh Group rests on a thick succession of interbedded lithomarge, pyroclastic deposits and lacustrine sediments which comprise the uppermost part of the Antrim Lava Group in this area.

Coagh deposit*

Prior to 1984 there was no evidence that lignite beds occurred in the area lying between Coagh and the shore of Lough Neagh some 7 km due east. On the 6-inch field maps, however, prepared by the geological surveyors in 1878 and 1879, "Pliocene Beds", comprising, "classy with lignite" are recorded to the south of Salter's Castle (Irish Grid H952 824) in a belt 2.5 km wide fringing the west shore of Lough Neagh. These are shown on the One-Inch to One Mile map, Sheet 27 (Cookstown), published in 1880 and described in the Geological Memoir as comprising mainly clay and sand occurring within 3 m of the surface – particularly along the Ballinderry River east of Ballinderry Bridge and the area south of the river. The clays were variably coloured in shades of green, blue and red with layers of white sand and "lignite", while lignite and wood fragments were ubiquitous. Since the range of drift thickness recorded in the 12 boreholes drilled by the Geological Survey in 1984 is 16-36 m (Figure 3.6), there must be some doubt as to the veracity of the Tertiary age ascribed to the near-surface deposits recorded during the original geological survey.

The seismic surveys carried out in 1981-2 and 1983 indicated that in the area between Ballinderry Bridge and Ardboe (Figure 3.6) there was a prominent, shallow basin-like structure defined by a prominent reflector. This was interpreted as the top of the Antrim Lava Group and the overlying

* Although Coagh is not in the basin, it is the nearest village to the deposit, hence the use of the designation, Coagh deposit.

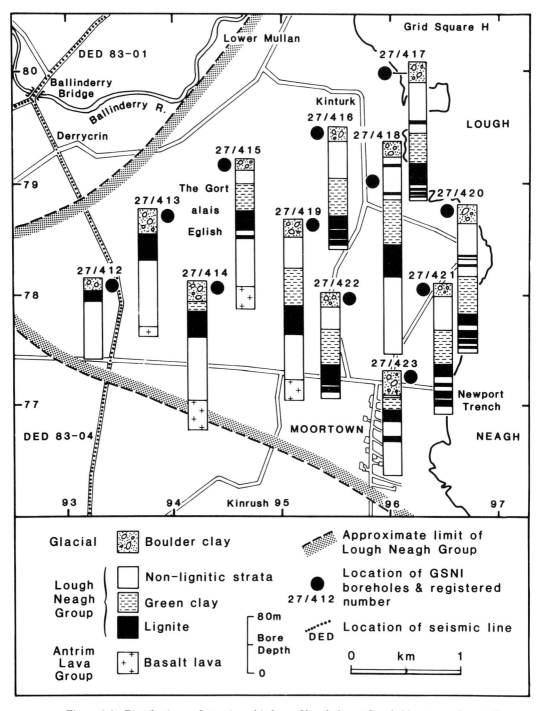

Figure 3.6 Distribution and stratigraphic logs of boreholes at Coagh-Moortown, County Tyrone.

low velocity layer was considered to represent deposits of the Lough Neagh Group. Thus, by 1983, although there was evidence for the existence of Tertiary sedimentary strata in the area east of Coagh, there was little evidence of their nature. Further investigation by drilling was therefore planned.

In order to penetrate, at an early stage in the exploration programme, the maximum possible thickness of strata of the Lough Neagh Group, the first borehole was located close to the centre of the "seismic" basin. This borehole (27/413) which was drilled in June 1984 at The Gort (alias Eglish), to a depth of 183.8 m demonstrated the existence of strata of the Lough Neagh Group, containing in total some 34 m of lignite, mostly in one seam, and then penetrated highly weathered basalt of the Antrim Lava Group at 171.2 m. Eleven further boreholes all proved the existence of lignite either in a single seam as in the western boreholes or, towards the lough, as a multiple seam deposit (Figure 3.6). Although the full extent of the basin has not yet been defined the strata appear to be disposed in a simple basin, deepening towards the Lough at a dip averaging about 10%.

The Lough Neagh Group in the vicinity of Coagh consists of four easily recognised lithological units. The lowest stratigraphic unit of the Group consists of variably coloured, mainly blue-grey and brown clay, sandy clay with ironstone bands, beds of lignitic clay up to 2 m thick and rare, thin beds of lignite. Although conglomeratic beds commonly occur towards the base of the Group, the precise junction with the top of the underlying Antrim Lava Group cannot always be accurately defined as the lavas are usually deeply weathered and consist of lithomarge and multicoloured clays.

The lower lithological unit is overlain by lignite with a gross thickness of between 19 and 49 m (the 19 m occurs in borehole 27/423 in the south-east corner) occurring either in a single seam or in thinner multiple seams. The base of the main lignite seam is not clearly defined as the lignite passes downwards through alternating layers of clayey lignite and lignitic clay into the underlying clays. The upper surface of the lignite is invariably and abruptly overlain by distinctive, olive-green clays between 18 and 65 m thick with occasional ironstone (siderite) bands. With the exception of two boreholes, in the north-west (35 m in 27/415) and south-east (18 m in 27/423) of the Coagh Basin, the complete thickness of green clays varies only from 51 to 65 m.

Lying above the green clays and representing the highest beds of the Lough Neagh Group in the Coagh Basin is a variable sequence of brown, grey and blue-grey sand, sandy clay and clay with ironstone nodules and bands; and numerous thin layers of lignitic clay, clayey lignite and lignite rarely more than 1.5 m thick. The transition zone between these beds and the underlying green clays is never more than 1m thick and consists of layers of alternating coloured clays with rare wood fragments. The maximum thickness of strata assigned to the Lough Neagh Group in the Coagh Basin is 283 m (unbottomed).

Crumlin deposit

As has already been mentioned, the occurrence of clays, lignite and silicified wood in the vicinity of Crumlin, County Antrim, was known locally from an early date but the full extent of the lignite deposits has been revealed only gradually during the systematic exploration carried out over the past 10 years and still in progress.

Within this area the Lough Neagh Group is poorly exposed as it is generally covered by 15-20 m of unconsolidated deposits of Pleistocene boulder clay with lenses of sand and Recent alluvium, river terrace and raised beach gravel and blown sand. As nearly all the geological information of the Crumlin area is commercially confidential the generalised sequence given below is based on the Geological Survey's own drilling programmes and information published by Northern Strip Mining Ltd.

Lough Neagh Group: Succession in the Crumlin Basin

Clays – clays and silty clays, medium to dark
 blue-grey, generally laminated, firm to
 stiff, thin beds of lignite, lignitic
 clay, sand and ironstone   - 0-100 m

Upper Lignite -   multiple beds of clayey lignite,
 significant lateral variation with
 interbedded clays and lignitic clays;
 splits to the east   - 0-25 m

Clays -   clay and silty clay, blue-grey to
 brown, occasional beds of sandy clay
 and ironstone   - 35-90 m

Lower Lignite -   multiple lignite beds interbedded with
 think clay and lignitic clay; laterally
 persistent and uniform   - 17-42 m

Basal Clays -   clay, pale grey, stiff, overlying the
 Antrim Lava Group   - 15-40 m

The vertical and lateral distribution of these strata is shown in Figure 3.7 as a section drawn across the southern part of the deposit.

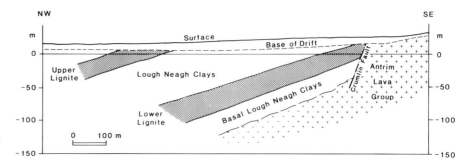

Figure 3.7 Diagrammatic section of the southern part of the Crumlin Basin.

From the borehole data the Lough Neagh Group is now known to be bounded to the north-west and south-east by two sub-parallel north-east-south-west trending faults, the Lennymore Fault and the Crumlin Fault respectively. Only in the northeast does the Group probably rest unconformably on the underlying Upper Basalt Formation of the Antrim Lava Group.

Gold

The presence of alluvial gold in the Sperrin Mountains has attracted attention intermittently over the years; Briggs et al. (1973) showed that it was used in the Bronze Age for gold ornaments, and they also reported trace amounts of alluvial gold from the area. A company called New Industrial Issues obtained a concession for mining gold in 1935 and published an extremely optimistic account of the presence of gold in streams around Newtownstewart and Faughanvale. There is, however, no record of gold having been mined or indeed of any systematic exploration until the 1970s, although a number of gold occurrences were recorded by prospectors.

From 1973 to 1975 part of the Sperrins was held under a prospecting licence and grains of gold were recorded from six localities in bedrock belonging to the Upper Dalradian Mullaghcarn Schists. During the Geological Survey of Northern Ireland's Mineral Exploration Programme carried out over the Sperrin Mountains area between 1973 and 1975, alluvial gold was described from nearly 30 sites, mainly on Upper Dalradian metasediments. Most of the gold occurred as flattened flakes but the source of the gold was not located.

Since 1981, much of the Sperrin Mountains has been held under licence by Ulster Minerals Limited (Ennex PLC). For the first time gold has been discovered in bedrock and in the Ennex Annual Report for 1984 gold in boulders is referred to from over 130 sites in an area of about 13 km^2 and gold in outcrop is shown from 22 localities. Clifford (1986) reports that the gold mineralisation is predominantly associated with quartz veins. One area, at Curraghinalt, has been the focus of intensive exploration since 1983. The float boulders containing gold reflect the presence of 16 mineralised vein structures. On the basis of trenching and drilling, a geological ore reserve of 1,000,000 short tons grading 0.28 ounces gold (cut) per short ton has been calculated (Ennex PLC 1986).

With the results of these investigations becoming more widely known, most of the remaining outcrop of Dalradian rocks in Northern Ireland has been licenced for exploration. Alluvial gold is known elsewhere in the province; in County Down it has been described from five localities along the Leitrim River and also in bedrock in the Mourne Mountains Granite, and exploration is now turning towards these areas.

References

Barton, R., 1757. *Lectures in natural philosophy designed to be a foundation for reasoning pertinantly upon the petrifactions, gems, crystals and sanative quality of Lough Neagh in Ireland.* Dublin.

Bazley, R.A.B., 1976. The Tertiary and Quaternary sediments of Lough Neagh – a consideration of the economic potential of the clays, lignites and ironstones. *Geological Survey of Northern Ireland Open File Report No.55.*

Bennett, J.R.P., 1978, *in Geology of the Causeway Coast II*, 143-56 by Wilson, H.E. and Manning, P.I. Belfast.

Bennett, J.R.P., 1983. *The sedimentary basins in Northern Ireland.* London.

Briggs, S., Brennan, J. and Freeburn, G., 1973. Irish Pre-historic gold working: some geological and metallurgical considerations, *in Bull. Historical Metallurgy Group* 7, 18-26.

Clifford, J.A., 1986. A note on gold mineralization in County Tyrone, *in* Andrew, C.J., Crowe, R.W., Finlay, S., Pennell, W. and Pyne, J.F. (eds) *Geology and genesis of mineral deposits in Ireland.* Dublin.

Ennex PLC, 1986. *Quarterly Report to Shareholders, Sept. 1986.*

Griffith, R., 1837-8. *Second report of the commissioners appointed to consider and recommend a general system of railways for Ireland*, H.C., XXXV, 34.

Stewart, D.S., 1800. Report to the Dublin Society, *in Trans. Dubl. Soc.* 1, 142.

Mineral Exploration Programme Volumes 1-9, 1984. *Geological Survey of Northern Ireland, Belfast.*

4 Inland Waters

R. B. WOOD

Director, Limnology Laboratory; University of Ulster School of Environmental Science, at Coleraine

There is a strongly held belief in Northern Ireland that civilisation ends at the River Bann. This is as tenaciously held by those of us who live to the west as those in the Belfast area, although there is naturally some difference of opinion as to whether a traveller leaves civilisation moving west or eastwards.

This is a rather tenuous way of introducing a piece on freshwaters and their contribution to Belfast's setting, but the boundary is of freshwater and the Bann does divide the Province effectively in two (Figure 4.1), rising in the Mourne Mountains some five miles from Ulster's southern boundary in Carlingford Lough and discharging into the Atlantic Ocean at Castlerock on the North Coast. More usefully it sets a westerly limit to Belfast's region which, although arbitrary, includes those things I want to write about. Given the excellence of roads in the Province, the whole of Ulster is within easy reach of Belfast but, with due respect to the beauties of the Erne, the Foyle and the Roe, my inland water resource base of Belfast is east of the Bann.

The River Lagan

Belfast probably would not be there at all without a deep water harbour at the estuary of the River Lagan, and the river is clearly a major feature (Figure 5.2). Principally of amenity value now, it was significant in water-borne navigation in the 18th/19th century, linking Belfast with Lough Neagh, to the coal of County Tyrone and to small trading centres such as Ballyronan (McCutcheon, 1965 and 1980). It is around the river and the canal that the Lagan Valley Regional Park was formed.

The Park is a valued amenity accessible to the populations of Belfast and Lisburn and is administered by a committee drawn from Belfast, Castlereagh and Lisburn Councils, the National Trust, the Sports Council, the Ulster Countryside Committee and various Government departments, under the general guidance of the Department of the Environment for Northern Ireland (DoENI). It covers over 4,000 acres and, as well as the old canal works, the Park with its associated small lakes, Galwally and

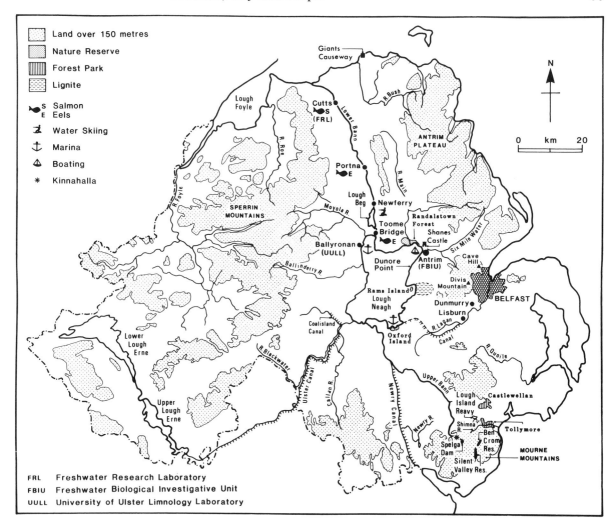

Figure 4.1   Location map with places mentioned in the text.

Ballydrain, supports interesting aquatic bird life, including kingfishers, dippers, wagtails, little grebes, herons, pochard and tufted duck. Plant life on the mixture of habitats offered by river and silted up canal is varied and includes Himalayan Balsam (*Impatiens glandulifera*) and *Anthriscus sylvestris* (Cow Parsley). Further details of the Park, particularly of noteworthy buildings and monuments, can be found in *The Lagan Valley* (HMSO, 1977).

For those more active in using the Lagan's amenity resource, anglers and boating folk perhaps have cause for complaint. The Lagan has not for many years supported salmon, and, certainly until recently, very low values for dissolved oxygen in some reaches have been common. But trout, pike and other fish flourish in the upper reaches and, with current refurbishment of sewage works, improvement can be expected. In recent years £25 million has been committed by DoENI for improving the sewerage system in Belfast and for upgrading four sewage works which discharge into the

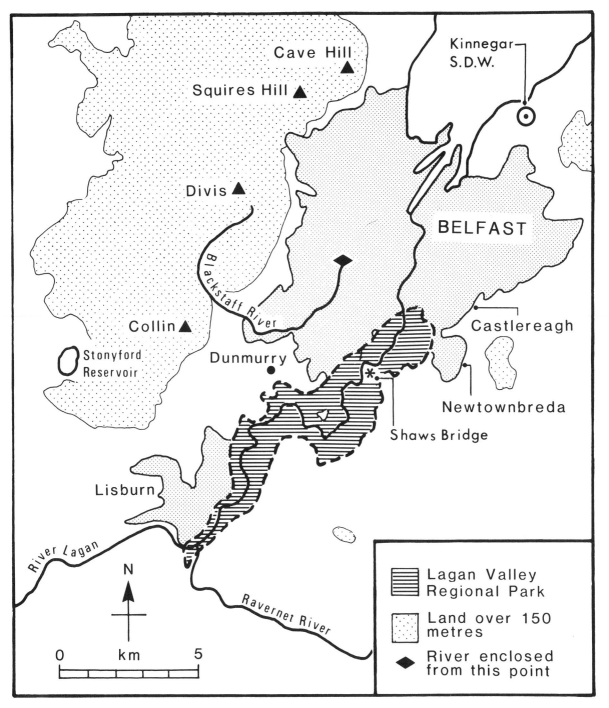

Figure 4.2   Lagan Valley
Regional Park.

The Lagan Valley at Lisburn, County Antrim, looking north-east towards Belfast seen in the distance. The river and the adjoining canal once provided a commercial link between Belfast, Lough Neagh and the linen manufacturing towns of the Lagan Valley; now it forms a green corridor for outdoor recreation as the Lagan Valley Regional Park.
(C.F.S. Newman)

non-tidal reaches of the Lagan. Dunmurry works is complete and is now producing a much improved 5/5 effluent (Biological Oxygen Demand/Suspended Solids) against a 10/10 consent and the normal Royal Commission Standard for discharges of 20/30. Upper Falls and Newtownbreda are scheduled for completion in mid-1987 and New Holland (Lisburn) works will be started in mid-1987. Nine major industrial polluters of the non-tidal Lagan have been identified and eight of these, since 1970, have been improved so that they can now discharge through the sewage works. The long-term aim of DoENI is that below Lisburn, the Lagan shall achieve at least Grade 2 status, and above Lisburn, Grade 1.

Those viewing the Lagan in Central Belfast will perhaps question the optimistic note of the previous paragraph. At low tide ugly and rubbish-covered mud banks are exposed, the polluting skills of an industrialised community conserved for all (particularly the Belfast and Queen's University Boat Clubs) to appreciate. Even allowing for man's great capacity for fouling his own nest, the Lagan does present certain special problems. Something approaching half a million people live within its catchment and heavy industry is still significant. Yet the river itself drains a small area and has a mean discharge of only some 8.7 m^3 sec^{-1}, resulting in, at times, a ratio of low flow to sewage volume of 1:1. To avoid pollution, the sewage has to be of exceptionally high quality.

Improvements are afoot even for the more heavily populated and industrialised tidal reaches of the Lagan. A major hydrological survey of the estuary is almost complete and decisions on the siting of new weirs will be made, balancing the covering or dredging of the accumulated muds, the desirability of a free flow of freshwater and the restriction of the tidal zone to further downstream. These will clearly be major and recognisable works. Less spectacular but equally valuable was the commissioning in the late 1970s of the new sewage disposal works at Kinnegar serving the east of Belfast (£7 million including associated works) and the comprehensive survey and refurbishment of inadequate sewers within the city, many a century old, against a background of urban renewal and shifting population.

Lough Neagh

In joining the Upper and Lower Rivers Bann, Lough Neagh provides about 15 miles of my boundary between Belfast and "the rest". Like the River Lagan it represents a considerable amenity resource but unlike the Lagan it is Belfast's biggest water supply resource with a current operational capacity through Dunore Point (Figure 4.1) of 127 Ml d^{-1} compared with the 112 Ml d^{-1} capacity of the Silent Valley (see below). That Belfast preferentially uses the Silent Valley supply reflects the very different costs involved. Silent Valley is an upland reservoir (gravity fed to Belfast) of remarkable purity requiring little treatment. Lough Neagh water requires expensive pumping over the Divis Mountain/Cave Hill high ground to the west of Belfast and is of comparatively poor quality. The story of that poor quality and its rectification is worthy of special comment as it involves a very considerable scientific and environmental effort on a national scale in recent years and appears to be having a happy ending.

In the middle 1960s Belfast Water Commissioners seeking new water resources investigated the 365 10^9 m^3 reservoir, Lough Neagh. While the effects of any abstraction on lough levels and discharge (and hence fish migrations) in the Lower Bann were being considered, Lough Neagh, in 1967, produced a spectacular bloom of *Anabaena flos-aquae*. Great concentrations of these algae impaired water filtration to the point of almost closing the British Enkalon Factory in Antrim, killed fish held in keep-boxes in the Lough, generated unpleasant sights and smells, and generally brought into question the Lough as a resource, for water supply, for sustaining Europe's largest eel fishery and as a wild life habitat of international repute.

The embryonic New University of Ulster had previously decided to make freshwater biology one of its major specialisms and had recruited its first staff to its lough-side Laboratory near Ballyronan. Following the 1967 bloom, a government laboratory, the Freshwater Biological Investigative Unit (FBIU) was also established under the Department of Agriculture for Northern Ireland (DANI) to seek out the causes and remedies for the poor quality of Lough Neagh. With excellent co-operation between the two laboratories and with other groups such as the Water Service of DoENI, the Water Quality Branch of Department of Economic Development for Northern Ireland and the Fisheries Laboratory of the Department of Agriculture of Northern Ireland (DANI), the problem has been thoroughly studied, and remedies identified and recently applied. It is not possible here either to précis or even list all the 200 or so scientific papers which the two principal laboratories have published, and the countless departmental minutes, memoranda and meetings which have been generated in the past 20 years.

In outline, Lough Neagh was shown to be among the world's most eutrophic or enriched lakes (Wood and Gibson 1973) supporting algal populations of species (*Oscillatoria redekei, Oscillatoria agardhii, Stephanodiscus astraea, Melosira italica*) and quantities (with chlorophyll *a* values increasing to peaks of 130 μ l^{-1} by 1981-82) typical of enriched lakes elsewhere (Gibson et al., 1971; Gibson, 1975a; Gibson and Fitzsimons, 1982). Photosynthesis by phytoplankton and its controlling factors (Jewson, 1975, 1976, 1977a and b; Jones, 1977a,b,c,d, 1978, 1979), Lough Neagh's notorious midge populations (Carter 1975, 1976, 1980) and the lough's levels of dissolved oxygen and algal nutrients (Gibson, 1975b, 1981, 1984a; Smith, 1972, 1975) all confirmed the initial diagnosis and showed phosphorus to be the key nutrient setting the upper limit to phytoplankton growth (Stevens, 1978). Laborious studies of nutrient budgets and sources both external (Smith, 1973, 1975; Alexander and Stevens, 1976; Parr and Smith, 1978; Smith, 1977; Smith and Stewart, 1977; Stevens and Stewart, 1982; Smith, 1984) and internal (Stevens and Gibson, 1977; Rippey, 1977, 1983) were carried out. Soluble phosphate originating from sewage disposal works and creameries was recognised as a significant fraction, perhaps

Plain of Myroe, County Londonderry   *N. C. Mitchel*

Northern Ireland has splendid natural resources of scenery and habitat, though really good agricultural land is limited.

The Roe Valley (above) is one of the best arable areas, its large flat fields seen here with ripening grain. This area of County Londonderry is known as the Plain of Myroe, and is backed by the dramatic basalt scarp of Binevenagh, where peregrines soar and rare arctic-alpine flora clings to the inaccessible cliffs. This is ideal country for gliding and hang gliding.

Island of Muck, County Antrim   *Ulster Trust for Nature Conservation*

Sand and Gravel Quarry, County Down

C. F. S. Newman

Islands often provide a refuge for wild life. Here on the Island of Muck off the east coast of County Antrim, young volunteers are carrying out a vegetation survey. The Island was acquired by the Ulster Trust for Nature Conservation by inviting people to buy a 'yard of Muck'.

Glacial activity in the uplands has endowed the province with vast resources of glacial sands and gravels which are used in the construction industry, either as aggregate or converted into concrete blocks. This quarry is in one of the morainic deposits which mask the lower slopes of the Mourne Mountains in County Down.

Whitepark Bay, County Antrim   *C. F. S. Newman*

All the Counties in the Province have their share of beautiful scenery –
Lakeland in Fermanagh, Sperrin Uplands in Tyrone and Derry, apple orchards
and Slieve Gullion in Armagh, and Strangford Lough and the Mournes in
Down, and spectacular coastline in Antrim. Dark basalt cliffs and white
pristine beaches are the breathtaking scenery of the Causeway Coast of north
Antrim. This area is still relatively unspoiled, and needs careful planning to
keep it that way.

Springhill, County Londonderry   *R. H. Buchanan*

Mourne Mountains, County Down

R. H. Buchanan

Springhill, near Moneymore, County Londonderry. Ulster has its share of interesting country houses in public ownership. This National Trust property has a decidedly Ulster flavour and charm to its simple seventeenth century facade, in tune with its traditional rural surroundings.

The rugged granite peaks of the Mourne Mountains form a scenic backdrop to much of County Down's gentle rolling topography. They are most impressive when seen, as here, rising steeply from the sea above Newcastle.

as high as 40 per cent, of the active phosphate and, equally importantly, the fraction most susceptible to control. After extensive work on a bauxite (=laterite) quarried in County Antrim which proved to be an excellent phosphorus coagulant, a process was developed for application not only to sewage disposal works but also to the decolourising of drinking water (Sutton, 1976; Gray, 1985). Over the past two to three years phosphorus reduction has been gradually introduced in ten major sewage disposal works with some 60 tonnes (of an estimated annual input from all external sources of some 250 tonnes) prevented from entering the lough. With fine-tuning at the works, the 60 tonnes may be raised to near 100 tonnes which, with anticipated lessening of anoxia and P-loading from the sediment of the lough, and changing practice in creamery operation and septic tank disposal, may be expected to bring about significant improvement. Already, allowing for year to year variation, there is evidence that the steady upward trends in phosphorus and phytoplankton concentrations observed from 1968 to 1981 have been halted and possibly reversed (Gibson, 1986; Wood and Smith, 1987 in press). Of particular relevance to Belfast's water supply, improved water quality may revive prospects of increased water abstraction from Lough Neagh thereby easing environmentally less acceptable new impoundments in the Mournes as recently proposed for Kinnehala (Dennison and Sweetnam, 1979). Economic recession (and vigorous waste detection) have given breathing space for the better planning of new water supplies and Lough Neagh's improvement may be most opportune.

Lough Neagh studies have not been restricted solely to current eutrophication. For example, palaeolimnological reconstruction of the history of the Lough in recent centuries from analysis of dated sediment cores has, through the evidence of fossil diatoms (Battarbee, 1978), chironomids (Carter 1977), and various trace metals (Rippey, 1982; Rippey et al., 1982) enabled us to identify the timing of the rate of deterioration, describe the less disturbed condition and set targets for Lough Neagh's rehabilitation. Many other studies have been made, for example, a ten-year analysis of zooplankton populations (Andrew & Fitzsimons, in press), the finer details of algal ecology (Foy, 1980, 1983; Jewson et al., 1981; Gibson and Foy, 1983; Gibson, 1984b; Riddols 1985a,b), inshore invertebrates (Murphy & Carter, 1984), and the fish populations, in particular pollan (Wilson, 1983, Wilson & Pitcher, 1979, 1983, 1984a,b; Dabrowski, 1981, 1982a; Dabrowski et al., 1984; Ferguson, 1974; Ferguson et al., 1978), brown trout (Crozier, 1983) aspects of eel and salmon runs (Kennedy and Vickers, in a major review soon to be published) and a somewhat superficial synthesis of the brown and silver eel catches by the Lough Neagh Fishermen's Cooperative over the past 22 years (Wood, 1984).

When a similar volume to this was written for the 1952 British Association meeting in Belfast, the biological treatment was essentially a description of interesting and perhaps unusual species and associations. We can update reference to one or two features of Lough Neagh's unusual biota. Pollan (*Coregonus pollan* Thompson) still survives but is less rigorously

Eel weir at Portna on the River Bann in County Antrim. Eels have been fished on the Bann since prehistoric times, and now form an important export, mainly to continental Europe. (N.I. Tourist Board)

fished than in the past. Wilson and Dabrowskis' excellent population studies have already been referred to, while of zoogeographical interest is Ferguson's demonstration, using modern electrophoretic analysis of enzyme proteins, that Lough Neagh (and Lough Erne) pollan are conspecific with Alaskan and Siberian populations (which, in marked contrast to the Lough Neagh fish, migrate between fresh and salt water and inhabit waters of very low temperature) and are more distantly related to the *Coregonus* found in Scotland, England and Wales. Ferguson postulates an invasion of Irish fresh waters at the edge of the last retreating ice-sheet at a time when a persistent pocket of ice kept the rivers of Great Britain ice-bound. When eventually unfrozen, those rivers were invaded by more warmth-tolerant stock at that time occupying the warmer ambient oceanic waters.

Another glacial relict, *Mysis relicta*, mentioned in the 1952 volume remains numerous and makes significant contribution to the food of fish. A two year study of its populations will be published shortly by Andrew & Woodward. An unusual feature of *Mysis relicta* is that elsewhere it appears to have a brackish water preference and a high dissolved oxygen requirement, neither of which obtains in Lough Neagh.

The eel and salmon runs into the Lough system remain of very great biological, economic and social importance. Since the last British Association meeting, the eel fishery has formed into a very successful co-operative, employing some 500 men and with a turnover of between £2 million and £3 million per annum. The bulk of the labour is involved in fishing for brown eels in the open lough in all weathers, but the men share the proceeds from the less labour-intensive silver eel fishery which catches (using the permanent engines at Toomebridge and Portna) nearly mature eels as they migrate to the sea from August to November. Financial returns to individual fishermen remain modest but in Northern Ireland 500 jobs are very welcome. The commercial salmon fishery too, based on permanent engines just upstream of Coleraine has recently been reorganised and a more coherent policy of conservation and exploitation should follow, with angling assuming its proper role.

The fish of Lough Neagh, though perceptibly more fully studied than they were in 1952, still represent a large gap in our knowledge. Perch populations in the late 1970s increased noticeably and for a brief period provided a lucrative local fishery. For uncertain reasons (but probably including over-fishing and/or natural causes and/or severe competition from the recently introduced and explosively increasing populations of roach) that fishery collapsed in 1983 but shows some signs of recovery. Scientific studies of both perch and roach are now in hand at the University Laboratory (by Winfield, Tobin and Montgomery) and are generating data which should be of great value in establishing valid criteria for fishing regulations; at present no study of the ecology of young eels is in hand. The enormous populations of the "trash" fish roach are particularly worrying in the context of competition with commercially important fish; although for coarse angling, the roach are naturally very popular, having been the basis of numerous world records in angling competitions in the Erne.

Sport angling in the Lough Neagh system is almost entirely restricted to rivers. It is not possible to quantify the number of anglers using Lough Neagh rivers, but in Ulster 2,000 anglers are registered members of Angling Clubs, vigorous Associations fish the River Main, River Six Mile Water, Rivers Upper and Lower Bann and it seems likely that Belfast folk participate significantly, even if sea angling is closer to hand. Many stretches of the rivers support excellent game fishing but it would be misleading to imply that all is well. Impoverished reaches undoubtedly exist variously due, for example, to outdated pockets of industry with inadequate effluent treatment – perhaps struggling to stay in business – to the unsubtle efforts of drainage engineers seeking to improve farm land, and to negligence by farmers who leak farm effluent into rivers. Significant fish kills, coincident with silage harvesting, show that much remains to be done and sewage and water treatment works have not been blameless.

It is their waters which are the basis for the internationally recognised significance of Lough Neagh and Lough Beg with regard to their wildfowl populations. In a soon to be published review of the birds of Lough Neagh and Lough Beg, J. Furphy rightly regrets the absence of sustained scientific study of the avifauna and pays tribute to the amateur Northern Ireland Ornithologists' Club which, over the years, has carried out wildfowl counts. More recently wardening staff of the DoENI, Craigavon Borough Council and the Royal Society for the Protection of Birds have contributed significantly. Wintering populations of 24,000 Tufted Duck, 20,000 Pochard and 5,000 Golden Eye have been recorded, while late summer populations of 7,000 Mallard and 4,000 Coot have occurred. Scaup (up to 1,400) show peaks in spring and autumn (perhaps indicating that the Lough Neagh

Coarse angling competition on the Erne in County Fermanagh. The Erne has some of the finest coarse angling waters in western Europe, and major facilities for anglers have been provided by the Department of Agriculture and the local council. (N.I. Tourist Board)

system is a staging post on their migration route) and there are significant populations of Teal, Pintail, and Shoveller. The ten pairs of Gadwall although tenuously few, actually represent a recent increase and the beautiful Great Crested Grebe appears to be surviving well, with approximately 300 birds, mostly in the vicinity of the Oxford Island Nature Reserve. An imaginative management policy (helped by a 100 mile coastline) seeks to accommodate the needs of both conservation and gun clubs.

In the previous British Association volume, Small (1952) quoted Tansley's observation (1939) that the Lough Neagh fen lands were "probably the most extensive in the British Isles still remaining comparatively unspoiled". Little has been published on the non-algal flora of Lough Neagh since the work of Praeger and Stellfox in the 1930s, but Harron's field studies which have just been published (Harron and Rushton, 1987, in press) have shown significant changes in distribution and abundance of some species and the major decline of others such as *Lathyrus palustris* (the Marsh Pea) and *Carex acuta* (the Slender Spiked Sedge) seems most likely to be the result of lowerings of the Lough up to the mid-1950s. At present both Lough Neagh and Lough Beg have been declared Areas of Scientific Interest (ASI) largely on the strength of their bird fauna and wetlands flora, and, within the global ASIs, conservation of the flora is of particular concern in the Nature Reserves at Oxford Island, Rea's Wood, Shane's Castle, Randalstown Forest and Farr's Bay.

Lough Neagh offers another major amenity, water sports. Although Belfast has ample access to the sea, thriving sailing clubs at Antrim, at Kinnegoe Bay, and, geographically more remote from Belfast, at Ballyronan (with its excellent new marina) provide valuable amenities particularly in winter. Vast non-tidal waters mean that sailing and water-skiing, as at New Ferry, can be enjoyed with little disturbance to wildlife, fishermen and other legitimate users of the multipurpose resource.

By the time Belfast next hosts the British Association meeting, Lough Neagh will have had to cope with environmental pressures of a new order. Lignite deposits at Crumlin will probably be exploited (Chapter 3); prospecting for other deposits is in hand; mining, processing, power generation and the necessary infra-structure are all likely to need careful control if the Lough's recent upturn in quality is to be sustained.

Other inland waters

Many readers will doubtless complain that this essay is grossly unbalanced, devoting 1,800 words to the featureless and boring Lough Neagh while lumping the beautiful waters of the Mournes, the tarns of the Antrim Plateau, the locally popular Quoile Pondage and the excellent fisheries on the River Bush in a final section called "others". Those many critics are probably right, but east of the Bann offers, by high Irish standards, relatively few, although locally valued, water bodies.

The lower reaches of the River Quoile and a small part of its associated marshes are a Nature Reserve noted for its avifauna, particularly Greylag

Hire cruiser on Lough Erne at Enniskillen. A major tourist industry based on the lakes and waterways of the Erne system has been developed over the past two decades. (N.I. Tourist Board)

Geese, and Widgeon. In spite of indifferent effluent from various towns along its feeder rivers, the Quoile Pondage was noted for its rudd fishing and recent improvements to sewage disposal works should at least prevent further deterioration.

Unique among British salmon rivers is the River Bush, draining westwards then northwards from the Antrim Plateau to discharge into the Atlantic just west of the Giant's Causeway. Its uniqueness is not that its waters sustain the world's oldest (and best) legal whiskey distillery, but that, by agreement between the riparian owner and the Government, an entire and important salmon river is under single management and subject to detailed study. In 1973 the Fisheries Research Laboratory (DANI) began a 30-year study (optionally renewable for a further 30 years) of all fish runs, stocking, returns, spawning, catches, etc. Published results are beginning to emerge from this very important study and Kennedy and Johnson (1987) have recently reviewed the project in print. For those who see little future for Northern Ireland, take heart! The Fisheries Research Laboratory still plans to be gathering its data on River Bush salmon in AD 2033.

Epilogue

Belfast, in its Northern Ireland setting, has enjoyed a pretty poor image in recent years, much of it undoubtedly deserved. In the context of its inland waters, although Ulster avoided the worst excesses of environmental degradation from industrialisation, it nevertheless developed major problems in the River Lagan, in Lough Neagh and in many stretches of other rivers. Many problems still remain and much has to be done. Effluent disposal, both urban and rural, industrial and agricultural, is very far from perfect as many fish farmers will confirm; drainage work, doubtless with the best intentions of improving agriculture, has scarred many rivers and impoverished angling; the public at large seem to have limitless supplies of old sofas with which to furnish our water ways; new pressures will arise from mining, intensive agriculture, fresh water abstraction and Ulster's desperate need to accommodate any enterprise offering employment. Against these must be set the real advances made in recent years. The Lagan and Lough Neagh appear to be improving; water quality black spots are being gradually turned grey if not virginal white; drainage engineers, in addition to building fishing stands and riverside walks are receiving training in conservation and the reinstatement of fisheries; the farming community seems to be increasingly aware of its responsibilities as well as its rights to the countryside. Throughout Ulster's recent troubled past much good work has been done on Belfast's freshwaters. Of course "they" (the authorities) are at times secretive, obtuse, misleading, inert, even wrong, but "we" (the good guys) seem to be more readily listened to as Ulster seeks to manage positively its resources for the common good, thoughtfully exploiting, and sometimes modifying or blocking development. Perhaps the most encouraging sign for the future is the positive response of the Government to the recommendations of the Balfour Report (Chapter 6) calling for increased support for conservation work, in the best sense of that over- and often mis-used word. It is not only the Thames which may soon carry salmon through a capital city.

Acknowledgements

My thanks go to many who have made available to me information which has not been published. Particularly I thank George Alexander, Joe Furphy, Jack Gault, David Logan and Brian Rushton. Throughout, misinterpretations, errors, bouquets and brick bats originate with the author.

References

Alexander G.C. and Stevens R.J., 1976. Per capita phosphorus loading from domestic sewage, in Water Res. 10, 757-64.
Battarbee R.W., 1978. Observations on the recent history of Lough Neagh and its drainage basin, in Phil. Trans. R. Soc., B28, 303-45.
Carter C.E., 1975. Emergence periods of the main species of chironomidae (Diptera) of Lough Neagh, in Ir. Nat. J. 18, 245-46.
Carter C.E., 1976. A population study of the chironomidae (Diptera) of Lough Neagh, in Oikos, 27, 346-54.
Carter C.E., 1977. The recent history of the chironomid fauna of Lough Neagh, from the analysis of remains in sediment cores, in Freshwat. Biol. 7, 415-23.

Carter C.E., 1978. The fauna of the muddy sediments of Lough Neagh, with particular reference to eutrophication, *in Freshwat. Biol.* 8, 547-59.

Carter C.E., 1980. Methods of summarising survey data from lakes illustrated by reference to Lough Neagh Northern Ireland, *in* Murray, D.A., *ed.*, *Chironomidae: ecology, systematics, cytology and physiology.* London, 217-24.

Crozier W.W., 1983. Population biology of Lough Neagh brown trout *(Salmo trutta L.)* Ph.D. Thesis, The Queen's University of Belfast.

Dabrowski K.R., 1981. The spawning and early life history of the pollan *Coregonus pollan Thompson* in Lough Neagh, Northern Ireland, *in Int. Rev. ges. Hydrobiol.* 66, 299-326.

Dabrowski K.R., 1981. Seasonal changes in the chemical composition of fish body and nutritional value of the muscle of pollan *Coregonus pollan Thompson from Lough Neagh, Northern Ireland, in Hydrobiol.* 87, 121-41.

Dabrowski K., Muranska E., Terlecki, J. and Wielgosz, S., 1984. Studies on the feeding of *Coregonus pollan* (Thompson) Alevins and Fry in Lough Neagh, *in Int. Rev. ges Hydrobiol.* 69, 529-40.

Dennison M. and Sweetnam R.J.N., 1979. *The Kinnehala Scheme: public enquiry.* Belfast.

Ferguson, A., 1974. The genetic relationships of the coregonid fishes of Britain and Ireland indicated by electrophoretic analysis of tissue proteins, *in J. Fish. Biol.* 6, 311-15.

Ferguson A., Himberg, K-J.M., and Svardson, G, 1978. Systematics of the Irish pollan *Coregonus pollan* Thompson: an electrophoretic comparison with other holarctic coregoninae, *in J. Fish Biol.* 12, 221-33.

Foy R.H., 1980. The influence of surface to volume ratio on the growth rates of planktonic blue-green algae, *in Br. Phycol. J.* 15, 279-89.

Foy R.H., 1983. Interactions of temperature and light on the growth rates of two planktonic *Oscillatoria* species under a short photo period regime, *in Br. Phycol. J.* 18, 267-73.

Gibson C.E., 1975a. Cyclomorphosis in natural populations of *Oscillatoria redekei* Van Goor, *in Freshwat. Biol.* 5, 279-86.

Gibson C.E., 1975b. A field and laboratory study of oxygen uptake by planktonic blue-green algae, *in J. Ecol.* 63, 867-80.

Gibson C.E., 1981. Silica budgets and the ecology of planktonic diatoms in an unstratified lake (Lough Neagh, N. Ireland), *in Int. Rev. ges Hydrobiol.* 66, 641-64.

Gibson C.E., 1984a. Eutrophication, oxygen and Lough Neagh, *in DoENI Conference on Lough Neagh and its Rivers. Antrim.*

Gibson C.E., 1984b. Sinking rates of planktonic diatoms in an unstratified lake: a comparison of field and laboratory observations, in Freshwat. Biol. 14, 507-15.

Gibson C.E. and Fitzsimons A.G., 1982. Periodicity and morphology of planktonic blue-green algae in an unstratified lake (Lough Neagh, Northern Ireland), *in Int. Rev. gest Hydrobiol.* 67, 459-76.

Gibson C.E. and Foy R.H., 1983. The photosynthesis and growth efficiency of a planktonic blue-green alga, *Oscillatoria redekei, in Br. Phycol. J.* 18, 39-45.

Gibson C.E., Wood R.B., Dickson E.L. and Jewson D.H., 1971. The succession of phytoplankton in Lough Neagh 1968-1970, *in Mitt. Internat. Verein Limnol.* 19, 146-60.

Gibson C.E., 1986. Preliminary results on phosphorus reduction in Lough Neagh – assessing the effect against a background of change, *in Hydrobiological Bulletin* 20, 173-82.

Gray A.W., 1985. Removal of phosphate at sewage treatment works and the implications on phosphate loadings into Lough Neagh, *in J. Inst. Wat. Eng. Sci.* 39, 1137-54.

Harron, J.E. and Rushton B.S., 1987. *Flora of Lough Neagh.* (In press, Belfast).

HMSO 1977. Department of Agriculture for Northern Ireland. *Ann. Report on Research and Technical Work.* Belfast. 79-91.

HMSO 1977. *The Lagan Valley: A guide to Ulster's first Regional Park.* Belfast.

Jewson D.H., 1975. The relation of incident radiation to diurnal rates of photosynthesis in Lough Neagh, *in Int. Rev. ges Hydrobiol.* 60, 759-67.

Jewson D.H., 1976. The interaction of components controlling net phytoplankton photosynthesis in a well-mixed lake (L. Neagh, Northern Ireland), *in Freshwat. Biol.* 6, 551-76.

Jewson D.H., 1977a. A comparison between *in situ* photosynthetic rates determined using 14^C uptake and oxygen evolution methods in Lough Neagh, Northern Ireland, *in Proc. R. Ir. Acad.* 77B, 87-99.

Jewson D.H., 1977b. Light penetration in relation to phytoplanktonic content of the euphotic zone of Lough Neagh, N. Ireland, *in Oikos* 28, 74-83.

Jewson D.H., Rippey B. and Gilmore W.K., 1981. Light penetration in relation to phytoplanktonic content of the euphotic zone of Lough Neagh, N. Ireland, *in Oikos* 28, 74-83.

Jones R.I., 1977a. Factors controlling phytoplankton production and succession in a highly eutrophic lake (Kinnego Bay, Lough Neagh) I. The phytoplankton community and its environment, *in J. Ecol.* 65, 547-60.

Jones R.I., 1977b. Factors controlling phytoplankton production and succession in a highly eutrophic lake (Kinnego Bay, Lough Neagh) II. Phytoplankton production and its chief determinants, *in J. Ecol.* 65, 561-78.

Jones R.I., 1977c. Factors controlling phytoplankton production and succession in a highly eutrophic lake (Kinnego Bay, Lough Neagh) III. Interspecific competition in relation to irradiance and temperature, *in J. Ecol.* 65, 579-86.

Jones R.I., 1977d. The importance of temperature conditioning to the respiration of natural phytoplankton communities, *in Br. Phycol.J.* 12, 277-85.

Jones R.I., 1978. Adaptations to fluctuating irradiance by natural phytoplankton communities, *in Limnol. Oceanogr.* 23(5), 920-26.

Jones R.I., 1979. Notes on the growth and sporulation of a natural population of *Aphanizomenon flos-aquae, in Hydrobiologia* 62, 55-8.

Kennedy G.J.A. and Johnston P.M. A review of salmon research on the River Bush, *in Proc. Inst. Fish Management N.I. Conference,* 1987 (in press).

McCutcheon W.A., 1965. *Canals of the North of Ireland.* Newton Abbot.

McCutcheon W.A., 1980. *The industrial archaeology of Northern Ireland.* Belfast.

Murphy P.M. and Carter C.E., 1984. A summer survey of the littoral macroinvertebrate fauna (excluding the chironomidae) of Lough Neagh, N. Ireland, *in Proc. R. Ir. Acad.* 84(9), 103-8.

Parr M. and Smith R.V., 1976. The identification of phosphorus as a growth limiting nutrient in Lough Neagh using bioassays, *in Water Res.* 10, 1151-4.

Riddolls A., 1985a. Aspects of nitrogen fixation in Lough Neagh: 1. Acetylene reduction and the frequency of *Aphanizomenon flos-aquae* heterocysts, *in Freshwat. Biol.* 15, 289-97.

Riddolls A., 1985b. Aspects of nitrogen fixation in Lough Neagh: 2. Competition between *Aphanizomenon flos-aquae, Oscillatoria redekei* and *Oscillatoria agardhii, in Freshwat. Biol.* 15, 299-306.

Rippey, B., 1977. The behaviour of phosphorus and silicon in undisturbed cores of L. Neagh sediments, *in* H.L. Golterman (ed.) *Proc. SIL/UNESCO Symposium: Interactions between sediments and freshwaters* JUNK/PUDOC, 348-53.

Rippey, B., 1982. Sediment-water interactions of Cu, Zn and Pb discharged from a domestic waste water source into a bay of Lough Neagh, Northern Ireland, *in Environmental pollution* (series B) 3, 199-214.

Rippey, B., 1983. A laboratory study of the silicon release processes from a lake sediment (Lough Neagh, Northern Ireland), *in Arch. Hydrobiol.* 96, 417-33.

Rippey B, Murphy R.J. and Kyle S.W., 1982. Anthropogenically derived changes in the sedimentary flux of Mg, Cr, Ni, Cu, Zn, Hg, Pb and P in Lough Neagh, Northern Ireland, *in Environmental Science and Technology* 16, 23-30.

Small, J., 1952. Botany, *in Belfast in its regional setting.* Belfast, 51-65.

Smith R.V., 1972. Secondary pollution: Lough Neagh's problem, *in Agriculture, Northern Ireland,* 47, 223-5.

Smith R.V., 1973. Freshwater pollution in Northern Ireland: evaluation and significance of the agricultural contribution. *N.I. Inst. Agric. Sci. J.,* 1972-3. 6-12.

Smith R.V., 1975. Nutrient budget of the River Main, Co Antrim, *in Tech. Bull. Minst. Agric. Fish Fd.* London, 32, 315-39.

Smith R.V., 1977. Domestic and agricultural contributions to the inputs of phosphorus and nitrogen to Lough Neagh, *in Water Res.* 11, 453-9.

Smith R.V., 1984. Nitrate loading to Lough Neagh, *in J. Sci. Fd. Agriculture,* 35, 853-4.

Smith R.V. and Stewart D.A., 1977. Statistical models of river loadings of nitrogen and phosphorus in the Lough Neagh system, *in Water Res.* 11, 631-6.

Stevens R.J., 1978. Phosphorus – the critical nutrient, T.A. Stewart (ed.), *I.O. Biol. Symposium on Lough Neagh: the algal problem and its solution.* Belfast. 33-5.

Stevens R.J. and Gibson C.E., 1977. Sediment release of phosphorus in Lough Neagh, Northern Ireland, *in* H.L. Golterman (ed.) *SIL/UNESCO Symposium on Interactions between sediments and freshwater.* JUNK/PUDOC, 343-7.

Stevens R.J. and Stewart B.M, 1982. Some components of particulate phosphorus in river water entering Lough Neagh, *in Water Res.* 16, 1591-6.

Sutton G.K., 1976. *Phosphorus reduction programme for sewage disposal works. IPHE Symposium on Eutrophication of lakes and reservoirs.* Killarney.

Tansley A.G., 1939. *The British Islands and their vegetation.* Cambridge.

Wilson J.P.F., 1983. Gear, selectivity, mortality rate and fluctuation in abundance of the pollan, *Coregonus autumnalis* pollan Thompson in L. Neagh, Northern Ireland, *in Proc. R. Ir. Acad.* 83B(24), 301-7.

Wilson J.P.F., 1984. The food of the pollan, *Coregonus autumnalis* pollan Thompson in L. Neagh, Northern Ireland, *in J. Fish Biol.* 241, 253-61.

Wilson J.P.F. and Pitcher A.J., 1983. The seasonal cycle in condition in the pollan, *Coregonus autumnalis* pollan Thompson of L. Neagh, Northern Ireland, *in J. Fish Biol.* 23, 365-70.

Wilson J.P.F. and Pitcher A.J., 1984a. Fecundity of the pollan, *Coregonus autumnalis* pollan Thompson in L. Neagh, Northern Ireland, *in J. Life Sci. R. Dubl. Soc.* 5, 21-8.

Wilson J.P.F. and Pitcher A.J., 1984b. Age, determination and growth of the pollan *Coregonus autumnalis* pollan Thompson of L. Neagh, Northern Ireland, *in J. Fish Biol.* 24, 151-63.

Wood R.B., 1984. The present status of Lough Neagh as a fishery, *in Proc. Inst. Fish. Management (NI) Conference*, Londonderry. 61-82.

Wood R.B. and Gibson C.E., 1973. Eutrophication and Lough Neagh, *in Wat. Res.* 7, 173-87.

Wood R.B. and Smith R.V., 1987. Lough Neagh: 100 years of man's influence on the water quality of a major inland fishery, *in Proc. Inst. Fish Management: N.I. Conference* (in press).

Conservation

P. J. NEWBOULD

Professor Emeritus of Environmental Science, University of Ulster at Coleraine

Dentists, museums and ecologists all practise conservation. Your present author is an ecologist. Even in the context of ecology, conservation may be applied somewhat narrowly to wildlife or nature conservation or more broadly to resource conservation, including landscape. In this chapter the emphasis will be almost exclusively on nature conservation although in Northern Ireland the twin themes of nature conservation and countryside conservation have been more closely interlinked than in Britain. The subject will be reviewed chronologically from 1949 to the present, concluding with an assessment of the present situation and future prospects.

Historical review 1949-65

Nature conservation came of age in Britain in 1949 with the National Parks and Access to the Countryside Act and the establishment by Royal Charter of the Nature Conservancy. However, the British Association handbook of 1952, *Belfast in its regional setting*, contained no reference to conservation or to the fact that the rich diversity of fauna, flora and habitats described were in any way threatened; nor was there at this time much conscious or formal effort to conserve nature in Northern Ireland.

In 1960 Brian Faulkner, then Minister of Home Affairs, appointed a committee under the chairmanship of the Duke of Abercorn "to consider the protection of the natural fauna and flora and the physical features of scientific interest in Northern Ireland and to make recommendations on measures for their conservation and control including the protection of wild life." The committee reported promptly, stressing the need for urgent action, but it was not until 1965 that the Amenity Lands Act was passed, incorporating many of their proposals. In this Act the Ministry of Development was empowered to establish Nature Reserves, National Parks and Country Parks and to designate Areas of Scientific Interest and Areas of Outstanding Natural Beauty (AONB). Two committees, the Nature Reserves Committee and the Ulster Countryside Committee were set up to

Scrabo Tower in north County Down. The tower, erected in memory of a member of the local land-owning family, dominates the northern end of Strangford Lough. It is now a country park.

advise the Ministry on these matters. They shared a secretariat, administrative staff and field staff. The context of these events and this legislation are more fully described by Buchanan (1982) and also by Furphy in Forsyth and Boyd (1970).

Historical review 1965-70

These committees first met in 1965 and 1966. The Nature Reserves Committee was a most unusual committee. It included a lot of expertise, and was supported by a small but totally dedicated field staff. The Committee decided therefore to become fully involved in the work of site appraisal, frequently donning wellington boots and going into the field, even to the extent of camping on Rathlin Island. The CT (Terrestrial Conservation) section of the International Biological Programme gave a grant to assist in the process of site selection. This was used to fund a series of visiting groups, which involved distinguished scientists coming from Britain to assist in this process. The main visiting groups were concerned with woodland, bogland, coastal areas, grassland and heath, wildfowl and freshwater respectively. Members of the Nature Reserves Committee accompanied these visiting groups during their field visits. The Committee also paid visits to England and Scotland to learn from the Nature Conservancy operation there.

The activities of the Nature Reserves Committee are recorded in their successive annual reports. Their initial priority was to determine sites for potential Nature Reserves or Areas of Scientific Interest. The Committee decided to adopt a systematic habitat approach, rather than emphasise the protection of endangered species, though these were not ignored. Visiting groups were set up, as described above, and by 1970, European Conservation Year (ECY), the Committee was able to present to Brian Faulkner, then Minister of Development, a list of 44 sites proposed as National Nature Reserves (NNR) and a further 103 sites proposed as Areas of Scientific Interest (ASI).

The achievement in the period 1965-70 was very considerable. It culminated in a major European Conservation Year conference on *Conservation in the development of Northern Ireland*. This was based on the reports of three study groups, on Urban Development, Industry and Conservation; Outdoor Recreation, Tourism and Conservation; and Agriculture, Forestry and Conservation. The reports were discussed at the conference and recommendations formulated. The prompt publication of the conference reports and proceedings (Forsyth and Boyd, 1970) gave the government and other bodies and individuals involved in conservation a blueprint for the 1970s.

In opening the ECY Conference on *Conservation in the development of Northern Ireland*, on 12 September 1970, Brian Faulkner said:

> I can certainly undertake that the Government will, in the next five years, protect all the 147 areas, either by designation as "Areas of Scientific Interest" or by managing them as "Nature Reserves". We will aim at the complete protection of most of the 44 areas which have been recommended for declaration as "Nature Reserves". In this way we shall ensure that conservation is given its place in the planning of very large tracts of land and water throughout Northern Ireland and that a fully representative series of sites of the various habitat types are established, managed and used as Nature Reserves.

This sincere declaration of intent was to be overtaken by political events, the fall of Stormont, direct rule, followed by the brief interlude of the Northern Ireland Executive and Assembly and reversion to direct rule in May 1974. The political climate and the resources were not available to implement the full programme of nature conservation that had been envisaged.

The achievements 1970-85

Some good things happened in the seventies. A very good working relationship was established between the Conservation Branch (the executive arm of the Nature Reserves Committee and the Ulster Countryside Committee) and the Forestry Division of the Ministry of Agriculture, later renamed the Forest Service. Several of the early NNRs were established in forest areas and had joint management committees. Later a whole network of second-tier Forest Nature Reserves (FNR) was established, all with diverse fauna and flora and with educational potential but not quite meeting the criteria for NNR. By 1985 there were 14 NNRs on forest land and 38 FNRs (see Forest Service, 1986). Also nine Forest District Conservation Committees were set up, one in each of the Forest Districts, to advise on nature conservation in the forest areas of that district.

The functions of the Wild Birds Advisory Committee were transferred from the Ministry of Home Affairs to the Ministry of Development. Nine Bird Sanctuaries had been established under the Wild Birds Protection Act (NI) 1931 and a tenth was declared later. Two Wildfowl Refuges were designated on Lough Neagh.

In 1976, after nearly ten years of negotiation with the National Trust, the Murlough Dunes National Nature Reserve at Dundrum was declared as a co-operative venture between the National Trust and Conservation Branch. The Portandoo (now Portrush) Countryside Centre in Portrush, a major interpretive centre oriented towards nature conservation was opened in 1978.

Two small handbooks exemplify the enthusiasm of the early seventies. The first is a handbook of centres in Northern Ireland which could be used for field studies or outdoor pursuits. It was compiled by an ad-hoc committee meeting at Queen's University under the chairmanship of the late Professor Muskett and was published in 1972. It listed about 30 centres and 12 youth hostels. The second handbook is a guide to field study sites in Northern Ireland edited by Mrs P.M. Thomlinson, and issued by the Belfast Teachers' Centre based at Queen's University, in 1975. This contains an introduction with suggestions for the proper conduct of field visits, lists of literature sources, organisations, etc. and then a list of rather over 200 sites suitable for field study. The philosophy behind both handbooks is that it is desirable to get school children and adults out into the countryside, in properly conducted groups where conservation principles can be enunciated and practised, so that they can learn about wildlife, and come to respect it and to wish to conserve it. There has been a conscious effort to avoid the "Nature Reserve – KEEP OUT" philosophy wherever possible.

Conservation Branch discovered afresh, as the Nature Conservancy had in Britain twenty years before, what a slow and painstaking process reserve acquisition can be. By 1985, however, 40 National Nature Reserves had been declared, although some of these were sites not on the 1970 list. In number this looks good, but in area they are small. As I wrote (Newbould, 1982) "the whole Northern Ireland NNR acreage would fit easily into the Moor House NNR or the Beinn Eighe NNR. It would fit several times into the Cairngorms NNR. These small nature reserves are just too vulnerable to change outside their boundaries". Also by 1985 there were only 47 ASIs (compared with about 4,150 in Britain). This represents not only shortage of staff for surveying ASIs and notifying owners, but also, I suspect, a degree of disillusion about their effectiveness. In general the conservation euphoria engendered by the 1970 ECY Conference declined through the seventies.

The reorganisation of local government in 1973 brought many changes. Six County Councils and some 76 Urban and Rural District Councils were replaced by 26 District Councils, with greatly reduced powers. Many of the important functions such as planning, roads, water were centralised in Government departments in Belfast. Education, and Health and Social Services were regulated by Area Boards, leaving very little for the District Councils to do. While they have a potential role in conservation as will be seen below, the District Councils have yet to achieve much in this area.

Another area of interest is the liaison between agriculture and conservation. In Northern Ireland the patterns of land tenure and agriculture, and the social structure of the rural population are quite different from Britain producing different impacts on the environment. While there has been considerable hedgerow removal, average field size is still quite small. Quite a lot of the hedgerow management is poor, producing neither a stock-proof barrier nor a valuable wildlife habitat. Many mature hedgerow trees have been felled in recent years and few replanted, and the value of shelter around farm houses as well as around fields is not always appreciated.

Wet climate and heavy soils accentuate the need for field drainage and associated arterial drainage (Chapter 2). This has caused the loss of considerable areas of wetland habitat, especially the small marshy areas. Few farm ponds remain, since piped water is commonly available. In 1986 the Department of Agriculture and the Department of the Environment jointly issued a booklet *Ponds on the farm*, commending their retention or re-establishment and indicating methods of management. Silage has largely replaced hay for winter feed and water pollution incidents attributable to silage effluent or slurry have increased considerably. This is one component of the general eutrophication of lakes and rivers which reduces the habitat available for oligotrophic species.

There are a few large estates like Shane's Castle near Antrim or Baronscourt in Tyrone where farming, forestry, recreation and conservation are fully integrated. Wherever pheasants are reared and shot, a number of other species are conserved along with the pheasants; in other words the habitat management is generally beneficial to nature conservation.

In Britain the movement to integrate an element of nature conservation into farm management developed from the Silsoe Conference (Barber, 1970). This led on to the formation of a national Farming and Wildlife Advisory Group (FWAG) which in turn gave rise to local FWAGs, mainly at the county level. By all accounts these have been successful, advising farmers on hedgerow management, the establishment of copses, farm ponds and so on. Suggestions for a similar organisation in Northern Ireland have hitherto been rejected but in 1986, following a successful Institute of Agricultural Sciences conference on Agriculture and the Environment and a further lecture by Eric Carter, Director of the British FWAG, it was decided to establish a FWAG in Northern Ireland. It will be called the Farming and Wildlife Advisory Group (Northern Ireland).

It was partly the perceived failure of the Government conservation service, with its minimal resources, to cope with the job in hand that

stimulated the inauguration of the Ulster Trust for Nature Conservation (UTNC) in 1978. This followed a meeting convened by the Department of the Environment and Queen's University Belfast Extra-Mural Department on the subject of Field Clubs and Conservation. The UTNC followed the well-defined pattern of conservation trusts in Britain, and like them, is affiliated to the Royal Society for Nature Conservation. A single trust for the whole province resembles the situation of the Scottish Wildlife Trust.

The UTNC has achieved quite a lot in its first 8 years, but is having difficulty in building up membership, currently about 1,000. Membership of conservation trusts in Britain varies between 0.5 and 10.0 per thousand of population, and the UTNC which is the youngest of all the trusts is near the lower end of the table. In 1986 it was able to expand its staff to 20, mainly by employing full-time or part-time Action for Community Employment (ACE) workers. These jobs are limited to one year duration and therefore create considerable problems of continuity for the Trust.

The four main areas of activity of the Trust are (1) the establishment and management of nature reserves, (2) education and spreading awareness of conservation, (3) developing policies and campaigns on conservation issues like peat extraction, afforestation, drainage and scrutinising planning applications and (4) giving conservation advice to landowners, District Councils, etc. The Trust has 16 nature reserves, which is a creditable achievement and active management is in progress on most of them, often with the assistance of either Conservation Volunteers Northern Ireland or Grassroots Conservation Corps.

In 1986 the UTNC launched an appeal for funds under the title of the Northern Ireland Wildlife Campaign. One of the main objectives was to support the Crossgar Nature Centre, a new project being undertaken by the Trust. The Centre is based on an old walled garden, conservatory and outbuildings, situated at the Passionist Monastery at Crossgar, Co. Down. The idea is to re-create four different habitat areas within the walled garden, to create a butterfly house in the conservatory, and to develop the whole complex as an educational centre. The conservation of the buildings is being carried out jointly with the Ulster Architectural Heritage Society (UAHS). The whole project will provide a splendid focus for UTNC activity, but creating the habitat areas will probably be slow and difficult.

There are several other voluntary bodies, independent of government although in many cases eligible for government grants. The National Trust and the Royal Society for the Protection of Birds (RSPB) are both well-funded bodies with a sizable membership. They are UK organisations although the National Trust for Northern Ireland has a fair degree of autonomy. Both can get advice from their parent bodies on the mainland. The RSPB is primarily concerned with nature conservation, the National Trust with conserving properties, large houses and estates but also visual amenity, and, in respect of several important sites, with nature conservation. The RSPB, with a Northern Ireland membership of about 4,000, employs 11 full-time and part-time staff, several of them under the ACE scheme.

The use of state forests for recreation was recognised at an early date by the Forest Service of Northern Ireland who pioneered the concept of forest parks, now well established elsewhere in the United Kingdom. (Arts Council)

Another sector of activity impinging upon or promoting nature conservation is sport. The Sports Council is concerned with outdoor sports like mountaineering, canoeing, orienteering. In the areas of hunting, shooting and fishing, a number of bodies are active in Northern Ireland, for example, the British Association for Shooting and Conservation (formerly WAGBI) and the Ulster Game and Wildfowl Society. The various clubs co-ordinate their activities under an organisation entitled the Council for Country Sports in Northern Ireland. A successful scheme to co-ordinate shooting and conservation on Strangford Lough has been run by the National Trust since 1966 under the title of the Strangford Lough Wildlife Scheme. Lough Neagh and Upper and Lower Lough Erne also have designated shooting areas and wildfowl refuges. The Fisheries Division of the Department of Agriculture manage a number of fishing waters throughout the province and in a number of cases, in response to demand, have established game fisheries in water more naturally populated by coarse fish. A reasonable balance, however, now seems to be maintained. The Forest Service game farm at Seskinore in County Tyrone rears pheasants and ducks for supply to shooting estates and also gives advice on management, including that of grouse moors. As in other parts of the UK, the genuine conservation orientation of sporting organisations, who understand the need to conserve habitats and ensure breeding success in target organisms, is partly frustrated by unlicensed and often illegal operators.

The Ulster Society for the Preservation of the Countryside is a body of long standing concerned with countryside conservation and visual amenity. There are also a number of local Field Clubs whose membership and activity levels tend to fluctuate with time. Several of these voluntary bodies are attempting to co-ordinate their activities through a small informal body called the Northern Ireland Environment Group which meets two or three times a year. The Ulster Museum has the function of receiving, sorting and storing biological records in Northern Ireland, in conjunction with the National Biological Records Centre at Monkswood and the Irish Biological Records Centre run by An Foras Forbartha in Dublin.

The Balfour Report and new legislation, 1981-6

By the end of the seventies there was considerable disquiet about the conservation situation. The Nature Reserves Committee and its staff started to produce a draft document setting out the provisions needed in new wildlife legislation here. This was overtaken, however, by events since the Wildlife and Countryside Act, largely as a result of European Community and other international pressure, was under preparation in Britain. It was felt that the Northern Ireland legislation should follow rather than precede the GB legislation. Drafting resumed here in 1981 and in 1983 the Access to the Countryside (Northern Ireland) Order was enacted and two major items of legislation, the Nature Conservation and Amenity Lands (Northern Ireland) Order and the Wildlife (Northern Ireland) Order were published in draft form. These three Orders represented an attempt to bring Northern Ireland into line with the Wildlife and Countryside Act 1981 and between them cover similar ground to that Act.

At this time there was strong pressure from the voluntary organisations for the establishment of an appointed body with responsibility for conservation. Rather than delay the legislation any further, Dr Jean Balfour (past Chairman of the Countryside Commission for Scotland) was commissioned in 1984 to prepare a report for Chris Patten, the Minister with responsibility for the Department of the Environment (Northern Ireland). She consulted widely and her report *A new look at the Northern Ireland countryside* was published in October 1984.

Two main thrusts emerged from Dr Balfour's report. First, she stressed the need for more resources, more staff and a higher status for conservation and secondly the need for closer co-operation and co-ordination between all the agencies involved. While she understood the pressure in favour of a more independent "Appointed Body" along the lines of the Nature Conservancy Council or the Countryside Commission in Britain, Dr Balfour believed that the interests of conservation in Northern Ireland would be best served by increased resources and status within the Department of the Environment for Northern Ireland. She recommended a new and strengthened Conservation Service, headed by an Under-Secretary, with two divisions each headed by an Under-Secretary. The Countryside and Wildlife Board would deal with the activities of the existing Conservation Branch in relation to nature conservation, wildlife and countryside amenities; and the Historic Monuments and Buildings Division would have responsibility for the care and conservation of ancient buildings and monuments.

The Government accepted her recommendations in principle but not their full resource implications. The senior post became an Assistant Secretary and the other posts were downgraded accordingly. However, conservationists are delighted that the Director of the Conservation Service post has been taken by John Phillips, formerly Chief Forest Officer, and the post of head of the Countryside and Wildlife Branch has been taken by Dr John Faulkner, a research scientist from the Department of Agriculture and a former Chairman of the Ulster Trust for Nature Conservation.

Meanwhile the 1985 legislation has brought Northern Ireland broadly into line with Britain. The Nature Conservation and Amenity Lands (Northern Ireland) Order 1985 completely replaces the Amenity Lands Act (Northern Ireland) 1965. The Department of the Environment (Northern Ireland) can now commission relevant research as well as establish and manage nature reserves. The Department may get other bodies to manage land for it including the National Trust. The Department may grant-aid approved conservation bodies. The Ulster Countryside Committee remains intact with a somewhat wider remit but the Nature Reserves Committee is replaced by a Committee for Nature Conservation also with a somewhat wider remit including the functions formerly discharged by the Wild Birds Advisory Committee. In this respect the legislation differs from Dr Balfour's recommendations for she suggests merging these two committees

Castle Coole, the late eighteenth century mansion of the Lowry-Corry family, and now one of the many properties owned by the National Trust in Northern Ireland. (Arts Council)

into a new Northern Ireland Countryside Committee. Her recommendation will be implemented as soon as the necessary legislation is passed.

The 1983 Access to the Countryside (Northern Ireland) Order requires District Councils to undertake the assertion and protection of public rights of way, and enables them to create new public paths and long distance routes and to secure public access to areas of open country for recreational purposes. Under the 1985 Order they must also be consulted by the Department of the Environment about the establishment of Nature Reserves and notified about Areas of Special Scientific Interest (ASSIs). They also have the power themselves to establish Nature Reserves. There is little sign, however, that District Councils will in practice become active in conservation.

There are special provisions for establishing Marine Nature Reserves. The conservation clause declares that all public bodies "... in exercising functions relating to land ... shall have regard to the need to protect (so far as reasonably practicable) flora, fauna and geological and physiographical features of the countryside ...." Finally, the provisions concerning ASSIs resemble those of the (British) Wildlife and Countryside Act, inasmuch as the scientific interest must be clearly specified and those operations or activities likely to damage that interest must also be specified. Where this provision is harmful to the landowner, compensation may be paid. These replace the Areas of Scientific Interest of the 1965 Act.

The Wildlife (Northern Ireland) Order 1985 is the first Northern Ireland piece of legislation conferring protection on species, other than the Wild Birds Protection Acts of 1931, 1950 and 1968 and the Grey Seals Protection Act of 1933, all of which it replaces. It gives general protection to all bird species, making exceptions for pest species and for game species during the open season. It affords protection to a list of animals including several mammals and some butterflies. It makes it an offence to dig up wild plants without permission of the landowner, and for a schedule of some 55 rarer plant species it becomes an offence to pick, remove, uproot or destroy them. Other provisions of the Order limit the introduction of alien species, allow for the establishment of wildlife refuges and the protection of deer and empower the Department to grant licences for scientific or research activities which would otherwise involve committing an offence under the Order.

In her report Dr Balfour comments on the inadequacy of the present co-ordination of countryside activities and suggests how this could be improved. Her comments are perhaps aimed more at recreation planning than nature conservation, although some apply broadly. Liaison and co-ordination are required within the Department of the Environment, between that Department and other government departments such as Agriculture, Economic Development and Education, and between the Countryside and Wildlife Branch and the voluntary bodies and District Councils whose conservation activities it is now able to grant aid. As an example of successful cooperation between central government, District

Councils and voluntary bodies Dr Balfour cites the Lagan Valley Regional Park.

Within the Department of the Environment, the Conservation Service will need constructive dialogue with both Roads and Planning over ASSIs and AONBs, on general policy and on particular sites; with Water Service and with the Environmental Protection Division. Co-operation with the Department of Agriculture will be in the areas of farming, forestry, fisheries and drainage. As has been indicated, co-operation with the Forest Service is already very effective. Co-operation with Drainage Division is reasonable at the level of minor modification of particular drainage schemes in favour of conservation interests. This has been the situation since the public enquiry into the River Main drainage scheme in 1971. Liaison was maintained by Drainage Division having an observer on the Nature Reserves Committee, and by one member of the Drainage Council being appointed to represent conservation interests. Unfortunately the Drainage Council is more of a rubber-stamping than a policy-making group. Liaison with Fisheries has varied in the past, but will become necessary, if the new legislation on Marine Nature Reserves is followed up. Liaison with farming should develop from the inauguration of the Farming and Wildlife Advisory Group (Northern Ireland) described above.

The situation today

1986 appears to be a turning point in conservation in Northern Ireland. There is new legislation and a newly structured Conservation Service with new names at the top. The Balfour Report will serve as a blueprint for the next decade and the Northern Ireland Environment Group mentioned above is, as a priority, monitoring the implementation of the Balfour Report. The Report's recommendation for additional resources has been granted in part. Also the Conservation Service is now housed under one roof. Public support for conservation, stimulated by television, is stronger than ever before. The Government now recognises the value of the voluntary organisations, who can harness the commitment and expertise of their members to provide cost-effective conservation activity, and the Government is grant-aiding them accordingly. Dr Balfour stresses in her report that grant aid to voluntary bodies (and presumably also to District Councils) should be (as is now required by law) accompanied by advice, based on the expertise which will be built up by the Countryside and Wildlife Branch over the next few years; it is important that such advice is both proffered and accepted. The farming community, under pressure to reduce the production of its traditional products, is seeking to diversify and has also been caught up in the new wave of environmental awareness.

While all this activity sounds impressive, it is important to see how far it has led to effective conservation of nature in Northern Ireland. One criterion to look at would be protected sites in the province. National Nature Reserves and former ASIs are listed in Table 1 and their locations shown on Fig. 5.1. In terms of number of sites, this looks impressive but in terms of land area protected it is much less so. Table 2 attempts to make

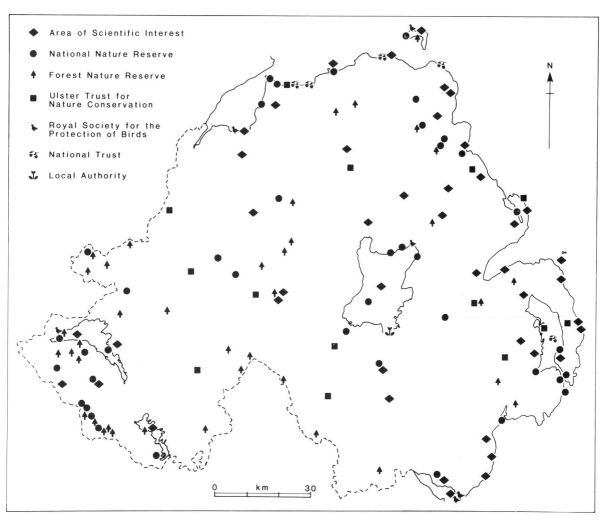

Figure 5.1 Northern Ireland: protected areas.

some comparison with the situation in Britain, indicating that in terms of percentage of the total land area, the Northern Ireland protected areas are about one third of those in Britain. The only sector where the comparison favours Northern Ireland is that concerned with Forest Nature Reserves.

As has been indicated, the UTNC is the youngest of the UK Naturalists' Trusts. If it were to have a nature reserve holding comparable on the basis of land area to the trusts in Britain, this would amount to about 90 reserves totalling around 3,000 hectares, nearly as much as the Conservation Service manage at present. It seems probable that the National Trust has a somewhat greater involvement and achievement in conservation in Northern Ireland than in Britain but this is difficult to quantify since conservation is a component in the management of most of their properties rather than being specifically related to nature reserves.

The main thrust of work in the Countryside and Wildlife Branch at present is concerned with the designation of ASSIs which now requires much more detailed work than hitherto: A declaration shall specify –

(a) the flora, fauna, or geological, physiographical or other features by reason of which the land is of special scientific interest, and

(b) any operations or activities appearing to the Department to be likely to damage that flora or fauna or those features.

Owners, occupiers and District Councils must be notified and may raise objections. The designation should prove a much more effective conservation tool than hitherto, although judging by the experience of the Wildlife and Countryside Act in Britain it may produce a further set of problems. In Britain the scientific basis for the new wave of Site of Special Scientific Interest (SSSI) designations was derived from the Nature Conservation Review (Ratcliffe, 1977); no study in comparable depth exists in Northern Ireland other than the rather limited and outdated (but still valuable) visiting group reports. Hence, the Countryside and Wildlife Branch now have a major habitat survey under way, designed to indicate where ASSIs should be designated.

In Britain in 1984 there were 4,150 SSSIs totalling nearly 1.5 million hectares, or 6.6% of the land surface. While strict comparison by area is inappropriate, it is notable that to achieve the same percentage cover in Northern Ireland, Countryside and Wildlife Branch would need to designate about 270 ASSIs covering nearly 94,000 hectares. Even with their expanded staffing, the workload would be enormous.

A perusal of the annual reports of the Nature Reserves Committee, 1-18, 1967-85, illustrates the slowness in establishing Nature Reserves. There are many reasons for delay. There have been very few field staff to carry out all the necessary survey work. Owners may be unwilling to sell at the price set by the District Valuer, or may find some clauses of a Nature Reserve agreement too restrictive. Valuers, land agents and lawyers tend to be busy men and difficult to hurry. Many desirable areas, especially the peatland sites, are in multiple ownership, or subject to multiple and ill-defined turbary (turf-cutting) or grazing rights. The Department is understandably reluctant to use its compulsory purchase powers except, for example, where the owner is willing to sell but cannot establish title. The Nature Conservancy Council in Britain established its 150,000 hectares of nature reserves at a relatively steady rate over 30 years – it may be that the Countryside and Wildlife Branch are halfway there after nearly 20 years.

Any attempt to discuss which habitats are adequately conserved and which are not is of course subjective and speculative. Geological sites fared quite well under the old ASI designation, and should do even better under the new ASSI designation. A number of Nature Reserves also have high geological interest, for example, the Giant's Causeway (a major tourist attraction, owned and managed by the National Trust).

Very little deciduous woodland survives in Northern Ireland. The iron smelting and other major uses of charcoal in the 17th and 18th centuries (described by McCracken, 1971) were followed by a big demand for fuelwood in the overpopulated years of the 19th century. A few old estate woodlands survive, often over-mature by forestry standards. In general the small remnants of woodland which are conserved in Nature Reserves constitute quite a good representation of what is left of this habitat. It is very desirable that new areas of deciduous woodland should be established.

Wetland habitats are much less adequately represented. Peat cutting, drainage, agricultural reclamation and afforestation have all taken their toll. Accelerated eutrophication of major water bodies is attributed to domestic and other effluent (Chapter 4). Silage and slurry incidents harm the streams and rivers. New, small, peat extraction machines are the latest threat. There are relatively few, if any, raised bog sites left worth conserving, and some of these are seriously threatened. ASSI designation may not be particularly effective since compensation could add up to the total value of the peat resource. Some existing bog Nature Reserves are vulnerable to fire damage. Many of the upland blanket bog areas, for example, on the Antrim Hills or the Sperrins, are in an advanced stage of erosion. Small areas of blanket bog are not suitable for conservation. What is required here is the acquisition of a large area, a whole hydrological and landscape unit, including a diverse range of bog, moorland and grassland habitats.

Brackagh Moss NNR, an old cutover bog with a good range of bog and fen vegetation, is proving quite difficult to manage. It is one of the sites where *Spiranthes romanzoffiana*, an orchid of especial biogeographical interest, survives. This species seems to be diminishing here and in some of its other Northern Ireland sites; this is probably a symptom of the reduction in the area of wetland habitats, attributable largely to drainage.

There is very little salt marsh in Northern Ireland and there is an urgent need to protect more of what remains. The protection of sand dune systems by the Countryside and Wildlife Branch, the UTNC and the National Trust combined is probably adequate, or at least as much as can be hoped for, given the pressures of recreational use including golf on this habitat. Techniques now exist for the agricultural "improvement" or "reclamation" of hill pasture. This would be highly destructive from a conservation point of view of the wide range of grassland and moorland habitats in Northern Ireland. At present the agricultural acreage seems more likely to contract than expand so the threat is not imminent but it may return in the future.

There are several large wild areas which should be under unified management, so that pressures and resources can be properly balanced. There are the big lake systems like Lough Neagh, Upper and Lower Lough Erne, the marine Loughs Strangford and Foyle; there are the mountains like the Mournes, the Sperrins, the Fermanagh limestone hills; coastline like the North Antrim Coast, Rathlin Island, the South Down coast. In less populated regions such areas could be made national parks, that is national parks by the international or IUCN definition rather than the UK definition. Since this is not possible, the fall-back position is to establish an advisory council where various interests can discuss mutual problems. Two such councils are the Mournes Advisory Council and the Strangford Lough Advisory Council. These have no statutory existence or powers but none the less provide a useful discussion forum. A similar body has now been established for Lough Neagh. Another positive measure is that the Nature Conservation and Amenity Lands Order enables the Countryside and Wildlife Branch to prepare management plans for AONBs. There is also the facility for the Department of the Environment and the Department of Agriculture jointly to designate Environmentally Sensitive Areas (ESAs) under the recent European Agriculture Directive and indeed the Mournes ESA was recently designated.

Conclusion

The present legislation, with a few minor changes which are envisaged, is probably adequate to provide for a reasonable level of nature conservation in Northern Ireland. But conservation is an element in the strategy of land and resource use which will be greatly influenced by, for example the Common Agricultural Policy as it affects the future of Northern Ireland agriculture, by incentives to forestry, by changing patterns of outdoor recreation, and so on. The voice of conservation must be heard in the formulation of this strategy. The Conservative government has made formal endorsement of the World Conservation Strategy and the other political parties at Westminster are demonstrating great enthusiasm for the environment in the run-up to the next election.

However, the resources available for conservation are still inadequate and seem likely to continue to be so. If the voluntary bodies can harness the commitment of their members and work hard and constructively together with the government Conservation Service, which can support them with grants and expertise to implement their conservation plans, much can be achieved within the meagre resources available. Such an achievement will be based on the commitment of that section of the population who care about the future of our wildlife.

Acknowledgement

I am most grateful to Joe Furphy of Countryside and Wildlife Branch of the Department of the Environment for Northern Ireland for his helpful comments on an earlier draft. Responsibility for the opinions expressed and the accuracy of the information remains my own.

Table 1

Nature Reserves and ASIs in Northern Ireland
(Designated and managed by Countryside and Wildlife Branch, DoENI)

National Nature Reserves

No.	Name	Area ha	Features
1	Killeter[1]	22	Bog
2	Lough Naman Bog	41	Bog
3	Correl Glen[1]	34	Mixed woodland
4	Castle Archdale Island[1]	74	Mixed woodland
5	Marble Arch[1]	24	Moist ashwood on limestone
6	Banagher Glen	30	Mixed woodland, bryophytes
7	Portrush	1	Geology
8	Breen[1]	21	Oakwood
9	Slieveanorra[1]	49	Blanket bog
10	Randalstown[1]	6	Lake shore woodland
11	Swan Islands[2]	1	Tern nesting site
12	Belshaw's Quarry	1	Geology
13	Quoile Pondage Basin	195	Lake and shore, wildfowl
14	Rostrevor[1]	20	Oakwood
15	Granagh Bay	30	Mudflats, rocky shore, marine fauna
16	Meenadoan	20	Bog
17	Hanging Rock and Rossaa	15	Dry ashwood
18	Brackagh Moss	110	Cut-over bog, fen
19	Boorin	58	Heathland
20	Dorn	790	Foreshore, intertidal
21	Farr's Bay	6	Fen and carr
22	Kebble	123	Grassland, lake, seacliffs, heath
23	Roe Estuary	474	Estuary, saltmarsh, mudflats, seals
24	Cloghy Rocks	27	Rocky shore, mudflats, seals
25	Magilligan Point	57	Sand dunes
26	Ballymaclary	227	Sand dunes, wet slacks
27	Killard	68	Grassland, foreshore
28	The Murrins[1]	54	Heathland
29	Ross Lough[1]	9	Fen, meadow, wildfowl
30	Murlough Dunes[3]	283	Sand dunes
31	Castlecaldwell	7	Swamp, fen, carr, open water
32	Glenariff Waterfalls[1]	8	Damp woodland, bryophytes
33	Crossmurrin	96	Limestone grassland
34	Mullenakill and Annagarriff	99	Bog, scrub, wooded drumlins
35	Reas Wood[1]	27	Damp woodland, invertebrates
36	Bohill[1]	5	Holly blue butterfly
37	Glenariff North	20	Hazel scrub, rich grassland
38	Straidkilly	4	Hazel scrub
39	Lough Neagh Island		Birds
40	Reilly and Gole Woods	67	Oakwood, mixed woodland

NOTES Areas to nearest hectare but all sites less than 1 hectare are shown as 1
[1] on Forest Service land, jointly managed
[2] managed by RSPB
[3] owned and managed under agreement by National Trust.

Areas of Scientific Interest
(Designated by former Conservation Branch, DoENI)

1	Lower Lough Erne	Lake, shore, reedswamp, fen, birds
2	Carrickbawn	Heathland, Erica vagans
3	Ross Lough	Reedswamp, fen, wildfowl
4	Upper Lough Erne	Lake, shore, reedswamp, fen, birds
5	Dart and Sawel Mountains	Eroding blanket bog

Table 1—*continued*

No.	Name	Area ha	Features
6	Carrickhugh		Shingle bars, salt marsh
7	North Derry		Basalt escarpment, beaches, dunes
8	The Skerries		Geology, marine islands, seabirds
9	North Antrim Coast		Varied coastal habitats
10	Rathlin Island		Varied habitats, seabirds
11	Loughaveema		Glacial features, moorland
12	Glenariff Waterfalls		Woodland, rocky gorge, bryophytes
13	Tievebulliagh		Geology, archaeology
14	People's Park, Ballymena		Lake, birds
15	Slemish		Geology, blanket peat, grass
16	Sandy Braes		Geology
17	Lough Beg		Lake, reedswamp, fen, birds
18	Lough Neagh		Lake, shoreline, fen, birds
19	Ballycarry		Saltmarsh, mudflats, birds
20	Hazelwood		Hazel scrub
21	Cultra		Geology
22	Copeland Islands		Birds, geology
23	Roddan's Port		Geology
24	Coalpit Bay		Geology
25	Burial Island		Terns, seals
26	The Dorn		Marine
27	Brackagh Bog		Cut-over bog, fen, birds
28	Lough Shark (Acton Lake)		Reedswamp, rare plants, birds
29	North Mournes		Grasslands
30	Green and Blockhouse Islands		Terns, seals
31	Scrabo		Geology
32	Mourne Coast		Geology, beaches, grassland
33	Carrigullion and Heron Loughs		Lake, reedswamp, wildfowl
34	Clea Lakes		Lake, reedswamp, birds
35	Islandmagee		Geology
36	Doraville Ridge		Geology
37	Carnlough		Landforms
38	Scawt Hill and Sallagh Braes		Upland grassland, geology
39	Killey Bridge		Fossils
40	Tirnaskea		Fossils
41	Carey River		Glacial geology
42	Lougher Hill		Kame features
43	Movanagher		Kane and esker
44	South Mourne Coast		Cliff sections
45	Knockshee and Slievefadda		Soil, grassland
46	Clontyfinnan		Glacial features
47	Mill Bay		Mudflats, salt marsh

NOTE Areas not shown, category no longer valid, see text.

Forest Nature Reserves
(Designated and Managed by Forest Service, DoE)

No.	Name	Area	Features
1	Garry Bog	7	Raised bog
2	Glenariff Lakes	12	Acid lakes, wildfowl
3	Kinramer	59	Scrubby woodland on Rathland
4	Slieveanorra Moor	225	Red grouse
5	Tardree	1	Geology
6	Carnagh	12	Estate woodland, lakes
7	Hawthorne Hill	29	Mixed woodland
8	Belvoir Park	15	Mixed woodland, scrub
9	Cairn Wood	40	Mixed woodland, scrub
10	Hollymount	13	Alder carr, fen
11	Aghagrefin	40	Cut-over bog
12	Aghatrirourke	695	Limestone, scrub, bog
13	Bolusty Beg	7	Bog
14	Carricknagower	86	Lake, marsh, cliff

Table 1—*continued*

No.	Name	Area ha	Features
15	Castlecaldwell Heritage	1	Old conifer woodland
16	Conagher	120	Acid upland vegetation
17	Cornagague Wood and Lake	3	Scrub woodland, lake
18	Corry Point Wood	4	Mixed deciduous woodland
19	Dohatty Glebe	29	Limestone cliff
20	Glen Wood	5	Oakwood
21	Killesher	4	Ashwood on limestone
22	Magho	74	Mixed woodland, cliff, scree
23	Naan Island	5	Reed beds, mixed woodland
24	Craig-na-Shoke	90	Hill grassland, peat erosion
25	Loughan Island	2	Mixed deciduous woodland
26	Altadavan	2	Mixed deciduous woodland
27	Altamullan	8	Old Mixed woodland, scrub
28	Black Bog	48	Raised bog
29	Drumlish	1	Fungi
30	Favour Royal	23	Mixed woodland, fallow deer
31	Killeter Forest Goose Lawns	16	Bog, Greenland whitefronted geese
32	Knockaginney	6	Mixed deciduous woodland
33	Knockmany	31	Conifer stand, lake, scrub
34	Moneygal Bog	47	Raised bog
35	Mullyfamore	13	Bog
36	Pomeroy	22	Old estate woodland
37	Slaghtfreedan	19	Bog
38	Teal Lough	40	Bog

District Council Nature Reserves
(Acquired and Managed by Craigavon Borough Council)

1	Oxford Island		Lough Neagh shore, reeds

Royal Society for the Protection of Birds Nature Reserves
(Managed by the RSPB)

1	Castlecaldwell	237	Woodland, fen, reedswamp, lake
2	Greencastle Point	1	Seashore, mudflats, terns
3	Lough Foyle	1335	Seashore, mudflats, wildfowl
4	Rathlin Island Cliffs	50	Seabirds
5	Shanes Castle	32	Lough Neagh shore, wildfowl
6	Green Island	1	Terns, shingle

National Trust Conservation Areas
(Managed by the NT)

1	Downhill		Wooded glen, lake, seashore
2	Portstewart Dunes		Sand dunes
3	Giant's Causeway		Geology, cliffs, coast
4	White Park Bay		Landslip, grassland, dunes
5	Larrybane		Geology
6	Murlough Bay, Fair Head		Cliffs, woodland, grassland
7	Strangford Lough		Str Lough Wildlife Scheme

Ulster Trust for Nature Conservation Nature Reserves
(Managed by the UTNC)

1	Cottage Farm	13	Wood, bog, pond, riverbank
2	Termon Glen	10	Wooded glen, stream, lake
3	Blessingbourne	10	Estate woodland, lake
4	The Umbra	24	Dune, slacks, wet woodland
5	Rainey Island	16	Grassland, oakwood, shoreline
6	Edenderry	1	Fen, woodland
7	Inishargy Bog	4	Bog, fen, carr
8	Argory Mosses	17	Bog, birchwood
9	Milford	1	Old railway cutting, orchids
10	Upper Glen, Glenarm	336	Bog, grass, hazel, oak

Table 1—*continued*

No.	Name	Area ha	Features
11	Strabane Glen	12	Mixed woodland
12	Isle of Muck	6	Sea-birds
13	Creighton's Wood	4	Hazel, oakwood, bog
14	Ballydyan Railway Cutting	1	Marshland, grass, scrub
15	Tonragee, Upper Lough Erne	2	Wooded island
16	Isle Namannfin, Lower Lough Erne	2	Wooded island

Table 2

Nature Reserves and SSSIs in Great Britain and Northern Ireland

	Great Britain 1984*			Northern Ireland 1985		
	No.	Area ha	% land area	No.	Area ha	% land area
NATURE RESERVES						
National	195	150,003	0.68	40	3176	0.23
RSPB	93	43,278	0.20	6	1658	0.12
Conservation Trusts	c1400	44,090	0.20	16	460	0.04
Woodland Trust	102	1,214	0.005	—	—	—
Forest	11	2,448	0.01	39	1857	0.13
Local	105	14,371	0.06	1	—	—
Wildfowl Refuges	44	11,180	0.05	2	—	—
TOTAL	1950	267,034	1.25	103	7151	0.52
SITES OF SPECIAL SCIENTIFIC INTEREST						
Biological	3166			—see text—		
Geological	984					
TOTAL	4150	1,470,900	6.6			

* Nature Conservancy Council 1984

References

Balfour, J., 1984. *A new look at the Northern Ireland countryside*. Belfast.

Barber, D. (ed.), 1970. *Farming and wildlife: a study in compromise*.Sandy.

Belfast in its regional setting, 1952. A scientific survey. Belfast.

Buchanan, R.H., 1982. Landscape, *in* Cruickshank, J.G. and Wilcock, D.N. (eds). *Northern Ireland: environment and natural resources*. Belfast. 265-89.

Field Studies and Outdoor Pursuits, 1972. Committee on field study and outdoor pursuits centres. *A handbook of centres in Northern Ireland. Belfast*.

Forsyth, J. and Boyd, D.E.K., compilers, 1970. *Conservation in the development of Northern Ireland*. Belfast.

Furphy, J.S., 1970. *Nature conservation in Northern Ireland up to August 1970*. in Forsyth and Boyd (above), 76-8.

McCracken, E., 1971. *The Irish woods since Tudor Times*. Newton Abbot.

Nature Conservancy Council, 1984. *Nature Conservation in Britain*. London.

Newbould, P.J., 1983. Retrospect: countryside conservation since 1965 *in* Forsyth, J. and Buchanan, R.H. (eds.), *The Ulster countryside in the 1980s*. Belfast.

Ratcliffe, D. A. (ed.), 1977. *A nature conservation review*. Cambridge, 2 vols.

Thomlinson, P.M. (ed.), 1975. *Field study sites in Northern Ireland*. Belfast.

THE BUILT ENVIRONMENT

6 Town & Country Planning

*JOHN GREER AND PAT JESS**

Senior Lecturer, Department of Architecture and Planning, The Queen's University of Belfast
*Lecturer, Faculty of Social Sciences, The Open University in Northern Ireland

The phrase "town and country" evokes above all else the notion of sharp contrast, if not downright opposition between its constituent elements. The distinctions between "town" and "country" certainly go beyond the merely geographical: they conjure up marked differences in economic characteristics, land use and life style. In Northern Ireland this clear division between the two held good until some twenty-five years ago, "town" being associated with manufacturing industry or market functions, while "country" was the undisputed domain of the farmer. At the present time, however, the phrase has lost much of its earlier punch; the old certainties and imagery have been swept aside in the intervening period so that now the differences between town and country are more difficult to discern, and relationships between the two are much more complex.

This chapter outlines the developments and processes which have blurred the distinction between town and country in Northern Ireland, together with the underlying forces involved, and discusses the implications of the changing perceptions and use of the countryside in particular.

A question of balance

Whatever the internal distinctions between town and country may be, Northern Ireland as a whole has proven notoriously difficult to categorise in terms of its urban/rural character. There has been a tendency, for example, in EEC studies to look upon Northern Ireland as an essentially *agricultural* region. The point is well illustrated in a recent report which stated that

> the basic criteria indicate that the *whole* of the Northern Ireland region can be assigned to Group One (i.e. agricultural problem regions) in the classification scheme and although there are some problems associated with the weight of manufacturing industry around Belfast, the agricultural problem areas are sufficiently widespread to warrant a classification for the region as a whole (Black and Henrichsmeyer, 1984, 36).

Newtownabbey, County Antrim. A suburban area north of Belfast, where the development of light industry and warehousing has been facilitated by the M4 Motorway with its direct access to Belfast docks. (C.F.S. Newman)

Such a categorisation brackets the Province with regions in Southern Italy where the proportion of the workforce engaged in agriculture is very high (24.8 per cent in Basilicata, and 16.2 per cent in Calabria, as of 1981). This is patently not the case in Northern Ireland, where the proportion of the workforce engaged in agriculture is some 10 per cent, a figure relatively close to the average for the European Community as a whole (7.2 per cent for EUR 10 as of 1981) and quite far removed from that for Greece (30.1 per cent) or even the Republic of Ireland (17.2 per cent).

The classification of Northern Ireland as a rural region of the European Community is also not supported by reference to factors such as population density or the proportion of the population recorded as living in rural areas. Estimates based on the 1981 Census of Population point to an overall density of some 106 persons per square kilometre in Northern Ireland, which may be put in context when the United Kingdom figure of 229 persons is considered or the European Community (as of 1978) average of 170 persons. While many of the core urban regions of the community have population densities in excess of 400 persons per square kilometre, the peripheral regions, such as the Republic of Ireland, have densities as low as 50 persons per square kilometre. The population density in Northern Ireland is twice that of the Republic of Ireland as a whole, but even more importantly, it approximates to that of the Province of Leinster which contains in the Dublin complex, one of the fastest growing city regions in Europe.

Table 6.1

Population density per square kilometre within the European Community, 1978 and 1981

Area	Population Density
European Community (1978)	170
United Kingdom (1978)	229
Northern Ireland (1981)	106
Republic of Ireland (1981)	50
Province of Leinster (1981)	91

Sources: *The Regions of Europe Com* (80) 816. *Final: Census of Population, Northern Ireland 1981, Summary Report; Census of Population, Republic of Ireland, 1981*, Vol. 1.

The figures underline the long standing divide in Ireland between a relatively densely covered east coast and a much more sparsely populated interior. This cleavage is well illustrated in Northern Ireland where the figures for District Council areas in the West[1] of the Province show an average population density of some 53 persons per square kilometre in 1981: exactly half of the Northern Ireland average. This points to a fundamental division between the Belfast City Region and the rest of the Province.

The delicate balance between town and country in Northern Ireland and the consequent difficulties for classification of the region as a whole, are

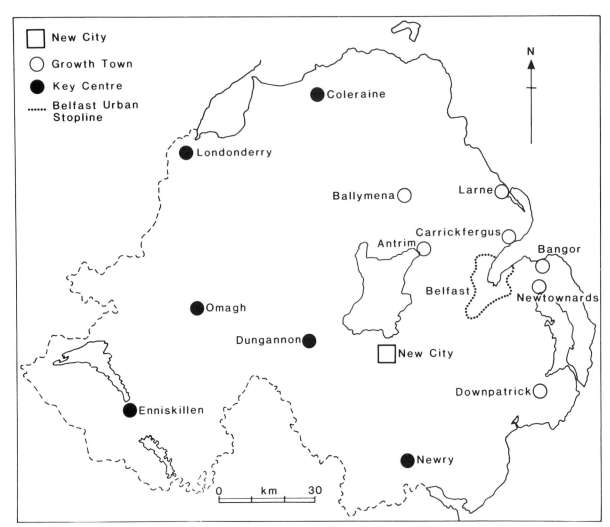

Figure 6.1   The Belfast
Regional Survey and Plan
Proposals, 1963

Source: Caldwell, J. and
Greer, J. Physical planning
for rural areas in Northern
Ireland *in* Jess, P.M. et al.,
(eds). *Planning and
development in rural areas,*
Belfast, 1984

highlighted in figures recorded for the percentage of the population living
in urban and rural areas. In a recent EEC report some 55.2 per cent of the
Northern Ireland population was classified as urban in 1980, which is very
similar to the 55.9 per cent in 1960 and 54.8 per cent in 1970 *(The regions of
Europe Com* (80) 816 Final). However, the equilibrium implied in these
figures is misleading in that they take no account of the large numbers of
people who work in towns and cities but, through the growth of private car
ownership, live in commuter villages or in the countryside, and are
therefore classified as rural dwellers for Census purposes. An earlier report
estimated that by 1970 some 70 per cent of the population of the Province
could be categorised as urban on this basis (Forsyth and Boyd, 1970).

In essence, data on the rural/urban nature of Northern Ireland
aggregated at the regional level, serve only to mask a fundamental divide
within the Province between (a) the Belfast city sub-region, with an

effective diameter of some 50 kilometres and a population of some 800,000 persons, the vast majority of whom are urban dwellers and (b) a large rural sub-region which accounts for no less than two-thirds of the land area of the Province, extending from North Antrim, through the Sperrins and Fermanagh, to embrace South Armagh and South Down. However, an important distinction must be drawn between the terms "rural" and "agricultural" in this context, since the sub-region contains not only a farming population but also a host of nucleated settlements, among them large administrative centres such as Omagh, Enniskillen and Armagh, whose fortunes are inextricably linked with those of their hinterlands.

The role of planning

Town and Country Planning in Northern Ireland is a comparatively recent phenomenon. The first legislation which enabled planning schemes to be prepared, and that on a voluntary basis, was passed only in 1931. In the event no such schemes were confirmed and the practice of Town and Country Planning up to 1962 was carried out on an informal basis, with interim planning schemes being produced for some urban areas, while development in rural areas was largely administered through building control regulations (Caldwell and Greer, 1984).

An exception to the prevailing laissez-faire attitude in the immediate post-1945 period is the work of the Northern Ireland Planning Advisory Board. Of particular note is the Report of the Board on the Ulster Countryside, published in 1947, which recommended among other things the designation of National Parks where appropriate, the preservation of the coast as a matter of national concern, and the establishment of areas of special control to improve amenities and conserve the best of the vernacular rural buildings (Buchanan 1982, 272-3). The report echoed similar concerns in Britain, and marked the beginning of a period of changing relationships between town and country, in which the latter was to experience a much greater volume and range of pressures for access and usage than anything that had existed hitherto.

The arrival of Town and Country Planning proper in Northern Ireland is commonly taken to accord with the appointment of Professor Robert Matthew in 1960 to prepare the Belfast Regional Survey and Plan, subsequently published in 1963. The choice of the Belfast Region in itself says much about the contemporary preoccupation of land use planning with urban issues. The 1961 Census had recorded a total population of some 1,425,000 of whom some 560,000 or 39 per cent were located in the Belfast Urban Area, a complex which contained not only elements of unregulated urban sprawl but also some of the worst inner city housing conditions in the United Kingdom. Hence the kernel of the brief given to Professor Matthew was the preparation of policies and proposals which would enable the other principal towns in the region to accommodate the growing demand for jobs and pressure on housing in Belfast, where there was already insufficient land upon which to implement any satisfactory redevelopment programme.

Craigavon, County Armagh: the shopping complex and office block which constitutes the centre of the new town, advocated by Professor Robert Matthew in his 1963 Plan for the Belfast region. (C.F.S. Newman)

Matthew made the following main recommendations which are illustrated in Figure 6.1:-

1. The development of a new regional centre, later known as Craigavon, which was to have a population of 100,000 in 1981, focussed on the existing market towns of Lurgan and Portadown
2. A stopline to curtail the physical expansion of the Belfast Urban Area to approximately 600,000 persons in 1981, surrounded by a Green Belt
3. The development of seven growth centres in the Belfast region to reduce the concentration of people and jobs in the urban area and prevent further loss of population from the rest of the Province
4. The establishment of six key centres in the remainder of the Province, where industry was to be concentrated (although significantly, no further elaboration of this proposal was made)
5. The setting up of a Central Planning Authority.

The prime object of the strategy, that of "demagnetising" the Belfast Urban Area while simultaneously expanding several of the larger towns within the immediate sphere of influence of the city, was a highly complex conception, requiring techniques of implementation and administration which were already running into difficulties where they had been tried in

Britain. The lynch-pin of the approach was that of growth centres which were not only to receive overspill population from Belfast but also to act as holding points or interceptor locations for people migrating eastward from the rural heartland of the Province in search of jobs and houses. These holding points were all firmly located in the historically-favoured eastern part of the region, thus further exacerbating the already marked dichotomy between east and west which had existed for centuries. In this sense the fixation of planning with the Belfast City Region relegated the rest of the Province to no more than a passive backdrop in the scheme of things and more particularly, identified planning efforts with the urban rather than the rural environment. The scale of the structural shift in the balance of settlement implied in the deployment of the growth centre policy may be appreciated in that, as of the mid 1960's, an additional 64,000 people were to be accommodated in Craigavon and the seven other urban areas outlined by Matthew. This meant that in 1981, some 55 per cent (912,000) of the Province's estimated population of 1,650,000 would live in these centres and the Belfast Urban Area. In planning terms, the Belfast City Region became almost synonymous with Northern Ireland as a whole.

The urban bias of all sectors of planning policy was consolidated with the publication of a major report on economic development (Wilson, 1965)

Craigavon, County Armagh: the expansive lay-out of residential development and associated road network, exemplified in the Legahory district. (C.F.S. Newman)

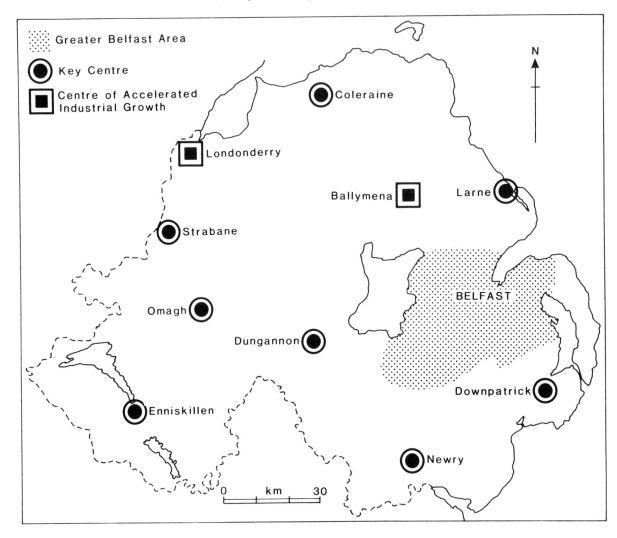

Figure 6.2 Northern Ireland Development Programme 1970-1975

Source: Caldwell, J. and Greer, J. Physical planning for rural areas in Northern Ireland *in* Jess, P.M. et al., (eds). *Planning and development in rural areas*, Belfast, 1984

which endorsed the spatial concentration of investment that was implicit in the Matthew rationale. When modest public disquiet was expressed about the implications of such a policy for economic and social opportunity in rural areas, the response invariably made was that the anticipated expansion of Craigavon and Londonderry would rapidly bring prosperity to the more remote parts of Ulster. However, with the publication of the Belfast Area Plan in 1969 (Building Design Partnership, 1969) arose the first major doubts about the efficacy of growth centre policy. The consultants found that by 1966 the population of the Belfast Urban Area had grown to 584,000 or 40 per cent of the total population in the Province, which was only 16,000 short of Matthew's estimated 1981 saturation point of 600,000. It was therefore becoming clear that growth centre policy was not having the intended effect of demagnetising the Belfast Urban Area, in that the centres chosen, and Craigavon in particular, were neither attracting families from Belfast on a scale sufficient to relieve pressure on the Urban Area itself, nor intercepting population migrating from the west, most of whom continued to locate in Belfast.

In spite of this evidence, official perception of the relevance of an urban-based solution remained unchanged, as evidenced in the subsequent publication of the Northern Ireland Development Programme 1970-75 (H.M.S.O., 1970). The Programme basically endorsed the previous proposals in principle, with a number of physical and economic policy modifications. Greater Belfast[2], Londonderry and Ballymena were to become "Centres of Accelerated Growth", thus reinforcing growth centre doctrine in an even more concentrated form. Eight other towns, referred to as "Key Centres" were also designated, four of these in the west of the Province (Figure 6.2). However, the Development Programme did acknowledge the existence of two distinct sub-regions in Northern Ireland with their attendant problems. On the one hand there was the problem of the under-developed areas outside Greater Belfast, which were regarded as essentially agricultural in origin; while on the other hand there were the problems of a declining industrial city region centred on Belfast. Significantly, the former areas were compared to the Highlands and Islands of Scotland, while Greater Belfast's problems were equated to those of Liverpool and Glasgow. Two strategies were therefore prepared separately for the Report and together they were to constitute a physical development strategy for Northern Ireland. Yet in spite of the recognition of the distinctive sub-regions and their different underlying economic structures, the recommended solutions to both were based on urban models derived from growth centre philosophy.

The policies outlined in the Development Programme soon disappeared beneath the avalanche of political and economic change which characterised Northern Ireland in the 1970's. The Planning Order (Northern Ireland) 1972 brought legislation into line with the British system, enabling plans to be prepared, for the first time, on a statutory basis and also accommodating public participation into the decision-making process. Local Government was reorganised into 26 new District Councils which were given very limited powers. Not only had they to relinquish planning functions, but public housing policy and house building programmes became the responsibility of the Northern Ireland Housing Executive. It was within this newly-devised system of centre-local relationships that the planning ministry, now known as the Department of the Environment for Northern Ireland issued a discussion paper in 1975 which was eventually to lead to the preparation of a regional physical planning strategy for the Province. The paper explored six main development options, ranging from the total concentration of resources in a huge linear expansion of Belfast, to a strategy which recommended a fairly widespread allocation of resources to obtain a relatively diffuse pattern of future development. The preferred option, based on public consultation, was a compromise solution known as the "District Towns" strategy. This formed the basis of the Regional Physical Development Strategy 1975-1995 which remains the main physi-

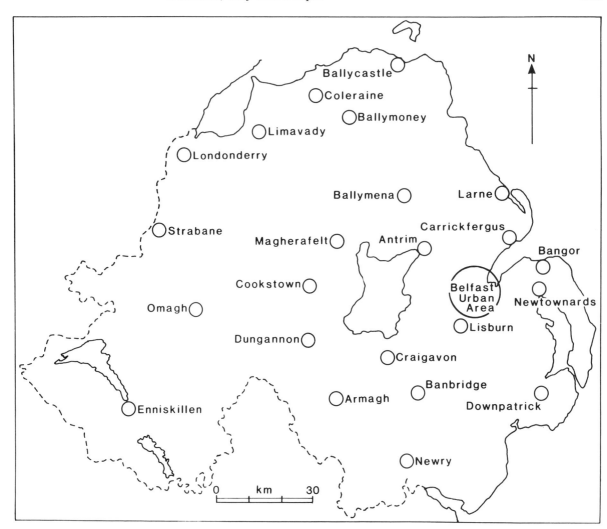

Figure 6.3 The District
Towns: regional physical
development strategy,
1975-95

Source: Caldwell, J. and
Greer, J. Physical planning
for rural areas in Northern
Ireland in Jess, P.M. et al.,
(eds). *Planning and
Development in rural areas*,
Belfast, 1984

cal planning policy instrument in the Province at the time of writing. The
strategy was aimed at a greater dispersal of resources than had existed
previously, by increasing the sixteen growth and key centres to twenty-
three (Figure 6.3). In effect, each District Council area was to have its own
growth centre, the corollary being that much less emphasis was placed on
concentrating all types of development in the main urban centres of
Londonderry, Ballymena, Antrim and Craigavon. In addition to the
District Towns, certain country towns were to serve as local centres, while
some of the larger villages were selected for more limited expansion,
provided they possessed adequate existing facilities and were situated near
District Towns. Finally, a number of small villages were to cater for very
modest housing development, primarily to replace unfit housing in the
open countryside. In essence, what this means is that some fourteen years
after the publication of the Belfast Regional Survey and Plan, a

comprehensive settlement policy had been prepared for the first time for the whole of Northern Ireland. In theory at least, a more equitable distribution of growth points had been established, reflecting a somewhat belated recognition of the important role played by the more rural parts of the province. The previous strategy based on solutions to the problems of the Belfast Region was abandoned, notably the ill-starred new city of Craigavon.

While it may be premature to comment on the final effects of the Regional Physical Development Strategy 1975-95, two issues which presently dominate the attention of planners in Northern Ireland are worthy of mention. The first is the revision of the Belfast Urban Area Plan; the only comprehensive review since 1969, being undertaken in a socio-economic climate that has changed utterly in the intervening seventeen years. The altered nature of the planner's task is put into perspective by indicating the main trends in population which have occurred over the decade 1971-81. First, the massive decline of some 100,000 in the population of the Belfast District Council Area; secondly, a marked increase in the population of the District Council areas adjoining Belfast such as North Down, Ards and Lisburn; and thirdly, an average increase in population of some 8 per cent in the District Council areas in the West of the Province as against 1.8 per cent for Northern Ireland as a whole. A recent report on the Northern Ireland economy, indicates that the trends established in the period 1971-81 have continued to date, if at a less dramatic rate (Coopers and Lybrand, 1986). The importance of these trends is that whereas the problem facing planners in Northern Ireland some twenty years ago was the halting of population drift to Belfast so that the urban area would not exceed 600,000 persons, one of the main objectives in the revised plan will be to ensure that the population of the same area does not drop below 500,000 in the next decade.

The second issue, which arguably has caused much more public debate than the first, is that of housing in the countryside. At present the number of recently built bungalows along the roadsides is perhaps the dominant feature of the rural landscape of Northern Ireland. In many cases their ostentation seems to belie the status of the Province as one of the poorest regions of the European Community while the range of architectural styles adopted seems to embrace virtually every tradition *except* that of the Irish rural vernacular – the very feature which the post-war Planning Advisory Board suggested should be conserved! The origins of the debate about the acceptability or otherwise of housing in the countryside may be traced back to an inventory of general planning principles documented by Professor Matthew (Matthew, 1961). He argued that restrictions should be placed on scattered and ribbon development because of the (assumed) disproportionate costs involved in servicing such development together with the loss of agricultural land and natural amenity. These principles, probably derived from planning experience in Southern England, were soon enshrined in a circular dealing with the erection of subsidy houses in rural areas (1964) and they became central to the philosophy of physical plan-

Village planning of the eighteenth century: Palatine Square in Killough, County Down, developed by the Ward family as a service centre and port for their estates. (Arts Council)

ning for rural areas in Northern Ireland. They were seen as an essential underpinning of the strategy of concentration of population in the growth centres, and tended to be rigourously applied to any proposals for housing in the countryside. In a further tightening of the restrictions, applicants were required to produce evidence of a *need* to reside outside a nucleated settlement, for reasons relating to their occupation in farming or other primary industry, or poor health. The public reaction to this policy may well be due to the broadcast nature of its application which tended to be oblivious to the very different socio-economic conditions existing between the east and west of the Province. Political opposition to the policy came equally from both sides of the community and welled up to such a degree that a review body, generally referred to as the Cockcroft Committee, was set up to consider the matter in 1977. The Committee's extensive set of recommendations was generally critical of prevailing policies and the nett result was a change in planning policy and a significant increase in the level of planning permissions for residential development in rural areas. This has meant that outside certain Areas of Special Control[3] applications for development in the countryside are judged solely against physical planning criteria and the "need" clause no longer applies. Heated debate still continues about the costs and benefits of the dispersed form of settlement, not least because it has added another, new, and indeed confusing dimension to the whole meaning of town and country in Ulster.

The changing countryside

The effect of the policy change on the rural landscape of Northern Ireland has been remarkable. Country towns and large villages, surrounded by their mantle of Special Control status are encircled beyond that by a girdle of "one-off" houses and bungalows which extends into linear development along the main roads between the towns. In some rural areas there are clusters of houses which reach suburban densities. Building continues apace. But why should this matter? After all, is it not simply an expression by individuals of where and how they want to live; an expression of "powerful cultural and commercial instincts which favour dispersal, privacy and a whole host of other values" (Smyth, 1986, 170)? To those who believe it *does* matter, the issue hangs on two aspects; amenity and access; that a proliferation of bungalows and houses, often ill-sited and of unsympathetic design, affects the quality of the landscape and, if there are too many of them, affects the freedom of the public to reach and enjoy the countryside.

These two factors, amenity and access lie at the heart of the countryside and conservation debate of the 1980s both in Britain and in Northern Ireland. In Northern Ireland thirty years ago, neither would have been the cause of public concern. At that time much of rural Ulster still reflected traditional patterns of rural life. There were few signs of affluence and the prevailing social ideology was of the land as an agricultural resource and in parallel with that, the private ownership and use of that land. Rural areas were places to live and work, usually in or related to agriculture, and "visiting" meant going to see family and neighbours rather than going for a picnic and enjoying "the view". There was, among a minority of largely urban and mainly middle-class interests, an awareness of the value of our varied landscapes and of the need to preserve them but there was no widespread sense of amenity and the present-day notion of access was probably never considered as such. Nevertheless, the Planning Advisory Board's Report (1947, noted above) acknowledged publicly, for the first time, "that the countryside was under pressure and that legislative action was necessary – (but) its proposals were greeted with almost total silence by the Government of the day, which not only ignored the Report but also allowed the Board to fall into abeyance" (Buchanan, 1982, 272-3). This is surely a clear illustration of the lack of public concern at that time. In fact it was to be nearly twenty years before legislation for amenity was enacted for Northern Ireland.

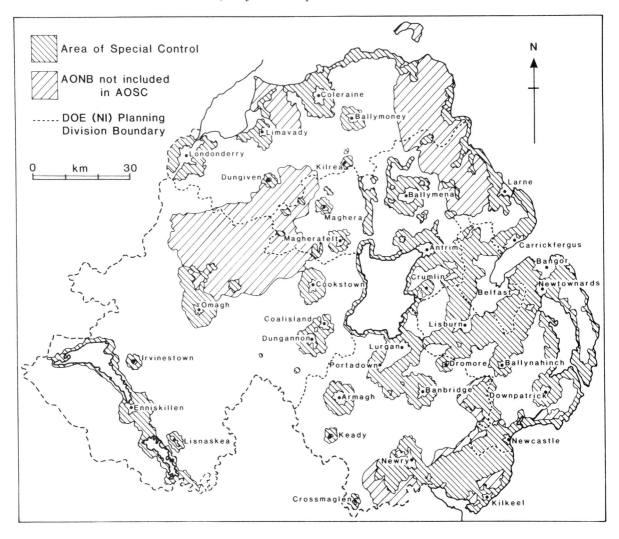

Fig 6.4 Areas of
Outstanding Natural Beauty
and Areas of Special Control

Source: Buchanan, R.H.
Landscape Cruickshank,
J.G. and Wilcock, D.N. (eds).
*Environment and resources
in Northern Ireland*, Belfast,
1982.

Despite that however, two significant events did take place during this
relative Dark Age of countryside management and planning. The first of
the Forest Parks, at Tollymore, was established in 1955 by the Forestry
Division of the then Ministry of Agriculture (Northern Ireland) and the
Ulster Folk Museum was founded in 1958. These two institutions have
developed over the years highlights of public provision for recreation and
education in Northern Ireland. They developed slowly but it is a monument
to the foresight of those involved that they were started at the beginning of
a period of significant social change, which was characterised by increases
in affluence, leisure time and personal mobility. These changes began in
the late 1950s and quickened during the 1960s. The growth in population
was largely urban based as indeed was the growth in affluence. Changing
patterns of employment, with marked expansion in the services and public
sectors as well as in "light" manufacturing industry raised many household

incomes and introduced car ownership to a wider range of social classes and ages. There was also much more leisure time, not only among those in paid jobs but also among young people, an enlarging and active retired population, and women. Added to this was a developing awareness of leisure and recreation through education, media, and the positive promotion of sport and leisure activities, a good deal of which focussed on the countryside. Alongside all this there were also other more tangible developments affecting the countryside. Roads were improved and new ones planned and built (Chapter 9). Industrial development became a major focus of activity, much of it on "greenfield" sites and adjacent to provincial towns and to suburban Belfast. Quarrying developed rapidly to supply base materials for the construction industry. New housing was planned. There were also considerable changes in agriculture: increasing specialisation and mechanisation, and an added emphasis on the nature of land as a resource; but at that time, few people asked, for whom and for what is the land a resource?

In short the 1960s was a period of growth and much of this carried quite widespread implications for the countryside and for relationships between town and country. Structural aspects of this have already been discussed above and the significance of adopted planning philosophies has been outlined. In the past the Northern Ireland landscape owed little to the practice of planning and management, but the 1963 Matthew Plan had firmly introduced the principles of post-war professional planning to Northern Ireland. Amenity was not one of Matthew's primary concerns but he did comment upon the "accessible and attractive countryside", "uncrowded roads" and "great potential value" of our type of environment. He also commented on "signs throughout the Region of neglect and indifference. There is little sign of appreciation of the value of the natural environment and in particular the special endowment with which many parts of the Region are blessed" (Matthew; quoted in Buchanan, op.cit., 274). In fact Matthew regarded planning for amenity and conservation as making sound economic sense; and this was probably the one thing likely to commend "amenity planning to the business and farming interests then dominant within the ruling Ulster Unionist Party. In 1965, three years after the Matthew Report was published, the Amenity Lands Act was passed by the Northern Ireland Parliament" (Buchanan, op. cit., 275). This legislation is of considerable importance because, along with the reorganisation of local government it provided the framework for environmental management and planning in Northern Ireland and underpins the most recent legislation (1985, see below). It provided for the designation of National Parks and Areas of Outstanding Natural Beauty (AONB) as well as for more specific sites of scientific interest and nature reserves. It is the fate of the first and the progress of the second that concern us here, for these two features should be most relevant to countryside management and recreation.

Legislation is only enabling; it requires *will* to implement its provisions. For example, legislation cannot be blamed for the complete lack of National Parks in Northern Ireland but there are many who would blame a lack of

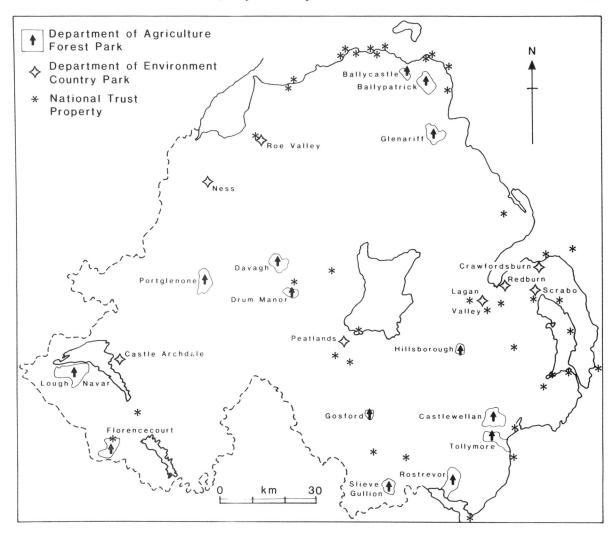

Fig 6.5 National Trust properties, DoE Country Parks and DoA Forest Parks.

Source: Buchanan, R.H. Landscape Cruickshank, J.G. and Wilcock, D.N. (eds). *Environment and resources in Northern Ireland*, Belfast, 1982.

conviction on the part of those with the power to designate – or perhaps more particularly, would point to the handling of the exercise which could have been the fore-runner of National Park designations, namely, the proposed AONB in Fermanagh. The details of this episode are referred to elsewhere: suffice it to say that in 1987 we have neither National Parks in Northern Ireland nor an AONB in Fermanagh – for which, it has to be said, some Fermanagh people have declared themselves profoundly glad! Designation does not have a good public image in Northern Ireland, where anything remotely resembling a real or imagined threat to the assumed rights of private property is strongly resisted. Despite this, we do have eight AONB, which have formed the cornerstone of management policy of the government department which is responsible for landscape and conservation. Probably equally significant for recreation and management has been the activity in the so-called "voluntary sector", notably the National

Trust; the Forest Parks run by the N.I. Department of Agriculture's Forestry Division; the activities of the N.I. Sports Council; and more recently, the developing role of the District Councils as providers for recreation.

Increased provision for countryside recreation, formal and informal, in the 1970s was a reaction to those social trends which had begun in the 1950s but while what actually happened was clearly local in character it was in fact related to much wider issues. What happens in Northern Ireland is a specific and local outcome of a much wider, complex set of interacting social processes which are evident at national and international levels, involving aspects of economic and political life, some of which may not immediately seem to have much to do with either countryside or the enjoyment of it. An example of this is the way in which agricultural policy decided in Brussels influences how farmers here use their land, which in turn affects the appearance of the countryside. Furthermore, changes in agricultural practices over the past twenty years are commonly blamed for environmental deterioration in large parts of England. Because of the smaller scale of our farming enterprises here and the greater emphasis on pasture rather than arable, we have largely escaped the ravages of prairie farming with the consequent loss of miles of hedgerows, the vast monotonous landscapes and more and more land being ploughed into production. (Blunden and Curry, 1985, ch.2). We have, however, had our share on the smaller scale, and we have also seen more effective fencing, afforestation, and land improvement schemes which, almost incredibly, seem to be continuing at a time when it might be thought that we should be taking land *out* of production, in the shadow of European and world-wide overproduction. As well as adversely affecting amenity generally and wildlife in particular such schemes also often impede access by the general public to the countryside in, for example, areas like the Sperrins and the Mournes. There are of course two sides to the access issue but in Northern Ireland it has been rare for the two sides ever to meet to discuss it.

Another adjunct to agriculture which has come into conflict with amenity and conservation issues is land drainage. Here the activities of one government department (Agriculture: Drainage Division) often seem to be in direct conflict with the interests of another (Environment: Conservation Division) and with the interests of specialist groups in the voluntary sector, such as the Royal Society for the Protection of Birds (RSPB) and the Ulster Trust for Nature Conservation (UTNC). A clear example of this is the scheme for the River Blackwater. Yet again, the recession of the mid-80's makes the economics of such schemes increasingly questionable.

Other changes in the wider context of political economy have had local effects with repercussions on the the interests of amenity and recreation. The widespread process of concentration and centralisation of services in both private and public sectors is particularly detrimental to a population which is dispersed rather than based on a hierarchy of villages and towns. It has most adversely affected the least affluent members of the rural population, particularly the very old and the very young, who lack ready

The Mall, Armagh: town houses reminiscent of Dublin, add dignity to Ireland's ecclesiastical capital. (Arts Council)

access to personal transportation. Since most people who visit the countryside for recreation prefer a "living" countryside to a deserted wilderness, any process or policy which encourages rural depopulation is detrimental to rural interests generally. This, of course, is an argument which has been used against planning controls but in fact, positive planning rarely fosters depopulation in any widespread way. Unfortunately many people feel that what they experience directly is negative rather than positive planning. This is clearly illustrated in the setting up, and the Report of, the Cockcroft Committee.

The issue of rural economic development has alrealdy been mentioned in terms of factories and roads. In the 1980s there is a very clear move away from a concept of large economic-industrial units and towards small-scale, locally viable economic activity. There seems absolutely no reason why this should not be perfectly compatible with amenity, conservation and recreation interests: in fact, it should contribute through the maintenance of self-sustaining local populations. The same should be true of tourism. In Great Britain there is a new impetus given to the idea of tourism in the local economy especially now that many people have taken early retirement or forms of voluntary redundancy from their paid employment. Northern Ireland has not in fact benefitted from international tourism as much as Professor Matthew had anticipated, largely because of continuing civil unrest. Nevertheless, the potential remains, especially among a local market and in the arena of activity and interest-based holidays. This concept could in fact be extended since not only the "retired" have leisure nowadays. Unemployment has conferred upon thousands of people in Northern Ireland, and millions elsewhere, the cruel paradox of having plenty of "free" time but not the money or resources to use it. This surely creates the major challenge to those concerned with countryside management and recreation in the 80's: how to involve people in creative experience, in the context of economic recession and government cuts in public spending.

Unfortunately the relative merits of development and conservation are not always resolved amicably, as the public enquiry over the application to extend limestone quarrying immediately adjacent to Navan Fort (Ulster's equivalent of Stonehenge), has recently demonstrated. In this case culture and environment may be seen to have won but only at considerable financial cost – again, a local example of much wider issues of extractive industry in areas of high amenity (cf. the recent cases in the Peak District National Park in the North of England) and of the costs involved in public enquiries (*Countryside Commission News*, 1986). These problems may arise again over lignite mining around Lough Neagh (Chapters 3 and 4). With the present weight of economic recession the problems involved become the more acute. Conservation must not appear to deny jobs and prevent progress, nor to be the plaything of the rich at the expense of the poor. The public debate must be broadened and the issues placed in their correct context of the quality of life and the kind of society we want for the future.

All of these issues are currently taking place against a growing crisis in the farming industry, brought about by changing economic and political circumstances, public attitudes and three years of adverse weather. Nationally, the first three factors combined to produce the 1981 Wildlife and Countryside Acts for England and Wales and for Scotland. Their provisions, and perhaps even more so, the campaign waged by a varied but vociferous "conservation lobby" prior to enactment, reflected changing public attitudes with regard to "the environment" in its widest sense. The ascendancy of agriculture over all countryside matters was no longer unquestioned: conservation in its widest sense was finally on the agenda for the future of rural Britain. Because of Direct Rule from Westminster and the consequent requirement for Orders in Council to be enacted to keep Northern Ireland at least broadly in line with the rest of the UK, the opportunity arose for the amenity factor to be strengthened in Northern

Ireland too. This opportunity was firmly grasped by the voluntary sector when it looked as though the review of amenity legislation which they believed necessary might not take place and the chance of change and progress might be lost. The Government responded to pressure from the voluntary conservation bodies by commissioning Dr Jean Balfour "to examine whether or not more appropriate administrative structures might be established" (Wilcock and Guyer, 1986, 124). The voluntary sector, co-ordinated through the ad hoc Northern Ireland Environment Group (NIEG) by R.H. Buchanan, presented their views on the Draft Orders to the Environment Committee of the Northern Ireland Assembly. The Wildlife (N.I.) Order 1985 and the Nature Conservation and Amenity Lands (N.I.) Order 1985 came into law in January 1985, three months after Balfour had reported and too soon to incorporate any of her specific recommendations but, together with the 1983 Access to the Countryside (N.I.) Order, they bring Northern Ireland's legislation (broadly) into line with that in Great Britain and with the UK government's obligations to international conventions and EEC legislation". (Wilcock and Guyer, 1986, 126).

The Balfour Report was widely discussed during the winter of 1984-85 and remains on the table in debate. The NIEG which includes conservation, recreation and area-based interests, politely welcomed the Report and its recommendations while expressing disappointment over the failure to recommend a semi-independent "countryside commission" style body for Northern Ireland. The report was however, given overall backing with the expressed hope that the recommendations would be fully implemented, especially in regard to financing for the voluntary sector and reorganisation within the Civil Service.

As a result, we now have in Northern Ireland an enhanced government Conservation Service within the Department of the Environment, with more staff, more money, and potentially more power to achieve viable management structures for the countryside within the existing legislative structures. However this depends, as Dr Balfour observed in her conclusion, on an active will within the Countryside and Wildlife Branch to *use* the legislation in a creative way and positively to activate co-operation within the Civil Service and with the voluntary sector. The necessary level of innovation required is a reasonably safe one, for while what is needed may not have been tried in Northern Ireland, various management strategies have been well tried and tested – and made work – in Great Britain. Principally this means National Parks *but* if this is not feasible – and it probably is not in the short-term of 5-10 years, then the Department's preferred tool, AONB designation, wanting thought it may be in several respects, can still be made to work much more effectively. The key to much of the desired success lies with the relationships between the Branch and the voluntary sector.

The role of the voluntary sector has been mentioned several times above. The term is deceptively singular and simple. In fact it covers a great range of bodies and activities, from very loose federations of people who pursue a similar interest somewhat independently, to the highly organised, large-membership groups like the RSPB; but also, associations of representatives of interest groups formed on an area basis, like the Mournes Advisory Council. These latter groups were formed specifically because of the lack of a clear lead in countryside management and in an attempt to resolve or better still prevent, local conflicts of interests and to liaise with the responsible government departments when issues arose which required their attention.

This kind of thing has already been recognised by the Countryside Commission in Great Britain. In a leaflet entitled *What is countryside management?* they comment that "small-scale conflicts between recreation, conservation, agriculture and development in the countryside are becoming more widespread, particularly in areas which are suffering from the stresses imposed by rapid landscape change, concentration of visitors or uncertainty over future patterns of development". Their now well-tried solution is a Project Officer "who is delegated financial and administrative powers ... to solve small-scale conflicts in the most effective way". The Commission goes on to point out that this method of "countryside management (at local level) offers real benefits to local planning authorities ... farmers ... local residents and amenity and recreation groups ... and to visitors".[4]

Such a method could be made to work very well in Northern Ireland where the local scale is highly significant in cultural and political terms. People here have a suspicion of centralisation and bureaucracy and a Project Officer working under a local management committee representative of local statutory and voluntary interests would act as the crucial link between locality and centre. However, to achieve this, the Department has to be willing and imaginative enough to provide adequate funding to the local level. They have the opportunity to do this in areas where local groups have already been formed.

Conclusion

The tale of town and country in Northern Ireland over the past thirty years is one of increasing complexity. Over the last ten years more people have expressed a desire if not a need to live in the countryside and more recently than that, the major task facing the planners has been identified as the need to arrest the sharp decline in the population of the Belfast Urban Area. These phenomena have added another layer to the development of our settlement pattern which was previously characterised by the rapid growth of Belfast and a network of provincial towns and smaller villages. In part this may be reaction to rigid physical planning policies favouring concentration but it owes something also to the nature of civil unrest during the early 1970s and to the other processes which led to an increase in out-of-city shopping. However, in parallel with the increase in numbers of people living in dispersed and small-scale settlement forms, fewer people are actually working in the traditional rural occupations based on farming while more and more are visiting the countryside for recreation. This aspect has introduced to the local scene in Northern

Ireland, the national debate about access. At a very general level it might well be claimed that we do not have a major access problem, such as that which led the Countryside Commission for England and Wales to develop the "Access Charter" but at a very local level there have increasingly been problems of access to scenic areas. The key question over access is how to enable the public to explore and use the countryside without impeding other rural activity by local people and farmers. This raises important and intimately related issues: how can greater public access actually be made to benefit local economies rather than create conflicts: and how can improved access be extended to the socially disadvantaged – the poor, the less mobile, the physically and mentally handicapped – to enable a far wider range of people to enjoy and benefit from countryside recreation. This leads to a further question; that of greater public *involvement* as well as access; how can we satisfy the growing public interest in the countryside in cost-effective, satisfying and useful ways (Countryside Commission News, 1985). This latter point is one on which the voluntary and statutory sectors are most likely to be able to co-operate; but in order for this, or indeed any of these aspects to work effectively in the countryside we require far greater levels of *integration*.

"Integration" has become a magic word. It is found in all texts and communications to do with rural development and conservation and is often imbued with the power of a panacea. "Integrated Rural Development" is the term widely used to imply a process whereby rural areas can be regenerated or achieve a viable place in modern society. But what is to be integrated; and integrated with what? and who is going to do it – and how? Basically we are talking about integration among uses and among users: this means agriculture and conservation; local people and visitors; extractive industry and amenity; car parks and privacy. This is exhibited at the local level, in local areas; but it requires integration also between the local level and the wider contexts of regional and national administration, provision and demand. That in turn introduces the so-called "top-down, bottom-up" debate: should decisions and implementation be initiated at local level or somewhere up in a hierarchy of bureaucracy: in other words, among those who are there on the spot or by those who are responsible to a wider set of considerations and crucially, responsible for budgets and their allocations. About the one thing which is quite clear in all of this is that the situation requires *management* and that someone, somewhere must generate plans and strategy and their implementation and evaluation. Such tasks are difficult but they have been tackled with some success elsewhere in the UK. There is a great deal to be gained for our society in facing the problems but one thing is sure: if we do not do so, the environment will make its impact back, with the ultimate loss of amenity, local economy and rural society.

Notes

1. District Council Areas in the West of the Province include Coleraine, Limavady, Derry, Strabane, Omagh, Magherafelt, Fermanagh, Cookstown, Dungannon and Armagh.
2. Greater Belfast was defined in the Programme as including the former growth centres of Antrim and Craigavon together with the major towns within a 20 mile radius of Belfast.
3. The Areas of Special Control, which were defined in consultation with District Councils, presently include parts but not all of the Areas of Outstanding Natural Beauty, the Areas of Scientific Interest, the Belfast sub-region and areas close to all other urban centres. The latter approximate to (1) a two-mile zone beyond the planned limits of each District Town and towns having a projected population of 10,000 or more and (2) a one-mile zone beyond the limits of towns with a projected population of 2,000 or more.
4. The Countryside Commission believe that countryside management offers real benefits to:

   Local planning authorities – by providing a means of putting broad planning objectives into practice; by clarifying countryside issues, particularly in urban-oriented authorities; by encouraging a multi-disciplinary approach to countryside issues; by providing a closer link with local farmers and communities on matters of landscape conservation and recreation provision; by highlighting problem areas where action needs to be taken.

   Farmers – by helping to reduce the problems caused by visitors on their land; by wardening and providing other facilities for recreation; by assisting with conservation work; by providing a general source of advice and liaison.

   Local residents and amenity and recreation groups – by helping to reduce the impact of visitors in the area – e.g. problems of noise, litter, parking; by enhancing the local landscape; by providing an opportunity for their involvement in the conservation management of the area.

   Visitors – by providing well-managed informal recreation facilities in an attractive environment which do not conflict with other uses of land in the area.

   (Reference, the Countryside Commission leaflet *An approach to countryside management*. undated).

References

Armstrong, J., 1986. Opinion: let's have fairer public enquiries, *in Countryside Commission News*, 19, 3.

Balfour, J., 1984. *A new look at the Northern Ireland countryside*. Belfast.

Black, W. and Henrichsmeyer, W., 1984. *Integrated regional development programmes. Commission of the European Communities: Information on Agriculture*, No. 89, Brussels.

Blunden, J. and Curry, N. *(ed.)*, 1985. *The changing countryside*. London.

Buchanan, R.H., 1982. 'Landscape', *in* Cruickshank, J.G. and Wilcock, D.N. *(eds.) Northern Ireland environment and natural resources*. Belfast. 265-89.

Building Design Partnership. 1969. *Belfast urban area plan*. 2 vols. Preston.

Caldwell, J.H. and Greer J.V., 1984. *Physical planning in rural areas of Northern Ireland*. Occasional paper no.5. (Dept. of Town and Country Planning, Queen's University) Belfast.

Commission of the European Communities, 1980. *The regions of Europe. First Periodic Report*. COM (80) 816 Final. Brussels.

Coopers and Lybrand Associates, 1986. *The Northern Ireland economy: review and prospects*. Belfast.

Countryside Commission. Undated leaflet. *An approach to countryside management*.

Countryside Commission, 1986. *Countryside Access Charter. Out in the country*.

Department of the Environment (Northern Ireland), 1975. *Regional physical, development strategy 1975-95*. Belfast.

Forsyth, J. and Boyd, D.E.K., 1970. *Conservation in the development of Northern Ireland*. Belfast.

HMSO, *Northern Ireland Development Programme 1970-75*, 1970. Belfast.

Matthew, R., 1961. *Belfast regional survey and plan: interim report, Belfast regional survey and plan; recommendations and conclusions*. CMD 451, Belfast.

Ministry of Health and Local Government. 1964. *Proposals for the erection of subsidy houses in rural areas, circular 56/64*. Belfast.

Planning Advisory Board, 1947. *The Ulster countryside. A report of the amenity committee.* Belfast.

Recreation 2000, 1985. *Countryside Commission News* 18. 4-5.

Review of rural planning policy, 1978: Report of the committee under the chairmanship of Dr W.H. Crockcroft, Belfast.

Smyth, W.J., 1986. The cultural geography of rural Ireland in the twentieth Century, *in* Nolan, W. *(ed.), The shaping of Ireland, the geographical perspective.* Cork/Dublin. 165-75.

Wilcock, D.N. and Guyer, C.F., 1986. Conservation gains momentum in Northern Ireland?, *in Area* 18.2. 123-9.

Wilson, T., 1965. *Economic Development in Northern Ireland.* Belfast.

7 Belfast: The Physical & Social Dimensions of a Regional City

F. W. BOAL

Reader, Department of Geography, The Queen's University of Belfast

In 1952, when the British Association last met in Belfast, the city was slowly recovering from the bomb damage of World War II and was still experiencing the effects of a war-activated surge in industrial employment. In that year I heard my first lecture on Belfast given by Emrys Jones, then a lecturer in geography at Queen's University, and later to become Professor of Geography at the London School of Economics. Jones (1952) also contributed a chapter ("Belfast: a survey of the city") to the volume on *Belfast in its regional setting* which was produced for the 1952 British Association meetings. Eight years later his classic piece of urban analysis, *A social geography of Belfast*, was published, dealing with the development of the city up to the time of the 1951 Census (Jones, 1960). Thus, 1952 serves as a particularly appropriate baseline year from which to start this examination of the city. The 35 years intervening between the two most recent meetings of the British Association in Belfast have been nothing if not dramatic.

Belfast has been physically controlled by its site and socially structured by the origins of its inhabitants. Recently, Robert Johnstone (Johnstone and Kirk, 1983) has described Belfast, viewed from the ever-evident backdrop of hills, as "... splurged below you, a spill of buildings gathered in by great arms, looking outwards to the narrow sea, but leaking round the coasts and back to the interior." (Figure 7.1.)

The steep escarpment of the basalt-capped Antrim plateau to the northwest looks down upon the subdued line of the Castlereagh and Holywood Hills to the south-east and, in between, the lowland of the Lagan Valley. The sea fills the lowest part of the valley, further constricting the site of the city.

Belfast is basically a creation of nineteenth century industrialisation, growing from a population of some 50,000 in 1830 to 350,000 by 1900. Linen manufacture and shipbuilding were the central components of this industrialisation which drew large numbers of migrants from rural Ulster. Jones has noted (1960, 134) that the population of Belfast is remarkably

125

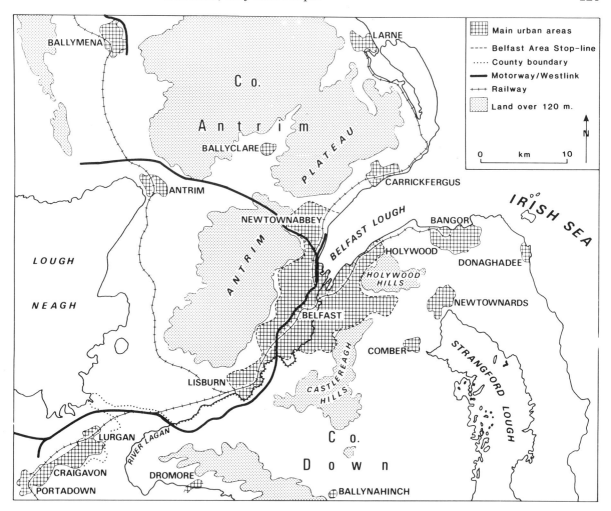

Figure 7.1   Belfast and its setting.

homogeneous – that is, it is overwhelmingly Ulster in origin. Be that as it may, the rural to urban migration involved both Protestants and Catholics to create an ethnic mosaic that denies the validity of Jones' perception of homogeneity or at least suggests that population heterogeneity can derive not only from international migration flows but also from population movements internal to a country.

The industrially driven growth of Belfast in the nineteenth century was of the greatest political significance in Ireland: firstly it meant that by 1900 Belfast was a larger city than Dublin, and secondly the city developed as an outpost of industrial Britain, causing her economic interests to be orientated in that direction rather than towards the agriculturally dominated society in the south and west of Ireland and its major urban focus, Dublin. Basically Belfast formed part of the great industrial triangle of the valleys of the Mersey, Clyde and Lagan. Indeed one might develop this notion by suggesting that Belfast in the nineteenth century was a British industrial city that happened to be on the island of Ireland. Like similar British cities (Glasgow, Liverpool, Manchester) Belfast received a substantial flow of Irish Catholic immigrants and, also like them, there was a series of riot situations generated by the native workers' response to the perceived threat of this immigration (Boal, 1980).

The growth of the city of Belfast levelled off during the first half of the present century, reaching a recorded peak of 443,000 at the time of the 1951 census (Table 7.1). However, growth continued beyond the city boundary and it becomes increasingly meaningful to recognise the existence of a wider "Belfast Urban Area" spilling along the Lagan Valley, lapping up the lower slopes of the surrounding hills and fingering out along both the north and south shores of Belfast Lough (Boal, 1967).

Table 7.1

The population of Belfast "City" and of the "Belfast Urban Area", 1937–81

Year	City[1]	Urban Area[1]
1937	438,086	492,238
1951	443,671	532,481
1961	415,856	563,518
1971	362,083	582,273
1981	310,000	510,000

[1] The "City" Area is that of Belfast County Borough. The creation of the Belfast District Council area in 1973 formed a larger unit, which is that used for the 1981 "City" figure. The 1971 figure for the then forthcoming District Council area was 416.679 (Vaughan and Fitzpatrick, 1978). The Urban Area is an approximation of the area delimited by the present planning "Stop Line". The data in the Table are from Boal and Royle (1986).

In 1951 this larger unit had a population of 532,000. Six years earlier, in 1945, the Planning Commission established by the Northern Ireland Government pinpointed a number of aspects of the urban area that required urgent attention (Planning Commission, 1945): control of haphazard suburban growth, co-ordination of transport and the decentralisation of industry, the relieving of population pressures in the inner Victorian city, improvement of housing conditions, and, finally, protection from urban encroachment of the striking edges of the Antrim and Down uplands and the green wedge of the Lagan Valley. In 1951 the Commission, in a further report, reiterated the concerns expressed in their 1945 document, giving particular emphasis to the requirement that the size of Belfast be restricted relative to the population of Northern Ireland as a whole. (Planning Commission, 1951).

The growth decade of the 1960's: planning

By the time of the 1961 census trends observable in 1951 had become much clearer. The City had experienced a net loss of almost 28,000 people in the previous decade with the rest of the Urban Area gaining 59,000 (Table 7.1). While the redistribution of population was occurring, the

Belfast: redevelopment on the lower Falls in west Belfast pictured in 1976. The controversial Divis Flats complex is shown in the centre of the photograph, close by St Peter's Cathedral. (C.F.S. Newman)

Urban Area itself increased its share of the Northern Ireland population to slightly under 40 per cent of the total. Thus concerns expressed by the Planning Commission in 1945 and again in 1951 had still great import for the Urban Area of 1961, except that the older parts of the city were now losing population. It was in these circumstances that the Northern Ireland Government commissioned Sir Robert Matthew to prepare an outline advisory plan for the Belfast region.

The Belfast Regional Plan was published in 1964. The prime objective of the Plan was ". . . to a modest extent, simultaneously to de-magnetise the Centre, and re-invigorate the many attractive small towns in the Region." (Matthew, 1964, 18). This was seen as a highly complex operation with two aspects – limitation and growth, which had to be complementary. Limitation was to be achieved by the imposition of a Stop-line round the Belfast Urban Area (Figure 7.1). This would not only act to restrict the population growth of the Urban Area both in absolute terms and relative to that of Northern Ireland as a whole, but also would protect the high amenity areas on the fringes of the conurbation.

Matthew expressed concern at the absence of effective town planning in Belfast ("in the sense recognised in Great Britain") and forcefully indicated the need for the integration, for planning purposes, of the whole Urban Area, a point made a few years earlier by Jones when he wrote that "planning in the city needs to be linked with planning outside . . ." (1960, 65). In addition Matthew noted that co-ordinated traffic planning was necessary and went so far as to suggest that "the driving of animals in the street might, with advantage, be prohibited at critical times" (1964, 24) (this referred to the movement of fat cattle from holding pens to the docks for shipment to the mainland U.K. and elsewhere).

Planning in the 1960's was dominated by the growth theme – the need to limit it in one location and to redirect it to others, although it is significant that a warning was sounded as early as 1964 that "Belfast is much the most important industrial base in Northern Ireland" and also that "Northern Ireland is not in the position to take the risk of losing (new incoming industry) or of cramping unreasonably the expansion of firms already within the Matthew Stop-line" (Wilson, 1964).

Planning and transportation consultants for the city were appointed by Belfast Corporation in 1965. The briefs were extended in 1966 by the Northern Ireland Government to encompass the whole of the Urban Area. The transportation consultants' immediate task was the planning, design and supervision of the Belfast Urban Motorway Scheme which involved a proposal, emanating in 1961 from the City Surveyor, for an elevated expressway system ringing the city centre, with links to radial motorways, the type of scheme very much in fashion in many cities in the U.K. and North America at the time (Figure 7.2). The final Transportation Plan that emerged in 1969 endorsed the urban motorway and proposed what was basically a "roads-only" strategy. (Travers Morgan, 1969).

The planning consultants were faced with the task of filling in the interstices of the road network, and included proposals for new public housing in the redevelopment areas that would have 15 to 20 per cent of the units as high-rise blocks, another current solution to problems of "put-back" of displaced inner city populations. The planning consultants also proposed a restructuring of the Urban Area by providing "district centres to enrich and widen opportunity in the outer areas" (Building Design Partnership, 1969, 6). There were to be twelve of these centres involving, in particular, a spatial reorganisation of inner city service provision from a pattern of commercial ribbons and corner shops to new, highly nucleated

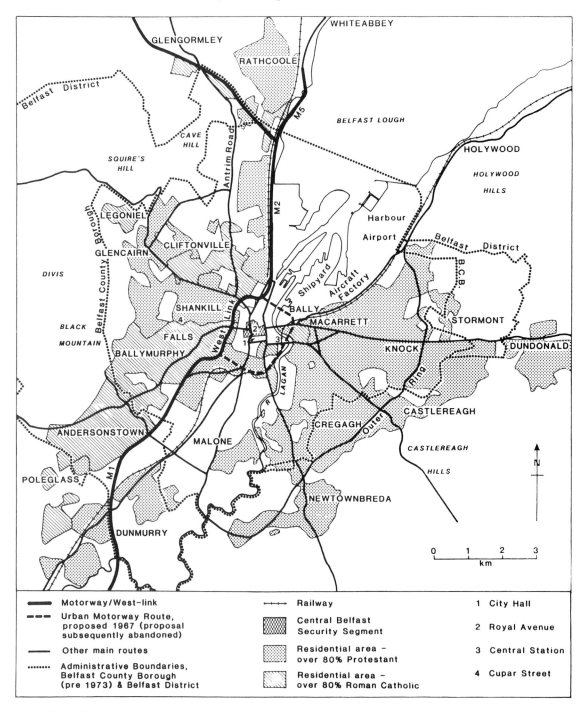

Figure 7.2   The Belfast
Urban Area, 1985 (excludes
Lisburn).

centres. One such district centre (Shankill) was to provide, as well as shops, sites for eight mission halls, all within a few metres of each other, in sharp contrast to the traditional scattered pattern.

The Regional Plan published in 1964 had set an upward limit of 600,000 people for the Belfast Urban Area. The Urban Area Planning consultants noted that the population had reached 584,000 by 1966 and that, in their opinion, it was likely to reach the planned limit of 600,000 as early as 1969. Thus the dynamic for growth seemed as strong as ever; a vigorous limitation and decentralisation policy was more urgently needed than it had been when Matthew reported in 1964.

The growth decade of the 1960's: employment and housing

While concern over growth was a dominant theme, very significant structural change in employment was underway. Between 1961 and 1968 employment in the Urban Area in manufacturing industry fell from 106,000 to 92,000, while service employment rose from 133,000 to 145,000 (Building Design Partnership, 1969). Shipbuilding reached its post-war peak in 1960 when about 20,000 were employed. The last great passenger liner to be built in Belfast, the *Canberra*, was launched in that year but subsequent shipbuilding activity was greatly influenced by intensified foreign competition and by a radical reorganisation of the Harland and Wolff shipyard during the 1960's, involving an assembly-line approach and a shift in production emphasis to large bulk carriers (oil, natural gas etc),(Harland and Wolff, 1985). It was to be one of the great ironies of shipbuilding that just as the Belfast yard became geared to the efficient production of super-tankers, so the market for such products collapsed. By 1969 employment in the yard had fallen to half its 1960 level. The linen industry also suffered severely as a provider of jobs. Fifty-one thousand residents of Belfast County Borough in 1926 had been employed in textiles. This had fallen to 31,000 by 1951 and to less than 13,000 by 1966 (Boal and Royle, 1986), with the bulk of the decline being in linen manufacture. During the 1960's total employment in the Urban Area remained fairly constant, but the traditional manufacturing industries were in rapid decline, the balancing growth coming in the service sector and in newer manufacturing enterprises such as aircraft, light engineering and man-made fibres.

In 1969 Building Design Partnership noted that housing had been the major problem of the Belfast Urban Area for the previous 20 years and that it would remain so for the next 20. The 1945 Planning Commission Report recorded 5,000 houses unfit for human habitation in the city, with, in addition, 9,000 married couples without separate homes. The Commission also observed that the inner city population of that time could only be rehoused on-site at acceptable space standards by resorting to flats of not less than six storeys for the whole population concerned. The Commission said, however, that they did not recommend such a solution for Belfast. The policy consequences of the rejection of high-rise flats was that much of the new development would have to be outside the city boundary. However, Belfast Corporation was unwilling to build outside its own area, and at the same time the Northern Ireland Government concluded that most of the local authorities in the Province had inadequate resources of their own to undertake large-scale public housing provision. In consequence, the Northern Ireland Housing Trust was established in 1945 to complement the housing programmes of the local authorities. In the Belfast area this meant that the Trust undertook the provision of public housing for Belfast overspill. By 1953 the Trust had provided 4,055 dwellings in the Belfast area (almost entirely outside the County Borough), this figure rising to 11,000 by 1962.

Despite house-building activity by the Trust and the Corporation, public sector housing demand continued to increase with the Planning Commission in 1951 estimating a need for 24,600 units. By 1959 over 18,000 houses were deemed unfit in the County Borough (Birrell et al, 1971). A 1962 study estimated that there was an overall demand in Belfast County Borough for 58,700 dwellings, with land available for only 7,800 in the city and 14,500 elsewhere in the Urban Area (Building Design Partnership, 1969). The whole housing situation seemed to be in a trap with a growing need, a lack of sites in the city and limited sites elsewhere in the Urban Area, due, in the middle 1960's, to the imposition of the Stop Line and due also to an unwillingness on the part of the local authorities that surrounded the city to see sites in their territory taken for Belfast overspill housing. Belfast Corporation had also failed to obtain a boundary extension, because of opposition from the same authorities, and due also, it is suspected, to opposition from the Northern Ireland Government, who were concerned that an expanded Belfast would emerge as an excessively powerful political unit. The lack of a boundary extension and the unwillingness of Belfast Corporation to build houses outside its corporate limits meant that inner city urban renewal was very slow to get underway, the first scheme only commencing in 1962. Renewal was also held up by the absence of legislation in Northern Ireland that would permit government subsidies on site preparation. This barrier was removed in 1956 with the passage of the Housing Act of that year. Again it has been claimed that the previous lack of such legislation was due to opposition of non-Belfast members of the Northern Ireland Parliament, who saw such subsidisation as merely channelling funds to the big city.

The great turnaround of the 1970's

In 1977 the Department of the Environment for Northern Ireland issued a report entitled *Northern Ireland: regional physical development strategy, 1975-95.* In this the Department declared that "Belfast faces a combination of economic, social, communal and physical development problems unparalleled in any major city in Europe." While Belfast was far from problem free in the 1960's, it is clear from the extremity of the Department's statement that radical changes must have occurred at the end of that

Shorts 360 Plane   *Industrial Development Board*

Ulster is no longer a predominantly agricultural area; in fact less than 10% of the work force is employed in agriculture. Conversion to an industrially-based economy has been an uphill struggle, due to lack of industrial resources and distance from markets.

Shorts is an aeronautical engineering firm competing successfully in world markets. The Shorts 360 is one of their recent contributions to domestic air transport, seen here skimming the eastern shore of County Down, wearing the livery of Air UK.'

Mural, Belfast City Hall   *Belfast City Council*

Ulster's earlier industrial base of linen and shipbuilding is symbolised in the John Luke mural in Belfast's City Hall. The wealth created by these industries is reflected in the City Hall's ornately plastered and marbled interior.

Silent Valley Reservoir, County Down   *N. C. Mitchel*

Plessey Factory, County Down

Industrial Development Board

Industry depends on plentiful supplies of water. Above is one of the Province's upland gravity-feed sources at the Silent Valley Reservoir in the Mourne Mountains, County Down. Lough Neagh in the middle of the Province provides a vast lowland fresh-water reserve, which has to be purified and pumped.

Light electronic industry is illustrated in this factory scene at the small market town of Ballynahinch, County Down. Such industry is ideally suited for rural locations and is vigorously promoted by the Province's Industrial Development Board.

Goliath Cranes, Belfast   *Harland & Wolff Ltd.*

Heavy industry still survives in the Harland and Wolff Shipyard, which has now been throughly modernised and diversified. The top photograph shows an historic moment when an enormous box-girder, made in the Yard, is being lifted by the two Goliath mobile cranes on to a waiting barge for transport round the coast to Londonderry where it forms part of a new bridge across the River Foyle.

The photograph on the right shows an Aviation Training Ship, 'RFA Argus' during conversion in the building dock in April 1987. The Yard has pioneered new types of vessel to service the off-shore oil industry, such as the BP 'SWOPS' which can be used to tap low product–ivity oil wells when market prices are favourable.

RFA Argus, Belfast

Harland & Wolff Ltd.

decade and during the early 1970's. Indeed a great deal did happen, starting in what must be a particularly critical year, 1969.

The violent political conflict that has occurred in Northern Ireland from time to time resurfaced in 1969. The so-called "Troubles" have not only affected Belfast, of course, but they have had a particularly sharp impact in the high density of an urban environment. There has been massive property damage, a large-scale forced population movement estimated at 60,000 (Darby and Morris, 1974), 1,050 deaths due to political violence in the Urban Area between 1969 and 1977, and a recorded 2,280 explosions in the same period (Murray 1982). The consequences have been massive. Beyond the unquantifiable human distress, there has been considerable damage to housing stock, further exacerbating an already bad situation. Planned population movements have been overwhelmed not only by the forced moves, but by the fear-generated constraints on people's willingness to be rehoused in certain areas. Employment has also been affected as has the appearance of parts of the city, including the centre, ringed as it now is, not by an elevated urban motorway but by barricades round the retail core in a reasonably successful attempt to prevent the placement of car-bombs.

The euphemistically named "Troubles" are only a part of the trauma of Belfast in the 1970's. In late 1969 a Review Body on Local Government in Northern Ireland was established. This, in many ways, was Northern Ireland following the example of the Maud-Wheatley Commission in Great Britain, although it was also consequent upon an earlier decision to establish a central housing authority for the whole Province. The Review Body reported in 1970 (Macrory, 1970) and a new system of local government was instituted in 1973. The new local authorities emerged with very limited powers, such as the provision of leisure facilities and cemeteries and the removal of rubbish. Housing provision, planning, education and

Belfast: the Peace Line in west Belfast at Cupar Street, built to improve security and reduce sectarian tensions along the divide between unionist and nationalist communities. (N.C. Mitchell)

social services were centralised in the Northern Ireland Government. The Belfast Urban Area fell within the ambit of five new local authorities. The former Belfast Corporation became Belfast District Council, one amongst 26 such bodies in Northern Ireland. There was a small boundary extension associated with the formation of the District Council but the fact that the Belfast Urban Area was still a fragmented unit at local government level was no longer a problem because fragmentation had been overcome by centralising all the important powers and functions at Provincial level. The former Belfast Corporation was left with the trappings of past glory, but little else. According to the Macrory proposals, political control of the important functions was to be given to the Provincial Parliament, but that body was itself prorogued in March 1972 (Douglas, 1982) and since that date, except for a brief five months in 1974, political control of housing, planning, education and social services has resided at Westminster. Thus the 1970's and 1980's have seen the Belfast Urban Area run by civil servants and semi-autonomous bodies – perhaps a bureaucrat's delight, but an abomination in terms of local democracy.

Employment aspects

Violent political conflict and an almost total loss of local democratic control are only the beginning of the list of Belfast's woes. The economic environment deteriorated markedly. An average male unemployment rate of 7.7 per cent in the Urban Area in 1972 (Doherty, 1982) rose sharply during the 70's reaching 21.3 per cent at the 1981 census, with localised pockets approaching 50 per cent. In May 1986 the male unemployment rate in the Belfast "Travel to Work" area stood at 22.8 per cent, with half of those unemployed in the Urban Area being under the age of 30 and half of the unemployed having been out of work for more than a year. Reports expressing concern about excessive growth of the urban area no longer appeared, being replaced by studies of social need such as that carried out for the Northern Ireland Community Relations Commisssion (Boal et al, 1974) and for the Government (Project Team, 1977). The "area of special social needs" delimited in these studies only emphasised the most spatially concentrated manifestation of the widely occurring economic and social malaise prevalent in the Urban Area. The economic base was the subject of greatest concern, with a further deterioration of the traditional industrial structure. The effect of this was now exacerbated by a combination of cut-backs and closures of newer industries (eg. electronics, man-made fibres) many of which had been attracted to the Belfast area in the economic boom times of the 1960's, and by an increased difficulty in attracting an inflow of new sources of employment. This latter problem was undoubtedly accentuated by the political turmoil, but the widespread ecomomic downturn in former source areas of capital investment (mainland UK, West Germany and the United States) was probably the most significant factor. High unemployment, a social disaster anywhere, becomes even more unfortunate in Belfast because it sharpens inter-ethnic rivalries.

The pattern of employment in the past 15 years can be examined in greater detail (Table 7.2). Basically what we see is a shift in employment composition occurring within the context of an overall decline in the number of jobs. Thus jobs in manufacturing industry had decreased from a situation where they formed 32 per cent of all employment in 1971 to one where they were the source of only 23 per cent (1981). Particularly hard hit have been electrical and mechanical engineering, textiles and clothing and footwear. Shipbuilding employment and that in the "vehicles" category (which includes aircraft manufacture) have had some success in maintaining job levels, this being particularly true of the aircraft firm of Shorts. Employment in the service sector has grown over the 1971-81 decade not only in its proportionate share (increasing from 60 to 72 per cent of all urban area jobs) but also absolutely. The growth areas have been in the insurance, banking and general finance fields, in professional and scientific services and in public administration and defence. Thus over only a decade the urban area has become much less of a manufacturing centre and much more a provider of services.

Table 7.2

Employment patterns, Belfast Urban Area 1971–81

Employment Category	Year			
	1971	1975	1978	1981
Manufacturing	71,798 (32.5)	63,849 (28.9)	53,641 (25.2)	46,839 (22.8)
Construction	16,210 (7.3)	15,210 (6.9)	12,204 (5.7)	9,598 (4.7)
Services	132,723 (60.0)	141,712 (64.1)	146,948 (68.9)	149,063 (72.4)
All	221,169	221,060	213,148	205,799

(The figures in parentheses indicate, for each year, the proportion of jobs in each employment category). The 1975, 1978 and 1981 data are for the Belfast Local Office Area of the Department of Economic Development. This area includes the Belfast District Council area, the town of Holywood and the continuously built-up sectors of Newtownabbey and Castlereagh Districts. The 1971 data refer to the aggregates of the then Belfast County Borough, Newtownabbey and Holywood Urban Districts and Castlereagh Rural District. Thus the 1971 data area is not exactly coincident with that used for the subsequent years. The 1971 data are from the population census of that year (Northern Ireland General Register Office, 1977). The other data were provided by the Department of Economic Development.

As a consequence of the conjunction and severity of Belfast's housing, economic and social problems, the Commission of the European Economic Community designated the city as one of two (the other being Naples) in which to develop an experiment in "Integrated Operations" with the objective of encouraging the concentration of national and community resources on the area and of overcoming administrative bottlenecks through a greater collaboration by the bodies concerned. A Belfast Integrated Operations Document was presented to the Commission in 1981, containing a series of proposals for schemes and projects that could be

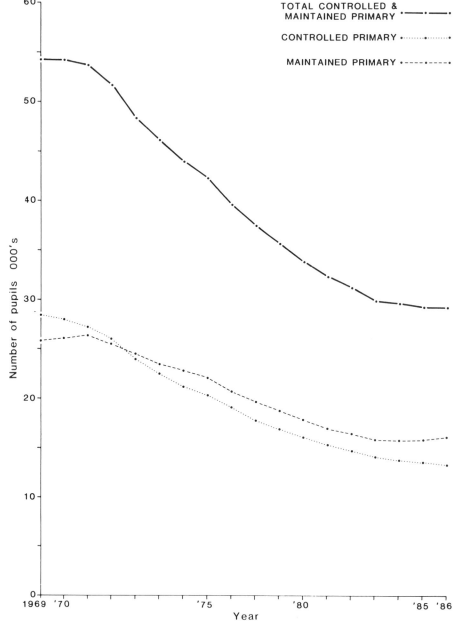

Figure 7.3 Primary school enrolments, Belfast District Council Area, 1969-1986

(Source: Belfast Education and Library Board)

linked together and which exemplified an integrated approach to the city's development. The cost of the proposals in the 1981 document was estimated at £486 million, with over half being related to housing and its supportive infrastructure. By 1986 almost all the housing schemes proposed had been completed, though various infrastructural objectives, such as a new cross-Lagan road and rail link, had not even commenced. (Integrated Operations, 1985).

Population and housing

The population of the Urban Area in the late 1960's came very close to reaching the limit of 600,000 set by Matthew in 1964. Thereafter, decline in numbers set in. Estimates of the volume of population change between 1971 and 1981 indicate a decrease in the Urban Area of some 72,000 people, the Belfast District Council area losing about 107,000 and the rest of the Urban Area gaining a little less than 35,000. The 1981 Urban Area population of 519,000 is 90,000 *below* the limit set by Matthew in the Regional Plan. Growth limitation has been achieved but to a much greater degree than intended and partly due to processes that practically no-one would have wished. (Table 7.1).

A planning report issued in 1977 (Department of the Environment for Northern Ireland, 1977) noted that the danger was no longer uncontrolled growth but rather an excessive loss of population from inner Belfast. This "excessive loss" must be attributed to the combined effect of civil disturbance, large-scale urban renewal clearance schemes and removal of housing along the line of the proposed motorway. The fall in population was also due, in part, to a low rate of natural increase in the inner part of the Urban Area, which in turn was affected by an increasing proportion of the population being elderly – in 1971, 12 per cent of the City's population was over the age of 65, rising to over 15 per cent by 1980. In some of the inner city wards those aged over 65 comprised as much as one quarter of the inhabitants. Thus a large decline in population numbers was combined with an unbalanced age structure.

School enrolments provide a sensitive indicator of urban population dynamics, displaying the combined effects of changing birth rates and population migration. If we examine the numbers of pupils attending those primary and secondary schools[1] located within the Belfast District Council area (basically the inner, older part of the Belfast Urban Area), we find that there were 80,000 in 1969, just under 60,000 in 1979 and just over 47,500 in 1986 – a decline, over 18 years, of 41 per cent. In the same period primary school enrolments fell from 54,600 to just over 29,000 – a decline of 46 per cent. However, in the past few years the number of children attending primary school has levelled out, reflecting a stabilisation of population numbers in the inner part of the urban area after a period of rapid, large-scale decline, with a small upturn in the birth-rate also being a contributory factor (Figure 7.3).

Although the rapid loss of population became a matter of concern, it should not be viewed entirely in negative terms. As the Department of the Environment noted (1977)

> A lower population in the Urban Area will reduce the pressure placed upon its services and infrastructure and as pressure for new housing eases, policies will be increasingly aimed at making Belfast a more pleasant city in which to live. This will call for significant changes in the policies applied

---

[1] Grammar schools are excluded.

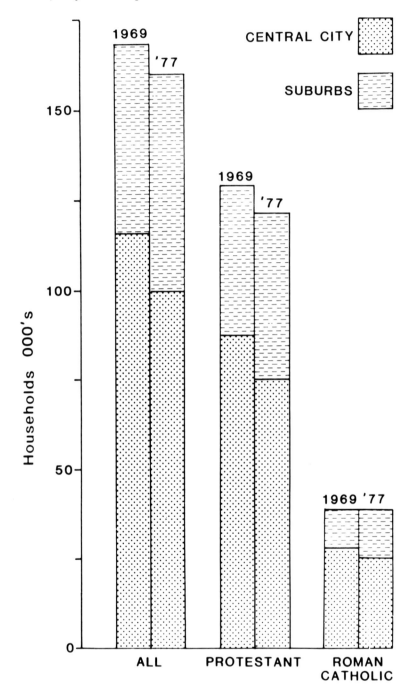

Figure 7.4 Belfast Urban
Area 1969-77: Distribution
of Roman Catholic and
Protestant households in the
central city (Belfast County
Borough Area) and suburbs
(area between central city
and Regional Plan stop-line,
excluding Lisburn)

Source: diagram constructed
from Keane (1985) Table
6.1c

to inner city areas. Redevelopment of areas already cleared will proceed as quickly as possible but more land will be available for open space zoning, recreation and other amenity purposes. It will also facilitate the provision of industrial sites in the inner city areas. (The Belfast Enterprise Zone was designated in 1980).

The slackening of pressure on inner city space also meant that there was no longer any need for high-rise housing. This corresponded with increasingly vigorous community opposition to maisonettes and tower blocks, and indeed with the demolition of a number of these structures.

Although population mobility in the Belfast Urban Area in the 1970's has been dominated by net outward movement, a concurrent set of relocations has also had a very significant effect on population distribution. These relocations have taken the form of movements that have accentuated the degree of ethnic segregation between Protestant and Roman Catholic. For instance in early 1969 (before the worst of the political disturbances) 69 per cent of households in the Urban Area were living in streets with very high levels of ethnic homogeneity. By 1977 this figure had risen to 77 per cent (Keane, 1985). This sharply increased segregation, to a level now probably higher than any experienced in the city heretofore, was significant both for its social impact and as a factor increasing problems associated with redevelopment and population overspill, ethnic territorial considerations becoming paramount. This is most dramatically illustrated by the proposal to build a large public sector housing estate at Poleglass on the outer edge of Catholic West Belfast. The site of the estate lies outside the original Matthew Stop-line, but the territorially constrained nature of Catholic housing demand meant that, following a public enquiry (Planning Appeals Commission, 1977) a relaxation of the planned urban limit was granted (Singleton, 1982). The rigidities of ethnic segregation have been further increased by the erection of a number of high barriers ("peace walls") at certain crucial Catholic-Protestant interfaces – most notably at Cupar Street between the Falls and Shankill areas of inner West Belfast. These barriers are placed to provide protection for those housed nearby but, as Brett (1986) has noted:

> The weaker (or more peaceable) party in any given locality invariably welcomes, if it does not actually demand, a wall on such a site. The stronger (or more aggressive) party invariably opposes its construction, or calls for its instant removal, on the grounds that it will perpetuate division and inhibit any possible return to integration of the two communities.

The latter demand may not be part of a genuine search for integrated housing, but part of a search for opportunities for territorial expansion by the group concerned.

Increasing levels of Catholic-Protestant segregation have occurred in a context of an overall decrease in population and a degree of redistribution from the central part of the urban area to the suburbs. Data on changes in the number of households between 1969 and 1977 (Keane, 1985) show that over that period the number of Catholic households remained constant – a loss of some 2,800 in the central city being balanced by a gain of 2,700 in the suburbs. On the other hand the number of Protestant households declined by about 8,000 – a loss of 13,000 in the central city being only partly compensated by a gain of 5,000 in the suburban areas (Figure 7.4).

From these figures it is evident that the loss in numbers of households in the Belfast urban area between 1969 and 1977 was almost entirely a Protestant phenomenon, with Catholics much less likely to migrate to the growth towns beyond the Stop-line. Consequently the relative size of the Catholic minority in both central Belfast and in its suburbs has grown, so that Catholics comprised about one-quarter of all households by 1977. Remarkably, in that same year, Catholic pupils already formed a majority of those attending primary schools in the central city (Belfast District Council Area) (Figure 7.3). Pupils attending "controlled" schools are over-whelmingly "Protestant" in background, while those attending "main-tained" schools are almost entirely "Catholic". "Controlled" and "main-tained" are particular forms of school management, the former being purely state schools; the latter, state supported Catholic church schools. An important footnote which needs to be added, however, is that a vigorous movement for integrated education has recently emerged – the pioneer school in this regard being Lagan College, founded in 1981. This school now gets government financial support through the maintained form of man-agement and the integrated sector seems likely to grow in the years ahead, a second integrated secondary school, Hazelwood College, having opened its doors in September 1985.

In contrast to the situation in the inter war period, Belfast is currently characterised by a remarkably high level of housing construction in the public sector. In 1972 25,800 dwellings in the Belfast District Council area were judged to be unfit. By 1984 the figure had been reduced to a little over 12,600 (Northern Ireland Housing Executive, 1985). After the tardy start to redevelopment in 1962, the 1970's and 1980's have seen a greatly accelerated programme in the Belfast Urban Area, with 16,501 public sector housing units completed between 1975 and 1986, on a combination of redevelopment and greenfield sites. A very striking feature of the pro-gramme is that high rise units form no part of it, such building having ceased by the late 1960's. In this respect the tardiness of redevelopment in Belfast has been a major blessing in disguise, for unlike many cities on the UK mainland, the inner city is notable for the presence of only eight tower blocks, while several large maisonette complexes of post-war vintage have been or are about to be demolished (currently only 2.9 per cent of public sector dwellings in the Urban Area are at four or more floors above ground). The other feature of the housing programme is the marked shift to "improvement", reflective of central government policies, but bringing in tow the advantage of limiting community disruption. All-in-all, public housing policy in Belfast is now meeting with major success. In addition to the construction of dwellings, there has been a large building programme for leisure centres, with fifteen such units now open. The provision of leisure facilities is very good, though cynics might argue that the large numbers of unemployed need to be given something to do.

The transportation plans of the late 1960's have also seen radical revision. A new central railway station serving commuter towns has been opened but plans for much of the inner elevated urban motorway have been scrapped, partly due to economic circumstances and partly due to very strong community-based opposition. Indeed, at one stage it was suggested that it would be very difficult to get any contractors to undertake such motorway construction as they would have been threatened with dire consequences by one or more of the paramilitary groups in the city. Much of the motorway proposal was abandoned officially following a Public Enquiry on a review of transportation strategy (Department of the Environment, Northern Ireland, 1978), but the linking of the two Northern Ireland motorways using a route through the inner west side redevelopment area was indicated as still a top transportation priority. This "West Link" is now open (Figure 7.2), but none of it is elevated, the northern portion being in a cut as a response to environmental concerns and the southern portion being at ground level, mainly because of cost considerations. The roads-only strategy of the late 1960's was somewhat downgraded as a result of the 1978 Inquiry, in which suggestions for the improvement of public transport included a further integration of the suburban rail network, the construction of a central bus station and the elimination of "Black Taxi" competition. The black taxis started operating a kind of "jitney" system in 1969, in both the Roman Catholic and Protestant segments of West Belfast. This, together with a perhaps not unrelated penchant for burning buses, deprived the official bus system (Citybus) of some of its highest density, and therefore most lucrative, routes.

Commercial development and the city centre

Retail provision was an important component of the 1969 Belfast Urban Area Plan. However, the strategy to sustain a strong city centre and to create a system of 12 District Centres within the built-up area went astray in the 1970's. There was a lack of investment during that decade in Belfast city centre by the major UK property companies despite the fact that an estimated £200 million a year in insurance premiums and pension fund payments was being extracted from Northern Ireland. There was also an unwillingness among planners to constrain out-of-town shopping development, as, in the investment famine of the 1970's, any capital expenditure was to be welcomed, no matter where it was located. In consequence several large out-of-town shopping centres were constructed, including one at Newtownards which was the largest of its type in the whole of Ireland (Parker, 1985). A close observer of the retailing scene in Belfast (Brown, 1984) has noted that:

> The rate of retail decentralisation in Belfast has exceeded that of any other British city. It is difficult to avoid the conclusion that recent retail trends in Belfast have been more akin to the American pattern of unrestricted

Old and new: the Edwardian elegance of Belfast City Hall in contrast with the stark functionalism of Windsor House office block (N.I. Tourist Board)

urban growth (in retailing) and City Centre decline, than they are to the pattern that prevails elsewhere in the United Kingdom.

The security situation was a major, although by no means the only, factor in retail decentralisation. Commercial premises in the Central Business District (CBD) were, indeed, a "favourite" target for the bombers in the early 1970's, which certainly discouraged potential shoppers. Measures taken to counter the bombers may have also added to discouragement (no unattended parking of cars on streets, barriers and concomitant searches at all entry points to the CBD core) although these measures did seem to be reasonably effective in reducing bomb attacks, thus renewing shopper confidence. The exclusion of most vehicular traffic from the CBD core also created the opportunity for large-scale pedestrianisation which markedly increased the attractiveness of some of the main shopping streets.

Although there has been a significant recovery in the fortunes of the city centre since 1975, there still has been no major central area shopping complex developed, such as that at Eldon Square in Newcastle-upon-Tyne. However, a large site has now been cleared at the north end of the CBD and plans have been approved for an enclosed shopping mall, which will be the single largest commercial development ever undertaken in Northern Ireland (Brown, 1985). This complex, to be named Castle Court, will also contain substantial office space, with the Northern Ireland Department of the Environment already committed to occupy 9,000m^2 of it.

Location policy for government offices can be seen as having two strategic objectives: firstly as an input to the revitalisation of the City Centre, and secondly as a means of making available government employment in what is perceived as ethnically "neutral" territory, unlike the governmental complex at Stormont in east Belfast, which is perceived by many Catholics as being in "Protestant" space. The notion of the city centre as a neutral, ethnically shared space has a certain irony to it, however, considering the battering the very same area took at the hands of Irish Republican Army bombers in the early 1970's.

One other development of recent years has been the emergence of an area lying south of the City Hall and extending to the edge of the campus of Queen's University. This area has been referred to as "the Bright Lights District" or the "Golden Mile", and is a linear complex of theatres, up-market restaurants of quite cosmopolitan variety, coffee bars, pubs, discos, second-hand book shops and various other manifestations of a lively night-life (Fitzgerald, 1986).

Conclusion

Belfast grew rapidly in the second half of the nineteenth century, developing in a similar fashion to other British industrial cities. The economic base for this growth was provided by specialisation in engineering (particularly shipbuilding) and textiles (linen). As was the case with Glasgow and Liverpool, large numbers of Irish Catholic immigrants were drawn into a predominantly Protestant urban social fabric. Inter-ethnic rivalries emerged as a significant part of this mosaic.

Following the First World War, a long-term decline in Belfast's key industries set in. This decline was temporarily halted by the economic boom associated with the production demands of the Second World War and was partly veiled during the boom-time of the 1950's and 1960's. However, as is the case with the urban industrial UK as a whole, the 1970's have seen the decimation of traditional industry and of some elements of the 1960's new industry as well.

Belfast has not only been a British industrial city in the island of Ireland, it has also been characterised by a transfer of mainland UK housing and planning philosophies and practices. However, much of the importation displays considerable temporal lag, with public housing being relatively insignificant in Belfast until the 1950's, and effective urban and regional planning for the area being delayed until the 1960's. Thus, in terms of British cities, Belfast is characterised both by parallelism and contrast. Contrast takes the form of a particularly virulent inter-ethnic conflict and a tendency to adopt change later than elsewhere. Indeed the latter phenomenon may be partly explained by the former, in that Catholic-Protestant rivalries have served to divert the working class of the city from issues, such as housing conditions and employment, that provide the force for the organisation of a strong Labour Party contribution to politics in urban industrial Britain. Belfast, up to the early 1970's, tended to be governed by a business-orientated group, while the Provincial Government was formed by a coalition of business, landed and agricultural interests.

In many ways Belfast has been paying a very heavy price for the period of rapid development experienced towards the end of the nineteenth century. Obsolescence of the housing and industrial fabrics produced at that time has reached a critical stage in recent years. The tackling of these problems would be a massive task in its own right without the vicious manifestations of ethnic, indeed nationalist, conflict to boot. And yet many of these problems have been tackled with vigour in recent years. The physical fabric of much of the city centre and the inner Victorian ring of housing and industry has been transformed – the city centre by piecemeal replacement of old buildings with new, the inner ring by massive clearance and reconstruction. Housing conditions for many have been radically changed for the good. On the other hand, ethnically riven social structures have been replanted in the new built environment, and while the demolition of obsolescent housing usually leads to replacement with new attractive dwellings, demolition of obsolescent factories symbolises the seemingly insoluble unemployment problem. Thus, as Belfast moves towards the twenty-first century, within the development framework of a soon to be presented Area Plan (Department of the Environment, 1986), and a set of proposals for the transformation of the lower reaches of the Lagan (Consultancy Team, 1987) there are many recent achievements upon which the future may be built. And yet the ethnic differences between Protestant and Catholic, rather than being a source of enriching diversity, are the basis of an at times savage division. In addition, the deep malaise of unemployment, which Belfast shares with most of the cities in the other peripheral regions of the UK, is an intolerable state-of-affairs, and one that throws a long shadow over the future.

References

Birrell, W.D., Hillyard, P.A.R., Murie, A. and Roche, D.J.D., 1971. *Housing in Northern Ireland*. London.

Boal, F.W., 1967. Contemporary Belfast and its future development, *in* Beckett, J.C. and Glasscock, R.E., (eds.) *Belfast: origin and growth of an industrial city*, London. 169-82.

Boal, F.W., 1980. Two nations in Ireland. *in Antipode*, 13, 38-44.

Boal, F.W., Doherty, P. and Pringle, D.G., 1974. *The spatial distribution of some social problems in the Belfast urban area* Belfast.

Boal, F.W. and Royle, S.A., 1986. Belfast: boom, blitz and bureaucracy, *in* Gordon, G. (ed.) *Regional cities in the U.K. 1890-1980*. London. 191-215.

Brown, S., 1984. Retail location and retail change in Belfast city centre. Unpublished Ph.D. Thesis, The Queen's University of Belfast.

Brown, S., 1985. Smithfield shopping centre, Belfast, *in Irish Geography*. 18, 67-9.

Brett, C.E.B., 1986. *Housing a divided community*. Dublin.

Building Design Partnership, 1969. *Belfast urban area plan*. 1. Belfast.

Consultancy Team, 1987. *Laganside*. London.

Darby, J. and Morris, G., 1974. *Intimidation in housing*. Belfast.

Department of the Environment for Northern Ireland, 1977. *Regional physical development strategy 1975-95*. Belfast.

Department of the Environment for Northern Ireland, 1978. *Belfast urban area plan : review of transportation strategy, public enquiry*. Belfast.

Department of the Environment for Northern Ireland, 1986. *The Belfast Urban Area Plan 1986-2000*. Belfast.

Douglas, J.N.H., 1982. Northern Ireland: spatial frameworks and community relations, *in* Boal, F.W. and Douglas, J.N.H. (eds) *Integration and division: geographical perspectives on the Northern Ireland problem*. London. 105-35.

Doherty, P., 1982. The geography of unemployment, *in* Boal, F.W. and Douglas, J.N.H., (eds) *Integration and division : geographical perspectives on the Northern Ireland problem*. London. 225-47.

Fitzgerald, C., 1986. Bright lights beckon along golden mile, *in Belfast Newsletter*, 24 June, 15-16.

Harland and Wolff, 1985. *A short history of Harland and Wolff, Belfast*. Belfast.

Integrated Operations, 1985. *Integrated Operations Belfast Urban Area*. Belfast.

Johnstone, R. and Kirk, B., 1983. *Images of Belfast*. Belfast.

Jones, E., 1952. Belfast: A survey of the city, *in* Jones, E. (ed) *Belfast in its regional setting*. Belfast. 201-11.

Jones, E., 1960. *A social geography of Belfast*. Oxford.

Keane, M.C., 1985. Ethnic residential change in Belfast 1969-1977: the impact of public housing policy in a plural society. Unpublished Ph.D. thesis, The Queen's University of Belfast.

Macrory, P.A., 1970. *Review body on local government in Northern Ireland*. Belfast.

Matthew, Sir Robert H., 1964. *Belfast regional survey and plan 1962*. Belfast.

Murray, R., 1982. Political violence in Northern Ireland 1969-77, *in* Boal, F.W. and Douglas, J.N.H. (eds) *Integration and division: geographical perspectives on the Northern Ireland problem*. London. 309-31.

Northern Ireland General Register Office, 1977. *Census of population 1971: economic activity tables*. Belfast.

Northern Ireland Housing Executive, 1985. *Northern Ireland house condition survey, 1984*. Belfast.

Parker, A.J., 1985. Shopping centres in Northern Ireland, *in Irish Geography*, 18. 63-6.

Planning Commission, Government of Northern Ireland, 1945. *Planning proposals for the Belfast area*. Belfast.

Planning Commission, Government of Northern Ireland, 1951. *Planning proposals for the Belfast area – second report*. Belfast.

Planning Appeals Commission, 1977. *Poleglass area public enquiry*. Belfast.

Project Team, 1977. *Belfast: areas of special social need*. Belfast.

Singleton, D., 1982. Poleglass: a case study of division, *in* Boal, F.W. and Douglas, J.N.H. (eds) *Integration and division: geographical perspectives on the Northern Ireland problem*. London. 178-94.

Travers Morgan, R., 1969. *Belfast transportation plan*. Belfast.

Vaughan, W.E. and Fitzpatrick, A.J., 1978. *Irish historical statistics: population 1821-1971*. Dublin.

Wilson, T., 1964. *Economic development in Northern Ireland*. Belfast.

8 Belfast: Housing Policy & Trends

D. A. SINGLETON

Lecturer, School of the Built Environment, Department of Architecture and Planning, The Queen's University of Belfast

What is your image of Belfast – a city wracked by violence, with high unemployment, social deprivation, poor environment and the worst housing conditions in the United Kingdom? Journalist Simon Winchester, Northern Ireland correspondent of *The Guardian* in the early 1970's, described his first view of Belfast from the overlooking hills of County Antrim on his way from the airport:

> ... it's the houses that make the first impression ... what strikes so very hard when looking at Belfast, are the row upon row of grimy, uninteresting sorry and forgotten rows of workers' houses ... that was Belfast from eight hundred feet: a city of so obviously poor, hardworking and probably intensely proud and lovable people, forced to live in damp, cramped, rotten, rat ridden, dirty and dying houses : houses they would adorn with all the glitter and tribal gaiety possible, to stop the creeping doom of community despair (Winchester, 1978).

In 1987, the image of Belfast from the same viewpoint is somewhat different. Paradoxically, it continues to be a violent city of intensely proud and paradoxically lovable people, with massive unemployment and, in the inner-city areas in particular, acute social deprivation, poor environment and bad housing conditions. Yet a closer inspection reveals that many of Winchester's "dirty and dying houses" have disappeared and have been replaced by new or rehabilitated dwellings which are among the best in the United Kingdom. This chapter outlines how this overdue improvement in Belfast's housing conditions has come about and discusses some of the policies by which further improvement might be expected.

Context

The snapshot of Belfast depicted by the 1981 Census is of a city of approximately 300,000 population, over 18 per cent of whom are of pensionable age. The average household size is 2.8 (compared with the Northern

*Belfast: nineteenth century
industrial housing at
Millfield in west Belfast, in
process of redevelopment,
1980.* (C.F.S. Newman)

Ireland average of 3.3) and 25 per cent are persons living alone. The census figures also reveal that 50 per cent of households are in owner-occupied accommodation and 30.7 per cent are in accommodation rented from the public authority. Viewed in isolation the statistics mean little, but compared with the 1971 Census they illustrate a city in decline. Population numbers have fallen by almost 115,000 (27 per cent) since the previous census and the proportion of elderly single person households is substantially greater than in 1971. Owner occupation increased by 7 per cent between 1971 and 1981, and public authority housing by 5 per cent. These increases have been largely at the expense of a rapidly declining private rented sector. The condition of the housing fabric in the city has generally improved throughout the 1970s and 1980s, but housing and household conditions remain, in comparison with cities in Great Britain, as some of the worst in the United Kingdom. One qualification needs to be made however. Belfast as a "Bricks and Mortar" city has long outgrown its former county borough boundary. The current Belfast District Council boundary, to which the statistics relate, generally accords with the old county borough boundary. Therefore the data relates to what might loosely be termed as "inner city" Belfast and in that sense the demographic trends described mirror those in many cities throughout the United Kingdom. The major difference in Belfast is that the effects of civil unrest have magnified these trends. In addition Northern Ireland's position as a "branch plant economy" during a period of widespread recession has exacerbated Belfast's economic decline.

Creation of the housing legacy

In 1885 the Royal Commission on housing in Ireland found that housing conditions in Belfast were among the best in the United Kingdom (Brett, 1986). In 1974 the Northern Ireland House Condition Survey indicated that over 24 per cent of Belfast's housing stock (29,750 dwellings) was unfit for human habitation. Confining analysis to particular inner city wards revealed that of a total dwelling stock of 38,010, 18,840 or 49.6 per cent of the dwellings were unfit for human habitation (NIHE, 1975). Housing issues played a prominent part in the Civil Rights campaign in Northern Ireland from the mid 1960's on. When the British Government intervened more directly in the administration of the Province in 1968, it identified housing as one of the major areas of grievance in Northern Ireland, and it became one of the main elements of the subsequent reform programme. How was it that housing conditions deteriorated so much in Belfast, during the period 1885-1968, to the point at which it was decided that a radically new initiative in the form of the United Kingdom's first comprehensive regional housing authority was considered necessary?

A recently published history of Belfast describes it as "pre-eminently a late Victorian city". Between 1830 and 1900 the population increased sevenfold from 50,000 to 350,000 (Bardon, 1982). This growth, fuelled by the influx of the rural poor, put the urban fabric under great strain. It was punctuated by frequent outbursts of sectarian strife, as Protestants, the majority community in the city, came to regard Roman Catholics as rivals for jobs, housing and other resources. The pattern of religious residential segregation in Belfast was thereby established and has generally persisted ever since. The housing stock of the city quadrupled between 1870 and 1900. Bardon comments that "it was above all the growth of shipbuilding and engineering which led to the spectacular development of private housing in the 19th century". The vast majority of the new dwellings were for rent but by 1900, even though there was great housing need in the city, some 10,000 houses lay vacant because those in need could not afford the rents. Belfast's building boom was over and the Corporation was reluctant to build public sector dwellings in such circumstances.

The inter-war period (1919-1939) saw housing policy in Northern Ireland diverge from that in Britain in two crucial respects. First, the level of subsidy for public sector housing was lower in Northern Ireland than in Britain, and second, greater reliance was placed upon private builders than local authority provision in the Province. The concept of housing as a social service was anathema to the Northern Ireland Government. Approximately 28,500 dwellings were built in Belfast during the inter war years but of these only 2,600 were built by Belfast Corporation. There is no city in Britain whose housebuilding record in the inter-war years, whether in the

*Belfast: nineteenth century
housing awaiting
redevelopment.*
(N.I. Tourist Board)

public or private sector or taking the two together, was worse than that of Belfast (Brett, 1986).

By 1944, following German air raids on Belfast in which 3,200 houses were destroyed and 53,000 damaged, it was estimated that 71 per cent of Belfast's dwellings required repair, and 23,591 new dwellings were needed (Boal and Royle, 1986; Birrell et al, 1971). After the war housing became a high priority. A new body, the Northern Ireland Housing Trust, which in several ways was a forerunner of the Northern Ireland Housing Executive (NIHE), was established to supplement the local authorities' individual programmes.

Northern Ireland's post-war house building programme was well up to the United Kingdom average. It was insufficient, however, to reduce the backlog of neglect. Progress in tackling Belfast's housing problems during this period was particularly disappointing. Between 1945 and 1972 the average number of new dwellings built by the Corporation was only 470 a year, far short of the need, assessed by the city surveyor in 1959 at 2,500 a year over a twenty year period. (Brett, 1986).

In defence of the Corporation it must be noted that it was denied a boundary extension by the Northern Ireland Government in 1947. The Northern Ireland Housing Trust therefore began to fulfil the role of building for Belfast overspill. Boal (Chapter 7) aptly describes the evolving housing problems faced by Belfast Corporation as a "housing trap". The fixed local government boundaries simply did not measure up to the dynamic housing processes of an expanding city. Housing schemes in Belfast were confined to green field and infill sites until the passage of the Housing Act 1956 facilitated the adoption of a programme of slum clearance and redevelopment of the inner city. The first of such schemes commenced in 1962 but it was not until the early 70s that any significant results could be seen on the ground. So while the pattern of Belfast's growth during the 19th century mirrored that of many British cities, the lack of building and re-building especially during the inter-war period, and the delay in tackling some of the worst housing problems in the 1950s and 1960s left Belfast with a housing problem much more serious than that of other cities in the United Kingdom. Planning initiatives dating from the 1960s compounded some of the housing problems in the city. Further consideration will be given to these initiatives later in the Chapter.

Tackling the housing legacy

The radically new initiative to tackle the Province's housing problems announced in 1969 was part of a political reform programme imposed on Northern Ireland by the British Government. The rationale in establishing the Northern Ireland Housing Executive was to centralise housing provision. The expected benefits included, "a common public authority rent structure throughout Northern Ireland ... an end to allegations about sectarian discrimination in housing allocations, ... but above all a new opportunity to solve Northern Ireland's housing problems in the foreseeable future". (HMSO, 1969). The fact that the Belfast Urban Area was still a fragmented unit at local government level was no longer a problem because fragmentation had been overcome by centralising housing powers. Further centralisation of powers and functions took place with local government reorganisation in 1973 (Boal and Royle, 1986).

The Northern Ireland Housing Executive took over the housing function from Belfast Corporation in 1972. It inherited massive housing problems which had been compounded by the results of sectarian violence and perhaps misconceived planning policies. In the sixties when the population of Northern Ireland was growing steadily and the economy was relatively buoyant the attraction of Belfast as capital city gave cause for concern in some quarters. It was claimed that the city was becoming congested at the centre and low density suburbia was spreading rapidly into Belfast's agriculturally rich and high amenity hinterland. The planning strategy adopted for the city was to contain the physical growth of suburban Belfast by means of a Stop-line on development and to redevelop the inner city.

This strategy, however, was jeopardised not so much by the scale of population movement as by its selectivity in age and socio-economic terms. As economic circumstances deteriorated in the seventies the already weakened economic base of inner cities throughout the United Kingdom declined further. These trends were magnified in Belfast. Additionally,

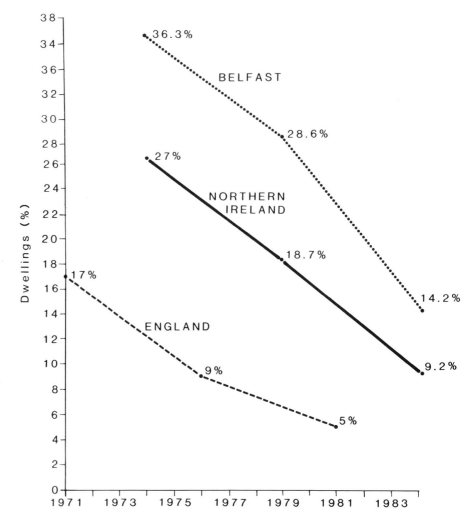

Figure 8.1 Housing
unfitness – England,
Northern Ireland and
Belfast.

Sources: *English House
Condition Surveys* 1971,
1976 and 1981; *Northern
Ireland House Condition
Surveys* 1974, 1979 and
1984.

businessmen and families anxiously sought opportunities to move away
from troubled areas, most of which were in the inner city. Mass evacuation
of families from the "interface" areas in 1969 and in the early 1970s left the
population largely polarised on a sectarian basis. Protestants tended to
move to outlying estates or growth centres, and Roman Catholics moved to
areas in west and north Belfast, much of which had been traditionally
Roman Catholic. This population movement led to contrasting conditions
in different areas. In west Belfast it resulted in significant overcrowding
and a lack of overspill sites for Roman Catholics who would be displaced by
inner city redevelopment. In parts of north Belfast the large number of
vacant and bricked-up houses accelerated deterioration in general housing
conditions. The sharp increase in segregation posed an immediate housing
crisis in west Belfast for the fledgling NIHE. It saw the solution as the
development of a large 4,000 dwelling public sector estate at Poleglass on
the outer edge of Catholic west Belfast. The scheme was controversial from

its inception with claim and counter-claim as to which community the site rightly belonged. Following a public enquiry, approval was granted for a 2,000 dwellings scheme which necessitated a breach of the Belfast Stop-line (Singleton, 1985).

Some critics hailed the decision as a brave attempt to overcome sectarianism. Others reached the opposite conclusion, claiming that the Executive had failed to confront and overcome a blatant example of sectarianism (Graham, 1984). A former Chairman of the NIHE has commented that: "the decision was a highly controversial one, and was to cause endless sectarian antagonism over the ensuing years – on a few occasions inside the boardroom as well as outside it" (Brett, 1986).

There is no doubt that the response time from the identification of the "housing crisis" in 1973 to the first houses on site in 1980 was appallingly long. However the crucial question is, perhaps, would the scheme have been built at all on the current site if Northern Ireland's government and institutions had remained unchanged from the 1960s? The answer must surely be "no", or "very unlikely". This begs the possibility, however, that mixed estates would have been common place in the absence of violence. In such circumstances specific territorial claims might have become unimportant by the 1980's.

Part of NIHE's inheritance from Belfast Corporation was an ambitious redevelopment programme comprising about 25,000 dwellings within more than 30 redevelopment areas. It was based on large scale clearance and the proposed replacement of terraced streets by generally high density medium to high rise flats and maisonettes. Those which were built, however, were often of poor design and proved unsuitable for families with children. They subsequently became extremely unpopular and have rapidly deteriorated as suitable places in which to live. In 1979 the Executive decided to demolish about 800 of these unpopular, and in many instances unlettable, homes. Selective demolition of such blocks has continued throughout the 1980's. It culminated in 1986 with an announcement that virtually all of the notorious Divis Flats complex would be bulldozed. The inherited redevelopment programme soon evoked the wrath of many inner-city communities. The difference between the community response in Belfast compared with cities in Britain was what has been termed "power in participation" (Weiner, 1976). In other words, the paramilitary bodies on both sides of the community divide provided community groups with the power to stop redevelopment taking place or at least to change its emphasis from high rise to more traditional dwelling forms. Against this background the NIHE became convinced of the need to involve local communities more in the developing of ideas and programmes to improve existing housing conditions. The Executive's subsequent decision to build mainly two storey traditional terraced housing to good quality design standards (Parker Morris minima) in redevelopment areas was generally welcomed and has since proved popular and acceptable to new residents.

In 1974 the Executive carried out the first Northern Ireland House Condition Survey. It documented great differences in housing conditions

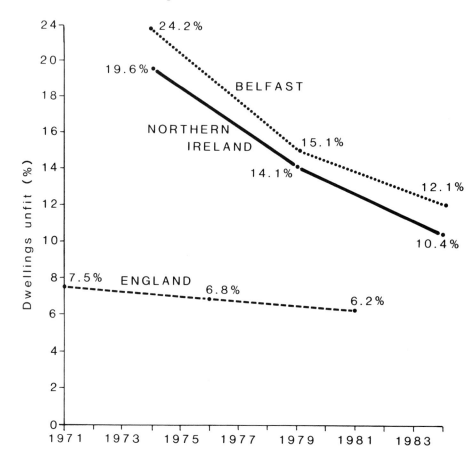

Figure 8.2 Dwellings lacking at least one basic amenity – England, Northern Ireland and Belfast.

Sources: *English House Condition Surveys* 1971, 1976 and 1981; *Northern Ireland House Condition Surveys* 1974, 1979 and 1984.

between Northern Ireland and England. It presented a very bleak picture for Belfast. A total of 44,710 homes (36.3 per cent) lacked at least one basic amenity such as a fixed bath or shower or an internal lavatory. Less than half of the houses in the city were in good condition and almost 25 per cent of the stock was deemed unfit for human habitation (Figures 8.1 & 8.2).

Community groups in Belfast increased their resistance to redevelopment of any kind in the mid 1970s. Coincidentally and partly as a reaction to community lobbying, the 1976 Housing (Northern Ireland) Order introduced Housing Action Areas (HAA) to the Province and the rehabilitation strategy was enthusiastically taken up in Belfast following the initial traumatic experiences of large scale redevelopment. An improved Renovation Grants Scheme was introduced, aimed at bringing a major improvement in private housing conditions by encouraging the uptake of grants by owner occupiers and landlords.

In December 1976 the Minister announced a new drive on Belfast's housing problems. He stated that the emphasis would switch more towards solving Belfast's problems within its boundaries, rather than encouraging overspill to surrounding towns and growth centres. With an emphasis on using rehabilitation as a method of housing action, a new housing programme was prepared. Significantly, however, within a year of its adoption the NIHE voiced its concern that the cost of carrying out rehabilitation works had spiralled to the point where it was almost approaching the cost of replacement by a new dwelling.

In 1980 public expenditure on housing was cut back for the first time in the Executive's history. This resulted in a moratorium on contracts in Belfast. Funding was restored a year later when the personal intervention of the Secretary of State elevated housing to No.1 priority among social and environmental programmes in the Province. Special priority was to be given to the housing needs of Belfast.

In 1981 as the inherited Redevelopment programme was nearing completion, the Northern Ireland Department of the Environment defined the fundamental planning issue in Belfast as the regeneration of the inner city and the prevention of the further spread of urban decay. The Department of the Environment felt that the situation required policies and proposals which sought to achieve a balance between meeting the short-term needs of an ageing population, particularly within Protestant areas, and the provision of facilities to attract younger households, upon which the long term future of the inner city would depend. It was within this planning context that the Housing Executive published its *Belfast housing renewal strategy* in October 1982. (NIHE 1982)

Belfast housing renewal strategy

Although there had been significant progress during the 1970s in relieving some of Belfast's housing problems it was felt that two important trends necessitated a review of strategy. These were, the continuing deterioration in housing conditions in some neighbourhoods, and, the marked changes in the city's population size and age structure. The *Belfast housing renewal strategy*, published following the review was, in the words of the Executive "a conscious decision to provide a wider range of initiatives embracing both the public and private sectors". The strategy recognised the fact that while inroads had been made in dealing with homes lacking amenities and in severe disrepair, there were, and would continue to be, large areas of pre 1945 housing falling into disrepair. Despite the impact made by the Renovation Grants Scheme and rehabilitation by the NIHE, the socio-economic characteristics of these households made it unlikely that this disrepair trend would reduce. A much greater commitment to improvement of homes in disrepair was required, therefore, if large areas of the City were not to continue to fuel redevelopment programmes. The main proposals in the renewal strategy encompassing about one quarter of the city's housing stock were: the designation of a further 42 redevelopment areas containing 6,500 dwellings in addition to those already identified in previous redevelopment programmes; the inclusion of a further 15 Housing Action Areas containing 7,500 dwellings to be declared over a two year period; the designation of Private Investment Priority Areas which comprised about 1,600 dwellings, and while having no statutory basis, would be seen as areas where people would have confidence to repair and

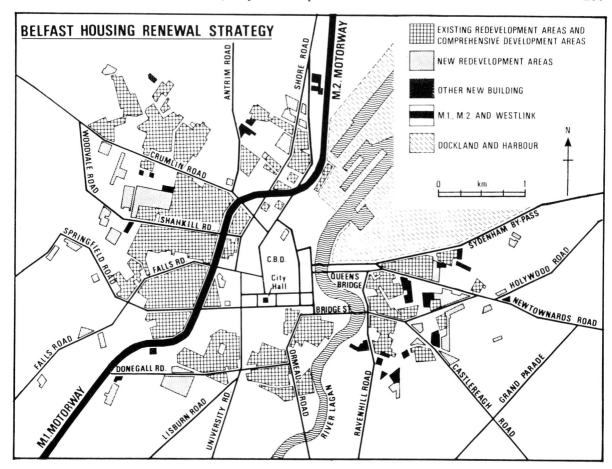

BELFAST HOUSING RENEWAL STRATEGY

EXISTING REDEVELOPMENT AREAS AND COMPREHENSIVE DEVELOPMENT AREAS

NEW REDEVELOPMENT AREAS

OTHER NEW BUILDING

M.1., M.2. AND WESTLINK

DOCKLAND AND HARBOUR

Figure 8.3 Spatial extent of housing redevelopment and comprehensive redevelopment areas, compared with the small scale redevelopment areas and new buildings in Housing Action Areas proposed in the Belfast Renewal Strategy.

improve their homes by the use of the renovation grants scheme and building society support. Together with a continuing programme of public sector house sales to sitting tenants, a range of initiatives aimed at encouraging improvement of private sector housing was thus proposed.

Redevelopment

The most contentious aspect of the housing renewal strategy when it was published in 1982 was the extent of redevelopment proposals. The Executive explained its thinking on the matter in the strategy document: "If we are to help prevent population drift and attract back younger families to a more attractive environment we feel that more emphasis must be given over the next ten years to small scale redevelopment in certain areas". Elsewhere in the document the Executive alluded to problems which had been created by the radical swing to rehabilitation in the mid 1970s, implying that the pendulum had swung too far in this direction:

> Full rehabilitation does not replace the main fabric of very old dwellings in poor condition and rarely does it extend their lifespan to even half that of a newly-built house. The relatively low space standard achieved after rehabilitating certain types of smaller houses together with recurrent mainte-

nance problems causing tenant dissatisfaction have combined with rising costs to make it a less effective solution than replacement for small old terraced housing.

For these reasons the redevelopment areas proposed were on a much smaller scale than those tackled in the 1970s (Figure 8.3). In spite of NIHE assurances about the sensitivity of its modern approach to redevelopment, the ghosts of previous efforts have proved difficult to exorcise. This is hardly surprising given the decimation of communities which occurred in the early 1970s. It is summed up in figures for one Belfast community, the Shankill (Table 8.1).

Table 8.1
Shankill Redevelopment Area

	1968	1983
Number of houses	7,000	1,100
Small businesses	200	11
Corner Shops	202	1
Mission Halls	23	1
Pubs	68	0
Playgrounds	3	0

The "put-back" levels in redevelopment schemes have assumed an importance in Belfast undreamt of in Britain. The Housing Executive can put forward valid technical explanations about such levels but rational explanations tend to get lost in political rhetoric about so-called sectarian plots to depopulate particular areas. Little progress seems possible in resolving this particular issue (Singleton 1985). By September 1986, of the 42 redevelopment areas proposed, only 32 had been declared. The remainder were excluded after consultation, or are areas where no housing put back is approved by DoE Planning Service.

Housing action areas and renovation grants

The emphasis in Housing Action Areas (HAAs) is on relieving housing and social stress through rehabilitation rather than redevelopment. The financial mechanism for private owners is through the uptake of renovation grants. Between 1976, when enabling legislation was introduced, and 1982, 28 HAAs were declared in Belfast. The renewal strategy proposed the declaration of 15 more HAAs, comprising about 7,500 houses. By September 1986, all 15 had been declared and a further 3 HAAs added to the programme.

The concept has met with mixed success in Belfast. In some areas few owner occupiers have availed of the grants. This has led to deterioration to such an extent that improvement and repair costs particularly of small kitchen houses, have been prohibitive and poor value for money compared to new buildings. An important new venture in HAAs since 1982 has been the involvement of the major building societies. Over 20 areas have been "adopted" and assistance with loans for the purchase and improvement of properties has been given by the societies. As more rehabilitation has been carried out in HAAs it has been increasingly realised that such refurbishment is not necessarily less disruptive than redevelopment. Frequently rehabilitation work is so extensive that tenants are required to live elsewhere during construction work.

Private investment priority areas

The 1984 Housing Condition Survey indicated that in addition to almost 13,000 unfit dwellings in Belfast there were 42,000 dwellings requiring repairs over £2,500 of which 20,000 required repairs of over £7,000 (NIHE 1985). Many of these dwellings were in existing or proposed HAAs. However, in addition to these areas, there was a zone fringing the inner core of the city where dwellings were ageing and in need of repair and improvement, but where NIHE has hopes, based on grant uptake records, that improvement can be effected mainly by residents with some intervention from the public sector and with the support of building societies. These areas, 25 in total containing 16,000 dwellings, were identified as Private Investment Priority Areas (PIPA).

The PIPAs are seen as a crucial private sector partnership initiative. Success, it is claimed, would obviate the need for renewal on a large scale in the future. Preliminary indications are that grant uptake in PIPAs has been better than in Housing Action Areas. The Partnership arrangements with the Building Societies has added considerably to the finance available for elements of the renewal strategy. In addition to adopting particular PIPAs, the Societies have provided substantial funding towards house sales to tenants, equity sharing and lending on older cheaper properties both within and outside Houing Action Areas. This inflow of finance reversed a former net drain on Building Society savings funds from the Province.

Priority estates

As the worst of the nineteenth century dwellings in the city have been replaced or improved, attention has been drawn to the problems of some post-war public sector housing estates. These are now among the most deprived housing areas in Belfast. Several of them have been defined as priority estates and the strategy for their improvement includes a more flexible allocation policy, greater tenant consultation, improved management and maintenance service, and dwelling and estate improvements. It has also been recognised that in some cases eventual demolition may be the only solution.

Estates are defined as "priority" for a number of reasons. Some have no vacancies but are unpopular and present management problems, whilst others are unpopular and "difficult to let". The problems are usually caused by a combination of factors such as housing design, high density, poor layout, inflexible allocation policies, tenants' behaviour, poor maintenance and management services and inadequate consultation with tenants.

Allocation policy, in particular, plays a crucial part in that tenants in urgent need who are not in a position to wait for a better offer, tend to be the economically deprived – the unemployed, low income families and single parent families. It is important that housing management activity is sustained in priority estates, otherwise, when the extra resources earmarked for them are withdrawn, the estates may well deteriorate again.

Private sector activity and sale of NIHE dwellings

Since 1979 successive Conservative Housing Ministers in the Province have made it clear that as much housing as possible should be provided outside the public sector. The past three years have witnessed a boom in private sector housing completions in Northern Ireland especially at the low cost end of the market. For example it has been estimated that in the period 1983-85, 3,800 low cost private houses were constructed in the District Council area of Belfast and the contiguous Districts of Newtownabbey, Lisburn, Castlereagh and North Down, each of which contain part of the Belfast Urban Area (Hendry et al 1986). In Belfast District Council area itself, private sector completions are subject to a large range of error and National House Building Council figures frequently conflict with official Government statistics. However, the increase in private sector activity during the past few years is not in doubt. Most of it has occurred outside the Belfast District Council boundary but within the Belfast Urban Area.

The extent of Government keenness to promote private sector house building in the Belfast area was illustrated by the Cairnshill proposal. In this case, following a public enquiry, the Government overruled a recommendation by the Planning Appeals Commission that permission for housing should be refused, and approved the development of 500 houses outside the Belfast Stop-line (Singleton, 1984). In announcing the decision the Environment Minister stated in 1983, "I attach high priority to private housing development particularly for first-time buyers, and this has been a major factor in my arriving at my decision to permit limited development". The Cairnshill development is now under construction and 30 detached houses have been advertised in the price range £43,500 – £65,000, hardly targetted at first time buyers (New Homes Marketing Board, 1986).

The scope for further private sector housebuilding within Belfast District is limited by the scarcity of suitable development land. However, private builders have developed many "infill" sites, especially for apartments, in the past two years. In addition the NIHE, as part of its remit as a comprehensive housing agency, has released several sites in Belfast District from its ownership to private developers. These initiatives are to be welcomed as long as they do not rob those in urgent need of public sector accommodation.

Since 1979 NIHE has sold off approximately 17 per cent of the public sector housing stock to sitting tenants. In Belfast District only nine per cent of the stock has been sold, the lowest figure for any NIHE region. This is hardly surprising given the special circumstances of Belfast, including its

Belfast: new public housing,
designed by the Northern
Ireland Housing Executive.
(NIHE)

demographic and social structure and the large number of new properties which do not qualify for the largest discounts.

Housing associations

The Housing Association movement in Northern Ireland has had a meteoric rise since 1976 when legislation was introduced providing favourable terms for area improvement and the establishment of Associations. The movement adds a welcome diversity of tenure to the monopoly position of the Housing Executive in public rented housing. The Associations have a particular contribution to make in the implementation of the Belfast housing renewal strategy.

Community based housing associations in Belfast achieve a degree of local democracy in particular areas in a context where the City Council has no housing powers. They are viewed as one way of bridging the gap between local people and a "remote" system of representation. There are currently more than a dozen community-based housing associations most of which operate in Belfast. Many are directly responsible for implementing Housing Action Area proposals included in the renewal strategy, having drawn up the Action Plans themselves. Working generally in small, tightly knit communities, the associations rarely bridge the sectarian divide, either in the composition of their committees or of their tenants. There are a few exceptions but there has been no ill conceived attempt to frame Housing Action Area boundaries with a view to experiments in "across the divide" social engineering.

Criticism has been levelled at community-based housing associations on the grounds that they are too small and therefore wasteful of resources and that they contribute little to the city's renewal strategy. Their proponents argue that community based housing associations devote time and effort to their communities which a large organisation such as the Housing Executive cannot possibly match. This sentiment is echoed throughout community-based associations in the Province and is a powerful argument for their retention. As housing conditions have changed in Belfast, so the priorities of individual associations have changed.

Belfast Improved Houses which is one of the largest associations in Northern Ireland was founded in 1975 with, as its name implies, the principal aim of rehabilitating older houses and providing rented accommodation for those in need. Ironically, given its original emphasis, the association's current programme indicates that it has more units of infill new build on site, than properties being rehabilitated. Other specialist housing associations have brought particular expertise to the implementation of aspects of the city's renewal strategy, principally in the provision of housing for the elderly. This expertise has been recognised by the NIHE with the transfer of several of its sheltered schemes to Associations for management.

One of the most successful aspects of the Housing Association movement's work in Belfast has been in co-ownership. The main objective of the scheme is to assist low-income first time buyers in the purchase of family type accommodation for their own occupation. It is an equity-sharing scheme largely pioneered in Northern Ireland and now available in Great Britain as Do-it-Yourself Shared Ownership. Applicants in Northern Ireland purchase a minimum of 50 per cent of the equity as the outset and may increase this in a minimum of 10 per cent steps to full owner occupation. In terms of the Belfast housing renewal strategy the scheme is an important support exercise for the private builder. It has possibly prevented builders from moving into large scale production of miniature starter homes because it has enabled people, who could not otherwise afford it, to buy properties of a larger size (upwards to 1,000 sq ft in many cases). Hopefully this will avoid the possibility of people becoming trapped in sub-standard accommodation as their needs change through the life-cycle. Forty per cent of co-ownership participants are former NIHE tenants and 13 per cent formerly rented from private landlords. Most of the remainder are newly-weds or single people who wish to form separate households (McPeake and Butler, 1985). The scheme therefore reduces some of the enormous pressure on scarce public sector accommodation by encouraging transfer from Housing Executive property to the "private" sector and through the removal of potential Executive tenants from the waiting list in Belfast.

From the array of initiatives outlined above it can be seen that the Housing Association movement has a major support role to play in the implementation of the Belfast housing renewal strategy.

Financing the housing strategy

The range of initiatives which together make up the Belfast housing renewal strategy require public expenditure in excess of £100 million per annum. Such levels of expenditure have been made available by Government in the past three years, although a cut-back was announced at the end of 1985. In December 1986 it was partially restored. Apportionment of the overall housing budget has reflected the special circumstances of Belfast and the scale of its housing problems. This has been further underlined by the pairing of Belfast and Naples as two cities within the EEC most deserving of grant aid for integrated operations in the area of urban renewal. It is likely that a sum of the order of £100 million of Community funds will be spent on urban infrastructural projects in Belfast during the next three years. Indeed expenditure on housing in the city has already been indirectly boosted by funds for such urban renewal schemes. The EEC requirement is that such funding is additional to the total volume of national expenditure allocated to urban renewal projects. Urban Development grants have also been available and have assisted private housing developers on difficult sites in the city. These, together with the increasing financial involvement of the building societies and capital receipts from house sales and the funding of housing associations in the city, represent a heartening commitment to Belfast's future development. However, such continuity of expenditure cannot be guaranteed in the future. Government has recently underlined that "value for money" criteria will increasingly be used to judge the success of the housing strategy.

One aspect of housing finance which has been a persistent cause for concern is the controversy over alleged contract frauds. A Civil Service report on the activities of the NIHE Commission in 1975 made several criticisms of the organisation including the lack of co-ordination within the housing authority and the problem of where exactly accountability for any particular problem lay. The criticism was underlined in the report of the investigatory commission into NIHE contracts published in 1979 (Rowland Report, 1979). The Commission investigated how the NIHE had placed and managed various rehabilitation contracts in Belfast and elsewhere. It reported that the NIHE's administrative procedures were inadequate and that the division of responsibility between it and Central Government was unclear. The Commission also found that funds had been siphoned off by paramilitaries, and concluded that "the reputation of the NIHE has been damaged by its performance in this affair."

In spite of Government attempts to tighten up the basis on which building contracts are awarded (see Singleton, 1985) the controversy persists. It arose most recently during a High Court case in January 1987 when the judge expressed great concern that public money was falling into paramilitary hands via building contract frauds. In the continuing circumstances of civil unrest in the city it seems unlikely that such frauds can be stamped out completely.

Conclusions

Much has been achieved in alleviating the appalling housing legacy in Belfast during the last ten years. While new-build and other programmes have been drastically pruned in cities throughout Britain, in Belfast the largest ever public sector programme is now under way in the city and it is complemented by large scale rehabilitation and other related programmes aimed at tackling disrepair. The results of the 1984 Housing Condition Survey (Figures 8.1 and 8.2) show how much has been accomplished but leave no room for complacency. Much remains to be done and the ten-year housing renewal strategy incorporates a versatile mix of elements to improve conditions throughout the city. Given the economic circumstances of the city it seems unlikely that private sector initiatives, although important, will eclipse the public sector to the extent that it becomes a residual tenure during the next ten years. Therefore, continued subventions from Westminster, and finance, however indirect, from the EEC, remain as essential elements in the strategy to improve housing conditions in Belfast. Overall, the proposed Housing Renewal Strategy is a worthwhile venture but it is a high risk undertaking in a declining economy, and several questions remain unanswered. For example, does regeneration of Belfast inevitably mean families moving from the suburbs and "growth towns" and if so, how can they be tempted back? Is it justifiable, in financial accountability terms, to build high quality houses in the inner city if they are to be occupied by families who may be vacating property elsewhere, which subsequently may not be able to be let?

Other considerations include the housing mix that should be built, and the balance which has to be struck between the needs of the existing inner city residents, especially the elderly, and the needs and aspirations of a future community which may have a very different age/sex profile.

The NIHE has now recognised the dilemma and publicly stated that in some long-established community districts, the two goals of catering for the existing populations and regenerating the local area are incompatible. It may mean the provision of a range of house sizes but in the short term, their allocation to and underoccupation by young single people or pensioners. This may entail problems of tenants' resistance to over-large houses and the high rents associated with them.

Belfast represents an inevitably uncertain context in which the Northern Ireland Housing Executive, the voluntary movement and private developers can only learn by doing. The Belfast Housing Renewal Strategy continues to face many obstacles to its implementation. Success is essential, however, if Belfast's housing and household conditions are to catch up with those in the rest of the United Kingdom.

References

Bardon, J., 1982. *Belfast – An illustrated history*. Belfast.

Birrell, W.D. et al, 1971. *Housing in Northern Ireland*. London.

Boal, F.W. and Royle, S., 1986. Belfast : boom, blitz and bureaucracy. *in* Gordon (ed.), *Regional cities in the UK, 1890-1980*. London. 191-215.

Brett, C.E.B., 1986. *Housing a divided community*. Dublin.

Cmnd 4178, 1969. *Text of a communique issued after discussion between the Home Secretary and the Northern Ireland Government*, HMSO, London.

Graham, D., 1984. Opposition restricts Poleglass project, *in Roof* (Shelter), Sept/Oct. 6.

Hendry, J. et al, 1986. *Private sector housebuilding in Northern Ireland: a supply side investigation*. Occasional Papers in Planning No.13, Department of Architecture and Planning, Q.U.B.

McPeake, J. and Butler, K., 1985. Shared ownership in Northern Ireland: the first five years of the co-ownership housing association, *in Housing Review*, 34, 5, 169-72. London.

New Homes Marketing Board, 1986. *Guide to new homes in Northern Ireland*. Belfast.

Northern Ireland Housing Executive, 1985. *Northern Ireland House Condition Survey 1984*. Belfast.

Northern Ireland Housing Executive, 1982. *Belfast Housing Renewal Strategy*. Belfast.

Northern Ireland Housing Executive, 1975. *Housing Condition Survey 1974*. Belfast.

Rowland Report, 1979. *Report of the investigatory commission into Northern Ireland Housing Executive Contracts*. HMSO, Cmnd 7586, London.

Singleton, D., 1985. Housing policy in Northern Ireland: an interview with the Minister, Chris Patten, M.P., *in Housing Review*, 34, 5, 155-4.

Singleton, D., 1985. Housing and planning policy in Northern Ireland: problems of implementation in a divided community, *in Policy and Politics* 13, 3, 305-26.

Singleton, D., 1984. Stop-Start Stopline, *in Planning*, 566 (Gloucester), 8-9.

Weiner, R., 1976. The Shankill: power in participation, *in The Planner*, May 102-3.

Winchester, S., 1978. *In Holy Terror*. London.

Services

M. H. GOULD AND ROBERT COMMON*

Senior Lecturer, Department of Civil Engineering, The Queen's University of Belfast
*Reader, Department of Geography, The Queen's University of Belfast

Since the Belfast Meeting of the British Association in 1952 the population of Northern Ireland has increased from 1.37 to c.1.6 millions and maintained its practice of living in towns rather than the countryside. Although the provincial average for urban population has now risen to 68 per cent this figure obscures the range that occurs between values of 90 per cent in the area around Belfast Lough and the Lagan Valley to 48 per cent in the west of the province. Socio-economic developments have also influenced the demand for the utilisation of a range of services designed to facilitate change and sustain improved conditions within the province. The collective services and amenities offered by these utilities provide an infrastructure which has been subject to considerable innovations over the last 35 years. While the demands for both water and electricity have risen in this period, the gas industry has endured a fluctuating decline as the result of financial uncertainty. In keeping with trends elsewhere in the UK, however, an increased reliance upon motor transport and improved road systems has been at the cost of Northern Ireland Railways. Greater accessibility to individuals, firms and official agencies through widening networks of national and international telecommunications has also been a revolutionary feature of the last fifteen years.

In the period under review the administration of local and provincial government services changed dramatically in October 1973. County, district and borough councils were replaced by a new system of district councils and the newly established Department of the Environment for Northern Ireland (DoENI) became responsible for the provision and maintenance of water and road systems within the Province.

Water supply and sewerage

Overall growth in demand for water means that 18,148 km of water mains now carry a safe supply of drinking water, as well as water for other uses in the homes, farms and factories of 90 per cent of the people in

Altaheglish reservoir, in the Sperrin Mountains, County Londonderry, a principal source of water for Londonderry City.
(C.F.S. Newman)

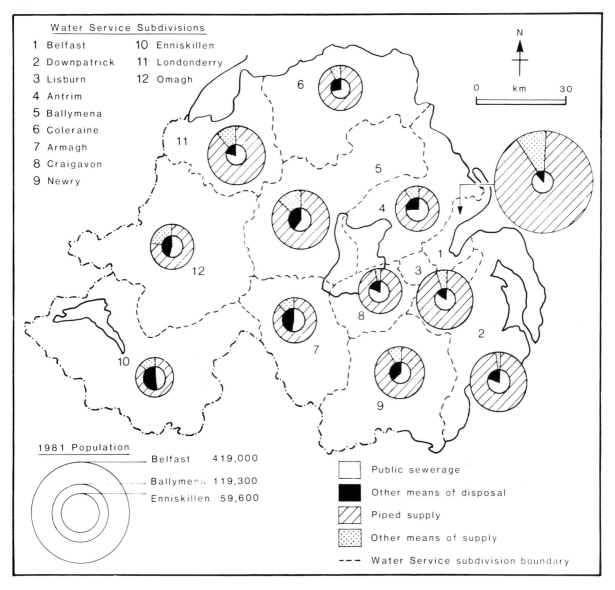

Figure 9.1 Supply and disposal of water, 1981.

Northern Ireland. The availability of piped sewer systems within the Province has also been improved, so that 8,997 km of sewers served the disposal needs of 75 per cent of the population by 1984. Supplementation through the use of septic tanks caters for the needs of another 16 per cent of the public, particularly within the Northern and Southern Divisions of the Water Service.

While the overall trend in quantities supplied has been upwards since 1952, divisional rates of water supply have fluctuated over the last 12 years and an initial check to provincial increases occurred in 1980-1981. As an inspection of Figure 9.1 will demonstrate, subdivisional supply rates are relatively high in the eastern half of Northern Ireland but the more

Spelga dam and reservoir in the Mourne Mountains, tapping the water catchment of the Upper Bann River. (C.F.S. Newman)

sparsely populated districts in the northeast, west and southwest of the Province are supplied at rates below the general average. Not surprisingly the services of an extensive sewerage system are best displayed in the economically favoured Eastern Division, for provision elsewhere still tends to be largely restricted to the vicinity of large centres of population.

It is worth recalling that only 55 per cent of the population possessed a piped water supply in 1945. Four small towns had no piped supply at all at that time but most settlements with less than 1,000 residents and most rural households possessed neither piped supplies nor proper sewerage facilities. The Water Supply and Sewerage Act (NI) 1945, required that water supplies should henceforth be provided subject only to the cost being "reasonable". Government grant aids were provided to the various water undertakings to enable this to be achieved and an average of £3.8 million per annum was to be spent upon water schemes until 1973. In that year new legislation produced a single Water Service within the DoENI and thus completed a process of rationalisation in the water industry that had been going on for several years. Grant aid from the Northern Ireland government generally met at least half the cost of these water schemes through the terms of the Water Supply and Sewerage Act; the Development Services Act (NI) 1948, which provided funds for winter relief schemes on water supplies; and the Industries Development Act (NI) 1945, which offered grants for water facilities at factory sites such as Maydown and Kilroot. By 1952 completed water supply schemes served only 13 per cent of the area in the three western counties and 17 per cent in the eastern three, but the momentum for growth was already well established. This was the year in which work on a tunnel for the Belfast City and District Water Commissioners allowed water to be transferred from the Annalong River to the Silent Valley reservoir and preparations to start work on the new Ben Crom dam nearby were also well advanced. Meanwhile ten joint supply boards and one Water Board were in operation within the province, and the first Joint Board for sewage disposal for the towns of Newtownards and Comber had been constituted in 1951. By 1960 it is estimated that communities with more than 250 residents had adequate sewage disposal works for 50 per cent of the inhabitants and a piped supply of water to 70 per cent.

Growth in water supplies is reflected by the fact that the volume consumed has more than doubled in the last 35 years. The percentage of the supply going to domestic uses has shown a steady and significant growth, whereas agriculture's share has only increased slowly. After earlier gains, the percentage utilised by industry and commerce has been almost halved in the past decade, mainly as the result of the industrial recession. As Figure 9.2 suggests, there are still considerable variations in the patterns of water use across the Province.

Sewage disposal schemes completed or under construction in 1952 affected 43 settlements in the three western counties and 86 in the more populous eastern ones. Thirty years later the disposal of considerable quantities of sludge or waste on land and into the sea is dependent upon the organised services of 116 sizeable sewage treatment works and 562 smaller ones, backed up by 2ll major septic tanks.

The need to find new sources of water supply, to improve the storage capacity of impounding or service reservoirs, to reduce waste from the existing distribution system and to provide water treated to desired health standards have all posed additional problems to the water industry over the last three decades. Public water supply in the three western counties was heavily reliant upon 16 lakes and impounding reservoirs, along with 13 other sources such as rivers, wells and springs in 1952. Contemporaneously, consumers in the three eastern counties depended largely upon 28 lakes and reservoirs, together with water from 22 other sources of supply. Thirty years on, the western counties are mostly supplied from 22 lakes and reservoirs, along with 19 other sources. Clients in the eastern counties, however, look to 42 lakes and reservoirs (including Lough Neagh), as well as 28 other sources for much of their supply. In the meantime the storage capacity of supply reservoirs had risen from some 30 million m^3 to more than 55 million m^3. Impounding reservoirs and lakes now supply 81 per cent of the water consumed and prove to be especially important in the Eastern and Southern divisions of the Water Service. River intakes contribute 11.7 per cent of the supply and represent important sources in the

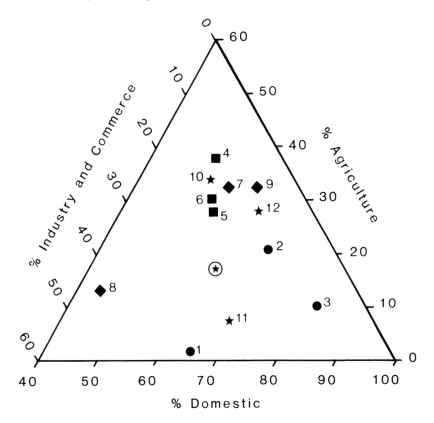

Figure 9.2   Percentage use
of water, 1981.

● EASTERN   1 Belfast
            2 Downpatrick
            3 Lisburn

■ NORTHERN 4 Antrim
            5 Ballymena
            6 Coleraine

◆ SOUTHERN 7 Armagh
            8 Craigavon
            9 Newry

★ WESTERN   10 Enniskillen
            11 Londonderry
            12 Omagh

⊛ Northern Ireland average

Northern and Western divisions. Groundwater sources of supply are widely scattered over the Province in drift and solid deposits. They also prove to be increasingly attractive to farmers in some districts, because of the rising costs of metered supplies (which now amount to 20 per cent of the total volume consumed). Over 460 service reservoirs store another 2 million m^3 of water throughout Northern Ireland. Although their numbers are evenly shared across the Water Service divisions, the capacity of the Eastern group is 56 per cent of this total whereas that of the Western division is only 26 per cent of this total. By contrast two-thirds of the 69 water treatment plants in the Province are located in the Eastern and Southern divisions.

The development and maintenance of an effective water supply and sewerage system by a government agency has involved financial expenditure heavily reliant upon exchequer aid. In the fiscal year 1983-84, for example, outlays on the supply and protection of water amounted to c.£60 million while expenditure associated with the treatment and disposal of sewage added another £27.7 million to the overall costs. Although the Water Service headquarters have been located at Stormont (Belfast) since 1973, the provincial organisation of its affairs is through four divisions centred upon Belfast, Craigavon, Ballymena, Londonderry and 12 subdivisions. A rationalisation of the labour force in this Service has reduced the numbers employed from 5,275 (1972-3) to 2,605 in 1983, when one quarter of those engaged were classified as professional, technical and scientific workers. The Water Service was established by Government order to supply and distribute water as well as providing and monitoring effective means by which to dispose of sewage and effluents. The management and conservation activities of the Service are also subject to scrutiny and advice from a provincial Water Council, which was established by the Water Act (NI) 1972. From what has already been stated about the distinctive supply and distribution arrangements within the Province, it is understandable that interdependent relationships should have been established between the Water Service, the Fisheries Conservancy Board and the Geological Survey of Northern Ireland, as well as the Drainage Division, Fisheries Branch and Freshwater Biological unit of the Department of Agriculture.

In the discharge of its duties, the Water Service is continually faced with the problems of adaptability and management that can arise from physical, socio-economic and political factors. The concentration of manufacturing industry and urban population in the eastern part of the Province, along with the limited availability of water in nearby catchments, has made Lough Neagh water an attractive source of supply since 1960. Unfortunately, problems arising from eutrophication in the Lough, commercial fishing and the desire to work the recently proven sources of lignite nearby, have all produced interest clashes in the area that will not be resolved readily. Lough and river waters within the Province have also been exposed to increased pollution risks from all sources since 1952. To offset this danger the Government has been subjected to demands for improved ecological standards since 1972, as the result of various EEC environmen-

Kilroot Power Station, situated at the mouth of the Belfast Lough, near Carrickfergus in County Antrim. (C.F.S. Newman)

tal directives. Ancillary activities in the Service, such as the monitoring of water quality and the protection of waters against pollution, have consequently proved increasingly important (Chapter 4).

The frequent occurrences of dry summers after 1970 and the shortfalls in rainfall required to top-up supply reservoirs have not only produced water restrictions to domestic consumers but drawn attention to the lack of storage capacity in many of the smaller reservoirs. Another legacy causing concern is the state of pipes in the supply and sewerage systems which, in some cases, have evolved over the past 100 years. Understandably the wear and tear on installations have produced leakages and demonstrated inefficiencies in need of remedial action. Leakages and other water losses form part of the nagging problem of unaccounted-for water, which is now unacceptably high in percentage terms. Management problems do not confine themselves to the present moment, however, for by its very nature the Water Service must also be concerned with future and possibly changed needs. Estimated percentage increases in demand for the period from 1980-2000 AD, vary from 1.7 per cent to 2.7 per cent depending upon the changes assigned to the various provincial consumers. Such estimates in their turn pose questions about the sources for the extra water that will be required, where it will be held and how it will be distributed at costs deemed to be reasonable. Not surprisingly, therefore, the subject of water continues to provide a frequent topic of conversation within the Province!

Electricity service

During the period under review there has been a considerable increase in the electrical supply system in Northern Ireland and in the number of units sold. It is estimated that sales in 1952 amounted to some 700 million units, whereas in 1985 the total number of units sent out from the generating stations was 5,244 million. Such a large increase in supply could not have been met without a considerable increase in the distribution system. In 1952 this system totalled 8,815 km, with 2,165 km in the Belfast area and 6,650 km throughout the remainder of Northern Ireland. By 1985, the distribution system amounted to 27,673 km of overhead cable and 15,717 km of underground cable. This, in turn, is fed by a 1,243 km of high voltage transmission system.

Generating capacity has also been increased to meet this growth in demand. There are now 4 major generating stations in Northern Ireland and the details of these are summarised in Table 9.1.

Table 9.1

Capacity, type, location of Northern Ireland Electricity Service Stations

Station	Fuel	Installed Capacity
Ballylumford B Larne	Oil	960 Mw
Kilroot Carrickfergus	Oil	500 Mw
Coolkeeragh Londonderry	Oil	360 Mw
Belfast West	Coal	240 Mw

(It should be noted that the first three stations also have smaller gas turbines, with a total capacity of 250 Mw. These are only occasionally used.)

It will be seen from Table 9.1 that Northern Ireland is very heavily dependent on oil for its power supply. Figure 9.3 shows the power usage in the period from 1959 to 1985. The sharp rises in oil price in and after 1973 led to a check in the previous steady rise in the number of units consumed until after 1978. Because of the rise in oil prices there has also been a considerable increase in the percentage of the running cost which is accounted for by fuel, i.e. up from 53 per cent in 1984 to 57 per cent in 1985. The electricity service is well aware of the problem of high energy costs and is now actively seeking ways of reducing the dependence of Northern Ireland on oil supplies.

Table 1 indicates that only Belfast West Power Station currently burns coal. This station produces 10 per cent of the installed capacity and is now 30 years old. Although work has recently been completed on refurbishing the station and in building new chimneys, any additional work at Belfast West is not considered to be economically worthwhile at present. Coolkeer-

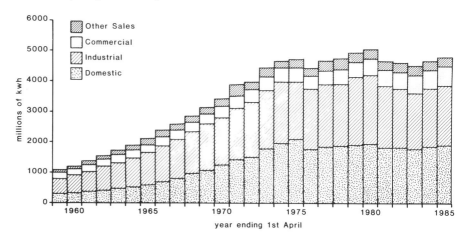

Figure 9.3 Power supplied by the Northern Ireland Electricity Service.

agh began generating electricity in 1961 and is now regarded as a comparatively expensive oil fired station. Accordingly its main purpose is to provide a voltage support for the north west of the Province.

In order to overcome the problem of a high dependence on oil, it has recently been decided to convert part of the newest power station, at Kilroot, to burn coal. It is estimated that the work which is currently being undertaken should cost some £2.5 million but then could save the Northern Ireland Electricity Service between £30 to £40 million a year in fuel costs. Such savings are highly significant in financial terms but equally important is the expectation that when this work is complete the proportion of electrical supply which is dependent on oil fuel will drop from 90 per cent to about 60 per cent.

The recent discovery of large lignite reserves in the Province provides another possible alternative to oil (Chapter 3). Serious consideration is now being given to the economic feasibility of mining lignite and using it for the generation of electrical power. First estimates suggest that there might be 100 million tonnes of lignite available but further investigations may prove that there is even more lignite than is presently thought. Calculations based upon the proved deposits of lignite already indicate that they are adequate to keep a 400/500 megawatt power station supplied throughout the normal lifetime of the plant in that station. No firm decisions have yet been taken concerning the mining of lignite and the location of a power station close to the extraction sites. Accordingly, it has been decided that the work presently being undertaken at the Kilroot Power Station will allow the existing boiler to be modified to burn coal while retaining the capacity to burn oil. It is also believed that this modified system will, if required, permit the burning of a processed form of lignite in the same boilers. For operational purposes coal will therefore be processed in a pulverising mill at the power station, and then blown into the furnaces in a fine powder form. It is estimated that the annual consumption of coal at Kilroot will be about three quarters of a million tonnes a year.

In addition to this work at the existing power stations and additional work on the various overhead power transmission lines, consideration is being given to the possibility of interconnecting the Northern Ireland grid network with that in the Republic and possibly with that in Scotland. Such proposals will have been given a boost by the recent successful completion of a similar cross-channel link between Britain and France.

As with the Water Service, the Northern Ireland Electricity Service was established in 1973 when it took over four separate undertakings in the Province. A Consumer's Council was created at the same time, with statutory responsibilities over the costs and the efficiency of Northern Ireland Electricity services to the 484,000 consumers in the province.

It is clear from this short review that Northern Ireland has a highly developed distribution system allied to a soundly based generating capacity which is capable of considerable and rapid expansion should the need arise.

Gas

The gas industry has been in decline in the period under review and, unlike the other services under discussion, no central organisation has been set up for gas supplies. In 1952 there was a number of small supply bodies, some private companies and some controlled by the local authorities. These had declined to 13 by 1985, and more of them are due to close in the near future. The largest authority is in Belfast, where the Belfast Gas Department expanded after 1960 by taking over those of Carrickfergus, Holywood and Lisburn and contracting to supply gas to Bangor and Newtownards. The traditonal method of manufacture from coal was replaced by a plant manufacturing gas from "tailings" of the oil refinery at Sydenham. This refinery was small and has been closed with the recent rationalisations which have taken place in the oil industry. In 1968 a new gas plant using naptha as a source was opened. The amount of gas sold dropped steadily from 7,339 million cubic feet in 1952 to 5,701 million in 1968. Gas sales then appeared to recover up to 1973 but in that year it was admitted that the quoting of this volume in cubic feet was misleading and future sales were given in millions of therms instead. Quoted figures for sales again showed a steady decline, from 36 million therms in 1974 down to 26 million therms in only five years.

The limited size of the Province's market, the need to interlink the small areas of supply and the dependence upon imported supplies of naptha for gas production were all inhibiting factors to the industry. In the last few years several studies have considered the possibility of bringing natural gas to Northern Ireland, either by pipeline from Scotland or from Kinsale in the Republic. It has been decided that the costs were not justifiable, even with EEC financial assistance. The future of piped gas supplies in Northern Ireland therefore looks bleak. Fortunately another substitute source of gas has become available, acceptable and increasingly important throughout the province, in the form of bottled gas. Indeed by 1979 the sale of 24 million therms of bottled gas had almost overtaken the 26 million therms being provided by piped supplies of gas.

Northern Ireland's first motorway, the M1, which links the south-west of the Province with Belfast. Here the road cuts through parkland at Dunmurry on the southern outskirts of the city; the Antrim hills form the background.
(C.F.S. Newman)

Roads

Under the former local authorities in Northern Ireland a roads policy was formulated by which everyone would have access to a paved road within a very short distance of their home. In many cases this meant that a farmer, for example, only had to travel about one kilometer before emerging onto a public roadway. The net result of this policy was that when the Roads Service of DoENI took over the function of roads authority in 1974, they inherited a network which is much larger than that in many other comparable areas of the United Kingdom. The total length of road presently in public ownership is 23,000 km and its character ranges from narrow, single carriageways (used primarily by agricultural traffic) up to two stretches of motorway, one of which incorporates a length with five lanes in each direction. The Roads Service is another responsibility of the Department of the Environment (NI) with headquarters at Stormont, divisional centres in Omagh, Craigavon, Downpatrick, Belfast, Ballymena and Coleraine and a labour force of some 5,000 employees.

The first motorway to be built, the Northern Ireland M1, runs south west from Belfast towards Dungannon. It was completed in 1968 and is about 60 km in length. The second motorway, the M2/M22, runs in a general north-westerly direction, by-passing Antrim and terminating at Randal-

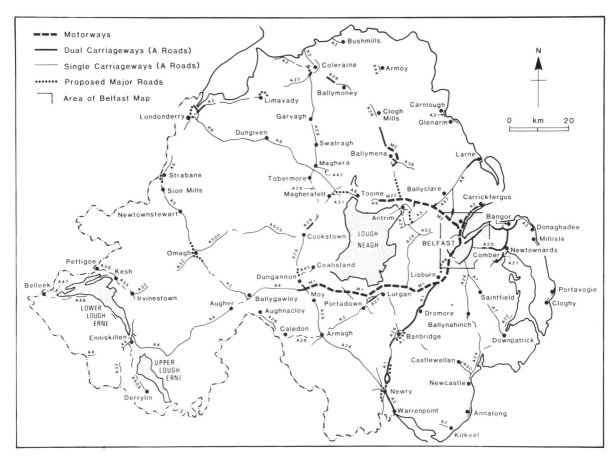

Figure 9.4a Map showing main road schemes in Northern Ireland, 1952-86.

stown. The length is approximately 30 km, but there is also a short spur from it, the M5, which runs along the foreshore of Belfast Lough towards Carrickfergus. These motorways, together with all of the other improved major roads, are shown on Figure 9.4. The only other length of motorway to be built was the Ballymena by-pass. The original intention was that this stretch of motorway would be connected to the M2 but financial restraints have resulted in a recent decision to improve the existing A26, instead. It therefore appears that the fifteen year period of motorway construction in Northern Ireland is complete, at least for the foreseeable future.

When these motorways were constructed there were three major modifications incorporated into them for safety reasons. Perhaps the most important of these modifications was the provision of a central barrier on all motorways. These barriers were made from earthen sods and were erected to a height which also prevented dazzle from oncoming traffic. The barriers soon proved their worth in deflecting vehicles, particularly those running into them at an angle, which had accidentally crossed from one carriageway to another. While these barriers were not without their own particular problems (for example, the lengths constructed of peaty sods are subject to considerable settlement), the concept has now been taken up

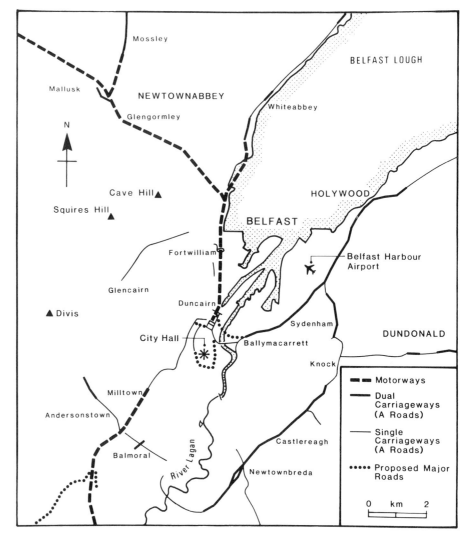

Figure 9.4b Map showing main road schemes in Belfast, 1952-86.

elsewhere. Very few major motorways are now being built anywhere in Britain without such a central barrier.

The Northern Ireland motorways were also the first in Britain to incorporate a definite kerb between the carriageway and the hard shoulder. These kerbs consisted of a rounded dome top, incorporating cross-drainage channels, and were set very low in the carriageway with the rounded dome protruding. Known commonly as "rumble kerbs" these provided an audible warning to a driver who was leaving the carriageway and, in certain circumstances, they also served to deflect a car back onto the carriageway. These devices have proved to be highly valuable as safety features, in spite of doubts that the inclusion of a kerb at this point in a carriageway would lead to cracks along the side of the motorway, with subsequent damages from water penetration. The most recent motorways now include a thermo-plastic strip in their construction which fulfils the same function as the original kerbs.

The third safety feature incorporated in all Northern Ireland motorways was a hard standing of 3.7 m width, at a time when the accepted standard in Britain was only 2.8 m. There was some criticism at the time because of the extra expenditure involved, but recent increases in the width of heavy goods vehicles have undoubtedly justified the extra width provided here. Motorways being constructed in the rest of the United Kingdom do now incorporate these wider verges for safety reasons.

Several of the basic problems confronting the road engineer in Belfast result directly from the geographical features of the city. While the location of the city at the head of Belfast Lough may have been very advantageous for the requirements of a port and shipbuilders, the growth of the urban area has taken the plan form of a Y. Inevitably this growth has made it very difficult to provide cross town links. The distinctive form and functions of Belfast have also resulted in all the through traffic being funnelled into the central area, with resulting traffic delays. Numerous proposals have been formulated over the years to overcome this problem of congestion but environmental rather than economic considerations have always prevailed. It is only within recent years that a link has been completed between the M1 and M2 motorways. Known as the West Link, this scheme was completed after a series of public enquiries and after considerable design amendments had been made to meet environmental objections. In fact this link road has very quickly proved its worth and is now carrying a considerable volume of traffic throughout the whole day. The other major traffic development within the city of Belfast has been the gradual completion of the Outer Ring Road. This road sweeps from the second junction on the M1 around the south and east of the city to join with the main dual carriageway leading towards Holywood and Bangor. Car ownership per capita is high, and an urban traffic control system has been installed in Belfast. Many of the traffic signals can be controlled and co-ordinated from a command centre, through TV monitoring of strategic street junctions. The system initially cost £600,000 in 1980; the computer control has since been modified to use a software package (called SCOOT) which produces a faster response to changing traffic conditions.

Throughout the remainder of Northern Ireland the Roads Service has maintained an inherited policy of major route development, with the result that very high quality roads link all the main provincial towns. Trunk Class 1 roads worthy of mention are those from Belfast to Bangor and the main cross-border route to Newry, as well as the roads leading from the Dungannon end of the M1 towards Fermanagh and its lakeland tourist attractions, or to Omagh. Another major road, subject to constant improvement, is that which links Randalstown with Londonderry. Improvements which have paid for themselves many times over are those which link the roll-on-roll-off port of Larne to the motorway network at Glengormley and the trunk road system at Ballymena.

These major road developments were not undertaken without consider-

Westlink, the dual carriageway which links the M1 and M2, shown as it skirts the central area of the city. The photograph is taken from the north, with the Belfast Cooperative Society's store and the College of Art in York Street in the foreground. (C.F.S. Newman)

able expenditure. Prior to 1974 developments were very reliant upon provincial grants made to the County Councils and to certain urban district councils which were also road authorities. From 1974 the Roads Service has undertaken its own developments. Figure 9.5 shows the expenditure on roads in Northern Ireland in the period from 1952 to 1978. The investment in roads outlined above means that Northern Ireland has a remarkably good network of both major and minor roads for its size.

Innovation and research in road design

Mention has already been made of the safety features incorporated into the motorways when they were being constructed. The formation of the Roads Service in 1974 resulted in a greater ability to undertake quantitative and basic research into various aspects of road design. The Service was quick to grasp this possibility and subsequently has undertaken research into several aspects of road design and maintenance. Much of this work has been undertaken in conjunction with the Department of Civil Engineering at The Queen's University of Belfast and therefore merits further comment here.

The assessment of highway pavement performance has to be undertaken in order that economic programmes of maintenance, reconstruction and rebuilding may be undertaken. The work which the DoE has undertaken in this respect is, in many respects, of a pioneering nature and certain of the concepts derived from it have been taken and developed further by other Road Authorities. Significant development work was undertaken by the Roads Service on an existing package for highway maintenance assessment, known as MARCH, and developed by the City Engineers Group. Northern Ireland engineers purchased the first British built deflectograph, the function of which is to measure the deflection of a pavement under wheel loads. This information may then be used to estimate the remaining serviceable life of a pavement. The Roads Service has an ongoing research project aimed at relating the structural condition of the pavement to the shape of the deflection "bowl" recorded by the deflectograph. Initial results of this research programme are encouraging.

The depth of rutting present in a pavement is often indicative of its condition. It is generally considered that a rut depth of 10-200 mm shows that the carriageway is in a critical condition, while a rut depth greater than 20 mm is found on a carriageway which may be considered to have structurally failed. Rutting is also important because the resulting depressions may hold water and lead to aqua-planing by vehicles in wet weather, with all of the safety problems which that involves. From a very practical point of view rutting can lead to a very irregular surface for the motorist. Recognising the importance of rutting, the Roads Service in conjunction with The Queen's University of Belfast, has developed equipment in Northern Ireland which allows the measurement of rut depth by vehicles travelling at high speed. This machine will take regular measurements on the roadway while travelling at 50 km/h and will clearly speed up the task of data acquisition. Eventually it is hoped that this equipment will go into commercial production.

The concept of an Integrated Maintenance System has been developed including the MARCH system, measured data from a bump integrator (a

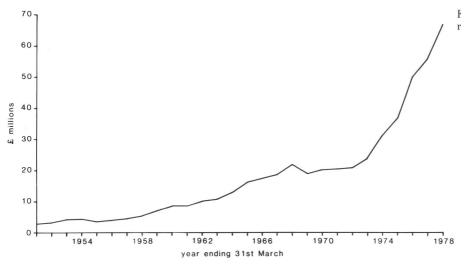

Figure 9.5 Sums spent on road works.

measure of riding quality), SCRIM (a measure of skidding resistance) and the deflectograph. The proposal is for this data to be incorporated into a data bank giving a historical record of any length of road, which together with data on pavement strengths, will allow an economic assessment to be made of any additional proposed strengthening. No pavement assessment technique may be undertaken without having measurements of the loadings to which the roadway is subjected, however. Loadings in the past have generally been measured statically: that is by use of a portable weighbridge which has been set up at the road side, with lorry wheels resting on their weighing pad. Many engineers, however, contend that it is the dynamic loading of a lorry when in motion which is more important and research is now being undertaken into the effect of dynamic loadings on the new Foyle Bridge. This elegant structure was constructed by Redpath, Dorman & Long and Grahams of Dromore, from steel box sections fabricated by Harland & Wolff Ltd, and was built across the river downstream of the centre of Londonderry. The present proposal is to monitor movements of the bridge under wind and traffic loads, measurements of which will be made while vehicles cross the bridge at normal speeds. This is one of the first, if not the first, attempts to relate such high speed dynamic weighing to the overall performance of a bridge.

Research undertaken by the DoENI has not omitted the question of the suitability of road construction materials. The Esso company has developed a new method for designing road pavement overlays. Their method was tested on the Coleraine Ring Road, in Northern Ireland, and this is believed to be one of the first occasions that this method has been used in the United Kingdom. The DoE recently commissioned a research study by the Department of Civil Engineering, The Queen's University of Belfast, into the fatigue performance of bituminous materials, including asphaltic concrete. Work has also been undertaken into the off-site recycling of bituminuous surfaces. Whilst some on site recycling, particularly of asphaltic surfaces, has been undertaken previously in the United Kingdom, this is another instance in which the Department is to the forefront with regard to new technology.

In addition to the work on the design of road pavements and the formalisation of assessment techniques on them, the Roads Service has undertaken structural research of the load distribution characteristics of both T-beam and PSEUDO-box type of bridge decks, using full scale load tests. This research required the very careful placing of mobile loads (normally loaded lorries), and a highly sophisticated set of measuring devices placed under the bridge deck. Results suggest that major savings in construction costs could be achieved by increasing the spacing of beams in a conventional bridge deck. However, if the beams are placed more widely apart then problems can arise over the strength of the slabs laid across the top of the beams. Accordingly, the research programme was continued in order to ascertain the effect of these changes on the bridge deck itself. Much of this work was undertaken on model decks cast and tested in the Department of Civil Engineering. A full scale experimental bridge was then built using the two sets of research data. Loading tests showed that it behaved almost exactly as had been predicted. As a result of this work it is estimated that savings of up to 25 per cent in the cost of certain bridges can be achieved using the revised design charts which have resulted from this research.

It will be seen from these brief notes that the Roads Service has a policy of continuing research which not only ensures the best utilisation of our natural resources but also has applications for road engineers elsewhere in Western Europe.

Acknowledgements

The authors wish to acknowledge the help given by:

Mr D. Stewart, Publicity Officer of Northern Ireland Electricity Service, and The Chief Engineer and staff of the Roads & Water Services of the Department of the Environment for Northern Ireland, in the preparation of this paper.

Bibliography

Northern Ireland Water Statistics – Water Service. Now published annually. Belfast.
Digest of Statistics, Northern Ireland. Published annually until 1979. Belfast.
Local Government Services. Published annually until 1974. Belfast.
Annual Report of the Northern Ireland Electricity Service. Belfast.

ECONOMY & EMPLOYMENT

Economy & Employment

C. W. JEFFERSON

Senior Lecturer, Department of Economics, The Queen's University of Belfast

Northern Ireland is a small region within the United Kingdom accounting for three per cent of the total population and producing two per cent of its output. Despite a strong industrial tradition going back to the middle of the last century and a vigorous and skilled workforce, Northern Ireland has retained the unenviable position over several decades of being the region of the United Kingdom with the lowest level of income per head, the highest rate of unemployment and one of the highest rates of outward migration. Although the rate of job creation in the Province has been high compared to other United Kingdom regions over the past quarter of a century, it has still failed to keep pace with the expansion in the labour force. The region's high rate of population growth, the highest in the United Kingdom, lack of natural resources and remoteness from principal markets have been fundamental difficulties which the economy has had to face. In addition, since 1969 the Province's political instability has adversely affected its economic performance in a variety of ways, but especially in deterring inward investment and tourism. This small open regional economy is highly dependent on the growth of the national economy, the level of local public expenditure and its ability to attract investment from outside the Province.

The period under consideration, 1960-85, can conveniently be subdivided into the 1960s, the 1970s and the 1980s. The 1960s was a period dominated by structural change. Jobs lost in the declining traditional industries, linen, shipbuilding and agriculture, were gradually replaced in the new government sponsored manufacturing industries, the construction industry and services. This was a period of rapid industrial expansion in the national and world economies and the local economy diversified and prospered.

A much harsher climate prevailed in the 1970s, partly due to the effects of the civil disturbances but more generally to the stagnation in the national and international economies in the wake of the 1973 "oil crisis"

Harland and Wolff's shipyard in east Belfast in the early 1970s, with the airfield at Sydenham – now Belfast Harbour Airport – and Shorts aircraft factory beyond. (IDB)

and the overall weakening of regional policy within the United Kingdom. The only area of major employment growth was in services which expanded dramatically as successive governments increased public expenditure in the Province to make up leeway on the level of national provision of social services relative to need.

The 1980s began with the worst recession since the 1930s. As in most other British regions the manufacturing sector in Northern Ireland suffered dramatic falls in output with consequent redundancies and closures. Even although the recovery eventually got under way around the end of 1982, industrial production in 1986 was still substantially below the level in 1979. The Conservative Government's conscientious efforts to reduce the rate of growth of public expenditure put an end to the expansion of public services and public sector employment in Northern Ireland. In addition, the cumulative effect of cutbacks in public sector civil construction projects since the late 1970s was to cause major redundancies in the construction industry. Unemployment virtually doubled during the recession to reach over 20 per cent of the workforce by the middle of 1982. Since then, despite three years of recovery, unemployment has continued to increase and is expected to go on increasing for the remainder of the decade.

The pattern of employment

The Northern Ireland economy supports a population of 1.5 million people. Official population forecasters in the late 1960s were predicting a population of two million by the end of the century; however, the events of the 1970s forced them to lower their estimates to a possible level of 1.6 million by the year 2001. In common with most European countries (with the exception of the Republic of Ireland) a fall in the birth rate substantially reduced the average annual rate of natural increase; from 11.7 per thousand in the 1960s to 7.1 during the 1970s. In addition, the level of outward migration, which averaged less than 7,000 per annum in the 1960s, rose dramatically in the early 1970s as a result of the civil disturbances. Estimates suggest that outward migration was at its highest between 1973 and 1975, the worst years of the "troubles", and involved some 14,000 persons in 1975. By the late 1970s, however, migration had fallen back to more normal levels, possibly due to the improved security situation and to the difficult economic conditions in Great Britain and abroad which had reduced the incentive to move.

A glance at Figure 10.1, which shows annual rates of unemployment, will confirm the similarity in the cyclical movements in the national and regional economies. The closeness in the relationship is hardly surprising since Northern Ireland is subject to the same national economic policies and operates within the same monetary and fiscal framework as any other region of the United Kingdom. The British economy is the principal market for Northern Ireland's exports and consequently fluctuations in national

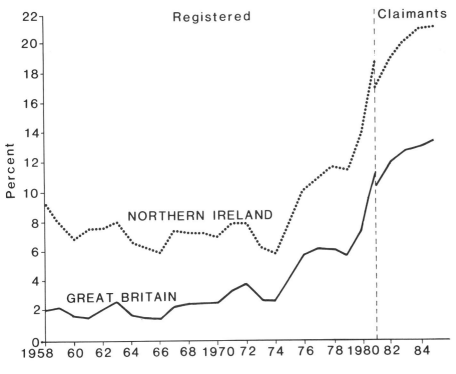

Figure 10.1 Unemployment rates in Northern Ireland and Great Britain 1958-85.

The figures for 1958-81 show registered unemployment rates; from 1981-85 they are claimant based.

Sources: *Official Statistical Sources, Northern Ireland and Great Britain.*

demand, together with local public expenditure, largely determine the level of activity in the regional economy.

The numbers in civil employment increased from 555,000 in 1960 to around 590,000 by the end of the 1970s. This increase in total employment averaging nearly 2,000 jobs a year, during a period when employment in agriculture, shipbuilding and traditional textiles declined by over 100,000, was due to the extensive diversification of manufacturing industry in response to the Northern Ireland Government's industrial development programme and to the sustained expansion in the services sector. Table 10.1 shows how job losses throughout the period from 1960-79 in agriculture, and in manufacturing and construction in the 1970s were more than compensated for by the growth in services. Comprising 41 per cent of civil employment in 1960, the service sector had grown to 58 per cent by 1979 and nearly 65 per cent by 1985. In 1960 manufacturing was dominated by engineering, textiles and clothing which between them employed 140 thousand people, 77 per cent of the total employees. The decline in shipbuilding and linen in the early 1960s was substantially offset by the flow of new enterprises attracted to the Province by the industrial development programme. Traditional textiles lost about 23,000 jobs in the 1960s, many of them for females. They were partly replaced by the growth of synthetic textiles, hosiery and knitwear, although most of the 10,000 jobs created were for men. The 14,000 jobs lost in shipbuilding were compensated for by the growth in electrical and mechanical engineering and metal goods so that the engineering group ended the decade with only 2,000 fewer jobs overall. The establishment of new firms in Other Manufacturing increased employment in that group by 10,000 over the decade.

Table 10.1

Northern Ireland civil employment (June), 1960–85

Sector	Industrial Order	1960	1970	1979	1985	Percentage of total civil employment		
					(000s)	1960	1979	1985
Primary*	1,2	100.8	66.4	59.2	57.5	18.2	10.1	10.7
Manufacturing	3–19	183.6	179.7	142.2	101.3	33.1	24.1	18.9
Construction	20	40.4	52.7	45.6	31.4	7.3	7.7	5.8
Services	21–27	230.0	267.4	342.4	346.4	41.4	58.1	64.6
Total	1–27	554.8	566.2	589.4	536.6	100.0	100.0	100.0

* Civil employment in Agriculture, Forestry and Fishing accounted for 97.7 thousand in 1960, 63.2 in 1970, 57.0 in 1979 and 55.3 in 1985.

Source: Department of Economic Development, Northern Ireland.

The worsening national and international economic climate during the 1970s, the oil crisis, the civil disturbances and international over-capacity

North Sea oil exploration in the 1960s secured orders for oil rigs for Harland and Wolff: here "Seaquest" is being launched for BP. (IDB)

in the man-made fibres industry all contributed to the dramatic fall in manufacturing employment. By June 1979, employment in manufacturing had fallen to 142,000 – a decline of 41,000 since 1970. All the individual groups had suffered but between them Engineering and Textiles had lost almost 30,000 jobs in this nine year period.

Employment in construction grew rapidly in the 1960s in response to the expanding public building programme (Chapter 8) and the generally rising level of prosperity. It peaked in 1968 with employment of over 54,000 but thereafter contracted slowly during the 1970s reflecting cutbacks in the public and private sector building programmes induced by the worsening economic climate.

Employment growth in the service sector in the 1960s and 1970s was principally due to the expansion in the public services. In education, medical services and public administration, employment increased by 220 per cent, from 68,000 in 1960 to 150,000 in 1979. This remarkable growth in the public sector was partly due to the increased emphasis on the provision of public services generally within the United Kingdom but the expansion was more rapid in Northern Ireland reflecting the drive to achieve parity of standards in areas where Northern Ireland lagged behind. HM Treasury's *Needs assessment study* (1979) indicated that Northern Ireland only achieved the same level of public expenditure per head as England in 1967/68. Relative to need (assessed at 31 per cent higher than England at the time) it was 1976/77 before Northern Ireland achieved parity of standards and by the end of the decade it had moved marginally ahead of England, Scotland and Wales.

Civil employment in the rest of the service sector grew by 18 per cent, that is, from 162,000 to 192,000 over the period 1960 to 1979. One would expect that the growing level of economic activity and prosperity would have induced similar expansion in marketed services and indeed there was substantial growth in Insurance, Banking and Finance (+10,000) and Miscellaneous Services (+29,000). However, a major part of the expansion in this latter group, which occurred mostly in the 1970s, was in publicly funded activities, principally in the employment of part-time workers by the welfare departments and in the new leisure centres created during this period.

The fall in employment in distribution was partly the result of major rationalisation within the industry and partly the effects of the civil disturbances. The retail trade suffered severe disruption as a result of the bombing campaign in the early 1970s; however, to a greater extent the fall reflects changes in the methods of operation in the industry whereby the traditional methods in the retail and wholesale trades were replaced by higher productivity, self-service supermarkets and cash and carry operations. The process of change was hastened in the late 1960s by the effects of Selective Employment Tax.

Despite the rise in employment in the 1960s and 1970s it was not sufficient to keep pace with the growth in the population of working age and this resulted in relatively high levels of unemployment, low activity rates and high outward migration. Unemployment in Northern Ireland has been continuously higher than any other region of the United Kingdom. Figure 10.1 indicates that while Great Britain was enjoying low levels of unemployment of around two per cent in the 1960s, local unemployment rarely fell much below seven per cent and this continued into the early 1970s. Unemployment in the Province reached a post-war low of 5.2 per cent early in 1975 but during the remainder of the 1970s it increased almost continuously to reach an average level of 11.3 per cent in 1979.

Within the Province there is considerable variation in local levels of unemployment; the heavily populated industrial area of Belfast and its hinterland have traditionally enjoyed the lowest rates while the rural areas in the South and West have experienced the worst unemployment. For example, in June 1979 there were 9.0 per cent unemployed in Belfast, while in Londonderry there were 15.2 per cent, in Dungannon 19.3 per cent, in Newry 19.5 per cent and in Strabane no less than 24.4 per cent. In terms of the scale of the unemployment problem it is important to note that the Belfast travel-to-work area accounted for 44 per cent of total unemployment and that some areas within the conurbation, notably West Belfast, have continually experienced rates similar to those in the worst affected rural areas.

One result of the continuously high level of unemployment in the Province is that the proportion of the population of working age in employment or actively looking for work is lower than in Great Britain. Activity rates for males and females from 1961 to 1981 are shown in Table 10.2. The decrease in the Northern Ireland male rate from 81.8 to 75.6 is due, in part, to the increasing importance of full-time education, a lowering of the average age of retirement and an increase in the number of males of working age. The increase in the female rate from 33.4 to 44.4 is due principally to the tendency for married women to return to employment after the child bearing period in response to the increased availability of attractive employment for females in the service industries and light manufacturing.

Table 10.2

Male and female activity rates, 1961–81
(Working population as a percentage of population of working age*)

	Northern Ireland		Great Britain	
	Male	*Female*	*Male*	*Female*
1961	81.8	33.4	85.2	40.6
1971	75.7	35.4	79.2	40.5
1981	75.6	44.4	78.3	45.4

* In 1961 and 1971 the population of working age includes those aged 15 and over. In 1981 it includes 16 and over because of the rise in the school leaving age.

Sources: *Official Statistical Sources, Northern Ireland and Great Britain.*

British Enkalon's plant at Antrim in 1973, one of several international companies which made Northern Ireland a major centre for the production of man-made fibres. A clean and plentiful supply of fresh water from Lough Neagh was one reason why Enkalon chose Antrim as the site for this major development which sadly is now closed.
(C.F.S. Newman)

Economic development

The industrial development programme in Northern Ireland had its origins in the inter-war period. The depression years of the 1920s and 1930s had shown the weakness of the traditional textile and engineering industries and the need to provide alternative sources of employment. The New Industries Acts of 1932 and 1937 attempted to meet that need by offering grants towards capital expenditure, interest-free loans and rates exemptions as inducements to attract new industry. In the post-war period industrial development policy in Northern Ireland developed within the context of United Kingdom regional policy. Northern Ireland has been able to offer grants and assistance similar to British Development Areas, but at somewhat higher rates to take account of its exceptional economic problems.

The mainstays of the programme have been the standard capital grants currently provided under the Industrial Investment (General Assistance) Act 1966 and subsequent legislation and the selective financial assistance provided under the Industries Development (Northern Ireland) Acts 1966 and 1971 and subsequent legislation. Under the former, capital grants are paid towards industrial building costs and capital expenditure on new machinery and equipment without employment conditions. This scheme was analogous to the Regional Development Grants Scheme in Great Britain. Under the Industries Development Acts selective financial assistance can be made available for creating employment in new industry or expansion projects, or for maintaining employment in firms whose continued existence is regarded as important. The level of grants and the composition of each package of assistance can be varied within certain limits and as a general principle the highest grants will be offered to firms establishing or expanding in areas of highest unemployment. This form of assistance is similar to that provided in Great Britain under Section 7 of the Industry Act 1972 to encourage both the creation and maintenance of employment.

In Northern Ireland selective financial assistance has been the main instrument to attract new industries. The amount of aid which can be given is defined by the confidential limits per job promoted and by the European Community rules in relation to the co-ordination of regional aids within the Community. The main forms of assistance have included: grants towards the purchase of new machinery and buildings at higher rates than the standard capital grants, the provision of advance government factories at preferential rentals, industrial derating, per capita employment grants and recently, the Corporation Tax Relief grant. In addition there has been a whole range of less significant types of assistance designed to enhance the operating efficiency of assisted industry.

As in other British regions the main thrust of the industrial development policy has been to reduce the initial costs of setting up new firms or the expansion of existing ones. With the exception of the Regional Employment Premium, in operation throughout the United Kingdom from 1967-76, and the employment grants mentioned above, the emphasis has been on assistance with capital expenditure. Since 1977 industrial development policy has been extended to offer the full range of incentives to private service industry; however, apart from the expansion of employment in a few small firms supported by the Local Enterprise Development Unit, there has been little in the way of positive results from this initiative.

Major successes for the industrial development programme came in the late 1950s and 1960s as a result of the vigorous promotional efforts of the Department of Commerce at a time of expansionary conditions in the national and world economies. As might have been predicted by economic theory, capital intensive industries such as synthetic textiles, chemicals and engineering began to expand rapidly in Northern Ireland to take advantage of the reduced real cost of capital. Investment in the man-made fibre part of the textile industry rose dramatically in the late 1950s and 1960s with the establishment of such international firms as ICI, British Enkalon and Hoechst and the expansion of existing firms such as Courtaulds, Monsanto and Dupont. Engineering companies such as Grundig, STC and the Ford Motor Company set up in the Province in the early 1960s and continued to expand throughout the decade. In other industries, major international companies such as BP, Michelin and Goodyear were induced to establish branches in Northern Ireland during the 1960s.

Courtauld's factory at Carrickfergus on the shores of Belfast Lough. This was one of the first artificial fibre plants to be built in Northern Ireland after World War II; it too is now closed (C.F.S. Newman)

Independent researchers agree that the operation of regional policy probably resulted in the net addition of about 40,000 manufacturing jobs in the 1960s. By 1970 sponsored employment accounted for 45 per cent of all manufacturing employment in the Province.

Output and Income

Both growth and structural change in the Northern Ireland economy continued up to the peak year of 1974 and were accompanied by a general increase in prosperity. As Table 10.3 shows, the rate of growth of total output was substantially above that in the rest of the United Kingdom especially in the 1960s, although still relatively modest in comparison with that enjoyed by other member countries of the EEC.

The historically rapid rate of growth of the local economy at this time can largely be attributed to the increases in labour productivity brought about by the structural changes in the economy. Output per head rose faster in Northern Ireland than in the United Kingdom as a whole. Having started the 1960s at about 81 per cent of the United Kingdom level, output per head

Toome Eel Fishermen, County Antrim   *N. C. Mitchel*

Toome Eel Fishermen.

Eels have been netted on the River Bann since the first people came to Ireland; the methods used are virtually unchanged. Wicker-work weirs are constructed across the river, converging downstream where the eels are collected in a long funnel-shaped net. Here two fishermen are opening the mouth of the net to empty the fish into a container with ice, for export to Belgium, the main market.

Castle Archdale Country Park, County Fermanagh   *N. C. Mitchel*

Ringhaddy Sound, County Down   *N. C. Mitchel*

Ulster's many sea and fresh-water loughs are a paradise for boating and fishing. The photograph above shows part of Castle Archdale Country Park on Lower Lough Erne in County Fermanagh, with a well sheltered marina in the foreground and a holiday caravan park beyond. The Fermanagh lakeland's peace and beauty is very popular with visitors from Europe, who come mainly for hire-cruising and fishing.

The lower photograph shows a tranquil deep-water mooring at Ringhaddy Sound on Strangford Lough in County Down. Unlike Lough Erne, this is a sea lough, which has unique marine flora and fauna. It also provides unrivalled sailing conditions.

Bloody Bridge, County Down   *R. H. Buchanan*

School group at Bloody Bridge.

The teaching of environmental sciences has become an important rural activity. The hills have always been used by hikers and climbers, but colourful congregations of oilskinned school children are an increasingly common sight. Such intensive use is causing problems, in Ulster as elsewhere, to the extent that management policies are becoming essential for the protection both of the environment and of the local inhabitants.

GP Championships, 1984   *R. H. Buchanan*

Exciting action during the 1984 GP Championships hosted by East Down Yacht Club, one of the fifteen yacht clubs whose members enjoy uncrowded sailing conditions on the 100 square miles of Strangford Lough.

in Northern Ireland climbed to 90 per cent by the end of the decade and remained around that level in the 1970s. This notable performance during the 1960s was due largely to the decline in the low productivity, labour intensive sectors such as agriculture and traditional textiles and the rapid growth in the high productivity, capital intensive industries such as synthetic textiles and chemicals.

Table 10.3

Output and output per person employed in all industries (1960 = 100)

	Output			Output per person employed	
	Northern Ireland	UK	EEC	Northern Ireland	UK
1970	148.2	130.3	158.4	145.3	129.2
1974	164.4	142.1	183.7	160.6	139.0
1979	182.3	153.7	208.0	171.6	149.8
1984	188.0	158.4	213.3*	196.6	163.5

* 1983 figure.

Sources: *Official Statistical Sources for Northern Ireland, United Kingdom and the European Communities.*

Along with the increasing labour productivity, average earnings rose rapidly over the period and more so than in the rest of the United Kingdom. Average male manual weekly earnings in manufacturing industry rose from around 83 per cent of the United Kingdom figure in 1960 to 97.5 per cent by 1979. For all industries the relative increase was from 81 per cent in 1960 to almost 93 per cent of the United Kingdom figure in 1979.

The statistics available from the New Earnings Survey for all employees in the 1970s tell a similar story of relative improvement for both men and women. Part of the reason for this improvement was increasing productivity, but other factors were also involved. Trade union policy was to achieve parity of wage rates for comparable occupations with those in Great Britain. The expansion of service employment in the Northern Ireland economy was also important in reducing wage differentials. This was especially the case in the public services, where almost all occupations enjoy British levels of wages and salaries.

Personal income per capita in Northern Ireland has been the lowest of any of the regions in the United Kingdom for many years. This is due not only to the relatively low levels of earnings and income in the Province but also to the fact that family size in Northern Ireland is greater than in any other region of the United Kingdom. Over the period from 1960 to 1979 personal income per head in Northern Ireland almost doubled and, growing more rapidly than the United Kingdom as a whole, rose from 68 per cent of the United Kingdom level in 1960 to 79 per cent in 1979 and 84 per cent in 1984.

Table 10.4

Personal income per capita in Northern Ireland (constant 1980 prices)

	£	Percentage of UK Level
1960	1,544	68.1
1970	2,224	74.8
1979	2,972	78.9
1984	3,103	83.6

Source: *Official Statistical Sources, Northern Ireland and United Kingdom.*

After the "oil crisis"

It is perhaps somewhat surprising that 1974 should be regarded as a particularly good year for the economy as the "troubles" had been affecting the Province since 1968. Although there was considerable disruption to commerce and distribution in town centres and severe effects on tourism, the damage to manufacturing activity was relatively slight. However, the indirect effects on the manufacturing sector of the economy gradually became evident. The inflow of new firms which had been contributing around 3,000 new jobs promoted annually in the late 1960s fell to a trickle in the early 1970s. Relative to the level of industrial movement within the United Kingdom, the inflow of new manufacturing firms into Northern Ireland fell from over six per cent of total moves in the 1960s to a mere 1.7 per cent for the period 1971 to 1975 (Hoare, 1981). The flow of new promotions in the early 1970s was maintained by the continued expansion of firms already established in Northern Ireland. Without the invigorating inflow of new firms, however, the expansion schemes began to diminish after 1972 and as the regional economy moved into the post-1974 recession in concert with the national and world economies, job creation became more and more difficult.

Some attempts have been made to quantify the longer term effects of the civil disturbances on employment in Northern Ireland. Such estimates are of course highly speculative but they are nevertheless in close agreement, suggesting an annual loss of two to three thousand potential manufacturing jobs throughout the 1970s.

After the peak of 1974 the economy of Northern Ireland was subjected to a harsh variety of problems. The oil crisis with its consequential effects on the costs of energy, transport and raw materials, had a particularly severe impact on peripheral regions and on particular industries. The national and world recessions were severe and prolonged with a resulting fall in demand for Northern Ireland's manufacturing exports. The poor performance in industrial development promotion between 1973 and 1977 left a gap in the inflow of new jobs and a consequential failure to absorb workers laid off in manufacturing industry.

The combined impact of these forces resulted in a loss of 27,000 jobs in manufacturing between 1974 and 1979, of which 6,500 were lost in engineering and 9,000 in textiles. These job losses occurred not only in the declining traditional industries but also among the government sponsored firms which had provided the impetus for growth in the 1960s.

In addition to the problems which were affecting manufacturing in the mid-1970s, the economy also felt the effects of the reduction in the rate of growth of the services sector. In an effort to reduce the rate of inflation, which was more than 20 per cent in 1975, the government began to cut back on the growth in public expenditure. As a result, public sector employment, which had increased rapidly during the early 1970s, continued to expand, but more slowly after 1975, thus hitting the local economy's main source of employment growth.

Following the recommendations of the Quigley Report of 1976, the government launched a package of new incentives in August 1977 designed to improve the attractiveness of Northern Ireland as an industrial location. Industrial and commercial electricity tariffs were reduced, bringing them into line with tariffs in Great Britain. Industrial incentives were increased and the marketing effort to attract new firms from abroad was stepped up. The package was announced at a time when the United Kingdom and the world economies were moving out of the 1975-77 recession and at the same time the security situation in Northern Ireland was improving. Partly as a result of these factors and the vigorous promotional efforts of the Department of Commerce there was a significant improvement in job promotions to around 6,000 in 1978 and 1979. Many of the new jobs promoted were in foreign firms; a considerable number from America, including the much publicised De Lorean Motor Company and Lear Fan Ltd.

The United Kingdom economy showed some signs of recovery from the recession during the course of 1978 and 1979 and reached a cyclical peak in 1979. Northern Ireland's participation in the recovery, however, was relatively slight and by the end of 1979 both national and local economies were moving rapidly back into recession.

The Great Recession, 1980-81

In 1980 and 1981 the United Kingdom economy experienced the most drastic recession since the Great Depression of the 1930s. Over the two-year period gross domestic product fell by 5.2 per cent compared to the fall between 1929 and 1931 of 5.0 per cent. Total unemployment, which stood at 1.4 million (5.6 per cent), at the beginning of 1980, had reached 2.9 million (12.3 per cent) by the end of 1981. Over the two-year period to December 1981, 1.7 million jobs were lost in the national economy and nearly half a million more were lost in 1982. Manufacturing industry accounted for two-thirds of these job losses.

The slackening of world demand,[1] high exchange rates, high interest rates and the Government's deflationary monetary and fiscal policy, combined to plunge the United Kingdom economy into recession. Pressure

---

[1] Output growth in the OECD countries excluding the United Kingdom fell from 3½ per cent in 1979 to 1½ per cent in 1980.

The De Lorean Motor Company's plant at Dunmurry on the outskirts of Belfast in 1981. The failure of this company after a comparatively short production run of its sports car dashed initial hopes that a viable motor industry might be established in Northern Ireland, and bring much-needed employment to west Belfast.
(C.F.S. Newman)

on United Kingdom exports came from an overvalued sterling exchange rate, boosted by high interest rates and increased oil revenue. In addition, the higher rates of wage and price inflation in the 1970s had eroded the competitiveness of United Kingdom exports. The high interest rates which accompanied the Government's deflationary monetary policy made company borrowing more expensive and companies reacted by running down their stocks, thereby fuelling the recession.

The Government's Medium-Term Financial Strategy, expressed in the March 1980 Budget Statement, was to reduce inflation and create conditions for sustained growth by reducing the rate of expansion of the money supply and reversing the growth of public expenditure. By the end of the financial year 1981/82 the application of restrictive monetary and fiscal policies together with the Government's firm stance on public sector pay settlements, were effective in cutting back on the growth of these policy variables and in substantially reducing the rate of inflation.

The bottom of the recession in Great Britain appears to have been reached in mid or late 1981 but the substantial growth which most forecasters expected in 1982 failed to materialise. The world recession in 1982 was the dominant feature hindering domestic recovery, by making it more difficult to sell exports. It also had the effect of helping to reduce inflation through the fall in commodity prices. Indeed, the only major success story in the economy in 1982 was the decline in inflation which fell from 12 per cent at the start of the year to 5.4 per cent at the end.

Bearing in mind its dependence on the national economy it is not surprising that the Northern Ireland economy fared badly in the recession. Between 1979 and 1981 manufacturing output fell by 12.7 per cent compared to the national decline of 14.6 per cent. Local manufacturing declined again in 1982 reflecting the further fall in textiles and the first annual fall in engineering output since the recession began. Unemployment, which at the end of 1979 was 63,000, increased throughout 1980 and 1981, and by June 1982 it had reached 116,000 (20.3 per cent).

Over the period from June 1971 to June 1982 manufacturing industry lost 35,000 jobs (25 per cent of employment) and construction 11,000 (30 per cent) with the most severe falls occurring during the second half of 1980 and 1981.

Although employment fell severely in all the manufacturing groups, textiles and clothing suffered most. In addition to the general recession both industries were badly affected by competition from low priced imports. Between June 1979 and June 1982 employment in textiles virtually halved while in clothing it declined by 30 per cent. The man-made fibre industry, which had been built up over the previous 30 years as a mainstay of the industrial development programme, collapsed with a succession of cut-backs and closures in firms which were national household names. Surprisingly, output and employment in the local engineering industry held up well in 1980 and 1981 due principally to exceptional growth in the output of valves, aircraft and vehicles. However, with the collapse of the De Lorean Motor Company early in 1982, output and employment fell substantially at a time when the national engineering industry had begun to stabilise.

Despite the intended cut-backs in real public expenditure in Northern Ireland, public financed employment continued to grow throughout the recession (by about 5,000 jobs from June 1979-June 1982) but at a much reduced rate of growth compared to the 1970s. A small fall in private sector services resulted in the overall numbers employed in the service sector remaining virtually unchanged.

Recovery came later in Northern Ireland than in Great Britain and it was not until the beginning of 1983 that industrial production began to rise. Led by the growth of national consumers' expenditure, industrial output grew by three per cent in 1983 and the recovery phase has continued up to 1985. Although employment stabilised in 1983 and has remained at that level since (536,000 in 1985), unemployment has continued to increase in line with a rapidly growing labour supply.

The mid-1980s

Although there have been three years of industrial growth since 1982, output in the production industries in 1985 was still 11 per cent below its 1979 level. There have been some major success stories in individual manufacturing firms and growth in locally based small firms but these have only managed to counterbalance the redundancies and closures in other parts of the industry. In the highly competitive international economy of the 1980s, Northern Ireland's poor media image abroad remains a major deterrent to inward investment and despite extensive efforts to alter the situation, the Industrial Development Board is obliged to rely mainly on indigenous industry to achieve its modest targets. While there has been some improvement in recent years and the Local Enterprise Development Unit has had substantial success with small firms, Northern Ireland has not been able to attract or generate sufficient major projects to renew the industrial structure. If this continues the manufacturing sector may have to rely even more on the rescue and maintenance function of the Industrial Development Board to prevent further job losses.

The construction industry has not recovered from the massive decline in the late 1970s and early 1980s and despite record levels of housebuilding in 1983 and 1984, construction activity still remains in the doldrums. The main reason is the industry's former heavy dependence on public sector capital programmes in a period of stringency in public expenditure. The rather limited public capital programme planned for the latter half of the 1980s suggests a lean future for the remainder of the decade. The high levels of housebuilding over the past decade have made substantial improvements in the Province's housing stock. For example, the amount of "unfit" housing in Belfast has been reduced from 24 per cent in 1974 to 12 per cent in 1985 but there is clearly a lot more to be done. Substantial improvements in the city's vitality and appearance have followed from the introduction of urban development grants in 1982 and the grants available for cosmetic improvements to buildings along the city's arterial roads and also from some major developments by the national retailing chains and financial institutions in the city centre.

As a result of the major structural changes in the Northern Ireland economy shown in Table 10.1 the service sector accounted for almost two-thirds of all civil employment in 1985. Of the 346,000 persons employed in services, some 207,000 were employed in public sector activities. Unlike the 1970s where the public sector provided the "engine of growth" in the local economy, since the start of the decade the Government has made it clear that the days of public sector growth are over and public sector employment has been static during the 1980s. What is more, the stationary numbers disguise a shift to part-time employment and a gradual loss of full-time job opportunities.

Northern Ireland's dependence on public expenditure can be seen in other ways. Projected public expenditure for 1985/86 is £4,270 million, equivalent to more than three-quarters of the level of gross domestic product. This works out at approximately £2,700 per person or £8,500 per household in the Province. More than one third of this expenditure can be attributed to the subvention from Great Britain. This compares very favourably with the figures for the United Kingdom as a whole which are £2,400 per person and £6,400 per household.

Energy prices in Northern Ireland have been especially high partly because of the heavy dependence on oil for electricity generation. It has been necessary to maintain electricity tariffs in line with those of the highest cost areas in Great Britain by means of a public subsidy. In addition, lack of access to natural gas has required the use of expensive oil-based naptha to produce town gas. In view of the Government's unwillingness to pipe natural gas from mainland Great Britain and the failure to negotiate a contract with the Republic of Ireland to supply natural gas from the Kinsale field, plans are in progress to phase out town gas. Contracts have been signed for the convertion of a major part of the generation capacity to coal-fired plant, a move which will reduce dependence on one particular form of energy. The dramatic falls in oil prices in 1985 and early 1986 may well make oil-fired electricity generation the most economical method in the short term but this situation is unlikely to continue in the longer term. However, it is the discovery of vast amounts of low cost lignite around Lough Neagh and elsewhere in the Province and its economic development for electricity generation which offers the prospects of low cost energy for Northern Ireland's producers and consumers in the early 1990s.

The existence of large scale unemployment has become an accepted feature of the 1980s. In December 1985 the total number of unemployed claimants (including school leavers) was over 121,000 or 20.7 per cent of the labour force, and this is after major downward revisions in the method of calculating the unemployment series. On the old basis which was in operation prior to October 1982 it is likely that there would have been of the order of 140,000 persons registered unemployed in December 1985. The full extent of unemployment is further masked by the fact that there are some 18,000 people on Employment and Training schemes; of these there are 8,000 on the Youth Training Programme and another 10,000 on adult programmes such as Action for Community Employment, Enterprise Ulster and Management Training.

Despite the discontinuities introduced into the unemployment series, the seasonally adjusted trend is still upward and likely to continue to be so for the rest of the 1980s and into the 1990s. On the assumption of static activity rates, official population projections suggest that the natural increase in the labour supply will be around 7,000 per year for the remainder of the decade. If it is assumed that half of these workers migrate, a figure consistent with a level of total outward migration of around 6,500 per year, it would require a net increase in employment of 3,500 jobs a year for unemployment to remain at its present level. Past experience suggests that, without growth in public sector employment, a net increase of 3,500 jobs a year is beyond the capacity of the Northern Ireland economy in present circumstances. Indeed it will do well to maintain employment at its present level over the next few years.

The improved security situation in the 1980s has produced some benefits. The tourist industry has revived, not only through the inflow of shoppers from the Republic of Ireland coming north to take advantage of lower prices, but also through visitors from outside Ireland coming to enjoy the Province's facilities. Another benefit has been the opening up of town and city centres with the consequent developments in shopping, catering and entertainment facilities. The ending of the civil disturbances and a return to completely normal conditions would no doubt bring substantial benefits especially through an increased inflow of foreign investment; however, with the limited amount of internationally mobile investment available and the widespread competition from many European countries and regions, it will be an uphill task. In addition, the "troubles" have created the security "industry" in Northern Ireland which currently employs more than 23,000. Presumably the return of peace and normality would mean the loss of a large proportion of these security related jobs.

Conclusion

The underlying problem causing Northern Ireland's economic difficulties is that the rate of growth of the labour force is greater than the rate of growth of employment opportunities. High levels of unemployment, outward migration and low incomes are the symptoms. Solving the problem requires either increasing the rate of growth of the employment, or reducing the rate of growth of the labour force or both. Because the problem is one of relative growth rates it is not sufficient to create, once and for all, a large number of new jobs, it is the long-term rate of net job creation which must be increased to be equal to, or indeed, if present levels of unemployment are to be reduced, to be greater than the long run growth of the labour force.

In the past quarter of a century the main growth of employment opportunities came in the private sector through government sponsored inward investment and through the expansion in the provision of public services. In the 1980s, however, both these sources of employment growth appear to have dried up.

In the present political climate the Government takes the view that self sustaining growth must be achieved in the private sector. In Northern Ireland with its lack of natural resources and remoteness from markets, past experience suggests that indigenous industry by itself cannot generate sufficient growth. It is of course essential to continually improve and upgrade the productivity and efficiency of local firms to enable them to survive in today's highly competitive markets; however, a substantial flow of inward investment of modern, efficient industry is needed to maintain industrial employment, let alone expand it.

The reduced level of mobile international investment makes it difficult for any of the many competing regions to attract substantial amounts and Northern Ireland with its continuing political instability is not regarded by national and international businessmen as a desirable location. The fact that many international firms already operate very efficiently from bases in Northern Ireland does not seem to alter their perceptions. Clearly everything possible must be done to attract viable new industry to the Province and the extensive work being undertaken and planned by the Industrial Development Board and other Government and private agencies is vital. However, at some point the question must be asked – how cost effective is industrial development policy?

At the national level the principle of redirecting industry from more efficient to less efficient producing regions has been called into question and regional policy has lost favour with the present Government. Formerly regarded as a means of equalising the distribution of excess demand for labour in the economy it is now regarded as a social measure for reducing regional inequalities.

Currently, the question is being asked as to whether the creation of private sector employment through the instruments of industrial development policy is really more cost effective than public sector employment. However, even if the answer were in favour of public sector employment the public services cannot generate self sustained growth and the present Government is unlikely to accept a policy of rapid long term growth of the public sector as a means of curing the region's economic ills. Nevertheless, it could be argued that from the point of view of the national economy, it may be economically more efficient to spend less diverting private sector firms from economically more efficient producing regions to less efficient regions and permit an increased provision of public sector services and employment, beyond the levels indicated by need, in the less efficient regions.

The other aspect of a solution to the Northern Ireland problem is to consider how to slow down the rate of growth of the labour force. In the medium term outward migration and lowering the participation rates are ways in which this can be brought about, however both have limitations. Outward migration usually results in a loss of the relatively more skilled and able members of the workforce leaving behind the relatively less skilled. Activity rates can be lowered by a variety of ways, such as altering the school leaving age or the retirement age or even by altering statistical procedures; however it usually results in a higher ratio of dependents to workers with a reduced income per capita. In the longer term, a major reduction in fertility and hence in the Province's rate of population growth is needed to reduce the rate of growth of the labour force.

In the medium term, from whatever source employment growth in Northern Ireland may come, the major prerequisites are a period of sustained growth in the United Kingdom economy and an end to the political instability in the Province. The present Conservative Government's economic policies together with the benefits which the international economy may derive from the major fall in oil prices, may possibly achieve the former condition but there appears to be no solution to the Province's political problems in the foreseeable future.

In historical perspective the performance of the Northern Ireland economy in the 1960s and early 1970s may be seen as the outstanding period of growth and development this century. The 1980s may come to be viewed in the same light as the 1930s, as a depression or trough between two long cycles of economic activity. One can only hope that solutions to the Province's economic and political problems can be found in the 1990s which will permit that decade to be known for its long-term recovery.

Bibliography

Economic and industrial strategy for Northern Ireland. (The Quigley Report). Belfast. 1979.
Needs assessment study, report of an interdepartmental study. London. 979.
Hoare, A G. Why they go where they go: the political imagery of industrial location, *in Transactions of the Institute of British Geographers, New Series 6*, 1981, 152-175.

Agriculture, Forestry & Fishing

W. I. HUNTER

*Lecturer in Agricultural Economics, The Queen's University of Belfast
and Principal Agricultural Economist, Department of Agriculture for Northern Ireland*

Farming is one of Northern Ireland's largest industries in employment terms, accounting for just under 10 per cent of the total in civil employment. In this respect the region is intermediate between the United Kingdom as a whole with three per cent and the Republic of Ireland with 17 per cent. A further three per cent of the region's workforce is employed in industries ancillary to farming. Forestry and fishing, although employing few people relative to agriculture, are also important in specific localities and in their share of the domestic market for timber and for fish. The emphasis in this chapter, however, is on agriculture as the predominant employer of the three industries.

The pattern of work in agriculture is established by physical and structural factors such as climate, topography and land tenure as well as by economic and policy influences including product pricing and the subsidisation of capital investment. While natural factors have altered little over the 35 years since the British Association last met in Belfast, the same cannot be said for structural and economic conditions affecting farming. These have changed dramatically, largely in line with agricultural developments in most advanced economies but influenced particularly by events such as membership of the European Communities (EC) since 1973. Together with physical and structural features peculiar to local farming, they have moulded the pattern of employment evident today. Developments in forestry and fishing have also occurred in response to different stimuli and are examined later in the chapter.

Physical and structural influences

Climate, topography and soils

The region has a temperate, equable but humid climate. Average rainfall is 1,100 mm (43″) per annum while the mean monthly temperature ranges from 4°C in January to 14°C in July. There is considerable cloud cover, the

Indoor feeding of cattle on silage is one of several major changes in livestock management which has occurred on Ulster farms. (DOA)

mean hours of sunshine per annum totalling just 1,300. Topography is varied, comprising a high proportion of land which is undulating, hilly or mountainous. Approximately 30 per cent of the region's area is above the 150 m line. Soil quality is also varied with only a small proportion classified in the top category. The majority of soils are medium or poor.

An indication of the combined effects of these topographical and pedological features can be gained from the fact that 75 per cent of the region's agricultural area is now designated by EC Directive[1] as Less Favoured. The remaining 25 per cent largely comprises the valleys of the major rivers – principally the Bann and the Lagan – and some lowland around the Co. Down coast. The presence of such a high proportion of Less Favoured Area constitutes a considerable constraint on the range of agricultural activities which can be pursued profitably and competitively. Farming is predominantly grassland-based with cropping concentrated on the relatively small areas of better land.

Land tenure

The pattern of land tenure in Ireland, north and south, is quite different from that in Great Britain. A series of Land Purchase Acts spanning the period 1885 to 1925, under which long-term loans were made available, enabled tenants to purchase their holdings and created a structure of relatively small owner-occupied family farms, unlike the situation in Great Britain where a significant proportion of farms are still tenanted and where

---

[1] *Mountain and hill farming, and farming in Less Forward Areas*, Directive 75/268/EEC.

average farm size is much higher. In Northern Ireland 99 per cent of farmland is owner-occupied compared with 60 per cent in GB. The operation of the Irish Land Acts, however, did result in consolidated holdings comprising relatively few parcels of land, in contrast to the situation in some western European countries where fragmentation of holdings has been common. Nevertheless fields in the region are small, creating the well known "patchwork quilt" appearance but also militating against large scale arable farming.

Virtually universal owner-occupation can impose a rigidity which would hamper desirable structural changes. Specifically, the market may not yield a sufficient supply of farmland to satisfy the demand from farmers wishing to enlarge, thereby pushing up land prices. This scenario is prevented, at least to a degree, by the widespread use of seasonal letting of land for periods of 11 months, a practice known locally as "conacre". Although the arrangements may continue between the two parties for successive years, title to the land remains with the owner and theoretically the "lease" is renogotiated each year. About one-fifth of the agricultural area is let annually, principally for grazing, but significant proportions of some crops, notably potatoes, are grown on conacre.

The impact of this local feature of tenure should not be under-estimated, particularly in socio-economic terms, for it simultaneously enables owners who wish to partially or wholly curtail their farming activities to do so without relinquishing title to the land, while at the same time enabling expanding farmers to satisfy their requirements for additional area. The effect on structure is quite marked, with some 30 per cent of holdings letting land in conacre, many thereby ceasing to be active farm businesses.

Farm size

Northern Ireland farms are small by UK standards. The region has 43,500 holdings, or units of ownership, with an average area of 20 hectares of crops and grass, compared with a UK average of 52 hectares. However, over 18,000 of these holdings are too small[1] to be regarded as farm businesses. The remaining 25,000 farm business units have an average area of 30 hectares of crops and grass, still well below the average holding size for the UK (where no distinction between holdings and farm businesses is appropriate as seasonal letting is not a common feature). The resources of many Northern Ireland farms are inadequate to generate income sufficient to support a family or to fund development.

The small farm structure in the region is a direct consequence of the tenure system and its origin. The transfer of ownership from landlord to tenant bore more similarity to agrarian reform in continental Europe than in Great Britain. Farm structure in Northern Ireland is, if anything, superior to that in many EC States, where the overall average size is 16 hectares (EC-10).

In common with trends in most advanced countries, structural change

---

[1] Having less than one European Size Unit (ESU) of business activity.

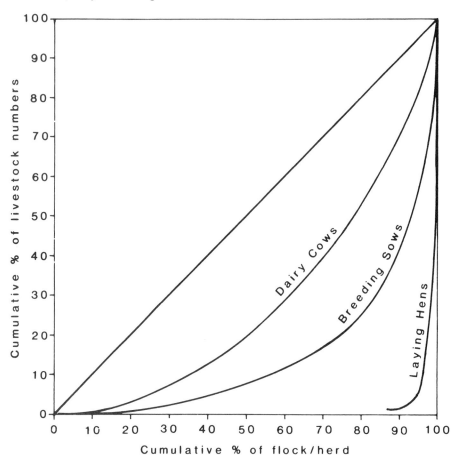

Figure 11.1   Lorenz curves of dairy cows, breeding sows and laying hens in Northern Ireland 1985.

Source: Derived from *June 1985 Agricultural Census*, DANI.

towards larger farms has occurred in Northern Ireland. As farming methods have advanced – largely through mechanisation, the use of agrichemicals and improved breeding of plants and livestock – economies of scale have increased and both the minimum viable size and the optimum size of unit have risen. Small farms have either disappeared as their resources have been amalgamated into larger businesses, or they have become genuinely part-time, the workforce combining some farming activity with other employment or supplementing it with state pensions or social security payments.

Specialisation

At individual farm level, specialisation on fewer enterprises has provided an alternative means of exploiting economies of scale. The greater financial certainty imposed by guaranteed price systems – both those found within the UK up to 1973 and those under the Common Agricultural Policy (CAP) of the EC since then – also encouraged specialisation, with the result that the traditional mixed farm with a wide range of enterprises, which would have predominated in the 1950s, has now become largely a thing of the past. Most farms in Northern Ireland now specialise in one main enterprise with perhaps one or two subsidiary enterprises. The distribution of farms by type (Table[1]1.1) reflects this quite clearly and also underscores the strong orientation towards livestock production.

Table 11.1

Distribution of farms[1] by type, 1985

Type	Number	%
Specialist Dairying	5,291	20.9
Other Dairying	1,984	7.8
Beef and Sheep	12,405	49.0
Pigs and Poultry	803	3.2
Cropping	1,530	6.0
Horticulture	536	2.1
Crops and Livestock	2,022	8.0
Mixed Livestock	740	2.9
All types	25,311	100.0

[1] Farms of 1 European Size Unit and over.
Source: *June Agricultural Census,* DANI, *1985.*

Many of the main enterprises are now concentrated heavily on these specialist farms. For example, in 1985, 77 per cent of dairy cows were found on Specialist Dairying farms; 78 per cent of beef cows and 79 per cent of ewes were on Beef and Sheep farms; 57 per cent of pigs and 75 per cent of poultry were on Pigs and/or Poultry farms and 50 per cent of potatoes were grown on farms classified as Cropping. Such specialisation obviously has direct implications for the pattern of farm work and many individuals, as well as farms, have become "specialist" in a particular branch of farming.

Enterprise structure

The structure of each enterprise has also changed fundamentally as a result of farm enlargement and specialisation, so that a high proportion of enterprise output is produced by a relatively small proportion of producers. This concentration is most marked in the intensive livestock sector, as seen from the Lorenz curves in Figure 11.1.

The deviation of each curve from the diagonal represents the extent to which each particular enterprise has departed from a situation in which all producers are of equal size. The intensive livestock enterprises, namely pigs and poultry, show the greatest concentration, but other farming enterprises have been moving in the same direction.

The effect of these structural changes has been to concentrate production of some farm products into relatively few hands: some examples serve to illustrate. Whereas in 1964 there were well over 25,000 producers with 50 or more laying hens, by 1985 the number was down to just over 500 and, of these, less than 100 kept almost 75 per cent of the total laying flock. Over 25,000 farms also kept breeding sows in 1964; by 1985 there were just under 4,000 and less than 300 of them accounted for well over half the female breeding herd. Similarly with dairying, the number of producers has fallen from over 21,000 in 1964 to less than 8,000 in 1985. Only beef rearing and finishing have remained well dispersed over a large number of the region's farms. In 1985, 17,000 producers kept beef cows compared with 27,000 in 1964; 22,000 farms also kept cattle for slaughter in 1985. Although cropping has normally been associated with the limited areas of good land, even in this sector significant concentration has occurred. In 1985 there were less than 8,000 cereal growers compared with almost 25,000 about 20 years ago. Over 12,500 farms grew one acre (0.4 hectares) or more of potatoes in 1967, but there were just over 3,000 farms with 0.5 hectares or more in 1985.

This catalogue of statistics is presented without apology to emphasise the extent of the swing which has taken place away from the traditional mixed farming of the pre- and immediately post-war era. It also serves to illustrate the flexibility and adaptability of the farming sector to respond to changing economic circumstances, contrary perhaps to public perceptions of the industry.

The changing economic environment

At the time of the British Association's last meeting in Belfast in 1952, the agricultural industry still reflected the effects of war-time measures to boost food production. For farming in the region, this meant an expanded tillage area, particularly of cereals, potatoes and flax and higher numbers of dairy stock and poultry (Table 11.2).

Table 11.2

Areas of crops and numbers of livestock, 1955–85

	1955	1965	1975	1985
Crops ('000 hectares)				
Cereals	106	116	61	54
Potatoes	47	25	11	13
Other crops	16	6	6	10
Total cropped area	169	147	78	77
Livestock ('000 head)				
Dairy cows	[1]...	196	239	294
Beef cows	[1]...	146	328	201
Total cows	255	342	567	494
Total cattle	904	1,116	1,626	1,514
Total sheep	870	1,074	934	1,590
Total pigs	686	1,248	645	617
Total poultry	11,272	10,394	12,056	10,061

[1] Not collected separately.

Source: *June Agricultural Censuses*, DANI.

In Northern Ireland as elsewhere, farming throughout the post-war period has been subject to a high level of state intervention and support. After the withdrawal in the mid-1950s of war-time measures including food

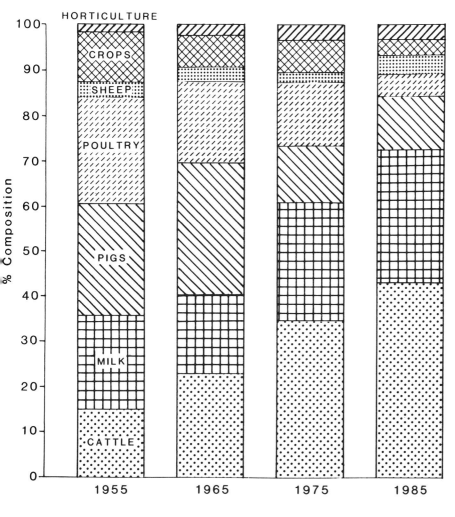

Figure 11.2 Composition of receipts from farming, 1955-85.

Source: DANI.

rationing, UK farm price support up to the early 1970s was based on a system of guaranteed prices and deficiency payments, established under the 1947 Agriculture Act. Although the major crops were included in this system of support, much of the adjustment in the pattern of farming was the eventual reversion to a more grassland-based agricultural economy with increasing emphasis on milk and beef cattle production.

The liberal import policy of the UK allowed grain to be imported into the region at relatively low world market prices, enabling the expansion of the intensive livestock sector whose foundations had been laid in the 1930s. Through the development of pig and poultry enterprises many farmers were able to expand their businesses on relatively small areas. By 1955 pigs and poultry were together contributing almost half of farming gross output (Figure 11.2). Significant ancillary sectors developed to supply inputs and process products, providing much needed employment.

However, dairy and beef production increasingly dominated the region's

Mechanisation has replaced hand-labour in most farm operations: a round bailer in operation on an arable field after harvest. (DOA)

agricultural economy throughout the 1950s, 1960s and early 1970s, with 26 per cent and 35 per cent respectively of total gross output by 1975. Dairying developed mainly on lower land not devoted to crop production while beef rearing, in particular, was concentrated on the upland areas, especially the Antrim Plateau and the Sperrin Mountains. Special support in the form of production grants was given to beef and sheep production in upland areas through the UK Hill Cow and Hill Sheep Subsidy Schemes. By the early 1970s, the region's livestock-based agricultural economy was exporting approximately two-thirds of its agricultural output, mainly to GB.

The European dimension

Following the UK's membership of the European Community in 1973, several anticipated and some less expected changes to the region's farming occurred. Adoption of the Common Agricultural Policy (CAP) – with its high-price régime for cereals, established through minimum import prices – was expected to lead to some contraction in the region's intensive livestock production as grain for feedstuffs would no longer be available at cheap world prices. As can be seen from Table 11.2, this expectation was justified and significant contraction in pig production has taken place. Production of both pigs and poultry is now concentrated on a relatively small number of specialised producers although, in the case of poultry, numbers of birds have been maintained through the expansion of the broiler (poultrymeat) sector.

Several of the other major adjustments, however, were unforeseen. The most major was the secular decline in the beef breeding herd from 1974 to 1983. From the theory of comparative advantage, it might have been expected that, along with dairying and sheep, beef production would have flourished with the introduction of a common market in Europe. That it did not was largely a consequence of international events. An acute world shortage of grain and protein, coupled with high levels of inflation globally around 1973, caused farming costs to escalate. At the same time – fuelled by the oil crisis of 1974 – living standards fell and the anticipated increase in demand for beef in the UK and in Europe did not materialise. The result was a collapse of the market price for beef, at a time when no satisfactory EC support system for beef had been introduced to replace the UK national support scheme. Confidence of beef rearers was eroded so severely that, for nearly a decade, the beef cow population declined and only from 1983 has it stabilised, albeit at less than two-thirds of its former level.

One of the few alternatives available to beef rearers, particularly those in the hill and upland areas, has been sheep production which has consequently experienced a long-standing and continuing expansion. This has been encouraged by the introduction in 1980 of an EC sheepmeat régime which has conferred benefits on British and Irish sheep producers. Northern Irish sheep producers have benefitted, through exports to the Republic of Ireland, and from the greater access for Irish sheepmeat to the important French market for lamb than has been available to producers in GB.

Milk production, based predominantly on grass both grazed and conserved, also increased very markedly up to 1984. Dairying has long been recognised within the region as the enterprise providing the greatest potential for high profitability and regular income, but with a concomitantly high and sustained input of labour and capital.

Until the introduction of milk quotas in 1984 (see later), the dairy cow population increased steadily, not only supplying the liquid market but providing raw material for milk processing. Indeed less than 20 per cent of milk produced in Northern Ireland is consumed in liquid form, the remainder being processed for export as cheese, butter, yoghurt and skim milk powder, thereby generating employment and added value.

Several other EC developments have had implications for farming and for agricultural employment. First, monetary and exchange rate instability has arguably had a greater effect on agriculture in the region than in other parts of the UK. This stems from the existence of the land frontier with the Republic of Ireland. The UK and the Republic of Ireland negotiated different transitional arrangements for bringing national agricultural prices up to full EC prices, giving rise to differential prices in the two parts of Ireland for commodities such as beef and pigmeat. The situation was further aggravated by exchange rate fluctuations including a break in parity between the UK and Republic of Ireland pounds, and by different approaches in the two countries to the question of agricultural or "green" rates of exchange between EC currency units and national currency. All of these have operated to generate, sporadically, significant price differentials both sides of the Irish border, creating circumstances favourable to movement (sometimes illegal) of agricultural products. Between 1975 and 1980 the situation for beef and pigs was so serious that a special subsidy payment to meat plants under the Meat Industry Employment Scheme, (MIES) was required to stem the flow of animals to processing facilities in the Republic of Ireland in order to protect employment in northern meat plants.

The second point concerns the control of European food surpluses which in the 1980s has become a major and well publicised issue already significantly affecting farming throughout Europe. The most direct effect on Northern Ireland farms has been felt in the dairy sector with the introduction of on-farm quotas for milk production and a punitive "super levy" on production above quota. These have already resulted in the arrest in 1985 of the long-standing expansion in dairy cow numbers. Milk quotas are seen as a harbinger of further supply controls in other sectors, notably cereals. Apart from requiring producers to examine the possibility of alternative and perhaps novel enterprises, production controls obviously have a knock-on effect on ancillary employment, an effect which the region can ill afford.

The third development has been an increasing emphasis within the CAP on special policy measures for specific groups of farmers and geographical areas. Such policy is permitted under the Treaty of Rome despite the basic philosophy of a *common* market and a *common* agricultural policy. Of particular interest to and impact in the region is the designation of Less Favoured Areas (LFA). In 1975, 45 per cent of the agricultural area, based mainly on the areas previously entitled to UK hill subsidies, was so designated, rendering farms eligible for headage payments known as Hill Livestock Compensatory Allowances (HLCAs) and for enhanced rates of grant on certain capital investments. In 1984, a further 30 per cent of the agricultural area was similarly designated though, since officially viewed as "disadvantaged" rather than "severely disadvantaged", lower rates of subsidies and of capital grants are payable. The underlying objective of the LFA directive is the maintenance of employment in such areas throughout the EC.

The introduction of Community programmes for specific regions within the EC has also been exploited to the advantage of farms in the region's LFAs. In 1982, a Northern Ireland Agricultural Development Programme was introduced, funded partly by EC and partly by UK funds. This provided *inter alia* for enhanced rates of assistance to particular categories of farmers in the LFAs in Northern Ireland and was designed to improve the viability of individual farms and to ensure the retention of rural population. Pending a review of the Programme, it was suspended in April 1986.

Mechanisation and modernisation

The pattern of employment in European agriculture has been influenced greatly by the adoption of modern farming methods and Northern Ireland has been in the vanguard of this movement. Space prevents a detailed

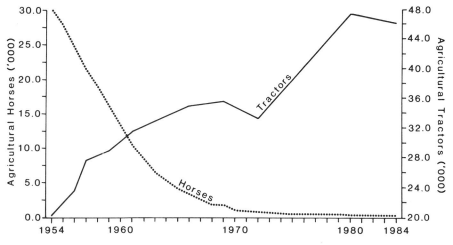

Figure 11.3   Numbers of agricultural horses and tractors 1954 to 1984.

Source: *June Agricultural Censuses and December/January Machinery Censuses*, DANI.

critique, but two comparisons serve well to examplify the twin concepts of mechanisation and modernisation.

Appropriate perhaps in the homeland of Harry Ferguson, a native of County Down and inventor of the original power-take-off system for tractors, has been the rapid adoption of the tractor as the modern "work horse" on Northern Ireland farms. Figure 11.3 portrays graphically the substitution of tractor for horse power. It is worth noting that there is one tractor for every 23 hectares of agricultural land in Northern Ireland compared with one per 36 hectares in the rest of the UK. The effect on labour productivity of this and other forms of mechanisation and of the myriad of other technological developments has been phenomenal.

The second comparison illustrates just one facet of the adoption of modern farming methods and again is fitting for a region which can boast two outright winners and two runners-up in the British Grassland Society's National Silage Competition between 1981 and 1985! A sustained switch from hay to grass silage as the dominant form of grass conservation

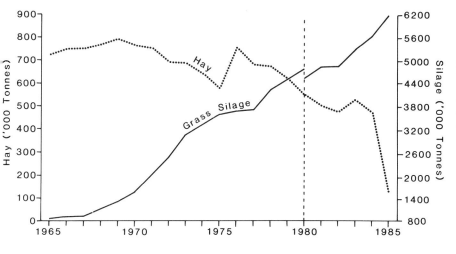

Figure 11.4   Production of hay and grass silage 1965-85.

Source: *December Agricultural Censuses*, DANI.

has taken place (Figure 11.4), primarily amongst dairy producers over 90 per cent of whom now rely on silage for winter feed. Silage is, of course, much less susceptible to unfavourable weather than is hay production and, furthermore, favours the use of self-feed and easy-feed systems. Together with other developments such as mechanical handling of farm waste and automated systems of meal feeding, reliance on silage has contributed towards higher productivity of those engaged in farm work.

Employment in agriculture

On-farm employment

Half a century ago there were some 170,000 persons working on farms in Northern Ireland. Today the figure is around 60,000. There were still over 150,000 persons employed in 1951, but the 1950's and 1960's witnessed a rapid drift from the land as a result both of the push of mechanisation and the pull of more rewarding jobs outside agriculture. By 1970 numbers on farms had fallen by half to approximately 80,000. The trend since then is shown in Figure 11.5 from which a decelerating decline is evident. Indeed the total farm labour force is now virtually static in aggregate. The high

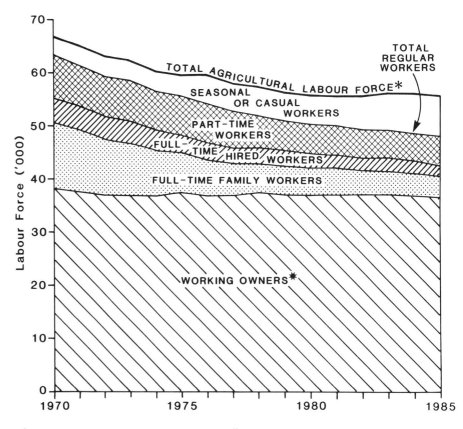

Figure 11.5 Agricultural labour in Northern Ireland 1970-85.

Source: *June Agricultural Censuses*, DANI.

*Excluding wives of owners   *Including partners and directors level of regional unemployment – running at over 20 per cent in the 1980's – is an important factor.

It can also be seen that the decline over the last 15 years has occurred mainly in full-time family and hired workers. The number of farmers, or "owners, partners and directors", is related much more closely to the number of farming units and is therefore linked to more fundamental processes of structural change such as farm amalgamation. It is also noticeable from Figure 11.5 that the contribution of part-time workers, especially seasonal and casual workers, has increased in recent years, an indication that farmers may be matching their labour supply more accurately to labour requirements.

Figure 11.6 gives some indication of the geographical distribution of the agricultural work force in terms of density per 100 hectares of agricultural land. As a generalisation the east, with greater emphasis on more intensive enterprises such as dairying, pigs and poultry, exhibits a higher density than the western areas of the Province.

Composition of the work force

With small family farms the norm, owners, partners and directors supply the greater part (65 per cent) of the region's agricultural labour force, against 47 per cent in the UK as a whole. When other family members are included, the farmer and his family together account for over 85 per cent of the region's on-farm work force. The 3,600 regular hired workers, representing just six per cent of the total, are found on only 2,200 farms and of these just 500 farms employ more than one regular hired worker. Indeed, when viewed in terms of the total regular work force on farms, including farmers themselves, over 50 per cent of farms are merely one-man units and 85 per cent are one or two-man units (Table 11.3).

Table 11.3

Distribution of total regular labour by numbers working on each farm, 1985

| Workers per Farm | Farms | | Workers | |
	Number	%	Number	%
1	15,823	51.4	15,823	29.9
2	10,280	33.4	20,560	38.8
3	3,223	10.5	9,669	18.2
4	979	3.2	3,916	7.4
5–6	358	1.2	1,890	3.6
7–9	65	0.2	495	0.9
10 and over	31	0.1	628	1.2
Total	30,759	100.0	52,981	100.0

Source: *June Agricultural Census, 1985*, DANI.

This predominance of one or two-man farms has a number of implications. For example, it creates a situation in which additional labour may be required at certain peak periods such as harvest. This demand is met by employing increasing numbers of seasonal or casual workers. Certain

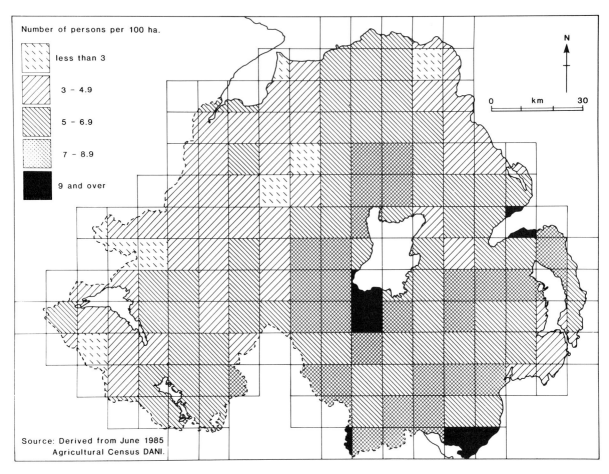

Source: Derived from June 1985
Agricultural Census DANI.

Figure 11.6 Density of
farm labour in Northern
Ireland 1985.

tasks such as slurry disposal and silage making, which require expensive, specialised machinery, can more economically be performed by the use of agricultural contractors. It is estimated that as many as 12,000 of the region's farms now employ contractors on a regular basis. Many contractors are themselves active farmers but, increasingly, firms specialising in agricultural contract services have been developed to handle tasks ranging from ploughing and slurry spreading to silage making, combine harvesting and hedge cutting.

An alternative to the use of contractors is the formation of small syndicates to co-operatively own and operate specialised machinery and equipment. This development has had official encouragement through the provision of grant aid, from both national and EC sources, provided through the Central Council for Agricultural and Horticultural Co-operation (now part of the Food From Britain organisation). Silage making and crop harvesting are two of their main activities, but groups to share equipment for milking and grain drying and handling have also been formed.

The combination of farming with other, normally off-farm, occupations is a feature increasingly found in the farming industries of many European countries, notably West Germany. Northern Ireland is no exception to this, but, with the high level of general unemployment and the attendant scarcity of alternative job opportunities, the scope is more limited here. Nevertheless a significant proportion of the farm work force is "dual-active". Results from the 1983 EC Survey of Agricultural Structure indicate that almost one-fifth of the region's farm occupiers have other employment in addition to farming and over two-thirds of these consider their other gainful activity to be their main employment. When other family members are included, the proportion of farms with dual-active family workers rises to over one quarter. Little is known about the range of non-farming activities engaged in, but over 90 per cent takes place off-farm.

Ancillary employment

With livestock and livestock products accounting for 87 per cent of the region's agricultural output, significant supply and processing sectors have been developed. It is estimated that 17,000 ancillary jobs are directly dependent upon farming (Table 11.4). Animal feed is the largest single expenditure incurred by farmers, and supplying and distributing this input is the main employment generated on the supply side. Fertiliser manufacture and distribution is also important. Both animal feed compounding and fertiliser manufacturing are located mainly in Belfast, adjacent to the docks for the importation of raw materials. Farm machinery manufacture and distribution and the provision of agri-chemicals are also important components of the supply sector throughout the region.

Downstream from farming, the conversion of milk into a wide range of dairy products is conducted at 35 creameries and milk processing plants around the Province, employing over 5,000 people. The processing of beef and sheepmeat provides employment for about 3,000 people. Of the 14 meat plants, 10 meet EC licensing standards for export. There has been considerable re-organisation, including rationalisation of ownership, of meat plant capacity in recent years with a high proportion now owned by South of Ireland based firms. The very high animal health status of livestock in both parts of Ireland enables meat to be exported to most countries of the world. To meet the increasing sophistication demanded by the market, meat processing has swung towards the provision of boned-out and vacuum-packed products, providing a welcome boost for employment and value added.

Despite the contraction in pig production, employment in pig processing is still important with 2,000 persons engaged mainly in bacon curing. About 60 per cent of the bacon produced is exported, largely to GB. Although the poultry sector has also contracted, this has been confined to commercial egg production; despite the decline, egg packing still employs 500 people. Poultrymeat, by comparison, has grown steadily and the 33 million broilers and turkeys produced annually provide the raw material for poultrymeat processing and packaging involving around 2,000 people.

Table 11.4

Employment in industries ancillary to farming, circa 1984

Sector	Numbers employed
Supply	
Animal Feed	1,350
Fertilisers	700
Farm machinery	700
Sub-Total	2,750
Processing	
Milk and dairy products	5,350
Beef, mutton and lamb	2,950
Pigmeat	2,000
Poultrymeat[1]	1,950
Eggs	500
Sub-Total	12,750
Miscellaneous[2]	1,300
Total	16,800

[1] Includes part-time working converted to full-time equivalents.
[2] Includes employees in horticultural processing, general agricultural merchants, auction marts, agricultural contractors, pharmaceutical firms, vets and animal nutritionists.
Source: *Department of Agriculture for Northern Ireland (estimates).*

With vets, agricultural contractors and so on making up the remainder, farming's ancillary sector makes an increasingly important contribution to total agriculture-dependent employment. In addition to this ancillary employment, scientific, professional and technical staff in the Department of Agriculture for Northern Ireland are engaged in agriculture and food research, education and advisory work, making an important contribution to advances in technology and their adoption on farms. The role of these personnel promises to be equally important in future as agriculture faces new challenges.

Some current issues

The agricultural industry in Northern Ireland, as in other regions of Europe, is presently going through a difficult period. Farming income in 1985 totalled £67 million, 48 per cent down on the previous year, and the lowest figure in real terms since 1980. While the adverse weather in 1985 accounted for a significant proportion of the drop in income, other underlying factors have also been at work which are likely to have a longer-term effect on the industry.

Turning first to agricultural policy, two paramount issues exist concerning the CAP. These are the twin and related objectives of controlling food surplusses in the EC and of arresting the spiralling cost of the CAP. Both have a direct impact on the region's farmers. Stated crudely, no longer can they look to expansion of production as the main source of increasing income; neither can they expect increased levels of support from the EC or national exchequers. The ramifications are many and just two of the more fundamental will be touched upon here. First, future prospects in farming will depend more upon cost minimisation than on revenue maximisation.

"Low input farming" has become a fashionable concept and, in Northern Ireland conditions, this will mean relying increasingly on grass and silage to replace bought-in feed. Additional cereals for use as home-grown feed will also be worth considering in certain areas. On some farms more use of clover, with its nitrogen-fixing properties, may be worthwhile at the expense of inorganic nitrogen. All of these avenues would obviously have negative employment consequences for the ancillary sector. Second is the greater need for diversification into alternative products. With the exception of sheepmeat, the major products of the region's agriculture are now in over-supply in Europe. Already interest has been shown in oilseed rape and in the reintroduction of flax which, if chemical retting can be achieved satisfactorily, offers the prospect of import substitution of up to 3,000 tonnes of fibre annually for use in the linen industry. But some alternative products may lie outside traditional farming itself. On marginal land, biomass production for fuel, using, for example, willows, together with more "orthodox" forestry, may become viable alternatives to food production. Horse breeding and rearing, already conducted on the fringe of agriculture, also provide opportunities for development.

Other pressures on farming exist in addition to those of CAP origin. Environmental issues have been the subject of increasing public concern throughout Europe in the last decade and conservation of the landscape and protection of wildlife have assumed an important place in public debate. Farming in Northern Ireland with its structure of small family farms and its orientation towards livestock, is less likely to be in conflict with environmental interests than is farming in other parts of the UK where continuous cereal growing in particular has been associated with such emotive subjects as hedge removal, straw burning and pesticide damage. Nevertheless, intensification of livestock production and concentration on silage as the main form of winter fodder in Northern Ireland have brought limited problems of water pollution caused by run-off of slurry and leakage of silage effluent. The farming industry here is alive to such issues, as witnessed by the discussions currently taking place about the establishment of Farming and Wildlife Advisory Groups (FWAGs) similar to those already existing in GB.

Public concern over animal welfare – including that of farm livestock – has been less vociferous in Northern Ireland than in GB. Nevertheless, EC standards for housing of intensive livestock will impose a further constraint on farmers' ability to respond to changing economic circumstances. Finally, farming will also be affected by consumers' greater awareness of dietary considerations, such as levels of fat intake and the existence of residues in meat – issues epitomised by the "health food" lobby. The region's farming industry is currently vulnerable to some of these developments, with its heavy dependence on dairying and on red-meat production. For Northern Ireland agriculture to survive as a major direct and indirect source of employment, it may well have to learn to adapt to changing market requirements in the future even more effectively than it has adopted new techniques of production in the past.

The forestry and fishing industries

While small in employment terms relative to agriculture, forestry and fishing, nevertheless, represent important activities in the region when judged on other criteria. Against the general backdrop of chronic, high unemployment, they are also important sources of work in specific localities.

Forestry

Although Ireland became predominantly tree covered following the last period of glaciation 10,000 years ago, clearance of natural forests to make way for agricultural use started as early as the Bronze Age and continued virtually unchecked up to the present century. As a result, Ireland north and south is the least afforested area in Europe, with the exception of Iceland. Despite a programme of state afforestation commenced in Ireland at the beginning of this century, the Province currently has just five per cent of its land under trees, compared with eight per cent in GB and an average of 20 per cent for EC countries.

Of the 70,000 hectares of forests in Northern Ireland, approximately 57,000 hectares are owned by the Forest Service of the Department of Agriculture, with the balance found largely on agricultural holdings. In 1983, 3,000 holdings recorded woodland with an average area of four hectares; over 95 per cent of holdings had less than 10 hectares of woodland each. Few are therefore engaged commercially in forestry. The remainder of this section will deal with State forestry operations.

Official forestry policy has been based on use of marginal agricultural land where the production and profitability of agriculture are low. Forestry land is therefore largely high level peat land or marginal hill land. Timber production is the primary objective of forest operations. Fast growing coniferous species therefore account for 94 per cent of all plantings, with 63 per cent under Sitka spruce. Lodgepole pine, however, is used for planting on the poorest upland sites. In recent years, approximately 100,000 tonnes of timber have been produced annually. This will rise towards the end of the century, as some large forests planted in the 1950s and 60s reach maturity, and will provide a significant proportion of the region's timber requirements in the future.

Recreation and conservation are two very significant by-products of forestry operations, and a secondary objective of State forestry has been to maximise these uses. Ten forest parks have been created, many more forests are open to the public and, in total, forests receive at least one million visitors each year. Concern for wildlife conservation has led to the establishment of over 50 Forest Nature Reserves, 15 of which have National Status.

These various activities currently provide direct employment for approximately 400 regular workers, often in more remote areas where few other job opportunities exist.

Fishing

The region's sea fishing industry is based primarily on the County Down fishing ports of Ardglass, Kilkeel and Portavogie, from whose harbours 185 trawlers of over 10 metres operate. Almost all local boats fish the northern section of the Irish Sea and land fish at ports in England,Scotland and the Isle of Man as well as in Northern Ireland. The total value of landings in 1985 exceeded £14 million of which £10 million was landed in Northern Ireland. Much of the fish landed here is absorbed by the processing industry. The species of most importance are prawns, whiting, cod and herring. Processed fish products are exported largely to GB, but also to continental and North American markets.

An EC Common Fisheries Policy (CFP) was introduced in 1983 and EC Regulations now govern access, fishing quotas and conservation rules. The CFP includes structural measures under which grants for scrapping, modernisation and construction of boats are provided. It is estimated that just over 2,000 jobs are dependent upon the sea fishing industry, 1,100 of which are involved in the catching sector. The remainder are predominantly engaged in fish processing, but also in marketing and distribution, boat building and harbour work.

A more recent development has been marine fish farming, located along the County Down coast in Strangford Lough and Dundrum Bay. Over 1.5 million oysters were produced for human consumption in 1985, primarily for markets in GB, the Republic of Ireland and other EC countries. Commercial fresh-water fish farming is also expanding with 16 farms currently producing almost 500 tonnes of rainbow trout, again for export mainly to GB and the Republic of Ireland.

A significant commercial fresh-water fishing industry is found on the region's inland waters. Over 100 tonnes of commercial salmon are caught each year as are some 800 tonnes of yellow and silver eels, worth £1.5 million per year. Almost 95 per cent of the eels come from Lough Neagh and the remainder mainly from Lough Erne.

Undoubtedly the best known aspect of the region's fishing industry is its angling waters. These are renowned for the quality of their coarse fishing, particularly roach and bream, while excellent salmon and trout angling is available for most of the year. Angling is now one of the region's major tourist attractions with parties of anglers coming from many parts of Europe. It is by the region's rivers and lakes, as well as in its forests and through its countryside, that the less publicised, tranquil aspects of life and work in Northern Ireland can most readily be appreciated.

PEOPLE & POLITICS

Population

P. A. COMPTON

Reader, Department of Geography, The Queen's University of Belfast

The chapter is devoted to a discussion of the more salient features of the demography of Northern Ireland – population distribution and change, religious composition and the characteristics of fertility, mortality and migration. It is assumed that Belfast and its region is coterminus with Northern Ireland.

With just over 1.55 million inhabitants in the mid-1980s, the population of Northern Ireland comprises around 2.8 per cent of the United Kingdom total. It is therefore the smallest constituent country of the United Kingdom, being roughly one third the size of Scotland and just over half as large as Wales, and is also smaller than East Anglia, the smallest of the English standard regions.

Northern Ireland is demographically distinct because it is here that those specific features, which distinguish the populations of Great Britain and the Irish Republic, overlap. This overlap is a function of the religious composition of the Northern Ireland population. Hence the demographic behaviour of Protestants, who comprise just over three fifths of the total, is broadly similar to that of the population of Great Britain. Marriage occurs relatively early and is virtually universal, divorce and remarriage are comparatively common, average family size is small and the birth rate and rate of natural increase are low. By contrast, the Catholic population, comprising around two fifths of the total, is to all intents and purposes indistinguishable demographically from the Catholic population of the Irish Republic. It is more pro-natalist in outlook and as a result Catholic families are comparatively large in size. In the past, because age at marriage was late and celibacy pronounced, high marital fertility was not translated into a particularly high birth rate; but more recently with the convergence of Catholic and Protestant marriage behaviour, although not for divorce and remarriage, the larger average size of Catholic families has been more exactly reflected in the birth rate and natural increase differentials between the two groups.

One obvious consequence of this demographic overlap is that the Northern Ireland birth rate and rate of natural increase lie roughly mid-way between the corresponding values for Great Britain and the Irish Republic. But there are in addition, age structure implications; because the proportion of children in any population is a direct function of the birth rate, young age dependency in Northern Ireland is higher than in Great Britain but lower than in the Irish Republic whereas old age dependency is lower than in Great Britain but higher than in the Irish Republic. As a result, the balance of provision needed for educational, health and welfare services varies between the three areas. Furthermore stemming directly from its younger population – the Northern Ireland crude death rate is substantially lower than that in Great Britain although, whether measured in terms of age specific rates or as life expectancy, the real level of mortality in Northern Ireland is substantially above the United Kingdom average. These relationships are quantified in Table 12.1 for the early 1980s. Because of the variability of net migration, actual population change cannot necessarily be expected to accord with this simple model.

Table 12.1

Demographic comparisons for the early 1980s

	Northern Ireland	Great Britain	Republic of Ireland
Birth rate per 1,000	17.5	12.8	20.4
Death rate per 1,000	10.2	11.5	9.4
Natural increase per 1,000	7.3	1.3	11.0
Per cent under age 15	25.9	20.8	30.3
Per cent aged 65 and over	12.0	15.0	10.7

Sources: *Population Trends 43, Office of Population Censuses and Surveys; The Northern Ireland Census 1981; Census of Population of Ireland, 1981.*

The 1960s was a phase of comparatively rapid population growth in Northern Ireland as numbers increased from 1,485,000 in 1961 to 1,536,000 in 1971 due to a combination of moderately high natural increase and relatively low net out migration. The precise characteristics of population change during the 1970s and early 1980s, however, are more debatable because of the unreliability of the 1981 census.

As in Great Britain the birth rate climbed steeply after 1955 to peak in 1964 but then declined even more sharply before bottoming out in 1977 at the lowest ever recorded rate of 16.5 per 1000. The death rate, by contrast, has moved within a comparatively narrow range since 1951. As a result the broad pattern of natural increase – the balance of births and deaths – has faithfully mirrored the trend in the birth rate, rising from around 1 per cent per annum in the mid-1950s, to almost 1.5 per cent in 1964 and then dropping to barely 0.5 per cent in 1977. Most recently the rate has fluctuated between 0.6 and 0.8 per cent per annum (Figure 12.1).

While natural increase is accurately known from the registration of births and deaths, an account of actual population change during the 1970s

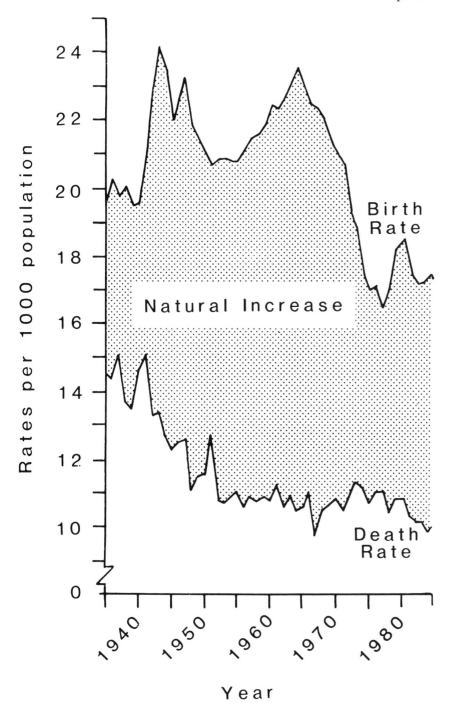

Figure 12.1 Northern
Ireland crude birth and
death rates and rates of
natural increase, 1935-84.

and early 1980s, which also takes account of net migration, must use the 1981 census of population as a bench mark. Yet, this census was conducted under uniquely difficult circumstances. A campaign of non co-operation involving intimidation and murder meant that census forms could not be collected in the ordinary way in many areas and the public were therefore urged to return uncollected schedules to the Census Office. In the event, returns were not obtained from an estimated 5,917 households, reckoned by the Registrar General to be equivalent to 18,988 persons. The initial count of the population for 1981 was therefore put at just over 1,507,000 persons, (1,488,077 persons actually enumerated plus the correction for non-enumeration), that is around 29,000 persons fewer than in 1971.

Shortly after this result had been published, evidence began to emerge that the Registrar General had understated the extent of non-enumeration. Investigation by the Policy Planning and Research Unit (PPRU), based on comparing child benefit and school census data with the corresponding census figures, showed that the under-enumeration of the child population alone was greater than the Registrar General's estimate of all non-enumerated persons. PPRU's estimate of the size of the Northern Ireland population on census night 1981 therefore involved a substantial upward revision of the Registrar General's figure. They placed it at 1,562,000, that is some 26,000 more than in 1971. (Inter-departmental Working Group on Census Revision, 1985.)

However, while there can be no doubt that the Registrar General seriously understated the extent of non-enumeration in 1981, there are now grounds for thinking that the PPRU revision in turn, erred on the high side. There are three substantial reasons for thinking this to be the case. Firstly, the discrepancy between the population aged 17 and over enumerated at the census and the corresponding population on the electoral register was virtually the same in 1981 as in 1971, when the enumeration is accepted as being more or less complete, whereas any sizeable under-enumeration of adults in 1981 should have appeared as a marked widening of this discrepancy. Secondly, the residuals between the enumerated population and the population that would have been expected in 1981 from natural increase alone confirm substantial under enumeration of children in 1981. The residuals at other ages, however, are well within the range that might be expected from a moderate increase in net out migration. Thirdly, the PPRU estimate is at variance with what is now known about net out migration over the intercensal period. Their estimate of 81,400 was based on the assumption that the flows between Northern and Southern Ireland were in balance, whereas it is now apparent that there was a net movement of 19,000 persons to the Republic over the period in question.

Quantifying these three considerations indicates that the population of Northern Ireland on census night 1981 most probably lay in the range 1,530,000 to 1,540,000; 1,534,000 has in fact been used elsewhere by the author as a working approximation of the total (Compton, 1985; Morris and Compton, 1985). Moreover, PPRU is also now persuaded by the strength of the evidence above; they too now accept a lower population total and have reduced their estimate of population from 1,562,000 to 1,532,000. This latter total is now the officially accepted figure for 1981.

These two estimates – 1,534,000 to 1,532,000 – are sufficiently close to the figure for 1971 to suggest that the Northern Ireland population was essentially static between 1971 and 1981. Since we know that natural increase amounted to 107,600 over the last intercensal period, net out migration was therefore in the range 108–110,000, equivalent to a rate of 0.7 per cent per annum. Although this is a much higher rate of net out-flow than between 1961 and 1971, it is still lower than the corresponding rate for 1951 to 1961, and is therefore well within the recent migration experience of Northern Ireland. Furthermore, it also fits in with the reasonable presumption that the troubles greatly intensified the propensity to migrate during the first part of the 1970s. The intercensal components of population change since 1951 are summarised in Table 12.2.

Estimated annual movements in the population since 1971 (mid-year to mid-year) are also presented in Table 12.2. The values for natural increase are accurate as they come from the registration of births and deaths. The net migration estimates, on the other hand, are more tentative as they have been derived by summing the respective estimated balances with Great Britain and the Isle of Man, the Republic of Ireland and the rest of the world. The results of this exercise suggest that the Northern Ireland population initially declined by around 16,000 during the last intercensal period from 1,537,800 in 1971-2 to 1,521,500 in 1978-9, but subsequently recovered to 1,536,000 by 1981-2 and to 1,544,000 by 1983-4. The recovery was caused by a drop in the rate of net out migration from the very high levels of the early 1970s together with greater buoyancy in the rate of natural increase after 1977. At present the population increase is probably within the range 0.3 to 0.5 per cent per annum.

Population distribution

Population distribution in Northern Ireland is uneven. Just over one third of the total live in the city region of Belfast, defined as the continuously built-up area from Carrickfergus in the northeast to Lisburn in the southwest and to Holywood in the east. The region immediately beyond the built-up area, lying within an arc of roughly 25 to 30 kms from the city centre, has close economic ties with Belfast and contains a further 15 to 16 per cent of the population of the province living in such towns as Antrim, Bangor and Newtownards as well as in smaller centres and rural places. Together these two areas comprise the Greater Belfast region which contains around half the total population of the province living on less than one tenth of the surface area.

Another way of assessing the distribution is in terms of population density by local government districts. The high degree of population concentration is exemplified by the fact that in only nine of the 26 districts is density above the provincial average of 108.5 persons per square kilo-

Table 12.2

Intercensal population change, 1951–81; annual mid-year estimates 1971/2–1984

Period	Population at beginning of period in '00s	Natural increase		Net out migration		Overall change	
		Number in '00s	Annual average increase in per cent	Number in '00s	Annual average loss in per cent	Number in '00s	Annual average change in per cent
1951–61	1,370,9	146,3	1.02	92,2	0.64	54,1	0.38
1961–66	1,425,0	97,4	1.33	37,7	0.52	59,7	0.81
1966–71	1,484,8	75,6	1.00	24,3	0.32	51,3	0.68
1971–81	1,536,1	107,6	0.68	108,7	0.69	−1,1	−0.01
1971–72	1,537,8	14,0	0.91	15,8	1.03	−1,8	−0.12
1972–73	1,536,0	12,1	0.79	16,6	1.08	−4,5	−0.29
1973–74	1,531,5	11,1	0.72	13,8	0.90	−2,7	−0.18
1974–75	1,528,8	9,3	0.61	11,8	0.77	−2,5	−0.16
1975–76	1,526,3	9,7	0.64	11,7	0,77	−2,0	−0.13
1976–77	1,524,3	8,6	0.56	10,9	0.71	−2,3	−0.15
1977–78	1,522,0	9,3	0.61	9,8	0.64	−0,5	−0.03
1978–79	1,521,5	11,1	0.73	5,7	0.37	5,4	0.36
1979–80	1,526,9	11,5	0.75	6,2	0.40	5,3	0.35
1980–81	1,532,2	11,3	0.74	7,5	0.49	3,8	0.26
1981–82	1,536,0	10,8	0.70	7,1	0.46	3,7	0.26
1982–83	1,539,7	11,3	0.73	7,0	0.45	4,3	0.28
1983–84	1,544,0						

Sources: *International Migration*, Office of Population Censuses and Surveys; *Annual Reports*, Registrar General for Northern Ireland.

metre. The figures also point to the strong contrast between the remoter regions of very sparse population where densities fall below 40 persons per square kilometre as in Moyle, Fermanagh and Omagh, and the much higher densities in the vicinity of Belfast, exceeding 300 persons per square kilometre in the districts of Carrickfergus, Castlereagh, Newtownabbey, North Down and Belfast itself.

The breakdown of the population by rural and urban area is partly a function of definition. If a minimum population size of 1,000 inhabitants is adopted as the definition of an urban settlement then just under 75 per cent of the population live in towns and just over 25 per cent in rural areas, although about half the latter depend upon urban centres for their livelihoods. Naturally the proportion of urban and rural dwellers varies around the province. Thus Fermanagh, Magherafelt and Ballymoney are the most rural districts while outside the Greater Belfast region, Londonderry, Coleraine and Ballymena contain the highest proportions of urban dwellers. Nonetheless, Belfast completely overshadows the other towns and cities and is some eight times the size of the second city Londonderry, and eleven times the size of the third ranking place, Bangor.

For more than three decades, two general trends have dominated the

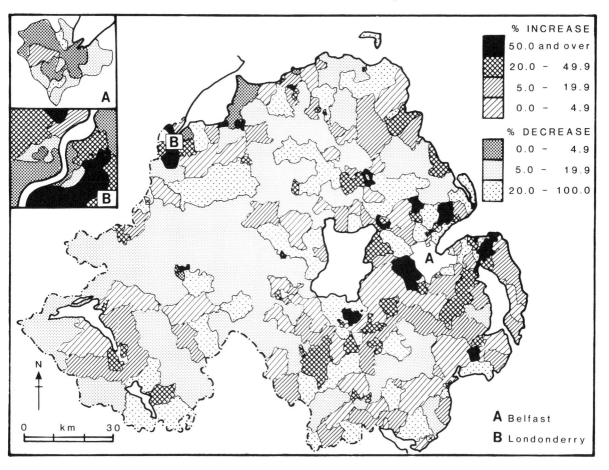

% INCREASE
50.0 and over
20.0 - 49.9
5.0 - 19.9
0.0 - 4.9

% DECREASE
0.0 - 4.9
5.0 - 19.9
20.0 - 100.0

A Belfast
B Londonderry

N

0   km   30

Figure 12.2 Northern Ireland: population change, 1971-81.

changing distribution of population in the United Kingdom and also in Northern Ireland. The first trend has been the continued movement of people from peripheral to core areas. The accession of the United Kingdom to the European Community in 1972 has enhanced the pre-eminence of the South East and has also accentuated the peripheral position of Northern Ireland. Set in this context, the net flow of more than 60,000 persons from Northern Ireland to Great Britain over the last intercensal period is not surprising.

The second general trend in distribution has been one of urban decentralisation and decline as population has shifted away from urban centres in search of more congenial residential living spaces. This process actually began in the 1930s in London, but subsequently spread to other large centres of population and most recently to the smaller cities and towns of the country. Several factors have contributed to the trend – the redevelopment of inner city areas, the associated development of suburban housing estates, the growing importance of private housing, the increasing number of households, rising car ownership; and the decentralisation of employment.

Seen in these terms, the 25 per cent drop in the population of Belfast
Local Government District between 1971 and 1981 is not remarkable, and
is, for example, no greater than the rate of decline recorded in Liverpool or
Glasgow for the same period (Compton, 1982). Nevertheless, the massive
reduction in the number of inhabitants of inner Belfast, as people have
migrated to the suburbs and beyond, has dominated the regional redistribution of population in Northern Ireland in recent years (Table 12.3). For
one thing, loss from inner Belfast has only been partly compensated by
population growth in suburban residential areas and as a result the
built-up area of the city suffered a substantial overall loss of population
amounting to around 15 per cent between 1971 and 1981. Furthermore
despite considerable population growth in the non-metropolitan parts of
the Greater Belfast region, this too has been insufficient to offset the loss of
pople from the city itself, with the result that the region as a whole has also
suffered an overall decline in population of the order of 5 to 7 per cent since
1971. By contrast, the populations of both the Fringe Bann and West of
Bann regions increased over the last intercensal period (terms explained in
footnote to Table 12.3). The most significant consequence of these regional
patterns of change is that the progressive concentration of the population of
Northern Ireland in the Greater Belfast Region has not only come to a halt
in recent years but has moved into reverse for the first time this century.
Thus between 1971 and 1981 the proportion of the total population residing
in the Greater Belfast region dropped from 52.7 to 49.5 per cent; by

Table 12.3
The distribution of population and components of population change by region,
1971–81

	1971	1981	Distribution (per cent)		Actual change 1971–81 per cent	Natural increase 1971–81 per cent	Net migration 1971–81 per cent
			1971	1981			
Greater Belfast (1)							
1. Belfast Local Government District	416,679	314,000	27.1	20.5	−24.6	1.2	−25.8
2. Fringe Belfast – inner ring	392,343	444,800	25.5	29.0	13.4	7.5	5.9
3. Belfast built-up area	612,570	519,500	39.9	33.8	−15.2	—	—
4. Rest of Fringe Belfast	198,452	239,300	12.8	15.6	20.6	—	—
1 & 2 The Region	809,022	758,800	52.7	49.4	−6.2	4.2	−10.4
Fringe Bann – intermediate ring (2)							
The Region	272,862	296,200	17.8	19.3	8.6	7.8	0.8
West of Bann – outer ring (3)							
The Region	454,181	480,000	29.6	31.3	5.7	11.4	−5.7
Northern Ireland	1,536,065	1,535,000	100.0	100.0	−0.1	7.0	−7.1

(1) The Greater Belfast Region comprises the following local government districts: Antrim, Ards, Belfast,
    Carrickfergus, Castlereagh, Larne, Lisburn, Newtownabbey and North Down.
(2) Fringe Bann includes: Ballymena, Ballymoney, Banbridge, Coleraine, Craigavon, Down and Moyle.
(3) West of Bann includes: Armagh, Cookstown, Dungannon, Fermanagh, Limavady, Londonderry,
    Magherafelt, Newry and Mourne, Omagh and Strabane.

contrast, in Fringe Bann it rose from 17.7 to 19.0 per cent and in West of Bann from 29.6 to 31.5 per cent over the same period (Table 12.3).

A closer examination of the geographical patterns serves to illustrate both the complexities of the spatial processes of change as well as to exemplify the generalities discussed above. In Figure 12.2, where the pattern of change between 1971 and 1981 has been mapped at ward level, the decentralisation of population away from Belfast and the corresponding build-up in the surrounding countryside and towns of north Down and south Antrim is clearly depicted. Moreover, in conformity with the general United Kingdom model, decentralisation of population away from the other main urban centres is also visible. Thus, inner Londonderry, like Belfast, has also lost population as have, for example, inner Newry and Coleraine. Depopulation now occurs only in the more remote rural areas.

Religious composition

The census of population has conventionally been the one comprehensive source of authoritative statistics on religious affiliation in Northern Ireland. However, the religious data published in the two most recent censuses are of doubtful reliability because of the refusal of a substantial section of the population to state their denomination; in all there were 142,500 refusals in 1971 and 274,584 in 1981. The figures as enumerated must therefore be corrected before trends and patterns can be analysed (Compton, 1985b).

Although corrected figures are subject to a margin of error, and the percentage breakdown of the population by major denomination presented in Table 12.4 are treated therefore with caution, there can be no doubt about the broad advance of the Catholic population in recent years. Thus

Table 12.4

Population change by religious affiliation – 1926–81

Intercensal period	Roman Catholics			All Other Denominations			Religious Break-down per cent Roman Catholic
	No. at beginning of period	Change Number	Per cent per annum	No. at beginning of period	Change Number	Per cent per annum	
1926–37	420,428	7,862	0.17	826,133	15,322	0.17	33.7
1937–51	428,290	43,170	0.68	851,455	48,006	0.39	33.5
1951–61	471,460	26,087	0.54	899,461	28,034	0.31	34.4
1961–71	497,547	62,253	1.19	927,495	32,805	0.35	34.9
1971–81	559.800	26,600	0.47	960,300	−19,600	−0.21	36.8
1981–*	586,400	—	—	940,700	—	—	38.4

* Estimated value

Source: *Northern Ireland Census of population* (various); Compton and Power, 1986.

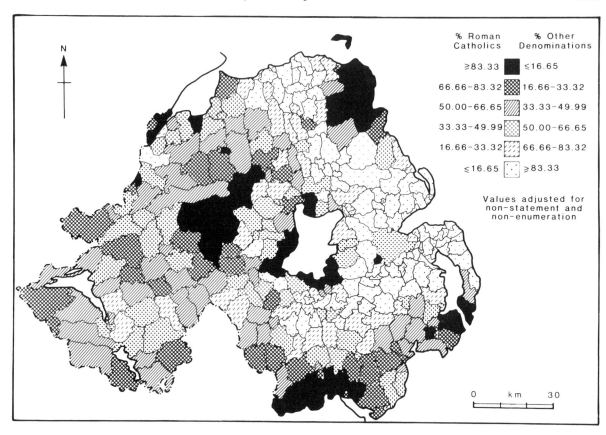

% Roman   % Other
Catholics   Denominations

≥83.33   ■   ≤16.65

66.66-83.32 ▨ 16.66-33.32

50.00-66.65 ▧ 33.33-49.99

33.33-49.99 ▦ 50.00-66.65

16.66-33.32 ▨ 66.66-83.32

≤16.65   ⋰   ≥83.33

Values adjusted for
non-statement and
non-enumeration

0   k m   30

Figure 12.3 Religious
distribution in 1981.

between 1961 and 1981, the estimates suggest that the number of Catholics grew at a rate ten times faster than the non-Catholic population – that is by around 18 and 1.5 per cent respectively – and now (1986) comprises around 40 per cent of the total compared with 34.9 per cent in 1961. As both groups have suffered from persistent net out-migration, Catholics more so than non-Catholics, the faster rate of Catholic growth is to be attributed to their substantially higher birth rate and consequently higher rate of natural increase.

The geographical distributions of Catholics and non-Catholics are quite distinctive, and there are clearly many areas of the province where the two communities are highly segregated (Compton, 1978). Three regions, generally areas of sparse population, can be distinguished where Catholics comprise the bulk of the population, i.e. in excess of 80 per cent of the total, namely in the western and central parts of Newry and Mourne district, mid-Ulster, and northeast Antrim (Figure 12.3). Additionally isolated areas of predominantly Catholic persuasion are to be found along the western and southern shores of Lough Neagh, at the southern tip of the Ards Peninsula, along the Fermanagh border with the Irish Republic, in and around Londonderry in the northwest, but most importantly in west Belfast, where between one quarter and one third of all Northern Ireland

Catholics are to be found. In contrast to the scattered nature of predominantly Catholic areas, Protestants comprise the bulk of the population in the east-central region of Northern Ireland. Outside this region, they form the majority in only isolated parts of the west, notably around Londonderry, Cookstown and Enniskillen.

As regards the cities and principal towns of the province, 14 may be described as predominantly Protestant – Belfast, Donaghadee, Ballyclare, Bangor, Newtownards, Dromore, Ballymoney, Whitehead, Coleraine,

Table 12.5

Estimated change in religious composition by local government districts: 1971 to 1981

Local government districts	Roman Catholics			Other denominations			Denominational breakdown			
	Number		Per cent change 1971–82[1]	Number		Per cent change 1971–81[1]	Roman Catholics		Other denominations	
	1971	1981		1971	1981		1981	1981[1]	1971	1981[1]
Antrim	10,400	14,800	42.5	23,000	30,000	30.0	31.1	33.0	68.9	67.0
Ards	7,500	7,500	−0.0	39,200	50,200	28.0	16.0	13.0	84.0	87.0
Armagh	20,300	22,900	13.0	25,300	26,200	3.5	44.5	46.5	55.5	53.5
Ballymena	8,600	10,400	21.0	40,100	44,200	10.0	17.7	19.0	82.3	81.0
Ballymoney	6,500	6,700	3.0	15,400	16,300	6.0	29.6	29.0	70.4	71.0
Banbridge	8,900	8,600	3.5	19,700	21,500	9.0	31.2	28.5	68.8	71.5
Belfast	140,200	118,600	−15.5	270,900	193,700	−28.5	34.1	38.0	65.9	62.0
Carrickfergus	4,400	2,300	−47.5	22,600	26,200	16.0	16.2	8.0	83.8	92.0
Castlereagh	6,500	4,800	−26.0	57,700	56,100	−3.0	10.1	8.0	89.9	92.0
Coleraine	10,600	11,100	4.5	33,600	35,500	5.5	23.9	24.0	76.1	76.0
Cookstown	12,800	14,900	16.5	13,200	13,400	1.5	49.2	52.5	50.8	47.5
Craigavon	26,100	30,800	18.0	41,300	42,200	2.0	38.7	42.0	61.3	58.0
Down	25,100	31,600	26.0	21,300	21,500	1.0	54.1	59.5	45.9	40.5
Dungannon	22,200	23,200	4.5	20,300	20,500	1.0	52.3	53.0	47.7	47.0
Fermanagh	26,600	28,100	5.5	24,000	23,300	−3.5	52.5	54.5	47.5	45.5
Larne	8,000	7,000	−12.5	21,700	21,800	−1.0	26.8	24.5	73.2	75.5
Limavady	12,100	14,700	21.5	11,000	12,300	12.0	52.4	54.5	47.6	45.5
Lisburn	11,500	18,700	62.5	57.700	65,100	13.0	16.6	22.5	83.4	78.5
Derry	53,600	60,800	13.5	29,800	28,000	−6.0	64.3	68.5	35.7	37.5
Magherafelt	17,200	18,400	7.0	14,200	14,100	−0.5	54.7	56.5	45.3	43.5
Moyle	6,800	7,300	7.5	7,100	7,000	−1.5	48.7	51.0	51.3	49.0
Newry & Mourne	51,400	56,500	10.0	20,600	19,900	−3.5	71.4	74.0	28.6	26.0
Newtownabbey	11,900	9,800	−17.5	54,300	62,200	14.5	18.0	13.5	82.0	86.5
North Down	5,900	6,100	3.5	46,000	59,900	30.0	11.3	9.0	88.7	91.0
Omagh	25,200	28,600	13.5	15,400	15,500	1.0	62.1	65.0	37.9	35.0
Strabane	19,500	22,100	13.5	14,800	14,100	−4.5	56.9	61.0	43.1	39.0
All Districts	559,800	586,400[2]	5.0	960,300	940,700[2]	−2.0	36.8	38.5	63.2	61.5[2]

[1] Rounded to the nearest 0.5 per cent.

[2] The marginal difference between these values and those given in Compton (1985b) are due to the use of homogeneous enumeration districts as opposed to homogeneous electoral wards in apportioning those refusing to state a denomination, and to the assumption of 45,000 non-enumerated persons as opposed to 46,000 non-enumerated persons.

Ballymena, Portadown, Kilkeel, Banbridge and Larne – while five are predominantly Catholic – Newry, Dungiven, Warrenpoint, Strabane and Londonderry. In Maghera, Newcastle, Enniskillen and Lurgan the populations are evenly balanced.

Since any evaluation of recent geographical change in denominational composition must be based on estimated figures, the findings discussed here can only be tentative. At district council level, the most clear-cut changes between 1971 and 1981 involved Cookstown and Moyle where small Protestant majorities in 1971 had been supplanted by equally small Catholic majorities in 1981 (Compton and Power, 1986). As a consequence, the number of districts with Protestant majorities dropped from 17 in 1971 to 15 in 1981, while the number with Catholic majorities rose from 9 to 11 (Table 12.5). However, changes of equal or even greater magnitude, although not affecting the majority/minority position are also suggested for Down, Londonderry, Fermanagh, Magherafelt, Newry and Mourne, Strabane, Armagh, Dungannon, Limavady and Omagh where moderate to high rates of Catholic increase combined with either static or modest rises in non-Catholic numbers. Such population dynamics have, of course, brought about a marked increase in the Catholic proportion in all of these districts.

By contrast, the non-Catholic population increased most rapidly in the districts fringing Belfast; between 1971 and 1981 growth in excess of 10 per cent was accompanied by a fall in Catholic numbers in Banbridge, Carrickfergus and Newtownabbey, and by a static Catholic population in Ards and North Down. Accordingly, these were districts where the Catholic proportion fell quite sharply. To these may be added Larne, Castlereagh, Ballymoney and Coleraine where the population dynamics again favoured non-Catholics.

These trends point to the emergency of greater denominational segregation at the macro-scale during the 1970s (Table 12.6); hence, all districts with Roman Catholic majorities in 1971 had become more Catholic by 1981. Similarly the majority Protestant areas also tended to become more Protestant with the notable exceptions of the districts of Belfast, Craigavon and Armagh. Furthermore there is some evidence of the physical retreat of Protestants from border districts. What is therefore suggested by the estimates is a relative retrenchment of Protestants in the east around Belfast, whereas Catholic expansion appears to be occurring elsewhere. What we are clearly witnessing is a demographic response to 18 years of political tension and uncertainty.

Fertility

For more than 40 years, the Northern Ireland birth rate has charted a broad cyclic trend with troughs occurring in the mid-1950s (29,000 live births) and in the mid-1970s (25,500 live births) while peaks have been recorded in the mid- to late 1940s (32,000 live births) and in the mid-1960s (34,500 live births) (Figure 12.1). It is in the very regularity of these cycles of roughly one generation in amplitude that an explanation can be found. Thus the small birth cohorts of the 1950s provided the parents of the small birth cohorts of the mid-1970s, while the large birth cohorts of the 1940s likewise were the parents of the large birth cohorts of the mid-1960s. In other words, in the absence of marked changes in family size, there is invariably a direct association between the size of a generation of parents and the number of their offspring. This has been termed the "echo effect", and it would lead us to expect the upturn in the birth rate since 1977, although apparently faltering in the early 1990s, to continue for a few years yet because a consequence of the rising birth rate of the late 1950s and early 1960s is an expansion of the population of reproductive age until the end of the decade.

Table 12.6

Population change in majority catholic and non-catholic regions 1971–81

Region	Number		Per-centage	Distri-bution	Per cent change	Per cent	Roman Catholics
	1971	1981	1971	1981	1971–81	1971	1981
O.D. Majority Region							
Roman Catholics	276,300	280,200	18.9	18.3	−2.5	27.2	27.2
Other Denominations	768,500	751,100	50.6	49.2	−2.3		
R.C. Majority Region							
Roman Catholics	272,500	306,200	17.9	20.1	12.4	58.7	61.8
Other Denominations	191,800	189,600	12.6	12.4	−1.1		

Source: Compton and Power, 1986.

In this cyclic pattern, the Northern Ireland birth rate has mirrored the trend in Great Britain – indeed the most recent peak of 1964 and the trough of 1977 exactly coincide in the two areas – although the local rate has always been substantially higher. In fact the gap has tended to widen in recent years and Northern Ireland now accounts for around 3.8 per cent of United Kingdom births compared with roughly 3.5 per cent during the 1960s.

An analysis of birth rates by age of mother helps illuminate these general trends. Thus it is clear from Table 12.7 that the local birth rate is higher than in Great Britain because the fertility of Northern Ireland women is higher across the whole age range, with the exception of women under the age of 20 where the high rate of illegitimacy in Great Britain becomes a factor. It is also apparent that the disparity widens with age so that for women aged 30 and over the Northern Ireland rate is now roughly double that in Great Britain. In other words, not only do Northern Ireland women have more children than their counterparts in Great Britain but they also go on bearing children to a later stage in their reproductive lives (Compton, 1986).

Table 12.7

Estimated age specific birth rates and total fertility rates 1970–1, 1974, 1977, 1980 and 1984 and comparison with Great Britain in 1984.

| | Age Group | | | | | | | |
	15–19	20–24	25–29	30–34	35–29	40–44	45–49	TFR(1)
1970–71	35	175	200	135	75	25	2	3.23
1974	35	150	175	110	55	20	1	2.73
1977	30	130	175	105	50	15	1	2.53
1980	30	145	180	120	55	13	1	2.72
1984	28	125	165	115	50	12	1	2.48
Percentage Change								
1970–71 to 1977	−14	−25	−12	−22	−33	−40	—	−22
1977 to 1980	0	+12	+3	+14	+10	−13	—	+8
1980 to 1984	−7	−14	−8	−4	−9	−7	—	−9
Great Britain								
1984	28	96	126	73	24	5		1.76
Ratio NI/GB × 100	100	130	131	158	208	—		1.41

(1) TFR – total fertility rate. The total fertility rate is the enumeration of the age specific birth rates. It shows the average number of children that a woman would produce if she bore children at those rates throughout her child-bearing life.

Sources: *Northern Ireland Census 1971:* Fertility Tables, Registrar General for Northern Ireland, *Annual Reports 1974–81*. Figures for 1984 are provisional.

The age specific rates also show that the most recent phase of fertility decline was greatest for oldest women. It was also greater for women under the age of 25 than for those aged 25-29, which suggests that the progressive deferment of births by young married couples was an important mechanism behind the decline. Deferment may in part have reflected a perceived worsening of economic conditions although there is no direct evidence to this effect. It may be noted that the decline in the fertility of women under the age of 25 would have been even steeper but for a sharp rise in the rate of illegitimacy.

Although the post-1977 recovery in the number of births is partly a function of a favourable shift in age structure, it was also associated with a rise in the actual fertility of all women under the age of 40, at least up to 1980, and by a marked increase in third and fourth order births. The recovery has, however, petered out since 1980 and, given the continued favourable shift in age structure, strongly suggests that we have entered a further phase of fertility decline.

The limited family size data available can be used to complement this brief discussion of trends in the Northern Ireland birth rate. The evidence suggests that average family size has fallen from around 4.7 children for

SOCIAL CLASS AND FAMILY SIZE

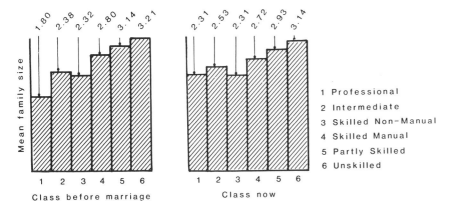

INCOME AND FAMILY SIZE

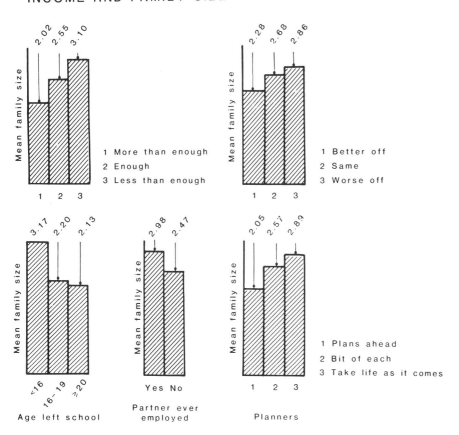

Figure 12.4 Fertility classified by social characteristics.

women marrying between 1900 and 1914 to about 2.5 children now. The evidence also suggests that, in marked contrast to the cyclic nature of the birth rate, the decline in family size has followed a reasonably consistent downward trend, although there have, of course, been periods of faster decline interspersed with periods of comparative stability or even resurgence in family size.

It is also clear that average family size in Northern Ireland remains substantially larger than in Great Britain. There are various reasons for this that include the greater importance of agriculture and hence of rurality in Northern Ireland, the more limited participation of women in the labour force, the ethos of the Catholic minority that favours large families, the impact of decades of emigration, a higher level of poverty and the occupational and social class composition of the population (Coward, 1981).

Current family size differentials are becoming clearer as the first results from the Northern Ireland Fertility Survey (NIFS) and the Continuous Household Survey (CHS) are published (Compton and Coward, 1987). The most salient findings are as follows. Firstly, although average family size in Northern Ireland continues to decline, NIFS suggests an overall drop of about 5 per cent between 1971 and 1983 from 2.78 to 2.65 children, the disparity with England and Wales still remains. As regards the religious differential, both surveys show that the gap has narrowed since 1971. For ever-married women under the age of 60, NIFS indicates that average Catholic family size has declined by 0.4 chidren from 3.64 in 1971 to 3.24 in 1983. The corresponding figures for other denominations are a decline of 0.08 children from 2.37 in 1971 to 2.29 in 1983. The religious differential in family size would therefore appear to have narrowed from 1.27 to 0.95 children (Compton and Coward, 1985).

As for other differentials, NIFS suggests the persistence of an inverse relationship with income, not so much with the actual amount of income coming into the family as with perceived income in relation to peer groups and with its adequacy. Educational attainment is also inversely associated with family size, as is the degree to which individuals plan their lives. Furthermore, those who at some stage during their working lives have been out of work have larger families than those who have not, while a reasonably clear inverse exists with social class (Figure 12.4). How these differentials should be interpreted will become clearer as more results from NIFS are published.

Mortality

In recent years the Northern Ireland crude death rate has fluctuated narrowly around an average value of 10.5 per 1000 population (Figure 12.1). It has also been consistently lower than in Great Britain – in 1983, for instance, the rate in England was 11.6, in Scotland 12.3, and in Wales 12.6, but in Northern Ireland only 10.2 per 1,000 population. However, because it is greatly influenced by population age structure, the crude death rate is a poor measure of actual mortality and therefore of the health of a

Opera House, Belfast   *Arts Council Northern Ireland*

Belfast can offer a very comprehensive range of indoor and outdoor activities to its visitors and citizens.

The Northern Ireland Arts Council sponsors entertainment of international standard, in the recently restored Belfast Opera House with its refurbished Matcham interior. The exuberant gilded elephant theme reflects the high-Victorian period of Empire when Belfast grew most rapidly.

Glass House,
Botanic Gardens, Belfast

Belfast City Council

Belfast City Council Chamber

Belfast City Council

Another neglected Victorian gem of Belfast's heritage was the curvilinear glass-house in the Botanic Gardens. It too has been restored to its former glory and delights the eye with its beauty of form and its horticultural content, thanks to Belfast City Parks Department.

Belfast's City Council can be seen below – perhaps approving the urban tree planting scheme which is doing so much to enhance the city's streets.

Mary Peters Track, Belfast   *Sports Council Northern Ireland*

At the annual Ulster Games in 1986. The Games are sponsored by a local Dairy and held in the arena constructed largely through the efforts of Ulster's Olympic Gold Medallist, Mary Peters.

The Province is unusually well provided with athletics and sports facilities of every kind, and has more indoor recreation centres per head of population than anywhere else in the British Isles. Sports activities and facilities are co-ordinated and grant-aided through the Northern Ireland Sports Council.

Ann Street, Belfast   *Belfast City Council*

Lunch time bustle in Ann Street, one of Belfast's central pedestrian areas. Shopping is a universal activity, catered for here by a wide range of small shops on the right with some historic 'entries' (narrow alleys) leading into Belfast's older heart-land.

population. Suffice it to say that age standardisation demonstrates that the real level of mortality in Northern Ireland is about the same as in Scotland but substantially higher than in either England or Wales (Table 12.8). This broad regional disparity has been attributed to a variety of economic, social and lifestyle factors, including lower living standards and a higher incidence of poverty in Northern Ireland and of course in Scotland, together with differences in diet, consumption of alcohol and smoking habits.

The principal characteristic of recent change is that female mortality has continued to decline more rapidly than that of males and as a result the very clear sex differential in favour of females has widened further in recent years. These trends are best summarised in terms of life expectancy (Table 12.9). Thus since 1950 the advance in female life expectancy at birth has been roughly twice that recorded by males; while at age 65 females have recorded a further substantial gain, little change has occurred in male life expectancy. The consequence of this trend is that the sex differential in mortality is now equivalent to 6 years of additional life at birth for females and to just under 4 additional years of life at age 65.

Table 12.8

Standardised mortality ratios, 1971, 1977 and 1982 (UK = 100)

	1971		1977		1982	
	Males	Females	Males	Females	Males	Females
England } Wales	99	99	99	99	98 115	98 103
Scotland	109	109	111	109	115	115
Northern Ireland	104	109	118	119	106	109

Source: *OPCS Mortality Statistics.*

Table 12.9

Trends in life expectancy

	At Birth		At Age 65	
	Males	Females	Males	Females
1950–52	65.5	68.8	12.1	13.5
1960–62	67.6	72.4	12.2	14.4
1970–72	67.6	73.7	12.0	15.2
1976–78	67.8	74.1	11.8	15.3
1981–83	70.1	76.0	12.6	16.3

Source: *Registrar General of Northern Ireland Annual Reports* (various).

Heart disease is the single most important cause of death followed by cancer and cerebrovascular disease. As regards differences by sex, cancer accounts for a slightly higher and cerebrovascular disease for a very much higher portion of deaths among women than men. Specific causes that have shown the greatest relative change in recent times are pneumonia and lung cancer which have risen sharply whereas deaths from bronchitis and infectious diseases have dropped away.

Viewed in the United Kingdom context, circulatory disease mortality in Northern Ireland is substantially above the national average and within this the situation with regard to ischaemic heart disease is somewhat worse than for other types of heart disease. Respiratory disease mortality is also above the national average, more so for females than males, as is mortality from congenital abnormalities, motor accidents and accidental poisonings and falls. The only important area in which Northern Ireland shows up rather well, particularly for males, is in the comparatively low rate of mortality from cancers, notably lung cancer. Patterns of cause of death are discussed in more detail in Compton 1986.

Although infant mortality continues to be significantly higher than in England and Wales, notable advances have been made in recent years and the rate was more than halved between 1960 and 1984, declining from 27.2 to 10.5 per 1,000 live births. In demographic terms, this improvement has largely occurred at the neo-natal stage and may be correlated with some rise in living standards despite unemployment, together with better hospital provision and health education. The reduction in the fertility of older women and the decline in the number of high parity births has also assisted in this process.

Migration

Between 1951 and 1981, Northern Ireland lost some 250,000 individuals net as a result of out-migration. The rate of loss, however, fluctuated during these 30 years and was high during the 1950s and 1970s, but very much lower during the 1960s, and seems to have broadly mirrored the relative fortunes of the local economy. Yet the more detailed trend of recent years depicted in Table 12.10 shows that this relationship with the economy may now be a loose one for as unemployment has risen since the mid-1970s, so the rate of net outflow has tended to decline. Table 12.10 also breaks down recent net migration into its Great Britain, Republic of Ireland and Rest of World components, geared to an estimated net out-flow of 110,000 between 1971 and 1981 – 63,000 to Great Britain, 19,000 to the Republic of Ireland and 28,000 to the Rest of the World.

Clearly, therefore, it is not just the performance of the local economy that explains these trends; opportunities outside Northern Ireland have also exerted a powerful influence. Hence it was "pull" factors sucking labour from Northern Ireland into a buoyant Britain as well as to other parts of the world, as much as a lack of opportunity at home, that accounted for the high rate of net out-migration during the 1950s. Nor, it may be presumed, would the rate of out-flow during the early 1970s have been so high had it not been for the continued existence of opportunities in Great Britain, as well as in the Republic of Ireland following its accession to the European Community. The fall off in net out-migration in recent years should not therefore be interpreted as some fundamental slackening of the desire to migrate. Rather it reflects the lack of opportunity at those destinations that have traditionally attracted migrants from Northern Ireland. In addition, overshadowing the migration of the last 18 years has been the "troubles" with their generally depressing effect and negative impact on job creation (Chapter 10).

Information about the characteristics of migrants from Northern Ireland is rather fragmentary. Traditionally it was largely the unskilled who migrated but this now seems to be changing. Thus a significant component of the gross out-flow to Great Britain is now made up of students going on to higher education. It is believed that the majority of these never return to Northern Ireland on completing their studies. The Great Britain census migration reports for 1981 (OPCS 19) also suggest that migrants from Northern Ireland are more likely to be economically active and less likely to be seeking work than the Northern Ireland population at large. Moreover, of migrants who are employees, a higher proportion are employees supervising others and a much higher proportion are apprentices and trainees. Furthermore, there have been as many skilled manual as semi- and unskilled manual workers among recent migrants to Britain, while the number of migrants in managerial and professional positions exceeds both these groups. These data provide the firm impression that migrants are now predominantly from the skilled segment of the population. But how far

Table 12.10

Net migration estimates, 1971–72, to 1982–83

Year	Number (in 00s)	Rate per 1,000	Balance with Rest of UK Number (in 00s)	Balance with Irish Republic Number (in 00s)	Balance with Rest of World Number (in 00s)
1971–72	−15,8	−10.3	−9,1	−2,7	−4,0
1972–73	−16,6	−10.8	−8,3	−2,6	−5,7
1973–74	−13,8	−9.0	−8,3	−2,4	−3,1
1974–75	−11,8	−7.7	−6,6	−2,2	−3,0
1975–76	−11,7	−7.7	−6,6	−1,9	−3,2
1976–77	−10,9	−7.1	−7,3	−1,8	−2,8
1977–78	−9,8	−6.4	−5,4	−1,6	−2,8
1978–79	−5,7	−3.7	−4,3	−1,3	−0,1
1979–80	−6,2	−4.0	−4,2	−1,3	−0,7
1980–81	−7,5	−4.9	−4,0	−1,2	−2,3
1981–82	−7,1	−4.6	—	—	—
1982–83(1)	−7,0(1)	−4.5(1)	—	—	—

(1) Data for 1982–83 are provisional.

Sources: Northern Ireland Registrar General: *Annual Reports 1972–82;* OPCS *International Migration 1974–82.*

this represents a real drain on Northern Ireland is difficult to assess without corresponding information about incomers to the province.

As regards the internal mobility of population the rate of movement declined during the 1970s; hence, whereas 8.7 per cent of individuals changed residence in the year preceding the 1971 census this had dropped to 5.6 per cent by 1981. As the majority of moves occur within the same local government district, the bulk of internal migrations may be described as short distance and probably occur for reasons other than those of employment, for example for reasons of housing, marriage and so on. Longer distance internal migration is largely directed towards the Greater Belfast Region, although not to Belfast itself.

Summary

The demography of Northern Ireland contains both British and Irish elements, which derive from the religious divisions within its population. As a result the province's crude birth and death rates as well as the rate of natural increase lie roughly mid-way between the coresponding rates for Great Britain and the Republic of Ireland. Because of the variability of net migration, actual population change has not always accorded with this simple model.

The study of recent population change is hindered by the unreliability of the 1981 census. It is known from the registers of births and deaths that natural increase, while remaining well above the Great Britain level, declined throughout much of the 1970s. Nonetheless, it still amounted to more than 100,000 persons over the last intercensal period, although this was almost exactly counter-balanced by the rate of net out-migration to give an essentially static population between 1971 and 1981. In regard to regional distribution, because the city of Belfast has lost one fifth of its people in recent years, the proportion of the Northern Ireland population residing in the Greater Belfast Region is now declining for the first time this century. This has brought to a halt the progressive concentration of population in the east of the province, and has resulted in some resurgence of numbers west of the Bann.

In recent years, the religious composition of the popultion has been marked by a sharp upward trend in the Roman Catholic proportion, which is now thought to amount to around 40 per cent of the total. Moreover, greater segregation by religious persuasion appears to be emerging at the macro-scale, with existing majority-Catholic areas becoming more Catholic and most majority-Protestant areas becoming more Protestant.

Since the end of the Second World War, the birth rate has followed a broad cyclic trend, whereas the crude death rate, after an initial decline, has remained essentially static. The sharp decline in the number of births in the United Kingdom between 1964 and 1977, was mirrored exactly in Northern Ireland, as has been the rather halting recovery since then. Although the province's crude death rate is lower than in Great Britain, this is entirely accounted for by the lower average age of the Northern

Ireland population. The real level of mortality, which measures the intrinsic health of the population, is substantially higher than in England and Wales but about the same as in Scotland. Information about migration is fairly rudimentary. The rate of internal movement appears to have declined markedly since the early 1970s. Net out-migration is also now very much lower than a decade ago although this has not been brought about by a reduction in the potential to migrate, but rather because of a lack of opportunities at the traditional destinations of Northern Ireland migrants.

References

Census of Ireland 1981, 1982. *Population of Ireland*. 1. Dublin.

Compton, Paul, 1978. *Northern Ireland – a census atlas*. Dublin.

Compton, Paul, 1982. The changing population, *in* R.J. Johnston and J.C. Doornkamp, (eds.), *The changing geography of the United Kingdom*. London. 37-74.

Compton, Paul, 1985a. The 1981 Northern Ireland Census of Population – estimates of non-enumerated population, *in Non-enumeration in the 1981 Northern Ireland Census of Population*, Policy Planning and Research Unit (Social Division), Occasional Paper no. 9. 24-40.

Compton, Paul, 1985b. An evaluation of the changing religious composition of the population in Northern Ireland, *in Economic and Social Review*, 201-224.

Compton, Paul, 1986. *Demographic trends in Northern Ireland*. Northern Ireland Economic Council, Report 57. Belfast.

Compton, Paul, Coward, John and Wilson-Davis, Keith, 1985. Family size and religious denomination in Northern Ireland, *in Journal of Biosocial Science*, 137-146.

Compton, Paul and Power, John, 1986. Estimates of the religious composition of Northern Ireland local government districts in 1981 and change in the geographial pattern of religious composition between 1971 and 1981, *in Economic and Social Review*, 87-106.

Compton, Paul and Coward, John, 1987. Fertility in Northern Ireland, Final ESRC Report (unpublished).

Coward, John, 1981. Ideal family size in Northern Ireland, *in Journal of Biosocial Science*, 443.

Inter-departmental Working Group on Census Revision, 1985. The 1981 Northern Ireland Census of Population – estimates of non-enumeration, *in Non-enumeration in the 1981 Northern Ireland Census of Population*. Policy Planning and Research Unit (Social Division), Occasional Paper no. 9, 8-23.

Morris, Chris and Compton, Paul, 1985. 1981 Census of Population in Northern Ireland, *in Population Trends* 40, Office of Population Censuses and Surveys, HMSO.

Northern Ireland Census of Population 1926. (1929). *General Report*.

Northern Ireland Census of Population 1937. (1939). *General Report*.

Northern Ireland Census of Population 1951. (1955). *General Report*.

Northern Ireland Census of Population 1961. (1965). *General Report*.

Northern Ireland Census of Population 1971. (1975). *Summary Tables*.

Northern Ireland Census of Population 1981. (1983). *Summary Tables*.

Office of Population Censuses and Surveys, *International Migration, United Kingdom, England and Wales*, (various), HMSO.

Office of Population Censuses and Surveys. (1986) *Population Trends* 43, table 1, 41.

Office of Population Censuses and Surveys. *Mortality Statistics*, table 13, (various).

Office of Population Censuses and Surveys and Registrar General Scotland (1983). *National Migration. Great Britain part 1*, London.

Registrar General of Northern Ireland, Annual Reports (various). Belfast.

Religion & Employment

R. D. OSBORNE

Senior Lecturer in Department of Social Administration and Policy,
University of Ulster at Jordanstown, and Associate Director, Policy Research Institute

This chapter aims to provide an assessment of Northern Ireland's occupational and employment structure and is concerned in particular with the different occupational and employment profiles of Protestants and Catholics. The appreciation of the nature of labour market differences between the two communities in Northern Ireland is central to the understanding of contemporary Northern Ireland society. Moreover, the objective of achieving full equality of employment opportunity between Protestants and Catholics has represented a significant aim of public policy over the past decade. The last ten years has also seen a major increase in information and analyses concerned with examining these issues thereby enabling a much more detailed consideration of the topic to be undertaken. This chapter will draw upon the growing output of social science research and the findings of the Fair Employment Agency (FEA), the body responsible for eliminating employment discrimination and promoting equality of employment opportunity between Protestants and Catholics. While the concern will be mainly with describing differences in the labour market circumstances of the two communities, a brief evaluation of policy will also be undertaken.

The approach in this chapter is to look at patterns of advantage and disadvantage in the distribution of jobs between Protestants and Catholics. The approach has been described as that of political arithmetic, that is the identification and measurement of inequalities of opportunity and the degree to which social policies have either directly or indirectly enhanced or restricted the growth of opportunities, (Cormack & Osborne, 1983). The guiding yardstick in measuring these distributions is that of *equality of opportunity*. The principle of equality of opportunity has been central to many progressive social policies pursued in the post-war period and political arithmetic has been primarily engaged in investigating the handicaps which diminish the opportunities available to specific groups in the population. Classically, in Britain, this has been concerned with social class but more recently gender and race have become a further focus of attention. In the Northern Ireland context it is religion which is of particular concern.

The situation prior to 1971

The recognition of the nature of the different labour market profiles of Protestants and Catholics in Northern Ireland can be attributed to the seminal work of Edmund Aunger in his detailed analysis of the 1971 population census (Aunger, 1975). Prior to this, limited work by Barritt and Carter (1962) found four different situations in the private sector:

(i) firms which only employed individuals from one community;
(ii) Protestant owned firms which employed Catholics only in lower paid jobs but not in supervisory positions;
(iii) firms employing Protestants and Catholics but segregating them by departments;
(iv) firms which mix members of the two communities within the same department.

Barritt and Carter, however, were unable to derive an overall measure of distortion in employment patterns produced by these practices. With regard to the public sector, they noted considerable under-representation of Catholics in the civil service and the widespread existence of discrimination in local authorities, both in employment and in housing allocations. Gallagher (1957) provides more detailed figures for employment patterns particularly in relation to local authority employment which Whyte (1983) has suggested are reliable. The Campaign for Social Justice were also active in collecting data particularly about the practices of local authorities in the 1960s. Rose (1971), using survey data (sample size, 1291) suggested that, whatever the case in particular areas, there was no discernible aggregate discrimination against Catholics in either the provision of public housing or public employment. Rose's conclusions conflict with most other observers of the period and may stem from a sample of respondents biased towards the middle class, especially in the case of Catholics. The official commission of inquiry set up to investigate the causes of civil disturbances at the end of the 1960s, the Cameron Commission (1969), suggested that "Social and economic grievances or abuses of political power were in a very real sense an immediate and operative cause of the demonstrations and consequent disorders after 1968."

Of course, aside from these attempts to assess employment patterns and practices, and the allocation of public housing, beliefs about malpractices or the evenhandedness of officials, were firmly entrenched in the two communities. On the one hand, Nationalist MPs routinely alleged discrimination against Catholics while Unionists equally firmly rejected such suggestions, although, as Nelson (1973) suggests, some Protestants would privately acknowledge discrimination, but argue that it was unavoidable when the minority challenged the existence of the state.

In recent years some attention has been given to attempting to assess the period up to 1971 both in terms of the record of the Unionist administrations and in terms of seeking to assess employment patterns and rates of social mobility earlier in the century. Whyte's (1983) assessment provides the most balanced review currently available and covers other areas as well as employment. His concerns are mainly with the policies and practices of Unionist central and local administrations and he concludes with a list of areas in order of demerit where discrimination was most prevalent: electoral practices, public employment, policing, private employment, public housing, regional policy. Whyte qualifies this list by suggesting that many of the sources of complaint stemmed from Unionist controlled local authorities especially in the west of the Province. Nevertheless he concludes: "The unionist government must bear its share of responsibility. It put through the original gerrymander which underpinned so many of the subsequent malpractices, and then, despite repeated protests did nothing to stop those malpractices continuing" (Whyte, 1983, 31).

Alongside the evaluation of governments and their policies, historians have been borrowing from the repertoires of sociologists to try and recreate the social structure of Belfast in 1901 and to attempt to evaluate patterns of social mobility in the earlier part of the century. Using the 1901 census, Hepburn and Collins (1981) provide a series of measures of religious segregation and industrial and occupational profiles of Protestants and Catholics for Belfast. The picture they reveal can be summarised in Tables 13.1 and 13.2.

Table 13.1

Industrial distribution by religion, Belfast, 1911
(Male household heads %)

	RC	OD
Construction	9	9
Manufacture	33	41
(engineering, shipbuilding, iron)	(9)	(16)
(textiles and dress)	(12)	(14)
Transport	10	9
Commerce	12	8
Financial services	2	5
General labourers	22	14
Public service, professional	8	6
Independent	1	1
Other	3	7
Total of sample	897	3,153

Note: OD includes all denominations except Roman Catholics
Source: Hepburn & Collins (1981)

Table 13.2

Social class by religion, Belfast, 1911
(Male household heads %)

	RC	OD	*Great Britain 1911
Classes I & II	13	13	15
Class III (non-manual)	8	12	7
Class III (manual)	31	35	33
Classes IV & V (semi-, unskilled)	36	45	—
Not classified	4	4	—
Total of sample	897	3,153	—

* From G. Routh 1965, *Occupations and pay in Great Britain, 1906–60*. Cambridge, 4–5.
Note: OD includes all denominations except Roman Catholics.
Source: Hepburn & Collins, 1981.

They note the lower proportion of Catholic male heads of household in manufacturing, predominantly because of low representation in engineering and shipbuilding. Higher figures are recorded in commercial occupations and shopkeeping, in general labouring, and marginally so in the public service and professions. Grouping occupations into social classes demonstrates, when compared with figures for Great Britain in 1911, that "the Catholic population of Belfast did not occupy an inferior position in relation to Britain as a whole, but rather that the Protestant population had obtained for itself a relatively advantaged position" (p. 226).

Hepburn (1983), using a random sample of manuscripts from the 1901 census and a sample of data from marriage register data from 1951, attempted to compare the socio-economic profiles of Protestants and Catholics and to assess the rates of social mobility at the two dates. Despite various problems associated with the data, Hepburn's conclusions firmly point to Catholic disadvantage in employment profiles and lower rates of upward social mobility:

> It is clear from our analysis that major differences existed in the employment profiles of Catholics and Protestants at the beginning of the century and that they did not, in general, narrow during the ensuing fifty years. The disadvantageous position which Catholics had increasingly slipped into during the second half of the nineteenth century was not alleviated during the first half of the twentieth ... The individual analysis of intergenerational mobility by religion confirms this general picture. (Hepburn, 1983, 61, 62)

Miller (1983) has also reported on a major analysis of social mobility drawing upon a large sample of adult males in Northern Ireland made in

1973-4. The survey of adults collected the employment histories of individuals and data relating to intergenerational mobility. The information spanned a substantial part of the twentieth century. Miller (1983, 76) concludes:

> In terms of the actual group experiences of mobility, the Catholic experience has been realised in a situation of somewhat of a disadvantage in origin exacerbated by a widening and clarified disadvantage in the present ... What the (above) results convincingly indicate is that it would be inaccurate and foolish to assume that present-day inequities are only legacies from the past that will somehow gradually fade into oblivion of their own volition.

These studies do not attempt to account for the patterns of advantage or disadvantage they reveal. They do reveal, however, that the patterns of relative advantage held by Protestants, and the disadvantage experienced by Catholics, were well established by the start of this century and showed little evidence of declining during the ensuing fifty or sixty years.

The situation in 1971

Much of the research reported above was sparked by the publication of Aunger's detailed analysis of the 1971 population census, the first cross-tabulation of census employment data by religion since 1911. The richness of Aunger's analysis laid out, for the first time, the detail of occupational, industrial and gender differences in the labour market between Protestants and Catholics. In summary Aunger suggested four dimensions of inequality: (a) skilled/unskilled: on the basis of "modal" averages, the "typical" Protestant male is a skilled worker, and the "typical" Catholic, unskilled; (b) employed/unemployed: although less than a third of the economically active population of Northern Ireland, Catholics constitute a majority of the unemployed; (c) masculine/feminine: occupations which can be identified as strongly Protestant tend to be male, while a significant number of those identifiable as disproportionately Catholic tend to be disproportionately female; (d) superordination/subordination: many of the occupations, involving levels of authority and influence, tend to be dominated by Protestants, while many of the lower status service occupations are disproportionately Catholic.

The crucial evidence of Aunger's analysis can be summarised in Tables 13.3-13.5. Table 13.3 shows the occupational class profiles of economically active men and women. This reveals that Protestants are disproportionately represented in non-manual and skilled manual occupations, while Catholics are disproportionately represented only in semi-skilled, unskilled and unemployed classes. While occupational disadvantage is evident for Catholics, it is also clear that a Catholic middle class does exist with 31 per cent of non-manual occupations although it is smaller than the 41 per cent of Protestants in those occupations. It is also apparent that the size of the Catholic middle class is substantially a product of meeting the

King William at the Battle of the Boyne: a familiar symbol of the Orange Order, here painted on the gable wall of a nineteenth century terrace in a Protestant area of west Belfast. (N.C. Mitchel)

needs of the Catholic community. Thus, 34 per cent of Catholics, in the professional and managerial class, are school teachers and clergymen compared to 19 per cent of Protestants in that class. On the other hand, Protestants show a much wider distribution in administration, finance and business services. These differences are even more marked when males alone are considered, emphasising the disadvantaged position of Catholic males. This is demonstrated particularly in Table 13.4 where Catholic males record the smallest proportion in non-manual occupations. Indeed, taking non-manual occupations, the majority of Protestants are male (69 per cent) while the majority of Catholics are female (51 per cent). Finally, when manual occupations are considered, Aunger observed a marked tendency for Catholics to predominate in lower status occupations in industries where they constitute a minority, and even in industries where they are more strongly represented. This is suggested in Table 13.5, where Catholics record lower proportions in low status occupations in both engineering, which has a low representation of Catholics, and in construction, which accounts for 40 per cent of Catholic male employment.

Table 13.3

Religion and Occupation Class (Men and Women), 1971 (%)

Occupational Class	Catholic	Protestant
Professional managerial	12	15
Lower grade, non-manual	19	26
Skilled manual	17	19
Semi-skilled manual	27	25
Unskilled, unemployed	25	15
N = 564, 682		

Notes: (i) based on those stating a religious affiliation and who are economically active
(ii) occupations classified on the Hall-Jones classification of occupations
(iii) this table omits two groups, farmers and the armed services

Source: Aunger (1975).

In drawing out these crucial differences it should be pointed out that the differences relate to *proportions*. As the above analysis makes clear not all Protestants are in secure well-paid jobs and not all Catholics are in the unskilled and semi-skilled categories.

It is difficult to do full justice to the comprehensiveness of Aunger's analysis in a brief summary. The publication of the paper coincided with the creation of the Fair Employment Agency (FEA) under the Fair Employment (Northern Ireland) Act of 1976 with a brief to promote equality of opportunity in employment and to secure the elimination of

Table 13.4

Non-Manual and Manual Occupations by Sex, 1971 (%)

	Non-Manual	Manual
Catholic men	21	79
Protestant men	33	67
Catholic women	48	52
Protestant women	55	45

Source: Aunger (1975).

employment discrimination. The FEA identified a need to keep both the patterns of employment identified by Aunger under review, but also to sponsor research to seek to identify those factors which might be contributing to patterns of advantage and disadvantage. As a result, far more has become known about changing employment patterns, unemployment and education than would have otherwise been the case. Moreover, the work of the FEA, in using its powers of investigation, has begun to reveal the detail of employment practices both generally and in specific employment situations. In the following section these areas are examined.

Unemployment

The 1971 census revealed that unemployment was substantially higher for Catholics than Protestants. Overall, the rate was 2.5 times higher but for males the rate was slightly higher at 2.6 (Table 13.6). Moreover, when examined geographically it emerged that Catholic male unemployment rates were higher than Protestant male rates in each of the 26 district council areas (Osborne, 1978; FEA, 1979). In the period since 1971 there

Table 13.5

Religion and Selected Occupations, Construction and Engineering, 1971 (%)

	Occupational Class	% Catholic
A. Construction		
Managers, building & contracting	I	18
Carpenters & joiners	III	35
Bricklayers, tile setters	III	51
Plasterers, cement finishers	III	51
Labourers, building & contracting	V	55
B. Engineering		
Managers, engineering	I	8
Fitters, n.e.c.	III	15
Electricians	III	20
Motor mechanics	III	27
Labourers, engineering	V	16

Source: Aunger (1975).

has been a substantial increase in the general level of unemployment. In the absence of unemployment rates disaggregated by religion there was a widespread feeling that with rates of unemployment increasing faster in the east of Northern Ireland, which is predominantly Protestant, and with major manufacturing plants in Protestant areas being major casualties of the recession, there was an evening-up in the experience of unemployment – an "equality of misery". One study, however, conducted on data collected on 3,500 males, who became unemployed in the early part of 1976 and whose labour market behaviour was followed over the next 12 months, challenged this conclusion (Miller and Osborne, 1983). The study found major differences in the experiences of Protestants and Catholics:

> ... Catholics were over-represented in the survey (compared with their representation in the economically active population), were more likely to have been unemployed in the previous three years, for that unemployment to have lasted longer, to experience a longer period before securing a job (for those obtaining a job), to receive from employment offices fewer job submissions, and to be disproportionately represented amongst those unemployed throughout the year. Moreover, the analysis demonstrated that these differences could not be accounted for by variations in education, skill level (as measured by social class), geographical mobility or general motivation. (Miller & Osborne, 1983, 98).

Table 13.6

Unemployment and Religion, 1971 and 1981 (%)

	1971			1981		
	Male	Female	Total	Male	Female	Total
Protestant	6.6	3.6	5.6	12.4	9.6	11.4
Catholic	17.3	7.0	13.9	30.2	17.1	25.5

Source: Osborne & Cormack (1986).

Particularly interesting in this study was the analysis of the Employment Officers' role in submitting individuals to job openings. What emerged was that when other variables were controlled for, the religion of the individual was associated with the number of job submissions. This implied that religion was being taken into account in the Offices. This could have been in the form of submitting individuals on the basis of "horses for courses" or that there was direct discrimination by officers in the Offices, or that both practices took place. By the time the data were analysed, however, Job Centres were replacing Employment offices and self-selection was replacing job submissions to vacancies. Nevertheless, the study may well have revealed circumstances, often alleged anecdotally, of religion being taken into account in official intervention in the labour market.

With the publication of the 1981 census[2] and data becoming available from a new major government survey, the Continuous Household Survey (CHS), it has become possible to assess the current situation (Osborne & Cormack, 1986). What emerges is that the unemployment differentials between Protestants and Catholics remain broadly the same as in 1971

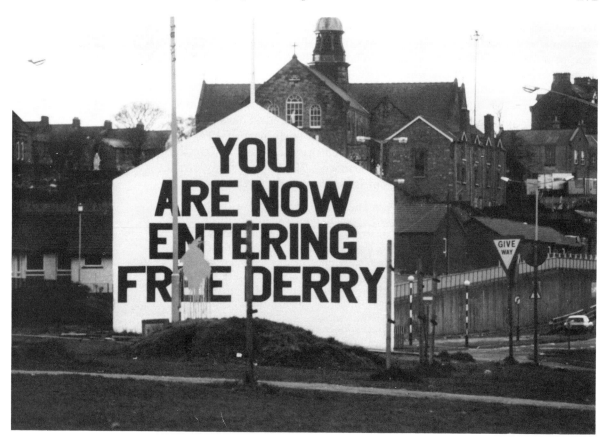

An explicit proclamation at the entrance to the Bogside in Londonderry 1985. A strongly nationalist area, with high levels of unemployment, this has been the scene of many confrontations with the security forces during the Troubles. (N.C. Mitchel)

(Table 13.6). Moreover, the new data reveal that when Catholics are compared to Protestants:

(i) Catholic male unemployment is higher in each of the 26 district councils except one (Castlereagh, where the Catholic population is very small). The picture is broadly the same for females, although the differences are generally smaller than for males (Census).

(ii) When unemployment rates are disaggregated by age groups, unemployment rates are substantially higher for Catholics for each age group (Census).

(iii) A higher proportion of Catholics have been unemployed for over a year (CHS).

(iv) When young people are considered, while unemployment rates are broadly similar for the 16-18 year olds, for 19-24 year olds, a group for whom remaining at school and entry to government training schemes is no longer an option, a much higher unemployment rate is recorded for Catholics than Protestants (CHS).

In short, the clear evidence is that unemployment is still not experienced as an "equality of misery" between Protestants and Catholics. The analysis of the causes of higher Catholic unemployment rates has sparked something of a debate and this will be outlined below. It is now appropriate to turn to evidence of changes in the employment profiles of Protestants and Catholics.

Employment

The assessment of change in the employment profiles of Protestants and Catholics can be undertaken through the use of the 1981 population census (Osborne & Cormack, 1987). The problems associated with the population census have been outlined (in Footnote 2) and they represent a significant handicap to the unqualified use of the census. There is an additional problem, associated with the attempt to compare patterns revealed in the 1981 census with those of 1971, caused by the changes in the systems of classification of occupations and the different questions asked on the two census schedules. For these reasons the best approach is to use only the 1981 census, acknowledging its deficiencies, and disaggregating the data in terms of age groups. The logic of undertaking such an analysis is that the change in occupational structure we are seeking to measure is likely to be relatively small. The expectation for marginal rather than wholesale occupational change is suggested by experience in the United States. In the late 1960s and early 1970s circumstances in the U.S. were highly propitious for securing improvements in the social and economic circumstances of blacks. An expanding economy with increasing job opportunities coincided with a highly supportive political and legal environment for vigorous public policies actively seeking rapid social change in a short time. Yet these circumstances failed to improve dramatically and conclusively the socio-economic profile of the black community (Farley, 1985). Such favourable circumstances have not characterised the decade of policy intervention in Northern Ireland. If it is rather unrealistic to expect a complete restructuring of employment profiles in Northern Ireland then the most likely evidence of change, if change is taking place, should be recorded amongst the newer entrants to the labour market. This assessment, therefore, loooks in particular for evidence of change in the employment profiles of those aged 16-35.

A. Social class

Table 13.7 shows the social class profiles of Protestants and Catholics. From this Table it is apparent that a higher proportion of Catholics are in the unemployed and manual categories, (65.1 per cent) than Protestants (54.4 per cent) and that Catholics show a much lower representation in non-manual groups perhaps most notably in social class III non-manual. However, it is also clear that a substantial part of the difference in these profiles results from the major differences in unemployment. When those who are unemployed are disregarded the profiles show a greater similarity. Catholic males in employment are under-represented in non-manual occupations and there is no evidence of this diminishing for the younger age groups (16-35). In general, the occupational differences between females are smaller between Catholics and Protestants than for males, albeit in the overall context of female disadvantage in the labour market.

Table 13.7

Religion and Social Class, 1981 (%)

| Social Class | Protestant | | | Catholic | | |
	Male	Female	Total	Male	Female	Total
I	4.5	1.0	3.2	2.8	0.8	2.1
II	22.9	20.1	21.8	17.4	23.7	19.7
III non-manual	11.9	34.8	20.6	6.8	24.3	13.2
III manual	29.5	6.6	20.8	25.2	6.8	18.5
IV	13.1	21.9	16.5	10.9	22.1	15.0
I	4.9	5.7	5.2	5.6	4.6	5.2
Unemployed	13.1	9.9	11.9	21.4	17.7	26.4

Note: Social class figures are based on the 'usually resident' population in employment; excluded are the armed forces and occupations 'inadequately described'. The exclusion of the 'inadequately described' from the denominator results in unemployment percentages which differ from those of Table 6.

Source: Osborne & Cormack (1987)

B. Occupations*

Examining the managerial and supervisory occupations in detail there is some evidence of change in Catholic representation. For example, while numbers of "managers in large establishments" increased by 145 per cent between 1971 and 1981, Catholic numbers increased by 244 per cent and Protestant numbers by 55 per cent. For all managers, Catholics represented 16 per cent of the total in 1971 and 18.5 per cent in 1981. Similarly, when supervisory occupations are considered some Catholic advance is recorded, especially for non-manual supervisory occupations although this increase is mainly evident for females. However, when these managerial occupations are examined in more detail, Catholics tend to record a higher representation in those areas considered to be of lower economic or strategic importance. Thus Catholics represent 40 per cent of those managers in "hotel, clubs, entertainment and sport", 25.3 per cent in "retailing and wholesaling" but only 14.5 per cent of "office managers" and 15.9 per cent of "production, works, maintenance etc managers". There is little evidence of change in the patterns of the younger age groups.

Examining other occupational groups suggests:

(i) Catholics show a high representation in "professionals in education, health and welfare" and in particular as teachers and nurses. Within this group of occupations, however, Catholics are not so well represented amongst "doctors and dentists", "pharmacists, radiographers and other paramedicals" and "higher education teachers". Generally,

---

* In the 1981 census Catholics represent 31.3 per cent of the economically active population who indicated a religious affiliation.

Catholics are not as well represented in the higher status occupations; but Catholics, both males and females, record increasing proportions in this group of occupations among younger age groups.

(ii) Catholics show a high representation in "construction and mining" with 48 per cent of construction workers recorded as Catholics. Moreover, disaggregation by age, suggests increasing Catholic representation in construction occupations.

(iii) Catholics show low representation in the key occupational group of "Professional and related support management (including senior national and local government managers)". Within this group there are big variations in individual occupations. Catholics account for 37.8 per cent of "judges, barristers, advocates and solicitors" but only 20.5 per cent of "economists, statisticians, computer programmers", 14 per cent of those in "marketing, sales, advertising and public relations", 15.9 per cent of those recorded as "general administrators – national government", 17.8 per cent of "senior local government officers" and 15.6 per cent of those recorded as "personnel and industrial relations managers". An increase is apparent, however, in Catholic representation in these groups amongst younger age categories.

(iv) In Aunger's analysis of the 1971 census, he noted that the occupations which recorded the highest proportions of Catholics were also largely female occupations and of low social status whereas the occupations which recorded the highest proportion of Protestants were predominantly male and of higher strategic or economic status. Repeating this analysis for the 1981 census suggests that while in essence this pattern is sustained, three occupations emerge in the Catholic profile which are of higher status (legal occupations, catering supervisors and managers in hotels and clubs). This provides further evidence of Catholic advance.

C. Industries

When the census is examined in terms of industrial distributions it is apparent that substantial differences remain. Catholics are still far more dependent on construction, an industry which now records more men unemployed than employed, than Protestants. Both communities have benefitted from the expansion of the public sector but in different ways. Perhaps most notably, Protestants record a particularly high representation in employment in security, an area of employment which has expanded considerably since the early 1970s. In this way Protestants have been partially able to offset the decline in manufacturing employment. Protestants are strongly represented in transport manufacture (shipbuilding and aircraft manufacture) while Catholics are more dependent on education and other personal services. Moreover, as O'Dowd (1986) has recently noted many of the jobs in services, especially in the public sector, have been part-time and low-paid jobs, often taken by women. Representation in agriculture is similar for both communities.

The evidence from the census suggests that to an extent patterns of advantage and disadvantage in the labour market remain. This is most stark in the case of unemployment. Some Catholic advance in employment, however, can be observed; to a significant extent, however, this has resulted from the growth of employment in the public sector. With the expansion of public sector employment now over, it must be questionable whether even the advances noted here can be sustained without determined policy intervention.

Investigations

In the past few years the investigatory work of the FEA into the employment profiles of individual employers has provided the level of detail for particular employment circumstances which sources such as the census cannot match. A significant number of the published reports deal with the public sector with comparatively few covering the private sector. Reports now cover the major banks, the building societies, Housing Executive, Southern Health Board, Northern Ireland Electricity Service and the Northern Ireland Civil Service among others. The circumstances found vary with each employment situation but generally speaking the data suggest that Catholic representation in employment is increasing. Typically, however, the increase in Catholic employment is at the lower occupational levels with often considerable underrepresentation still evident at more senior levels. However, there are exceptions, the Electricity Service, for example, which shows little sign of very low Catholic representation increasing. Perhaps the most significant employer investigated is the Northern Ireland Civil Service which responded to its investigation by creating an Equal Opportunities Unit to review employment patterns. This unit published its first review in mid-1986, providing the opportunity to examine changing employment patterns since the investigation by the FEA.

Northern Ireland Civil Service

The Northern Ireland Civil Service (non-industrial) is, with just over 20,000 employees, the largest single employer in Northern Ireland and is, therefore, of great economic and strategic significance. The representation of Protestants and Catholics in recent years has changed significantly as is shown in Table 13.8. When those who can be assigned to a religious category are examined for 1980 and 1985 the figures suggest that Catholic representation has increased from 30.7 per cent in 1980 to 36.4 per cent in 1985 representing a 21.5 per cent increase in Catholic numbers and a decline of 5.9 per cent in Protestant numbers. This increase included both the general service grades and the specialist non-general service grades. In the latter case, however, Catholics show a much lower representation than in general service grades with Catholics representing 28.5 per cent of the agricultural inspectorate, 34.9 per cent of those in the typing group, and also in the government training centre group, and 26.6 per cent in the scientific group compared with 41.4 per cent in the general grades. In terms of gender, a majority of Catholics in the civil service are female (55.1 per cent) while a majority of Protestants are male (51.7 per cent). Crucially, a higher proportion of Protestants enter the civil service at a higher level of entry than Catholics (partially explained by a larger number of Protestant entrants with degree level qualifications). Finally, perhaps the most significant indicator of change is an assessment of employment by the level or grade of the post held. The data for this assessment are shown in Table 13.9. The evidence suggests that the proportion of Catholics has increased at each grade, with the most notable increases taking place at the middle-management grades of deputy principal (from 19.3 per cent in 1980 to 27 per cent in 1985) and staff officer (22.1 per cent in 1980 to 27.2 per cent in 1985). Some increase is evident at the most senior grades but Catholic representation remains low.

On the whole the evidence from the investigations undertaken by the FEA do indicate general increases in the employment levels of Catholics especially in the public sector, but substantial under-representation is still evident in some areas, perhaps the most significant example being the Electricity Service. More generally, alongside the evidence of improvement continuing, Catholics have a low representation in more senior positions.

Table 13.8

Religious Representation in the Northern Ireland Civil Service, 1980 and 1985 (%)

	1980	1985
Protestant	64.5	58.6
Catholic	35.5	41.4

Note: Figures are for 'Amalgamated General Service' Grades.
Source: Equal Opportunities Unit, Department of Finance and Personnel (1986) *Equal Opportunities in the Northern Ireland Civil Service. First Report.*

Explanations

The work reported here on the labour market profiles of Protestants and Catholics has engendered a lively discussion about how to interpret and understand the causes of these differences. To a substantial extent the debate has focussed on the causes of the different rates of unemployment experienced by Protestants and Catholics although it can be equally applied to the overall patterns in the labour market. In broad terms this debate divides into three groups. The first, advanced from a traditional nationalist viewpoint, views the patterns of Catholic disadvantage as a product of a discrimination which is inherent to the socio-political structure of Northern Ireland (Farrell, 1976; Graham, 1984). In these terms, both the devolved Unionist administrations and predominantly Protestant employers conspired together to deliver relative employment advantages to Protestants thereby securing both Protestant political solidarity and a divided working class. According to this view, discrimination was systema-

Table 13.9

Religion and Level of Employment in the NICS, 1980 and 1985 (%)

	Protestant		Catholic	
	1980	1985	1980	1985
Senior Principal and above	91.5	90.2	8.5	9.8
Principal	82.9	81.1	17.1	18.9
Deputy Principal	80.7	72.9	19.3	27.0
Staff Officer	77.9	72.8	22.1	27.2
Executive Officer I	73.7	65.2	26.3	34.8
Executive Officer II	67.9	60.3	34.1	39.7
Clerk	60.1	52.5	39.9	47.5
Clerical Assistant	56.9	54.9	43.1	45.1

Note: These figures are for 'Amalgamated General Service Grades'.
Source: First Report of the Equal Opportunities Unit, Department of Finance and Personnel
(1986) *Equal Opportunities in the Northern Ireland Civil Service.*

tic, widespread and the only plausible or possible cause of differing employment patterns. On the other hand, the second group sees the disadvantaged position of Catholics in employment as a result of certain characteristics asserted to be intrinsic to the Catholic community and where discrimination is depicted as inconsequential, (Compton, 1976; 1981). In this context, geographical location, fertility and educational attainment provide the key explanations. The ideological underpinnings of these two positions result in exclusivist assignations of blame for Catholic disadvantage: either the "system" or "Catholics" themselves. The third position represents something of a mid-way stance. Whyte (1983) in his review of the period 1921-68 does not find sufficient evidence to sustain the position that discrimination is the only explanatory factor but that there is more than sufficient evidence of discrimination to reject the assertions of those who deny its importance. Similarly, Osborne and Cormack (1986) endorse this mid-way position and review the contemporary importance of the various explanatory factors. These are:

(i) Geographical location. A larger proportion of Catholics than Protestants live in areas of low employment opportunities, particuarly the west of the Province. It has been argued, therefore, that higher Catholic unemployment is predominantly a function of this distribution (Compton, 1981). However, such a view implies that Protestant and Catholic unemployment rates are similar in different areas. The data from both the 1971 and 1981 censuses reveal that Catholic unemployment rates are higher irrespective of area. Advocates of the importance of geographical location tend to neglect the role of the state in shaping the geography of job opportunities, while advocates of the "discrimination" explanation view industrial location policy, especially in the 1960s, as designed to benefit Protestant areas to the exclusion of Catholic areas. Most judgements tend not to go this far. Whyte (1983) finds regional policy one of the less serious areas for complaint by Catholics although a recent study of industrial location policy points out that, while in the period up to 1975, a large proportion of new projects went to the more economically advanced areas, since then areas of high unemployment have tended to benefit from location policies (Bradley et al, 1986). However, it is not possible to rule out the role of industrial location policies in the past in maintaining high unemployment in peripheral and predominantly Catholic areas.

(ii) Demography. The higher Catholic fertility rates and rates of population growth have prompted Compton (1981: 141) to suggest that:

> The only effective way to guarantee improvement in the relative position of Roman Catholics in Northern Ireland is through the encouragement of fundamental change in certain of the innate features of that community. Acceptance of the desirability to (sic) bring Roman Catholic family size and rate of growth closer to the national and European average would be an important step to greater equality.

The importance of fertility differences in accounting for higher Catholic unemployment can be queried on several grounds. First, analysis of the 1901 and 1911 censuses (Hepburn and Collins, 1981; Cormack and Rooney, n.d.) suggests that Catholic socio-economic disadvantage was already evident at a time when Catholic and Protestant fertility rates were similar. Second, and most important, this interpretation ignores labour market processes. Since it is asserted that there is little or no discrimination, the processes of entering the labour market and securing advancement within it are assumed to be fair. The role of exclusion, segregation and unfair hiring practices are ignored. Third, one of the asserted effects of larger Catholic families is through the operation of the 'poverty trap' which provides a greater incentive for those with large families (Catholics) to stay unemployed, rather than take a low-paid job. However, a study of 3,500 males, joining the unemployment register and, followed over the succeeding year, found little evidence of this disincentive effect, either in general or for those with large families, Protestant or Catholic. Finally, the most recent evidence suggests that the fertility differentials between Protestants and Catholics are declining quite markedly, (Compton et al, 1985). For these reasons it is argued that the role of demographic factors has been over-emphasised.

(iii) Educational attainment. There are differences in the educational attainment of Protestants and Catholics in Northern Ireland. The evidence from the CHS suggests that a smaller proportion of adult Catholics possess any qualifications: 39 per cent of Catholics compared with 46 per cent of Protestants. The 1981 census data, although only measuring more advanced qualifications, confirm this difference. Among school leavers, while slightly fewer Catholics gain GCE "O" or "A" levels than Protestants, and the subjects of their passes are skewed away from science subjects there is evidence of an evening-out of these differences (Osborne, 1986). However, current differences in the educational attainment levels of adults among the two religious groups reflect the range of opportunities available to them in Northern Ireland and also the level of migration in the past fifty years. Moreover, quite possibly a generation ago jobs and promotions were less closely related to qualifications than they are now. The crucial question is the extent to which increasingly similarly qualified school leavers are able to translate examination attainment into job access. In the Northern Ireland context there has been no research fully evaluating the 'tightening bond' between examinations and job access, similar to that reported for example in Scotland (Gray et al, 1983). However, careful scrutiny of the CHS data suggests that Catholics are more likely to be unemployed than Protestants irrespective of the level of qualification held and that this relationship is evident across age groups (Osborne & Cormack, 1987). Such evidence must further caution the weight given to aggregate differences in educational attainment in explaining employment advantage and disadvantage.

(iv) Discrimination. The extent and significance of job discrimination in the labour market remains the area of major disputation. Part of the problem stems from one of definition. Discrimination in terms of direct individual mistreatment needs to be differentiated from indirect discrimination where disadvantage results from actions or practices which of themselves are not necessarily designed to be biased. Undoubtedly discrimination both direct and indirect takes place in Northern Ireland. Moreover, at times of political tension as in 1986, for example, intimidation of workers on a sectarian basis does take place. However, in general terms most observers suggest that the volume of direct discrimination is falling and is considerably lower than that which existed in Northern Ireland during most of its history (Buckland, 1979). Indirect informal recruitment patterns even by employers with apparently well developed personnel functions help perpetuate longstanding employment patterns. The permitting of the display of political emblems and flags in the workplace by employers can present a threatening environment to an employee not drawn from the dominant tradition in that workplace. Employers who commit themselves to equality of opportunity need to follow this with firm action to ensure change. The adoption of new procedures and the monitoring of results by the Northern Ireland Civil Service is a good example of what is required. Many employers, in the private sector in particular but also including some in the public sector, have yet to take such vigorous action.

Overall, it is clearly not possible to endorse the view that only discrimination can account for labour market differences. Factors such as geographical location, educational attainment and demography can play a part although their importance is often asserted rather than carefully and logically assessed. On the other hand, religious discrimination, both direct and indirect has, and continues to be, a factor in the labour market. In this writer's view, it is indirect discrimination which is of greater current significance.

Policy

The final part of this chapter is concerned with a brief discussion of public policy. The main form of policy intervention has been the 1976 Fair Employment (Northern Ireland) Act which created the Fair Employment Agency. The powers and responsibilities of the FEA include the responsibility of investigating individual complaints of discrimination, the power to conduct general investigations of employers' employment practices to assess whether equality of opportunity is being provided. The FEA has been the subject of considerable criticism in the 10 years of its existence. Most unionist/loyalist spokesmen have bitterly opposed both the existence of the FEA and the work and reports produced by the Agency seeing its raison d'etre as antithetical to their community's interests. Nationalists on the other hand have either seen the FEA as a toothless sop to provide respectability to Direct Rule, or more supportively, as an underfunded body tackling a major problem without proper government support. More detailed commentaries have focussed on alleged inadequacies of organisation or methods of investigation (McCrudden, 1983; Miller, 1985). Nevertheless, a recent evaluation of the EOC and CRE in Britain (Appleby and Ellis, 1984) would suggest that in comparison the FEA has been far more active, interventionist and more effective than its British counterparts.

The question remains, however, of whether the existing form of policy intervention is adequate. From time to time, US style employment quota policies have been canvassed for Northern Ireland. Without covering both the advantages and the increasingly evident disadvantages of quotas there is sufficient scope for a significant tightening of policy within the existing pattern of intervention – by, for example, linking government contracts to employers' employment practices and profiles, through "contract compliance", and extending civil service style monitoring throughout the public sector, as proposed in a recent government discussion paper (Department of Economic Development, 1986). Moreover, in the light of the evidence of some improvement in Catholic employment profiles such a dramatic shift in policy towards quotas is unwarranted. The provision of full equality of opportunity for the two communities in employment must remain, however, a major task for public policy and one where policy effectiveness should be subject to continuous review.

Notes

1. Hepburn in a later paper reviewing religious aspects of employment change between 1871-1911 in Belfast notes some intra-Protestant differences notably between Presbyterians and Episcopalians and generally to the advantage of Presbyterians. He concludes, however, by highlighting the extent to which Catholic disadvantage relative to all Protestants worsened during the period. (A.C. Hepburn, 1983; Work, class and religion in Belfast, 1871-1911, *in Irish Economic and Social History*, X, 33-50.) By the time of the 1971 census, however, intra-Protestant variations in unemployment rates, for example, were very small and the major difference was between Catholics and Protestants.
2. The 1981 census presents two problems to the researcher. The first is of under-enumeration. Estimates of the level of under-enumeration vary between 45,000 and 70,000. The second problem is that of the non-response to the voluntary question on religious affiliation which at approximately 20 per cent was double that recorded at the 1971 census. These two problems do limit the extent to which the census can be used without due care but they do not render the census unreliable for analysis. See Osborne & Cormack (1986) for a discussion of these issues.

References

Appleby, G. and Ellis, E., 1984. Formal investigations: the Commission for Racial Equality and the Equal Opportunities Commission as Law enforcement agencies, *in Public Law*, Summer, 236-76.

Aunger, E., 1975. Religion and occupational class in Northern Ireland, *in Economic and Social Review*, 7, 1, 1-23.

Barritt, D. and Carter, C., 1962. *The Northern Ireland Problem*. London.

Bradley, J., Hewitt, V. and Jefferson, C., 1986. *Industrial location policy and equality of opportunity in assisted employment in Northern Ireland* 1949-81. Research Paper 10, Fair Employment Agency, Belfast.

Buckland, P., 1979. *The factory of grievances; devolved government in Northern Ireland, 1921-1939*. Dublin.

Cameron Commission, 1969. *Disturbances in Northern Ireland: report of the Commission appointed by the Governor of Northern Ireland*, Belfast. HMSO, Cmd. 532.

Campaign for Social Justice in Northern Ireland, 1969. *Northern Ireland: the plain truth*. Dungannon, Campaign for Social Justice.

Compton, P.A., 1976. Religious affiliation and demographic behaviour in Northern Ireland, *in Transactions (New Series), Institute of British Geographers*, 1, 433-52.

Compton, P.A., 1981, "Demographic and geographical aspects of the unemployment differential between Protestants and Roman Catholics in Northern Ireland in Compton, P.A., (ed.) *The contemporary population of Northern Ireland and population – related issues*. Belfast. 127-42.

Compton, P.A., Coward, J. and Wilson-Davis, K., 1985, Family size and religious denomination in Northern Ireland, *in Journal of Biosocial Science*, 17, 137-45.

Cormack, R.J. and Osborne, R.D., 1983. Introduction: political arithmetic and social policy, *in* Cormack, R.J. and Osborne, R.D. (eds.) *Religion, education and employment: aspects of equal opportunity in Northern Ireland*. Belfast, 1-23.

Cormack, R.J. and Rooney, E., Religion and employment in Northern Ireland, 1911-1971. Unpublished mimeo, Department of Social Studies, Queen's University of Belfast.

Department of Economic Development, 1986. *Equality of opportunity in employment in Northern Ireland, future strategies and options*. Belfast.

Equal Opportunities Unit, Department of Finance and Personnel, 1986. *Equal opportunities in the Northern Ireland Civil Service, first report*. Belfast.

Fair Employment Agency for Northern Ireland. *Second annual report of the Fair Employment Agency*, 1 April 1977 – 31 March 1978. Belfast.

Fairley, R., 1985. Three steps forward and two back? Recent changes in the social and economic status of blacks, *in Ethnic and Racial Studies*, 8, 4-28.

Farrell, M., 1976. *Northern Ireland: the Orange state*. London.

Gallagher, F., 1957. *The indivisible island: the story of the partition of Ireland*. London.

Graham, D., 1984. Discrimination in Northern Ireland: the failure of the FEA, *in Critical Social Policy*, Spring, 40-54.

Gray, J., McPherson, A.F. and Raffe, D., 1983. *Reconstruction of secondary education: theory, myth and practice since the War.* London.

Hepburn, A.C., 1983. Employment and religion in Belfast, 1901-1951, *in* Cormack, R.J. and Osborne, R.D. (eds.) *Religion, education and employment: aspects of equal opportunity.* Belfast. 42-63.

Hepburn, A.C. and Collins, B., 1981. Industrial society: the structure of Belfast, 1901 *in* Roebuck, P. (ed.) *Plantation to Partition.* Belfast. 210-28.

McCrudden, C., 1983. The experience of the legal enforcement of the Fair Employment (Northern Ireland) Act 1976 *in* Cormack, R.J. and Osborne, R.D. (eds.) *Religion, education and employment: aspects of equal opportunity in Northern Ireland.* Belfast. 201-21.

Miller, R.L., 1983. Religion and occupational mobility *in* Cormack, R.J. and Osborne, R.D. (eds.) *Religion, education and employment: aspects of equal opportunity.* Belfast. 64-77.

Miller, R.L., 1985. Fair employment in the Civil Service: report of an investigation into the non-industrial Northern Ireland Civil Service, *in L'Irelande Politique et Sociale,* 1, 99-125.

Miller, R.L. and Osborne, R.D., 1983. Religion and unemployment: evidence from a cohort survey, *in* Cormack, R.J. and Osborne, R.D. (eds.) *Religion, education and employment: aspects of equal opportunity in Northern Ireland.* Belfast. 78-99.

Nelson, S., 1974. Protestant "ideology" considered: the case of "discrimination", *in* Crew, I. (ed.) *British political sociology yearbook, 2: The politics of race.* London. 155-87.

O'Dowd, L., 1986. Beyond industrial society, *in* Clancy, P., Drudy, S., Lynch, K. and O'Dowd, L. (eds.), *Ireland: a sociological profile.* Dublin. 198-220.

Osborne, R.D., 1978. Denomination and unemployment in Northern Ireland, *in Area,* 10, 280-3.

Osborne, R.D., 1986. Segregated schools and examination results in Northern Ireland: some preliminary research, *in Educational Research,* 28, 43-50.

Osborne, R.D., 1986a and Cormack, R.J. Unemployment and religion in Northern Ireland, *in The Economic and Social Review,* 17, 215-25.

Osborne, R.D. and Cormack, R.J., 1987. *Religion and employment, 1971-1981.* Research Paper, II, Belfast, Fair Employment Agency.

Rose, R., 1971, *Governing without consensus, an Irish perspective.* London.

Whyte, J., 1983. How much discrimination was there under the Unionist regime, 1921-1968?, *in* Gallagher, T. and O'Connell, J. (eds.) *Contemporary Irish Studies.* Manchester. 1-35.

14 Administration

SYDNEY ELLIOTT AND R. A. WILFORD*

Senior Lecturer in Department of Political Science, The Queen's University of Belfast
*Lecturer in Department of Political Science, The Queen's University of Belfast

The pattern of administration in Northern Ireland has recently been studied *in vacuo* as an example of a unique experiment in devolution. However, the new regime of direct rule since 1972 requires some reference to the wider context of administration within the United Kingdom. In Britain, old orthodoxies have been recently contested: a challenge which has been reinforced by the experience of Northern Ireland.

One of the cornerstones of the United Kingdom constitution is that it is a unitary state. This has been maintained within the context of a multi-national state, with historic territorial communities in Scotland, Wales and Northern Ireland (and ethnic communities from the new Commonwealth in the large cities). Integrity has been sustained by a single bureaucracy and a national party system, resulting in a unified polity cohered by single party government, the doctrine of parliamentary sovereignty and the conventions of collective cabinet and individual ministerial responsibility. When the unitariness of the system was challenged by the rise of nation-alism in the 1970s, the referenda in Scotland and Wales showed that the centre could hold and that the periphery preferred the *status quo*.

Although constitutionally correct, in practical terms the unitary model needs to be qualified. Within Great Britain the pattern of government and administration is not uniform but extremely complex (Rose and Madgwick, 1982). To borrow a culinary analogy, it resembles less a symmetrical Battenburg than an irregular marble-layered cake. The whole has a shape and structure, but the ingredients are many and diverse, with the flavours and textures intermingling and cross-cutting. The ingredients of this mix include local government, the European Community, a bewildering array of quangos and a range of self-regulating interest groups upon whose support governments are dependent for policy formation and implemen-tation. Such bodies co-exist with central departments of state providing a system of sub-national government. Two central government depart-ments, the Scottish and Welsh Offices, enjoy a considerable measure of territorially defined administrative devolution further complicating the recipe. When the ingredients from Northern Ireland are added the diversity and richness of the mixture are even more apparent.

The focus on Northern Ireland is instructive in a number of respects. Not only does it offer a rigorous proof of the unitariness of the United Kingdom but it has also presented successive national governments with the problem of governing and administering a divided society (Rose, 1971; Lijphart, 1975). From the Act of Union 1801 until 1921 Ireland was part of the United Kingdom. In this legislative union laws were made at Westminster where Ireland had up to 105 representatives. However, Ireland was in practice administered by an executive in Dublin headed by a Cabinet Minister, the Chief Secretary for Ireland, and a separate civil service. The representative of the Crown was the Lord Lieutenant of Ireland. Increasing Nationalist pressure, aided by extensions of the franchise, especially in 1884, and Liberal dependence on the support of the Irish Parliamentary Party, led to the advent of a Home Rule policy. Despite the passing of the Home Rule Act in 1914 (suspended for the duration of the war), events during the war, especially the 1916 Easter Rising, and the 1918 general election, changed the future form of government in Ireland. The scheme for two devolved Parliaments within the United Kingdom, in Belfast and Dublin, proposed in the Government of Ireland Act 1920, was swiftly replaced in the twenty-six counties by dominion status negotiated in the Anglo-Irish Treaty of 1921. Northern Ireland alone faced the prospect of implementing an untried scheme for devolved government.

In this chapter we seek to outline and describe the pattern of government and administration of Northern Ireland from 1920 to the present. During this period there were two distinctive regimes. From 1920 to 1972 Northern Ireland possessed a system of regional government unique in the United Kingdom (Mansergh, 1936; Lawrence, 1965). However, for most of the past 15 years it has been subject to the equally singular system of direct rule (Birrell and Murie, 1980). Though the legacy of the pre-1972 period conditions the current political context of Northern Ireland, its administrative history can be divided into the pre- and post-direct rule periods. During the latter, successive governments have sought to restore a devolved system to Northern Ireland. Since 1972 there have been five concerted attempts founded on power-sharing institutions and a variable provision for an Irish dimension. The most recent initiative, the Anglo-Irish Agreement, signed at Hillsborough on 15 November 1985, advances the Irish dimension to the primary position and harbours the aspiration that devolution might follow. The Agreement confirms that Northern Ireland remains part of the United Kingdom until a majority of its population decide otherwise. But it also provides a structure through which the government of the Republic of Ireland is consulted about the governance of the Province. By itself, this innovation qualifies further the image of the United Kingdom as a unitary state.

The Stormont regime

The Executive

Before the first meeting of the Northern Ireland Parliament in 1921 the Lord Lieutenant of Ireland used his powers to establish a departmental structure. It comprised the Prime Minister's department and six others: Finance, Home Affairs, Agriculture, Labour, Commerce and Education which remained the core of the administrative system until 1972. A seventh ministry, Public Security, was added in 1940 but by 1944 was absorbed into Home Affairs. The Ministries Act (N.I.) 1944 empowered the Governor – who succeeded the Lord Lieutenant as the Crown's representative in 1922 – to transfer functions from one department to another and to alter the names of departments. This enabled some of the responsibilities to be adjusted in the light of developments and needs. For example, the Ministry of Health and Local Government was created in 1944, Labour and National Insurance in 1946, Health and Social Services, and Development in 1964. Finally, following the outbreak of civil disturbances in 1968, a Ministry of Community Relations was established in 1969.

The government departments were staffed by civil servants recruited to a separate Northern Ireland Civil Service formed in 1921. Originally many were from the United Kingdom Civil Service and existing Irish departments and new recruits to whom ex-service preference was applied. In time, however, the service became increasingly local in recruitment and in 1972 numbered 13,000 of whom 3,300 were temporary appointees. Their responsibilities were the transferred matters which were administered locally and for which there was accountability to the local Parliament. However, despite its separate status, the Northern Ireland Civil Service followed the administrative procedures and practices of Britain.

The heads of departments were designated ministers and were members of the Privy Council of Northern Ireland. In theory the ministers collectively, *viz* the Cabinet, constituted the executive committee of the Northern Ireland Privy Council and they aided and advised the Governor in the exercise of his executive power. In practice the Cabinet was the supreme organ of executive government, its members accepting the discipline of collective responsibility. Each minister had to be a member of the Commons or Senate, or to become a member within six months of appointment. Ministers could speak in either House on a bill but could only vote in the House of which they were members. The 1920 Act allowed the appointment of non-departmental ministers who were not required to sit in Parliament. This provision was used in 1971 when David Bleakley, a former Member of Parliament for the Northern Ireland Labour Party, was appointed Minister of Community Relations and G.B. Newe became Minister of State in the Prime Minister's Office. Bleakley resigned before the end of his six months without attempting to find a seat, while Newe, the first Roman Catholic to serve in an administration since 1921, went out of office with the fall of Stormont on 30 March 1972.

The power to appoint ministers rested with the Prime Minister, the

Lord Carson, revered Unionist leader of the early twentieth century, depicted in characteristic stance in a statue which forms a focal point in front of Stormont, built by the British government to house the Northern Ireland Parliament and now used mainly as government offices. (NITB)

leader of the majority party, on whose advice the Governor acted. The power to dismiss was rarely used, perhaps because electoral defeat never made it necessary and also because the area was small with a limited supply of talent. However, dissent existed and was probably responsible for the resignation of two out of six Prime Ministers, J.M. Andrews in 1943 and Captain T.M. O'Neill in 1969. Traditionally, the policy pursued and its tone stemmed from the Prime Minister: this was established by the long service of two of the first three Prime Ministers, Lord Craigavon serving for nineteen and Lord Brookborough twenty years.

The 1920 Act made Northern Ireland a self-financing region with its revenues separated from the national accounts. The appearance was one of independence with an imperial contribution included to defray the costs of defence and foreign affairs, two excepted matters, as the first charge on revenues. But financial autonomy was severely limited. From the outset some 88 per cent of revenue was raised by the British Government; the remainder came from sources at the discretion of the Northern Ireland Parliament. To be workable the system required a transfer of funds to Northern Ireland but this never materialised. The result was that finances became extremely tight especially in the economic circumstances of the 1930s. At times expedients such as raiding the road fund in 1934, were resorted to, in order to balance the budget. Moreover, attempts to increase transferred revenue by increasing the burden on ratepayers, through revaluation and an education levy, brought the regional government into conflict with local authorities, especially Belfast. In these circumstances the imperial contribution became a residual rather than a first charge.

In May 1938 Sir John Simon, Chancellor of the Exchequer, announced that Northern Ireland was entitled to the same social standards and services as Great Britain so that if a deficit occurred in its budget, which was not due to higher expenditure or lower taxation, means would be found to make up the shortfall. This parity principle – parity of services for parity of taxation – was extended in 1944 to enable Northern Ireland to make up the leeway in services. Since financial independence had proved illusory it was not difficult to accept this logical offer of parity. However, it also had consequences in other fields for it required legislative and administrative uniformity in order to obtain the financial benefits.

In the post-war period financial relations were determined by three agreements. Firstly, the guiding principle for relations between the two Exchequers was parity of taxation and services. This required the Northern Ireland Budget to be agreed annually between the Treasury and the local Ministry of Finance: divergences from parity had to be indicated, supplementary estimates approved and any new items exceeding £50,000 required express approval by the United Kingdom Treasury. Secondly, the National Insurance Act 1948 covered national insurance, national assistance and the health service and was administered on an equitable basis. Thirdly, the Social Services Agreement covered supplementary benefit, family allowance, non-contributory pensions and the health service. Both the National Insurance Act and the Social Services Agreement were reciprocal agreements with Great Britain paying 80 per cent of any deficit in Northern Ireland and *vice versa*: in practice the transfer was one way. In addition, Northern Ireland farmers and manufacturers enjoyed the same subsidies and regional employment premiums as in Great Britain. The benefits of these agreements gradually increased and their effects were evident in their final year of operation, 1971-2, when they totalled £115 million, equivalent to 27.5 per cent of total expenditure (Hewitt, 1986). Since only 74 per cent of revenue was raised in Northern Ireland and a further 11 per cent by borrowing, there was a dependence on a transfer of 15 per cent from Great Britain. The original intention of financial independence had proved illusory and administrative and legislative independence were also sacrificed for conformity and improvement.

Legislature

The legislature consisted of the Crown, the House of Commons and the

Lord Brookeborough, descendant of a seventeenth century English Planter, who became the longest-serving Prime Minister of Northern Ireland, holding office from 1943-63.
(N.I. Government Information Service)

Senate. From 1922, the Governor's duties included summoning, proroguing and dissolving of parliament, reading the Queen's Speech at the beginning of the session, and the giving or withholding of consent to legislation on the advice of the Monarch. The Governor also had power to resolve a conflict by convening a joint meeting of the Commons and Senate.

The 52 strong House of Commons was elected for a five year term. Originally the method of election in 1921 and 1925 was the single transferable vote: in 1929 it was changed to a simple majority system with single member constituencies. The Senate consisted of 26 members with two *ex-officio* members, the Lord Mayor of Belfast and the Mayor of Londonderry. The other 24 were elected by the House of Commons, using proportional representation, for an eight year term with half retiring every four years. The method of election ensured that the Senate was a reflection of the House of Commons and obviated the possibility of a Lords/Commons clash as at Westminster.

The legislative competence of the Northern Ireland Parliament was wide. It had power to "make laws for the peace, order and good government of the area subject to certain specific exceptions, reservations and restrictions". Among the "excepted" matters were the Crown and Succession, peace and war, defence and foreign affairs, citizenship, external trade and transport, communications, coinage, weights and measures and copyright. The "reserved" matters included postal services and related matters, the Supreme Court, land purchase, reserved taxes including customs and excise, income tax, surtax, profits tax or capital levy. The excepted and reserved services (other than the Supreme Court) were administered by lead departments based in London; as was the collection of reserved taxes.

Despite a wide legislative competence it was not used to promote radical change, partly due to political conformism and also the lack of financial freedom. A large proportion of British legislation was duplicated, thereby inviting the criticism that Stormont merely acted as a rubber stamp. On the other hand, the failure to follow Britain on aspects of electoral reform was contentious. For example, the retention of a property based franchise in local government, despite the assimilation of parliamentary and local franchises in Britain in 1945, produced a campaign issue for the Northern Ireland Civil Rights Association, under the slogan of "one man one vote", until it was conceded in 1969. However, on some issues, such as abortion and homosexual law reform, there was unity in a conservative community against following Britain. Stripped of polemic there was evidence that the legislative power was used to meet local conditions, either in adapting United Kingdom legislation or in meeting specific local needs. A survey of legislation 1965-70 showed that only 19 per cent of statutes and 25 per cent of Statutory Rules and Orders closely followed Westminster legislation (HMSO, 1973).

Parliamentary practice at Stormont, the seat of the Northern Ireland Parliaments, was modelled on Westminster. The presiding Officer was called the Speaker and his deputy, the Chairman of Ways and Means. The House normally met on Tuesday, Wednesday and Thursday afternoons (the Senate less frequently) with substantial recesses at Christmas, Easter and summer. The majority of bills were introduced in the Commons; all money bills had to be introduced there and the Senate, like the House of Lords, had no power to amend them. For private bills there was a single stage taken by a committee drawn from both Houses. The most important committee was the Select Committee on Public Accounts, appointed annually to review the expenditure of administrative departments.

Local government

Local government in Northern Ireland was not part of the Government of Ireland Act 1920 but stemmed from the Local Government (Ireland) Act 1898. This latter statute extended to Ireland the pattern of county councils, county borough councils, urban and rural district councils created in England and Wales by statues in 1888 and 1894. The two-tier structure, the allocation of functions and the financial arrangements were all similar. The only difference was the introduction of proportional representation (PR) for elections in the Local Government (Ireland) Act 1919.

At the top level in 1921 there were six county councils and two county boroughs, Belfast and Londonderry. The administrative counties were divided into a second tier of 35 rural district councils, 29 urban districts and 4 town commissions. The county council was the rating authority for the rural districts. It was also responsible for education, health and welfare, public works, planning development, tourist amenities, libraries, war memorials and museums. The county boroughs had similar functions, but in the case of Belfast it also had extensive municipal trading services. The urban district councils and non-county boroughs were responsible for water, sewerage, sanitation, street lighting and cleansing, housing, planning, non-trunk roads, harbours, recreation, museums and gas undertakings. Despite this distribution of functions it was common for some to be handed to the county. For example, a library service was often provided by the county as was the planning service. In addition, the Housing Trust, after 1945, often acted as a house building agent and estate manager for local councils.

However, the organisation of local government in Northern Ireland differed from England and Wales in two respects. First, the rural councils were not rating authorities: the county council set the rate with the rural council contributing its share. Second, with the exception of Belfast, the local authorities had no responsibility for the administration of the protective services, i.e. police, civil defence and fire services.

Local government services were financed by rates, government grants and loans and receipts from local trading services. At the end of the 1960s due to de-rating and sporadic revaluations, rate revenue accounted for only 40 per cent of spending; 60 per cent came from grants and loans raised from general taxation. Education, roads, water and sewerage, health and welfare accounted for about 80 per cent of total spending with education the single most expensive item at approximately 50 per cent. The expense of education and the way the rate for education was calculated at the expense of richer areas led many local authorities to support the centralisation of funding for the service.

With the future of local government in England under review by the Redcliffe-Maud Commission from 1966, a similar review was undertaken by the Northern Ireland Minister of Development, William Craig. It proposed to examine the structure, functions and finance of local authorities through a series of confidential discussions. With two county boroughs, six county councils, ten non-county boroughs, twenty-four urban districts and thirty-one rural districts – seventy-three local authorities, for a population of 1.5 million and a rateable value less than the city of Leeds – the review was opportune. Apart from Belfast, the units were too small to be efficient while their rate revenue was insufficient to attract professional staff. In addition, planned developments included proposals for a new city centred on Lurgan and Portadown, the development of the Antrim-Ballymena area and the Portrush, Portstewart, Coleraine area. Two White Papers, in 1967 and 1969, proposed the creation of area councils based on historic towns and boroughs and with responsibility for physical and environmental services. The original proposal was for between 12 and 18 area councils; the 1969 White Paper recommended 17 (HMSOa, 1967;

HMSOb, 1967). It also proposed to retain health, education, welfare and child care at county level but admitted to uncertainty depending on whether Redcliffe-Maud opted for a single tier or a two-tier system in England and Wales.

However, there was another dimension to local government which had a profound effect on the outcome of reform, namely, the impact of local political divisions on the administration of services. The rivalry predated partition but after 1920 it was intensified. Many nationalist controlled local authorities refused to recognise the new administration and local authority offices were the target of IRA attacks in border areas. The abolition of PR in 1922 added another political grievance to fan the flames of distrust.

Political rivalry between self-ascribed Unionists and Nationalists affected about two-thirds of the councils and was intense in some areas, not least because local government was regarded as a patronage system by both sides. Nationalists claimed that local electoral areas were extensively gerrymandered to favour Unionists and that the retention of the ratepayer franchise after 1945 placed them at a disadvantage. They also claimed discrimination in the allocation of public housing and public employment. Indeed it was a case of discrimination in the allocation of a council house that in 1968 ignited the fuse of the civil rights movement and ushered in the protracted period known colloquially as "the Troubles". The Cameron Commission inquiry into the disturbances in 1968 accepted claims that electoral boundaries in Londonderry, Omagh, Armagh, Dungannon and County Fermanagh did not reflect local majorities. It also accepted that housing policy had been distorted in these areas to preserve local majorities. The Commission thus considered these grievances to be "an immediate and operative cause of ... the consequent disorders" and as having "a substantial foundation in fact" (HMSO, 1969). These criticisms had an operative effect on electoral reform and the administrative reform of local government.

The whole future of local government was thrown into the melting pot by the civil disorders of August 1969. The Northern Ireland Government communique of 10 October 1969 announced an expanded housing programme and a central housing authority, the Northern Ireland Housing Executive, which had implications for other services, such as water, sewerage, roads, recreation, and staffing of councils. With the social services already under review, it was decided to set up a review body on local government to advise on "the most efficient distribution of all the relevant functions" (HMSO, 1970). There was no requirement to "sustain a viable system of local democracy" as in Redcliffe-Maud's report on local government in England and Wales (HMSO, 1969). Chaired by Patrick Macrory, and with equal Protestant and Catholic membership the review body reported on 25 June 1970. It recommended that functions be divided into two main categories: regional functions, requiring large units for administration; and district functions, administered by small units. The review team recommended that Stormont become responsible for regional services, which it defined as education, libraries, personal health, welfare and child care, road and traffic management, motor taxation, housing, water and sewerage, food composition, standards and labelling, tourism, electoral arrangements, criminal injuries and compensation, and trading services, such as gas and electricity, transport, major harbours, and the fire service. Except for the trading services each was to be under the appropriate ministry. Macrory's goal was a professional system of service delivery and he recommended that education and health and personal social services be administered through a system of Area Boards. The Boards, first mentioned in a Ministry of Health and Social Services Green Paper in 1969, were to be composed of technocrats and experts nominated by the relevant minister together with a minority of local council representatives. The district services were defined as minor environmental powers in health, street cleansing, drainage, public conveniences, crematoria and cemeteries, entertainment, culture and recreation. These functions, described locally and pejoratively as "bins, bogs and burials", were to be administered by 26 district councils. These services were to be paid for by a two part rate: a regional rate for regional services and a district rate levied by each council.

Macrory's report was debated by the Northern Ireland Parliament and the proposals were accepted in principle by the Government on 17 December 1970. They were incorporated in the Local Government Act (NI) 1972. As a consequence the elections due in 1970 were further postponed until the autumn of 1972.

The centralisation of so many local services would have added to Stormont the functions of a top tier of local government and increased its workload. The consequences were discussed in a Green Paper on the development of the local Parliament in 1971 (HMSO, 1971). It recommended three new functional committees of the House of Commons: Social Security, Environmental Services, and Industrial Services (to join the Public Accounts Committee). They were to be composed of nine members each, representative of party strength and with two chairmanships belonging to opposition parties; the chairmen were to be salaried and members paid. The Green Paper also recommended an increase of 20 to 30 members of the Commons and a Senate of 40. However, within five months the Northern Ireland Parliament had been prorogued.

Direct Rule

The momentous events between 1968 and 1972 culminated in the institution of direct rule on 30 March 1972. The Northern Ireland (Temporary Provisions) Act prorogued Stormont and transferred all legislative and executive powers to the United Kingdom Parliament and to a United Kingdom Minister, Secretary of State, for one year, in the first instance. Fifteen years later this "temporary" measure still applies. The year 1972 proved a watershed in the governance of Northern Ireland: the already contested legitimacy of the *ancien regime* was shattered.

The celerity with which direct rule was established provides an exemplary lesson in the sovereignty of Parliament at Westminster. In just thirty-three hours of debate, the powers vested in Stormont which had developed into a quasi-federal relationship with Britain were stripped away. At that stage the new regime of direct rule was intended as a short-term response to crisis management, providing a stable institutional context within which a political solution could evolve. The favoured policy since 1972 has been the creation of a consociational model to replace the adversarial Westminster one. The major elements of this preferred policy have been a consistent commitment to power-sharing in a devolved framework and a more variable commitment to an institutionalised Irish dimension. There have been five concerted attempts to achieve a solution founded on these principles. Four of them – the power-sharing Executive of 1974; the Constitutional Convention of 1975-6; the initiative of the then Secretary of State for Northern Ireland, Humphrey Atkins in 1980-1; and the scheme for "rolling" devolution fostered by his successor, James Prior, in 1982 – have proved abortive. The fifth, the outcome of the Anglo-Irish process conceived in 1980, is the Anglo-Irish Agreement signed in November 1985. Its gestation period was protracted, its birth troublesome, and its infancy has suffered from rather more than teething problems. To the sceptic, these frequent attempts to resolve the "Northern Ireland problem" along the lines mentioned above, recall Dr Johnson's maxim on remarriage: a triumph of hope over experience. While the high politics of the Province have remained uppermost on the agenda, direct rule provided the day to day administration in a divided society. Its durability since 1972 requires a more detailed examination.

The Northern Ireland Office

At executive level direct rule resulted in the creation of a new department, the Northern Ireland Office (NIO), headed by a Secretary of State of Cabinet rank, supported by two Ministers of State and up to three under Secretaries. Its direct responsibilities lay in the reserved and excepted categories, i.e. political, constitutional and security matters, and the co-ordination of the work of the local departments. The NIO was based at Stormont Castle and Dundonald House, with an Office in Whitehall to deal with UK Departments, inter-departmental matters and parliamentary business. The Secretary of State assumed executive powers while his colleagues were allocated the responsibilities for the existing eight local departments. To co-ordinate the whole, the Secretary of State instituted a thrice weekly meeting of ministers, senior civil servants, and the heads of the security forces thereby unifying civil, police and military administration. This structure was serviced by a newly created central Secretariat headed by a new permanent secretary, with the head of the Northern Ireland Civil Service ranking as a second permanent secretary. While the civil service heads of the eight local departments were not outranked by other NIO civil servants, the perception formed that the NIO, staffed by Foreign and Commonwealth Office personnel, provided overall policy direction. Another novel, albeit short lived, institution, the Northern

Ireland Advisory Commission, recruited from local opinion leaders, provided advice following the prorogation of the Stormont Parliament.

The Legislative process

The change in political control effected by direct rule involved fundamental changes in the legislative process for Northern Ireland. The Northern Ireland Temporary Provisions Act required that legislation on subjects formerly within the competence of the Stormont Parliament would be laid before Parliament at Westminster in the form of draft Orders in Council. They were then subject to either the negative procedure, whereby they came into effect immediately and remained in force unless negatived within a 40 day period, or the positive procedure, whereby explicit approval had to be given by both Houses within a period of 40 days.

Though both procedures were blunt, provision was made to enable local interests to influence proposed legislation. A draft Order originating from a Northern Ireland Department was first to be considered by a Policy Co-ordinating Committee of senior civil servants, approved by Ministers and then made available to local interests *via* the Northern Ireland Advisory Commission. It would also be circulated to interested parties and made available to the public in printed form through Her Majesty's Stationery Office. The draft Order was then scrutinised by the Commission at a meeting chaired by the Secretary of State with the responsible Minister and senior departmental officials present. Thereafter the Order was laid in draft at Westminster and referred to the Joint Committee on Statutory Instruments before being debated.

While this procedure appears exhaustive it was persistently criticised, especially in respect of the final stages at Westminster. Unlike Bills presented to Parliament in the normal way, draft Orders cannot be revised or amended. As Statutory Instruments they have the force of law and can only be approved or rejected by both Houses. In addition, debates on draft Orders tended to be held late at night with few Members in attendance and generally lasted not more than ninety minutes. Finally, the termination of the Northern Ireland Advisory Commission in 1973, in the expectation of the 1973 devolution scheme working, meant that after May 1974 there was felt to be insufficient local consultation on proposed legislation.

The Order in Council procedure has remained intact but a number of methods have been used to improve it. In 1975 the Northern Ireland committee was created at Westminster. It enjoys the status of a standing committee and comprises all the MPs from the province together with, originally, some 20, now over 50, other interested MPs. It considers matters relating to Northern Ireland, with the exception of security; but unlike the Scottish or Welsh Grand Committees it has no formal debating or legislative role. Secondly, in 1976 the Government provided for extended debates on draft Orders and agreed to transmit legislative proposals to the major parties before their introduction in Parliament. Finally, in the most recent attempt to restore devolved government, the Northern Ireland Act 1982, established a system of statutory committees in the Assembly (see below) with the power to preview planned Orders before they were laid at Westminster.

These changes in the legislative process and in the form of executive control were considered necessary, but temporary, arrangements while discussions took place on a new form of devolved government. After a period of consultation and debate the Government published a White Paper outlining its proposals on 11 March 1973. It proposed a return to devolved government but with attenuated legislative and executive power.

The Executive interlude

The Northern Ireland Assembly Act 1973 provided for elections to a new Assembly and the Northern Ireland Constitution Act 1973 provided for the restoration of a form of self government. The Constitution Act divided legislative responsibilities into three categories: "excepted matters" were the responsibility of Westminster and concerned the Crown, Foreign Affairs, Defence, titles, citizenship, appointments to the judiciary, elections, coinage; "minimum reserved matters" included public order, criminal law, the police, trade and navigation, postal service, communication, trade standards; "transferred matters" were those not included by the other categories. The Assembly could legislate on all transferred matters and the reserved matters could be devolved at a later stage. The right of the United Kingdom Parliament to legislate on any matter was retained, though it was anticipated that this would apply to transferred matters in only exceptional circumstances. All legislation had to be submitted through the Secretary of State's Office before reference to the Queen in Council: express consent was required for any measure involving excepted or reserved matters; legislation on transferred subjects could be referred back for reconsideration. Finally any measure was invalid if it discriminated against any person or group on religious or political grounds.

Members of the Northern Ireland Executive, meeting in January 1974. The Unionist leader, Brian Faulkner, seated third from left, was Chief Executive; his Deputy, Gerry Fitt (SDLP), sits facing him (third from right). Northern Ireland's only attempt at power sharing is further symbolised by the seating arrangements, in which Unionist, SDLP and Alliance Party members appear to be deliberately intermingled. (Pacemaker Press Intl. Ltd.)

Under the new arrangements executive power continued to be vested in the Queen, with the Secretary of State exercising the prerogative in respect of transferred matters. The devolution of power to a local executive was dependent on two political conditions. First, the Secretary of State had to be satisfied that an executive was capable of gaining widespread support throughout the community, thereby providing a reasonable basis for government by consent: in effect it prescribed power-sharing. Second, that satisfactory arrangements be made for a Council of Ireland linking Belfast, London and Dublin on matters of common interest to both parts of Ireland. Between the elections to the new Assembly held in June 1973 and the following November, the Secretary of State held talks with representatives from the Unionist, Social Democratic and Labour (SDLP) and Alliance parties on the shape and composition of the new Executive. Agreement was reached on 21 November. The Executive comprised six Unionist, four SDLP and one Alliance member, with Brian Faulkner (Unionist) as Chief Executive and Gerry Fitt (SDLP) as Deputy. There were four additional members, two SDLP, one Alliance and one Unionist, but they had no voting rights.

The new Executive required a reorganisation of departments into Commerce, Housing, Local Government and Planning, Health and Social Security, Finance, Agriculture, Education, Environment, Information Services and Law Reform. The non-voting members assumed responsibilities for Community Relations, Manpower Services, Executive Planning and Co-ordination and the functions of the Chief Whip.

During early December the Executive-designate met with representatives of both the UK and Irish governments at Sunningdale to agree a formula for a Council of Ireland. This was duly arrived at on the 9th of December 1973. It comprised a Council of Ministers, a Consultative Assembly and a Secretariat, with harmonising and executive functions, financed by both governments. An order was made devolving executive and legislative powers to the Executive on 13 December, effective from 1 January 1974. Within five months the Executive had collapsed as a result of political developments North and South. The main element was the failure to win the support of a majority of Unionists so that the February 1974 election and then the Ulster Workers' Council strike, May 14-28, proved to be mortal blows. But the challenge to the Sunningdale Agreement by Kevin Boland in the Irish Supreme Court and the inflexibility of the new arrangements were also significant factors. At the end of May the Assembly was prorogued and the UK government restored direct rule on an interim basis until July 1974.

Direct Rule Mark II

On 17 July 1974 the NI Act set out the new arrangement based on the NI Temporary Provisions Act 1972. The Secretary of State became responsible for the devolved functions and the Order in Council procedure was re-introduced. Where major or sensitive issues were involved, the Government undertook to proceed by a normal Bill. The first period of direct rule has been described as "passive" because it did not seek to bring NI into line with British legislation and policies. It also characterised the initial phase of renewed direct rule while the outcome of the Constitutional Convention was awaited. Its purpose was to recommend a new form of regional government. The Convention, elected by PR on 1 May 1975, was ostensibly free to frame its own proposals – the Government did not take a direct part in proceedings. However, it set three conditions which fixed the terms of the debate: the proposals had to provide for power-sharing; they had to recognise the Irish dimension; and finally, they had to be endorsed by Westminster. In the event a Report was produced but it was not unanimous: it was rejected by Westminster and the Convention was dissolved in March 1976.

While devolution remained on the agenda under a new Secretary of State, Roy Mason, the main thrust was towards a more "positive" form of direct rule. In this period a conscious effort was made to harmonise Northern Ireland legislation and policies with the rest of the UK. The Departments were re-organised into seven, namely, Agriculture, Commerce, Manpower Services, Education, Environment, Finance and Health and Social Services. These responsibilities were shared between the two Ministers of State and two Under-Secretaries of State. The main objective seemed to be the improvement of security and the demonstration of the "normality" of life in the province. By 1979 the main UK political parties seemed resigned to improving direct rule rather than chasing the more elusive devolution of power.

However, between 1979 and 1982 two further attempts were made by government to advance devolution. The second, the Northern Ireland Act 1982, created an Assembly of 78 members whose main purpose was to seek agreement for either the general or partial devolution of power. The second function was scrutinising the Northern Ireland departments administering the transferred services. In 1982 the seven departments were reduced to six when Commerce and Manpower Services merged to form Economic Development; in addition, Finance became Finance and Personnel when it acquired the Management Division of the Northern Ireland Civil Service. The function of scrutiny was intended to be accomplished through a system of statutory committees which were also able to advise on draft legislation. This meant that for the first time since 1974 there was provision for a decidedly local input into policy and legislation affecting Northern Ireland. But the main purpose of the Assembly was weakened from the outset by the abstention of the 19 representatives of SDLP and Sinn Fein. Furthermore, the largest Unionist party, the Official Unionists, demonstrated an ambivalent attitude to the new institution from the first.

Yet the gains achieved by the Assembly in rendering direct rule more locally accountable, have been jeopardised by the latest initiative, the Anglo-Irish Agreement of November 1985. The Agreement, in the form of an international treaty, was the culmination of a series of contacts begun in 1980 between the British and Irish governments which paralleled the devolution initiatives. Through the Anglo-Irish Conference and a joint Secretariat at Maryfield in Belfast, the Republic of Ireland was given a formal role in the governance of Northern Ireland for the first time. The

British Prime Minister and Irish Taoiseach clasp hands for the benefit of the press after the signing of the Anglo-Irish Agreement at Hillsborough on November 15th, 1985. Northern Ireland Secretary, Tom King and Foreign Secretary, Sir Geoffrey Howe, look on from behind. (Pacemaker Press Intl. Ltd.)

role, described officially as consultative, extends to political matters and the composition of various administrative bodies, security and related policy, legal affairs including the administration of justice and cross border co-operation. The Unionist parties tried to utilise the Assembly to oppose the Agreement, in the process prompting the withdrawal of the bi-confessional Alliance Party. Besides debating the issue, Unionists sought to use the Assembly's committee structure to evaluate the effects of the Agreement upon the Northern Ireland departments, a tactic firmly resisted by the government. Civil service staff were withdrawn from the committee early in 1986, effectively signalling the demise of the Assembly, which was finally dissolved by order on 19 June 1986.

Local government displaced

As we have indicated, the process of reforming local government began before the introduction of direct rule with the appointment of the Macrory review body, which reported in June 1970. Its proposals were enacted by the Local Government Act (NI), a matter of days before Stormont was prorogued. As a result the number of local councils was reduced from 73 two-tier to 26 single-tier districts whose boundaries were drawn by the independent Local Government Boundary Commissioner newly appointed in 1971. The then Secretary of State, William Whitelaw, decided to amend the scheme in providing for the elections on a single tranferrable vote system of proportional representation. As a result they were postponed until May 1973 following the grouping of the local wards into multimember constituencies by the Chief Electoral Officer. After the elections only half of the councils were controlled by a single party and in subsequent elections in 1977, 1981 and 1985 the number diminished further to three, four and two respectively.

The new arrangements came into effect on 1 October 1973 with the newly elected councils severely relegated as service providers in favour of central government. They had lost the entire responsibility for public housing in 1971 when the region-wide Housing Executive, announced in 1969, became operative. With the appointment of four Area Boards for Health and Social Services and five for Education and Libraries, the new councils retained only minor environmental and recreational functions. Though councillors were represented on these Boards they provided only a minority of their members – 40 per cent in Education and 30 per cent in Health and Social Services – and in each case were appointed at the discretion of the relevant Minister. The aspiration towards impartiality of local administration required, in effect, the relegation of representative democracy and the promotion of a professionalised service delivery system designed to provide economy and efficiency.

The nominated boards have not escaped criticism, whether on the grounds of quality of service provision or accountability. With services centralised, the vehicle of accountability became the short-lived NI Assembly acting as a top tier of local government. Since the end of the Assembly in 1974 responsibility for the relevant functions lay with the appropriate Minister in the already overburdened House of Commons. The second criticism became more prominent after an initial expansion of services between 1973-9: it was that the NIO set expenditure priorities, such as security and industry, leaving other services to live with the consequences. Hence, boards were criticised for cuts in services, thereby shielding the Minister. Among the most vocal in their criticism were councillors appointed to boards and a number of councils threatened to withdraw their members in protest.

Another criticism concerned the rating system used to finance local services. After 1972 rates were levied in two parts, a regional rate to cover centralised services and a district rate for expenditure by each district council. Only the latter was based on real expenditure. The regional rate was initially based on the cost of service provision in a similar region, said to be Humberside. Since then several other calculations have been used following criticism of the unreal nature of this formula.

While the centralisation of services improved the uniformity of their delivery, it would be idle to claim that it depoliticised the provision of public goods and services. While individual complaints about administration can be made to the Ombudsman and the Commissioner for Complaints, complaints about differential communal spending continue in areas such as housing. Moreover, while denuded of powers, the councils have functioned as the major indigenous arenas for politics during most of the direct rule period. Councillors have utilised their role as public representatives not only to criticise the administrative machinery of direct rule but also as a platform for campaigning on matters beyond their powers, including security policy and the Province's constitutional position. Though Unionist politicians in particular found their outlets enhanced by the 1982 Assembly, local government continues to provide an opportunity to engage in "high" politics. Currently, Unionist councillors have regularly adjourned business in 18 of the 26 district councils in protest at the Anglo-Irish Agreement. They refused to strike a rate for 1986-7 causing legislation to be passed to provide for commissioners to perform this function. They also withdrew from or disrupted the business of Area Boards.

Finance

In 1973 the cumbersome system of financial agreements between Northern Ireland and Great Britain were set aside in favour of a simpler block grant system. Thereafter revenue came from three sources, the attributed share of UK taxes minus reductions for reserved services, non tax revenue and a grant-in-aid approved by the Treasury. It was anticipated that the block grant system would enable a local executive to determine priorities, but with the fall of the Executive in 1974 the new arrangements continued in the hands of UK Ministers. Service provision continued on an expenditure rather than a revenue basis due to local needs and the low yield of tax income.

The province has benefitted from public expenditure under direct rule. As the poorest of the four nations within the UK, public expenditure increased by 17 per cent per capita 1972-9 compared with 2 per cent in Wales and an 8 per cent reduction in Scotland. Such growth reflected the narrow tax base, the relative poverty of the province and the leeway to be made up compared to Britain. Despite a national government committed to cutting public expenditure, since 1979 the Northern Ireland Programme has continued to grow at 2 per cent until 1984-5. This can be illustrated by government figures for per capita public expenditure in the respective parts of the UK. Standardising on England as 100, the figures in 1983-4 were Northern Ireland 150, Scotland 126 and Wales 114; in 1969-70 the figures were Northern Ireland 118, Scotland 131 and Wales 116. Expressed another way, Northern Ireland revenue financed about 73 per cent of expenditure by Northern Ireland Departments amd 66.5 per cent of the total Northern Ireland Programme (Hewitt, 1986(2)).

Since 1968 expenditure by Northern Ireland Departments has been fitted into the UK Public Expenditure Survey Cycle (PESC) and NIO expenditure has been subject to the control procedures of PESC since 1972. Currently, the planned public expenditure in Northern Ireland is in the region of £4.5 billion. All public expenditure relating specifically to the Province is shown in the PESC Report and subsequent White Paper as "the Northern Ireland programme". The "programme" appears in two sections: (i) Expenditure by Northern Ireland Departments, ie on matters transferred under the 1973 Constitution Act; (ii) Expenditure on Northern Ireland by UK Departments, ie reserved and excepted matters. The latter includes the NIO, Ministry of Defence and the Foreign and Commonwealth Office.

On transferred matters the Province conducts its own mini PESC exercise, co-ordinated by the Department of Finance and Personnel (DFP), which plays a similar role in relation to the remaining five Northern Ireland Departments as the Treasury plays in the UK PESC. The DFP subsequently conducts all negotiations concerning NI PESC allocations with the Treasury, with NIO assistance as appropriate: individual Northern Ireland Departments do not negotiate directly with the Treasury. The reserved and excepted areas are the subject of direct negotiations between NIO officials and the Treasury. NIO officials are responsible for co-ordinating both sections of the programme and the Secretary of State has overall responsibility. In this way the broad pattern of expenditure in the Province is integrated into the wider UK system of spending controls.

Conclusion

Throughout the period 1972-87, successive British governments have grappled with the problems of "governing without consensus" in Northern Ireland. The administration apparatus of direct rule, criticised by Nationalists, Republicans and Unionists alike as a form of neo-colonialism, does function. However, no government has regarded it as an end in itself. The post 1976 phase of "positive" direct rule has sought an alignment between British policies and legislation while not losing sight of the cultural distinctiveness of a Province containing two seemingly irreconcilable traditions. This is demonstrated, for example, by the fact that since the suspension of Stormont until the 1978-9 Parliament, 62 per cent of all laws made binding in Northern Ireland have been uniform UK legislation, while 38 per cent have been distinctive Northern Ireland Orders in Council or Acts of Parliament.

While direct rule enables the day-to-day routine of administration to proceed, the search for an alternative continues. The latest initiative, the Anglo-Irish Agreement, threatens to undermine the prevailing structure of local administration which, over the period, had acquired the status of the preferred second-best option within the majority of each community. In seeking to set the Irish dimension in place, *via* an international treaty, before an internally agreed scheme of devolution could evolve, the Agreement mobilised all major Unionist parties in opposition. The involvement of the Government of the Irish Republic in the governance of the North, albeit through a consultative structure, far from assisting peace and reconciliation, has polarised further an already divided society. Article 1 of the Agreement reiterates the status of Northern Ireland as a part of the UK, but only on the basis that a majority wish to remain within the Union. If, however, a majority wish to leave the Union and join the Republic then both the Irish and UK governments will make the necessary constitutional and other arrangements. Thus while diversity of administration within the UK is normal the "consultative role" given to the Irish Republic, together with Article 1, re-emphasise the contingent place of Northern Ireland in the UK, unlike the unconditional place of the other territorial communities of Scotland and Wales.

References

Birrell, W.D. and Murie, A.S., 1980. *Policy and government in Northern Ireland: lessons of devolution*. Dublin.

Hewitt, V., 1986. 'Public finance in Northern Ireland: historical background'; 'Principles and problems of devolved public finance'; Papers I and II, *Fourth report from the devolution report committee* (NIA 282). Belfast.

HMSOa, 1967. *The re-shaping of local government: statement of aims* (Cmnd 517). Belfast.

HMSOb, 1967. *The re-shaping of local government: further proposals* (Cmnd 530). Belfast.

HMSO, 1969. *Cameron Commission report on the disturbances in Northern Ireland* (Cmnd 532). Belfast.

HMSO, 1969. *Royal Commission on local government in England, report* (Cmnd 4040). London. (The Redcliffe-Maud Report).

HMSO, 1971. *The future development of the Parliament and Government in Northern Ireland* (Cmnd 560), Belfast.

HMSO, 1973. *Royal Commission on the constitution 1969-73*, 1, (Cmnd 5460), London.

Lawrence, R.J., 1965. *The government of Northern Ireland: public finances and public services, 1921-64*. Oxford.

Lijphart, A., 1975. The Northern Ireland problem: cases, theories and solutions, *in British Journal of Political Science*, 5, 83-106.

Mansergh, N., 1936. *The government of Northern Ireland: a study in devolution*. London.

Politics & Parties

PAUL ARTHUR AND B. M. WALKER*

Senior Lecturer, Department of Politics, University of Ulster at Jordanstown
**Lecturer, Department of Political Science and Assistant Director of
the Institute of Irish Studies, The Queens' University of Belfast*

When the British Association last visited Belfast in 1952, politics in Northern Ireland must have appeared rather uneventful and uninteresting. During that summer of 34 years ago the press reported little of political note. Today the situation is very different. The media regularly carry accounts of sectarian controversy, civil unrest and instability, and political murder. To understand this dramatic change and to explain the contemporary position it is necessary to look at the background to current events in Northern Ireland. In this chapter on politics and parties we have divided the material into two parts. The first deals with the origins of the political system in the region and looks at developments up to 1972 when the Northern Ireland parliament and government were prorogued and direct rule from Westminster was established. The second covers the period from 1972 to the present.

Politics pre-1972

The main features of party politics as they exist today in Northern Ireland date back to the late nineteenth and the early twentieth centuries. During the Westminster general elections of 1885-6 a clear political division emerged in Ireland between nationalists who sought independence (in a limited form) for the whole country, and unionists who wanted to retain full links with Great Britain (Walker, 1978; 1983). At the same time the electorate polarised sharply along religious grounds with most Roman Catholics voting for the nationalist party and most Protestants supporting the unionist party. These cleavages have remained important ever since in what became, after the Government of Ireland Act of 1920, Northern Ireland, comprising six of the north-eastern counties of Ireland with a unionist majority and a nationalist minority. The rest of Ireland, with its large nationalist majority (represented by Sinn Fein), became the Irish Free State and, later, the Republic of Ireland.

Elsewhere in many parts of Western Europe in this early period, party systems were also established which have remained influential to the present (Smith, 1984, 44-5). Some of the political divisions in these countries' formative years were similar to those in Northern Ireland. For instance, religious cleavage was, and indeed to some extent still is, important in Holland and Switzerland, while conflict over nationalism has been significant in the politics of countries as diverse as Norway and Scotland (Smith, 1984, 14-16, 305-21; Kaarwedt, 1980). Yet none of these states have the instability and lack of consensus to be found in Northern Ireland, a difference explained largely by three factors, crucial to the origins and development of the latter, which contrast sharply with the position elsewhere.

In the first place, unlike Holland and Switzerland, the religious division in the Northern Ireland community has largely correlated to, and has been strengthened by the other major cleavage in society, namely the nationalist/unionist division. In the second place, whereas the conflict over nationalism has in most other European countries been solved with either the victory of the local nationalist movement as in Norway, or in its relegation to relative insignificance as in Scotland, this has not happened in Northern Ireland and there survives a thorny, basic constitutional problem which has proved impossible so far to resolve satisfactorily. Finally, in both nationalist and unionist camps, there has been historically a tendency to resort to force or violence to achieve political ends, which creates a different situation from the other countries which have been mentioned. On the nationalist side, the Irish Republican Brotherhood, founded in 1858, and later the Irish Republican Army of 1916-21, were significant forces, while the Ulster Volunteer Force of 1912-14 played an important role on the unionist side.

Under the Government of Ireland Act, Northern Ireland remained part of the United Kingdom and continued to send MPs to Westminster but now acquired a local legislature and executive with considerable devolved powers. Over the next fifty-two years the new parliament and government developed a fair degree of autonomy. In the political life of the province, however, both in parliament and in local councils, the religious division and the split over the national question remained of paramount importance (Arthur, 1984; Harkness, 1983). The local parties were not divided on class lines, as in Great Britain, although there was some labour representation particularly after 1949. The unionist party, drawn from the Protestant community, ran the government and dominated the political world. The main voice of opposition was that of the nationalist party, based on the Catholic community (although often at odds with republican groupings in that community), which remained an ineffective party, deadlocked with the unionists over the constitutional question.

A comparison of the situation within Northern Ireland to that in the rest of Ireland reveals some interesting points. In the Free State and then the Irish Republic politics were likewise largely without social bases and constitutional matters were also of great importance (Whyte, 1974). The signing of the Anglo-Irish Treaty by representatives of the new Irish leadership in 1921 led to a split in the Sinn Fein party and the outbreak of a civil war. This has been the basis of the party system in the south ever since. But in spite of this similarity, there were important differences. First, the vanquished republican side eventually accepted the new state and took a full part in the political life of the country. Secondly, since the community was very largely Catholic, there was no serious religious division to freeze the constitutional split: Fianna Fail, the party of the defeated side of the civil war, increased its parliamentary representation and became the government in 1932. Both groups have held power at different times.

Between 1920 and the late 1960s the British government played little part in the internal political affairs of Northern Ireland although sovereign power in the state continued to reside at Westminster (Bew, Gibbon and Patterson, 1979). Northern Ireland remained an integral part of the United Kingdom, a position acknowledged by successive British governments, in particular with the constitutional guarantee of 1949. Another factor of importance to the local situation was the attitude of the government and people in the rest of Ireland towards Northern Ireland (Moody, 1974; Bowman, 1982). While the north was often ignored, the end of partition remained an important nationalist tenet and the 1937 Irish constitution contained articles which envisaged the eventual unity of all Ireland. This challenge to the Northern Ireland state, pursued intermittently and in different ways by various southern parties, was seen by northern nationalists as encouragement for their standpoint while unionists viewed it as a danger. At a very different level, members of the small surviving section of the Irish Republican Army sporadically posed an armed threat to the northern government, but in this early period they had limited impact.

The question of the position of the nationalist and Catholic minority in Northern Ireland between 1920 and the late 1960s is a controversial one. Nationalist spokesmen often claimed that there was widespread discrimination against their people while unionist spokesmen denied that it occurred at all. A recent study of the matter by Professor J.H. Whyte has dismissed arguments that there was wholesale discrimination but he has also stressed that the amount proved cannot be dismissed as insignificant (Whyte, 1983). In some parts, particularly in the west of the province, in areas such as electoral practices, public and private employment, and housing, there was discrimination against catholics, but in other parts the problem was not so significant. At the same time, while discrimination was part of the difficulty for the minority so also was alienation from a government and state in which they felt that they had no real political role and were not allowed full recognition of their cultural/religious traditions. The confrontation in Northern Ireland politics over the issue of the border created a permanent majority/minority situation: in addition the state and society were seen by many on both sides as predominantly Protestant and British. This conflict between the two factions assumed a position of stalemate that created a certain stability and an absence of heightened political tensions, which visitors to Northern Ireland in 1952 would have observed.

Terence O'Neill and Sean Lemass at Stormont on January 14th 1965, the first official visit by an Irish Taoiseach to Northern Ireland since Partition. (N.I. Government Information Service)

The 1960s, however, witnessed the beginning of important changes in the form of government and political society in Northern Ireland (Arthur, 1984; Moody, 1974; Flackes, 1983). In 1963 Captain Terence O'Neill became the new leader of the unionist party and Prime Minister of Northern Ireland. He set about not only modernising the economy but also improving community relations and the political atmosphere. He urged better relations between Protestants and Catholics. He held a meeting with the Taoiseach Sean Lemass at Stormont on 14 January 1965, the first time since partition that a southern leader had officially visited Belfast. These developments had a number of effects. First, they encouraged hope for significant reform among Catholics but this later created disillusionment due to lack of change. Secondly, they caused strong reaction within the unionist and Protestant side against O'Neill and change.

During 1968 a civil rights' campaign was launched to seek speedier reform. With their non-violent approach and demands for "civil rights and justice", the civil rights movement focused world-wide attention on its aims. Under this pressure O'Neill introduced a number of reforms such as a points system for local authority housing. With these civil rights marches went a growth in loyalist counter demonstrations and a rise in sectarian confrontation. Finally, serious rioting in Londonderry in August 1969, followed by mob violence in Belfast, led to the introduction of the army in the streets under the direct control of Whitehall.

In spite of this intervention, affairs in Northern Ireland continued to be conducted by the Stormont government, but under new pressure from London. O'Neill was replaced as Premier in 1969 by Major James Chichester-Clarke and he in turn was succeeded in 1971 by Brian Faulkner. In 1970 two new parties were established – the Social Democratic and Labour Party (SDLP), which replaced the old nationalist party, and the Alliance Party, which drew supporters from both sides of the denominational divide. An important new element in the situation was the forceful re-emergence of the IRA in 1970 which split into Official and Provisional wings. Republican violence was matched by the growth of Protestant paramilitary organisations, particularly the Ulster Defence Association (UDA) (started in 1971). During 1971 the Northern Ireland government came under increasing pressure from two sources: the escalation in violence and the withdrawal of the SDLP from parliament in opposition to government policies. As a result the Stormont parliament and government was prorogued in March 1972 and a new Secretary of State, directly answerable to the British cabinet, was appointed for Northern Ireland.

Direct rule

Initially, direct rule was viewed as a temporary measure but from the perspective of 1987 we can see how it has transformed the political, economic and social landscape in Northern Ireland. Indeed its continuation has a bearing on the political life of the British Isles in that it has cast the Northern Ireland question in a wider geographical setting and has made repeated calls upon the resources of the sovereign governments in Dublin and London. None of this was apparent when William Whitelaw took up office as first Northern Ireland Secretary of State in March 1972. After his appointment came the publication of a discussion paper in October 1972, followed by a White Paper in March 1973, which introduced the concepts of power-sharing and an "Irish dimension". Both of these have been on the political agenda ever since, although they have assumed varying degrees of importance, dependent upon the political will of the British government of the moment and the political environment inside Northern Ireland.

What *was* apparent in 1972, and has remained an important political factor, was the growing fragmentation inside the Protestant community. Elections held in 1973 and 1974 demonstrated a major split among unionists. The Official Unionist Party emerged as the largest group but was divided between anti- and pro- power sharing sections (the latter led by Brian Faulkner). Also there were smaller unionist groups, the Democratic Unionists (founded in 1971) led by Rev. Ian Paisley and the Vanguard Unionists (founded in 1973) under the leadership of William Craig. The split remains in 1987, but with the demise of the Vanguard Unionists and Brian Faulkner's party, leadership of the Protestant community is evenly divided between the Democratic Unionists and the Official Ulster Unionists, now led by James Molyneaux.

Political statement on a wall in Protestant west Belfast; UVF stands for the Protestant para-military organisation, the Ulster Volunteer Force.
(N.C. Mitchel)

These divisions are complex and have to be examined at a number of levels. In part the split emerged over the question of reform and the nature of the future society of Northern Ireland. After all, the Ulster Unionists had been in office since the foundation of the state and were used to a monopoly of power. While O'Neill and Faulkner had been willing to concede civil rights demands and broader involvement in participation in government others, particularly the Democratic Unionists, reacted against such developments as a betrayal of what they saw as their loyalist and Protestant heritage.

This takes us to a second level of division, and that concerns Northern Ireland loyalists' lack of trust of "the British". Since 1972 it can be asserted that the Protestant community has been engaged in an internal dialogue on its sense of identity. The most articulate exponent of a separate Ulster identity was William Craig, a former Minister of Home Affairs and an avowed enemy of Captain O'Neill. He had been sacked from the Cabinet in December 1969 because it was alleged he was attracted to ideas of Ulster independence. On the imposition of direct rule he was to argue that the union with Britain was never an end in itself but "was always a means of preserving Ulster's British tradition and the identity of her Loyalist people" (Miller, 1978, 153-4). The very act of proroguing Stormont meant that Britain "had unwittingly forged a nation that cannot entrust to them its security or national destiny".

Few presented the independence option so starkly but there is opinion poll evidence to suggest that a substantial segment of the Protestant community have not been enamoured by British rule for some considerable time. Indeed, in his Northern Ireland attitude survey of 1978, Edward Moxon-Browne (1983, 86) found that 85 per cent of Protestants agreed with the statement that "a loyalist is loyal to Ulster before the British Government", and that about 20 per cent of Protestants opted for an "Ulster" label as their first choice of identity. Given the measure of autonomy enjoyed by Northern Ireland before the "Troubles" and because of the degree of political power exercised by the Unionist community, few should be surprised by their sense of hurt and despair. But that sense was not uniform. Direct rule may have removed one layer of influence – Stormont – but we should remember that the province returned 12 MPs to Westminster (increased to 17 since 1979).

Since the Ulster Unionist Party returned the bulk of those members its leadership did not feel the same sense of isolation as the grassroots loyalist. Further, it could point to some concessions granted by the government especially in the period 1976-79 when a minority Labour Government relied on the smaller parties to keep it in office. It was during this period that unionists persuaded the government to increase Northern Ireland representation at Westminster and succeeded in diluting the concepts of power sharing and the Irish dimension. For that reason the Ulster Unionist Party leadership had more confidence in its ability to influence Westminster thinking and hence the greater British public. It was only with the signing of the Anglo-Irish Agreement on 15 November 1985 that they joined the larger throng in expressing strong mistrust of British political intentions.

This mistrust has manifested itself as a third political level of division among unionists, between devolutionists and integrationists. The former place little trust in British intentions and argue that the only way to maintain the integrity of the Union is through the safety of indigenous institutions. They realise that the *status quo ante* is no longer an option but they are prepared to consider modifications on it. Like the independence-minded people they accept that Northern Ireland is "a place apart" and that therefore mainland politicians and officials have not the sensitivity to rule it fairly. The integrationists (much influenced by Enoch Powell) seek what they see was the position of their forefathers, namely safety in numbers within the bosom of a fully integrated United Kingdom. They take as their role model, Sir Edward Carson, but just as he felt betrayed by Westminster in 1920 his latter day acolytes feel the same in 1987 and are conscious that there is not strong sentiment for integration among the mass of British people.

It would be wrong to attempt a simple demarcation of this complexity of division. After all, the DUP sailed under an integrationist flag for a period in the 1970s, whereas they are perceived as firm devolutionists in 1987. Moreover we have not discussed the role of those actors on the extraparliamentary level, paramilitary groups such as the UDA who played a key role in destroying the power sharing experiment in 1974 and who could be key players in the future. The UDA, for example, have produced some speculative papers on Ulster independence and, more recently, on "agreed government", and are to some extent more innovative than the conventional parties (UDA, 1979; 1987). Nor have we mentioned the degree to

A march on the Falls Road in west Belfast in March 1981, held in support of the hunger strike of Republican prisoners, housed in the H-blocks of the Maze Prison. (N.C. Mitchel)

which the unionist parties are divided on issues of class and religious fundamentalism. Both deserve more careful study. Suffice to say that since the introduction of direct rule there is strong intracommunity competition among the protestant population and that the intellectual ferment it has engendered is in effect a crisis of identity. At the same time, however, one should not too readily assume a collapse of the unionist monolith – again on Moxon-Browne's evidence (1983, 95) "what produces the greatest cohesion within the Protestant community are issues related directly to the status and security of Northern Ireland". It would not be too difficult to assert that virtually all that has gone on since 1972 has been concerned with those very issues.

We would be foolish to ignore a similarly intense but less consistent competition within the Catholic community. Catholics welcomed direct rule as a victory of sorts for them and the creation of a power sharing government (with an Irish dimension) on 1 January 1974 was seen as a tremendous gain. For the first time since the creation of Northern Ireland a nationalist party, the SDLP, had become part of the governing establishment. The collapse of that Executive in May 1974 should have dealt a severe blow to constitutional nationalists who were willing to work within the Northern Ireland framework. The very means of the government collapse, a province-wide industrial stoppage supported by the UDA and other paramilitaries, might have been expected to reinforce the Catholic folk-memory that it could not expect justice within Northern Ireland.

However, until the 1980s the SDLP had a virtual monopoly of the nationalist electorate for its constitutional nationalism and its advocacy of social and political reform within Northern Ireland, although sometimes conflict emerged from within the party as to which objective was more important. Other smaller nationalist parties were not properly organised and Sinn Fein, the political wing of the Provisional IRA, had ideological objections to contesting elections in a partitioned Ireland. Meantime, the Provisional IRA, the *soi-disant* protectors of the nationalist community continued its campaign of violence: allegedly engaged in a war against "the British war machine" the IRA managed to slaughter many of its co-religionists in the process and inflicted great economic damage on Catholic communities in the west and south of the province (New Ireland Forum, 1983). Still the IRA and Sinn Fein retained support among a small but important section of the nationalist community, particularly among the young and unemployed.

It was only with the emergence of a highly emotional issue, a hunger strike of republican prisoners protesting against the withdrawal of their political status by the authorities, that Sinn Fein saw the potential for eroding support for constitutional nationalism. It adopted the strategy of "the armalite and the ballot box", explained with ruthless logic in its organ, *An Phoblacht: Republican News* (16.9.82): "The essence of republican struggle must be in armed resistance coupled with popular opposition to the British presence. So while not everyone can plant a bomb, everyone can plant a vote." Sinn Fein won five of the 78 Assembly seats in October 1982 (10.1 per cent of first preference votes) and pushed its support up to 13.4 per cent in the Westminster election of June 1983, making it the fourth most popular party in the province. Such electoral prominence held out a threat to the SDLP in the first instance but ultimately to the legitimacy of government.

Before turning to London's strategy in face of this threat we must look briefly at "middle ground" politics in Northern Ireland. The bi-confessional Alliance Party had successfully achieved 9.2 per cent of the votes in the Assembly elections of 1973 and played a key part in the power-sharing Executive. Thereafter its vote has failed to improve significantly and at the 1983 Westminster election its portion of the poll stood at 8 per cent. Clearly the continued violence and polarisation between unionist and nationalist in the community at large has served to undermine the ability of Alliance to draw from both communities. While the Alliance Party has tended to be strongest in middle class areas, other middle-ground parties such as the Workers' party, have specifically aimed at working class communities but with relatively little success.

Undoubtedly government insensitivity, more ignorance than malice, compounded its problems inside Northern Ireland for it managed to alienate the zealots of both communities – at different times and to different degrees – a feat, it must be said, that is easy to achieve. It is not that it was not active; indeed Westminster entered its most creative phase in Northern Ireland since 1920 after the imposition of direct rule, culminating in the establishment of the power sharing Executive in 1974. London's problem was that it arrived with little detailed knowledge of the political landscape: it misunderstood the political culture – superficially British but British of an earlier imperial era; it appeared to have little of a consistent

Unionist opposition to the Anglo-Irish Agreement expressed on a banner at the offices of Lisburn District Council in Hillsborough, 1986, just across the road from Government House where the agreement was signed. (N.C. Mitchel)

policy beyond a desire to be of assistance and confusion as to whether it should concentrate on the economic, the constitutional or the security aspect. In consequence it tried all three, not in any harmonious fashion but simply as an exercise in conflict management. The result was a series of reactive policies and a failure to locate a patron or patrons with whom it could negotiate in confidence. It was learning that if anything united the two communities it was a shared distaste for direct rulers. In short it was paying for a policy of fifty years of benign neglect. In fairness, however, it must be said that the wisdom of Solomon would have been hard pressed in similar circumstances.

After the imposition of direct rule the first type of government backed by the authorities was a power sharing Executive made up of Unionists (led by Brian Faulkner), the SDLP and the Alliance Party. In May 1974, however, the new Executive collapsed. The immediate cause of its fall was the strength of a Protestant, paramilitary backed strike and the weakness of the British government in the face of this challenge. More importantly, this attempt at a cross-community form of government failed because of lack of broad support, particularly in the Protestant community. The concept of sharing power was still stoutly opposed by a sizeable and influential number of Protestants: at the same time, undue haste, by members of the

SDLP and the Irish government, in pursuing the "Irish dimension" created strong fears among unionists that this experimental form of government would fatally undermine the union. Continued activity by the IRA had also helped to destroy the effectiveness of the Executive.

Following this failure of power sharing, the authorities made three more serious efforts at constitution making. The first followed within a few months of the May 1974 debacle, if only to fill a political vacuum which might have been occupied by resurgent loyalist paramilitarism. In July the government published a White Paper to enable a constitutional Convention to "consider what provisions for the government of Northern Ireland would be likely to command the most widespread acceptance throughout the community". On this occasion the government was careful to distance itself from the deliberations of the newly elected Convention: this was to be the work of the indigenous politicians set the ultimate examination question of producing a "solution" to the Northern Ireland problem.

They failed, of course, split as they were on sectarian lines, although an interesting feature of the exercise was the futile attempt of William Craig to get his loyalist colleagues to accept the concept of coalition for the duration of the "emergency". The effort destroyed his party and ultimately his political career. With the Convention's failure British policy concentrated on the art of inertia. It is a curious feature of the period that any real innovation came from the Conservatives. Northern Ireland did not seem to fit into the Labour Party's accepted political parameters. Try as they might, they could not reduce it to a class cleavage. Labour had a distaste for anything which interfered with the crusade for an egalitarian Britain. Nationalism was an aberration. So both Merlyn Rees and Roy Mason, Secretaries of State between 1974-79, concentrated on the security and economic fields with very mixed results.

The return of a Conservative government in 1979 led to two further attempts at an internal settlement and, unwittingly, opened out the "Irish Question" which Lloyd George believed he had settled in 1920-21. Humphry Atkins attempted a Convention Mark 2 in 1979-80, although this time the Secretary of State chaired the Conference composed of small working parties from the DUP, the SDLP and the Alliance Party – the Ulster Unionists boycotted this particular exercise because the government had strayed from an integrationist strain in its 1979 manifesto. The result of these deliberations was another White Paper which narrowed the options to a variant of the power sharing theme or a system of majority rule with a minority blocking mechanism. This, too, proved unacceptable.

A final attempt at an internal settlement was made by James Prior who became Secretary of State in September 1981. His plan for "rolling devolution" was more subtle than earlier blueprints, built as it was on emphasising managerialism and gradualism. He suggested a new Assembly (it operated from October 1982) invested with scrutinising powers leading to the devolution of functional powers either partially or *in toto* if it could be demonstrated that it enjoyed a real measure of "cross-community agreement". It could not – the SDLP boycotted the exercise from the beginning since they saw no change of heart on the part of unionism, and the Ulster Unionists (divided on the intergration/devolution issue) were reluctant participants.

In any event the political environment was being changed radically by the resurgence of Provisional SF/IRA who made the hunger strike issue a major propaganda victory by stressing its "humanitarian" ethos, thereby enabling them to make the psychological leap from the margins of politics to the full glare of the international media. Four failed internal initiatives, resurgent republicanism generated by a growth in alienation among the minority community, and a more critical international awareness of the continuing Ulster saga, all induced Mrs Thatcher's government to launch a bold new initiative based on what has become known as the Anglo-Irish process.

Prior to the 1970s the Irish government had formulated no real policies on Northern Ireland. Lacking any deep understanding of the situation in the north its approach had alternated between policies of disinterest and aggression, although Sean Lemass had tried to improve the situation. With the spread of civil disturbances the Irish government found itself trying to assist the SDLP while co-operating with the British government in fighting republican paramilitary groups. Within the main political parties debate ensued about the best way to approach the northern situation. The result was the New Ireland Forum of 1983-4, an effort by Fianna Fail, Fine Gael and Irish Labour in conjunction with the SDLP, to produce a more reasonable and coherent nationalism. The *Forum Report*, an agenda rather than a blueprint, recognised that Irish unity was not simply a matter of "manifest destiny" and that both governments would have to co-operate to bring about peace, stability and good government in Northern Ireland.

On 15 November 1985 the British and Irish governments signed the Anglo-Irish Agreement at Hillsborough Castle. It has created a new asymmetry within Northern Ireland: a divided and demoralised unionist community facing a constitutional nationalist movement full of self-confidence. To appreciate this new departure we need to understand a number of factors. The Agreement has removed the debate from the "endogenous" to the "exogenous"; consequently it has proven much more difficult to destroy than the Sunningdale Agreement of 1973, and just as importantly it re-establishes the extent to which Northern Ireland is a subordinate part of the United Kingdom with a population of less than three per cent of the United Kingdom. The Agreement is not an end in itself but represents a burgeoning relationship between two sovereign states which recognise that they share a common problem. They have had to recognise that neither has been in absolute control of the political agenda and that constraints on bi-lateral co-operation have hindered the emergence of a solution. Hence since 1980 they have tried to work in closer harmony; there have been five summits – May and December 1980, November 1981, November 1983 and November 1984 – before the signing of the Agreement. Hillsborough represents, after several false starts, an exercise in mutual trust between London and Dublin in that it allows the

Irish government an input into the governance of Northern Ireland without derogation of sovereignty, and it guarantees Northern Ireland's constitutional status so long as that remains the wish of the majority of its people.

Protestant reaction has been profound and widespread, ranging from an attempt to make local government unworkable, to mass demonstration and to a virtual boycott of Westminster. The reasons are not difficult to find. Their self-perception is of a besieged community protecting a British way of life. They see themselves as victims of an IRA terror campaign launched in part from the Irish Republic with the possible connivance of the authorities there. They cannot understand how any British government could possibly allow such people any influence in Northern Ireland's affairs.

That is not the way the matter is perceived in London where it is accepted that the Irish authorities share a mutual detestation of the IRA. Unless both governments can work in tandem terrorism will flourish. Moreover, London cannot accept that Ulster loyalists do not realise that membership of the United Kingdom carries responsibilities as well as privileges. An obligation on the majority community, they believe, is to share power with the minority, in return for the nationalist community's acceptance of its duties and responsibilities within Northern Ireland. In effect, matters stand in 1987 as they did in 1920. It was the illusion of Ulster autonomy which spread in the intervening years which is a contributory factor towards a lack of solution. Until both communities accept their subordinate and inter-dependent status and seek out equality of status between them the elements of a solution will pass them by.

References

Arthur, P., 1984. *Government and politics of Northern Ireland*. London.

Bew, P., Gibbon, P. and Patterson, H., 1979. *The state in Northern Ireland*. Manchester.

Bowman, J. *De Valera and the Ulster Question, 1917-1973*. Oxford.

Flackes, W.D., 1983. *Northern Ireland: a political directory*. London

Harkness, D.H., 1983. *Northern Ireland since 1920*. Dublin.

Kaartwedt, A., 1980. The economic basis of Norwegian nationalism in the nineteenth century, *in* Mitchison, R. (ed.), *The roots of nationalism: Studies in Northern Europe*. Edinburgh. 11-19.

Miller, D., 1978. *Queen's rebels*. Dublin.

Moody, T.W., 1974. *The Ulster Question, 1603-1973*. Cork.

Moxon-Browne, E., 1983. *Nation, class and creed in Northern Ireland*. Aldershot.

New Ireland Forum, 1983. The cost of violence arising from the Northern Ireland situation since 1969, *in Northern Ireland Forum Report*.

Smith, G., 1984. *Politics in Western Europe*. London.

UDA, 1979. *Beyond the religious divide*. Belfast.

UDA, 1987. *Common sense: Northern Ireland – an agreed process*. Belfast.

Walker, B.M., 1978. (ed.). *Parliamentary election results in Ireland, 1801-1922*. Dublin.

Walker, B.M., 1983. The land question and elections in Ulster, 1868-86, *in* Clark S., Donnelly, J.S. (eds.), *Irish peasants: violence and political unrest, 1780-1914*. Wisconsin and Manchester. 230-68.

Whyte, J.H., 1974. Ireland: politics without social bases, *in* Rose, R. (ed.), *Electoral behaviour: a comparative handbook*. London. 619-53.

Whyte, J.H., 1983. How much discrimination was there under the unionist regime *in* Gallagher, T. and O'Connell, J. (eds.), *Contemporary Irish studies*. Manchester. 1-35.

16 Arts in Society

BRIAN FERRAN

Visual Arts, The Arts Council of Northern Ireland

To mark the Festival of Britain in 1951 *The Arts in Ulster* was published by the Council for the Encouragement of Music and the Arts (CEMA). Well-known authorities on poetry and drama, painting and sculpture, architecture and music, were invited to contribute essays to this survey which recorded for the first time the achievements of the Province's creative and performing artists. In his chapter on the painting and sculpture of the preceding ten years, John Hewitt concluded that "the general volume of Art work has notably increased and the average level has been rising slowly but perceptibly; in the schools of the Province there is a definite promise for the future; but so far no common denominators have become sufficiently remarkable to allow us to claim that we have as yet any distinctive Ulster School" (Bell, Robb and Hewitt, 1951). In the years since then no distinctive school has evolved but the amount of activity and its diversity have multiplied tenfold. More artists and new agencies reinforced and expanded the seeding work undertaken by established institutions concerned with generating and sustaining the artistic life of the region. In 1971 a more comprehensive book *Causeway* reviewed the decades from 1951 to 1971 (Longley, 1971). It included the role played in the arts by broadcasting and by the museums. Some of the essays took as their starting points the conclusions recorded in *The Arts in Ulster* while others considered jazz, Irish traditional music and the establishment of the Ulster Folk and Transport Museum. Since 1971 artistic activity has continued to flourish.

The Council for the Encouragement of Music and the Arts became the Arts Council of Northern Ireland in 1962 and remains the prime distributor of public support for the arts. Its annual reports succinctly chronicle the evolution of the arts in this community. Established in 1943, the Council's first funds were provided by the Pilgrim Trust and matched by the Ministry of Education for Northern Ireland. Since then, however, arts funding has been provided primarily by government with some local authority contri-

"Seated Figure", by one of Ireland's most talented young sculptors, Carolyn Mulholland, sited in Tannaghmore Gardens in Craigavon, County Armagh. (Arts Council)

butions. The annual budget of the Arts Council has increased from an
initial £3,000 to £3,477,000 in 1987-88. Unlike other arts councils in the
United Kingdom, the Council is a limited company whose affairs are
managed by a board consisting of twenty members. Its director is the
principal executive officer, and administrative support is provided by a
professional staff responsible for the council's ambition to increase the
public's access to the arts throughout Northern Ireland and to improve
standards of execution in all artistic disciplines.

Visual arts

In the visual arts, the Council creates opportunities for the public to
experience at first hand the work of Irish and foreign artists through
exhibitions, loan collections, public commissions as well as through the
making of films on distinguished Irish artists and the publication of
catalogues, magazines, monographs and surveys. The Council's awards,
bursaries, fellowships, exhibitions and other patronage assist painters,
sculptors, printmakers and craftsmen. The Council presents major exhibitions at the Ulster Museum, runs a gallery in central Belfast, and
operates a studio print workshop on the outskirts of the city. The visual arts
strategy comprises elements which provide the basic structure for bringing
the community and artists together. At present, there are approximately
25 art galleries in Northern Ireland, while in 1951 there were five. The Arts
Council Gallery in central Belfast is the Council's main platform in the
Province. Visited by up to 500 people each day, it generates exhibitions
which tour the region or are exchanged with other institutions in Ireland,
throughout the United Kingdom, or abroad.

The Council is mindful of community requirements and tours three
exhibitions to more than 20 centres each year. In 1985 these three local
exhibitions were: works by Tom Carr, a distinguished painter in the
academic tradition; works by David Crone, a mid-generation artist who, in
the past 25 years, has established a high reputation for the strength and
excellence of his painting, and NOVA an exhibition of works by younger
artists selected from open competition. The latter two exhibitions were
designed initially for showing at the Arts Council Gallery and modified in
scale to suit touring needs. The Tom Carr exhibition was one of a series of
major retrospective exhbibitions organised jointly by the two Arts Councils
in Ireland, as part of a continuing arrangement. It was shown at the Ulster
Museum in Belfast and the Douglas Hyde Gallery in Dublin and then
reselected for touring.

The Council also initiates projects designed to encourage the purchase
and commission of works of art. This is done primarily by providing, within
a set of rules, 50 percent of the cost of works purchased or commissioned.
Recent examples of this joint strategy are the two works commissioned in
1985 for Queen's University. One was a large canvas by Anne Carlisle for
the New Library and the other an outdoor sculpture by Clifford Rainey
located on the lawn adjacent to the University Library. Four new
sculptures are being made currently for the recently completed Belfast City

Hospital. These works, with many others, have added to the community's collection of art works, installed in public places and accessible to the widest population. Public access to important contemporary art works was considerably enhanced in 1958 when William Scott was commissioned by the architects Yorke, Rosenberg and Marshall to paint a long mural for the Altnagelvin Hospital in Derry. At the same time this architectural firm also invited F.E. McWilliam to design a sculpture for the main entrance to the hospital. These two Ulster artists were then among Britain's most celebrated contemporary artists and the community in the North West was given its first direct experience of new art. This example was followed in the early '60s by the commissioning of Mary Martin's relief sculpture for Musgrave Park Hospital and an Elizabeth Frink sculpture for the Ulster Bank in Shaftesbury Square. In 1951 the Arts Council made its first public commissions – a low relief stone sculpture for the Guildhall in Derry by George McCann and a painted mural for the Belfast City Hall by John Luke.

In a recent Northern Ireland information service publication entitled *Images*, (Evans, 1985, 11) David Evans observed that "in architecture as in speech the Ulsterman tends towards laconic understatement; though responsive to new ideas we like to follow fashion from a safe distance and view over-elaboration with suspicion". This assessment could be extended to embrace many of the arts. In the forties and fifties, celebration of abstract painting, moved from Paris to New York, and then in the sixties to London, Amsterdam and Dusseldorf, but in Belfast most artists' themes and subject matter remained true to a long relationship with the landscape. This preoccupation with figuration and with place continued to mark the work of Ulster painters so much so that many were readily associated with specific locations. Tom Carr's delicate and informed watercolours sang the praises of the Mountains of Mourne, while Terry Flanagan's sensitive painting charged the Fermanagh lakes and islands with emotive atmosphere, and Basil Blackshaw, with Cezanne-like dedication, exlored the mountains of South Antrim and the distant shoreline of Lough Neagh. These artists and many others working in this genre have, in style as well as location, the hallmark of individuality and are concerned primarily with the personality adjusting to the outer world. All Northern Ireland artists were not, of course, rooted in the landscape and there happily co-existed a rich diversity of approaches to all aspects of art. This versatility was most evident in the case of Colin Middleton, the best known and most appreciated painter in the community. The landscape is, nevertheless, a dominant element in his work, sometimes romantic or narrative or surrealistic, but always with a strong feeling of place. He exercised his imagination and talent on the topography of every county in the province.

From the turn of the century and for almost fifty years after, William Conor explored popular themes and stood almost alone in documenting the everyday life of Belfast's urban proletariate. He continued this practice until he died in 1968. In the fifties, for the first time, artists with some group identity emerged. This group comprised, among others, Gerard Dillon,

George Campbell and Arthur Armstrong, and they consolidated a romantic tradition based on post-impressionism and initiated here by Paul Henry and his followers who looked westward to Connemara and its people for their subject matter. Meanwhile, two of the founding fathers of contemporary Irish art, the Enniskillen painter William Scott, and the Banbridge sculptor F.E. McWilliam, were establishing their positions in London and New York, while at the same time helping their contemporaries at home achieve respectability and the beginnings of financial self-sufficiency. They also paved the way for the present generation of such young artists as John Aiken, Clifford Rainey, and Felim Egan, who now attract the attention of internationally important museums and collectors. The reasons for this rich diversity of works are as numerous as our artists themselves and year by year the range and nature of images produced increases. During the past five years issues and events have been forthrightly debated in *CIRCA* a contemporary art magazine published in Belfast, whose consistent approach to matters of social and political concern in the visual arts has gained it a high reputation. The emergence of new galleries has increased the accessibility of contemporary art and will generate public confidence in local artists.

Although Arts Council support strategies are governed by available resources the Council acknowledges that its subsidy and effort should also go towards helping provide facilities for artists. A place to work is vital. Grant aid is provided, for example, to the Artists' Collective of Northern Ireland to make studio space available at low rents. Access to specialist equipment is provided by maintaining a fully-equipped artists' studio print workshop for lithography, silkscreen printing and etching. The opportunity to see the work of other artists abroad is valuable and to this end the Arts Council provides travel awards for artists. It also regularly imports exhibitions from abroad and, from time to time, assists initiatives taken to present works abroad by local artists. Within its gallery programme the Council presents locally initiated exhibitons of an experimental nature and provides, for selected artists, working studio space abroad at the British School in Rome and at the Institute of Art and Urban Resources in New York. Annual awards and bursaries provide artists with opportunities to develop their talents, to buy time, and to purchase essential materials and costly equipment. In addition, short-term and long-term residencies at the Annaghmakerrig Centre in County Monaghan have been developed to provide a working sanctuary for creative artists of all disciplines. The overriding priority of the Arts Council is to help create a climate in which artists and their work are valued. This aim is assisted through commissioned films which, in recent years, have focused on the painter Colin Middleton, the sculptor F.E. McWilliam, the poet, critic and art curator John Hewitt, and on the painter William Scott. Although the William Scott film, unlike the other three, was not totally funded by the Arts Council, it was given a small measure of grant aid in the early planning stages of the film. In recent years the BBC, ITV and RTE and Channel Four have made numerous films on the arts and artists which have substantially increased public interest.

The ability of artists, however, to earn a living from their art is an aim which appears on the Arts Council's agenda. Thus the Council regularly purchases paintings, sculptures, prints, and drawings from artists it judges to be creating works of high quality and achievement. The first exhibition assembled in 1944 by CEMA was of 40 paintings by eighteen living Irish artists, most of which were purchased to serve as the basis of a touring exhibiton at a total cost of £154, and so the Arts Council collection was born. It now numbers almost 1,000 works most of which are continuously on show in public places and in schools and colleges. The collection today reflects changes in theme and treatment over more than forty years. Its scope was widened in the 1960s in order to circulate, in Northern Ireland, fine examples of contemporary British works by Victor Pasmore, Richard Smith, Robin Denny, David Hockney, Peter Blake, Bryan Winter, Keith Vaughan, Adrian Heath, and Roger Hilton.

In the early days of Northern Ireland's administration, the then Ministry of Education adopted a far-sighted policy of providing scholarships to the Slade and the Royal College of Art in London. The return of many of these students to active teaching duties in Northern Ireland shortened the traditional time lag of contact with international trends. So, as advances were made in art education, the aesthetic horizon of local artists changed. The rapid dissemination of information through touring exhibitions and art magazines, together with the greater mobility of artists, has radically changed the artistic environment. Artists in Northern Ireland are now as well informed and sensitive to current international preoccupations as are artists in London, New York, and Tokyo.

The opening of the Ulster Museum and Art Galleries at Stranmillis in Belfast provided direct contact in the late 1930s with authentically avant garde work. Young people saw in the opening exhibition five Henry Moores, four Barbara Hepworths and paintings by Ben Nicholson, Paul Nash, Edward Burra, and Edward Wadsworth. The Ulster Museum entered the competitive and expensive art collecting field late, so the museum sensibly decided that the collection would focus on Irish art and international contemporary art. The reputation of the collection steadily grew until 1980, when economic expediency forced a halt to purchasing. Even so, many commercial and subsidised galleries are now happily located close to the Arts Council Gallery and the Ulster Museum. They are the Tom Caldwell Gallery, the Octagon, the Bell Gallery, the Art and Research Exchange, Fenderesky Gallery, Malone Gallery, On the Wall, the Otter Gallery, Vasari Fine Art, Magee Gallery, and the Crescent Arts Centre. Others enter and leave the marketplace, but more galleries now operate than ever before in Belfast. In 1969 the art gallery in Derry, that from 1962 had presented a continuous programme of exhibitions, closed. Some seven years later a suitable central basement space was converted into an art gallery and re-named the Orchard. Here the Derry City Council now presents a successful programme of contemporary exhibitions which attract an annual attendance of more than 20,000 visitors. Its exhibitions are complemented by a successful commercial programme at the neighbouring Gordon Gallery.

Positioned in the centre of Belfast with a large shop window, the Arts Council Gallery invites not only the enthusiast but also the casual passerby to enter. It is the principal Arts Council forum for the visual arts, as well as a marketplace for books, publications, records, events, and video viewing. During the late 1960s, in an attempt to get the work of local artists into the streets and out of the rarified gallery atmosphere, the Arts Council commissioned artists to make images for the large advertising hoardings located throughout Northern Ireland. The images advertised nothing but themselves. They intended to activate visually city streets, gables, railway and coach stations and, by saturating the towns and villages with these images, to familiarise more of the population with artists' work, thus stimulating public imagination and discussion. As in commercial marketing, there was no tidy sequential link between the components, and the plan only marginally achieved its aims. However, the plan succeeded in getting aesthetically worthwhile images into public thoroughfares.

In the early 1970s, the Council adopted a more aggressive policy in presenting the work of living artists. The Council started a programme entitled "Art in Context" to encourage artists to turn their creative energies towards making either durable or ephemeral pieces for the environment. Artists were invited to submit proposals and public sites were found. Twenty proposals were completed, including concrete sculptures by Graham Gingles in Omagh; a mural by Gabriel Flynn at the University of Ulster; an outdoor play sculpture by Arthur Armstrong at Belmont School in Derry; a tapestry by Cecil King at the Ulster Hospital; a metal sculpture by Evin Nolan at the Loughshore Park, Newtownabbey; a mural by Adrian Hall at Dunmurry High School, and a low relief metal sculpture by Roy Johnston at the Christian Brothers School, Glen Road, Belfast.

Drama

In drama the Arts Council primarily ensures the survival of the province's theatres. The Grand Opera House in Belfast was taken into public ownership by the Council, rehabilitated, and then reopened in 1980. Vital financial support is given to the Lyric Theatre, the Civic Arts Theatre in Belfast, and to the Riverside Theatre in Coleraine. The Council also funds touring companies performing in Belfast and at regional centres. Many factors, but most particularly the civil disturbances in Northern Ireland throughout the 1970s, had a detrimental effect on theatre audiences and on the provision for live theatre in Belfast. Theatre buildings were damaged and audiences dispersed. At the beginning of the 1980s normal commercial and social life began its return to the city and the theatre and entertainment industry moved towards resuming its role in cultural and recreational life.

The new infrastructure, initiated by the reopening of the Grand Opera House, has now functioned well for six years. Organisations made homeless in the 1970s and others without access to a Belfast venue are handsomely accommodated in this well-equipped theatre. Many felt that the Grand Opera House in the city centre would draw audiences away from the other theatres, the Lyric and the Civic Arts, which are located outside the city

*Belfast's Grand Opera
House, built in 1895 and
reopened in 1980 following
restoration by Belfast
architect Robert McKinstry.
The building won a Europa
Nostra award.*
(N.I. Tourist Board)

centre, or from the small neighbouring Group Theatre. Initially this
happened, but gradually these smaller theatres recovered their audiences
or attracted new audiences to such an extent that the Lyric and Arts
recorded percentage increases on their audiences after the opening of the
Opera House. It was also felt that, because of programme similarities, the
Arts Theatre would lose a greater part of its audience to the Opera House
than would the Lyric. Detailed analysis, however, reveals no positive
evidence that the type of performance presented at any one of the four
Belfast theatre affects the size of audience at the other when either similar
or dissimilar programmes are presented. All live theatre in Northern
Ireland is unfortunately debilitated by low public spending and even lower
consumer spending on theatre.

When Belfast's Grand Opera House was built in the last decade of the
nineteenth century the local newspapers waxed lyrical over the splendours
of this "perfect eastern palace". On December 17, 1895 the *Belfast Newsletter* gave a detailed account of the theatre: "The auditorium is a large one,
constructed on the cantilever principle, and will accommodate at least
3,000 persons" (2,000 was a more accurate figure). Today, to satisfy the
audience's demand for comfort and to comply with safety regulations, the
auditorium seats an audience of 990. This has radically changed the idea of
profitability. Equally important is the fact that, in our television and video
age, live entertainment is facing hard times as the economics of the
industry become more dependent on rate and tax resources and as patterns
of recreation change. Seat prices in Belfast are pegged at approximately

the same level as elsewhere in the United Kingdom, and increases made to accommodate inflation have not so far resulted in noticeable market resistance. Although bookings for the Belfast Festival at Queen's increase annually, evidence suggests that promoters of live entertainment in Belfast are battling against the economic and social tide. Most income sustaining the live theatre comes from the box office takings, and the Arts Council is the main sponsor of entertainment which has cultural content, but both are proving vulnerable to the sustained pressures of the recession. Belfast theatres also have to meet the cost of transporting many artists to and from Britain. Charging its usual fee, a string quartet can cost twice as much in Belfast, because of air fares and accommodation.

The Grand Opera House was purchased in 1976 with funds made available for that purpose by government. The fabric was made structurally sound and the rescue of the building was then complete. Renovation and refurbishing then brought the Grand Opera House into operation as a modern working theatre. The auditorium was reseated with more generous spacing; the foyer and first floor circulation areas were redesigned; and the Grand Staircase was remodelled to take up less space. An

Performance of "Dockers" by Martin Lynch. This is one of a number of recent plays which deal with the contemporary political situation. (Arts Council)

Performance of "Boyd's Shop" by St. John Ervine. In contrast to the many recent plays dealing with the "troubles" this classic Ulster play, still widely popular, is concerned with countryside and town life. (Arts Council)

extension over Great Victoria Street at first floor level increased the first floor bar and general circulation area. Special provision was made for the disabled. The total capital cost of purchasing and renovating the Opera House was, in round terms, £3,000,000. The entire capital cost was met by government grants and the Arts Council, in running the theatre, was not compelled, like commercial theatre, to take into account capital costs. The Council therefore concentrates on meeting the running costs and production costs associated with the theatre.

The Arts Council encourages the Grand Opera House to present a mixed programme providing the citizens of the province with a wide range of cultural and entertainment experience. In respect of this requirement, the Arts Council will not enter into debates on definition, other than to encourage a reasonable balance between "popular entertainment" and events of "artistic significance". The objective of the Opera House is to secure maximum occupancy of the auditorium through a judicious balance between these two elements. Neither "majority" nor "minority" interests are over-riding considerations. In its programming, the Opera House aims to secure with the subsidy finance available the maximum audience response by catering for the widest possible range of tastes. The primary consideration is that every event is considered to be of acknowledged high quality in its particular field, and the Opera House endeavours to ensure that as much as possible of the annual programme is of artistic quality.

In 1945, actor-manager Hubert Wilmot opened a small theatre in Upper North Street with a capacity of 100 seats: eventually in 1961, under his direction, the Arts Theatre with 460 seats settled in Botanic Avenue close to Queen's University. Described by the contemporary press as "The first playhouse to be built in Belfast for over fifty years", it received help from CEMA, from the Belfast City Council, which for the first time made a direct grant to the theatre, from private patrons and from the Pilgrim Trust. In its early years, this theatre presented drama of the highest quality. In 1962 Hubert Wilmot announced that the Arts Theatre had had such a successful first year in its new premises that it had not been necessary to call on the CEMA guarantee: "We are very grateful for the CEMA guarantee. It is an umbrella which could be very helpful, but we are very glad and proud that we did not have to use it". However, the Arts Theatre now continues the policy stated by Hubert Wilmot in 1972 that "only by presenting enter-tainment can the living theatre survive the intense competition brought about by television and the rapidly-changing pattern of living in the last few years. Therefore we cannot afford to risk our existence by presenting serious plays for a minority audience who rarely support the theatre regularly enough, and in sufficient numbers, to keep our doors open". In coming to this conclusion Wilmot was assisted by a questionnaire addressed to the Theatre's predominantly middle-class audiences.

Based on an extensive knowledge of the Ulster playgoer Hubert Wilmot's opinion was that he could not stay in business and cater exclusively, or even largely, for the ten percent who wanted good drama. So, not surprisingly, the present policy at this theatre is to present a varied bill, although sophisticated comedy and musical entertainment feature predominantly. In the early 1970s the Arts Council provided capital finance for the renovation of the theatre. In return, it gained access to the theatre by mutual agreement for up to twelve weeks in any year for visiting com-panies introduced under Arts Council guarantee. The Ulster Actors Com-pany was then the resident company. Now the Theatre Ulster, a joint production board on which representatives of the Belfast Arts Theatre and the Riverside Theatre of Coleraine meet, sponsors productions that are shared by the two theatres and on occasions toured to centres throughout the province.

The Lyric Theatre was founded in 1951 by Pearse and Mary O'Malley to advance a crusade for the drama of Yeats, which they considered the Abbey Theatre in Dublin had neglected. The first presentations given in a private drawing room were *At the hawk's well* and *The dreaming of the bones* by Yeats, *Lost night* by Robert Farren and Valentine Iremonger's play on the death of Robert Emmet, *Wrap up my green jacket*. In the articles of association of the Lyric Players Theatre, an obligation of the trustees is the presentation of "plays of cultural and educational value from world theatre which shall include one play by William Butler Yeats, and in the selection of which special consideration shall be given to the work of Irish poets, writers

and dramatists". On June 12, 1965, Austin Clarke laid the foundation stone – or rather raised the portal stone – of the Lyric Players' new 304 seat theatre at Ridgeway Street, Belfast. With financial assistance from the Arts Council, charitable trusts and individual subscriptions, the theatre opened in 1967. This theatre's policy of presenting plays of "cultural and educational" value secures the continuing support of the Arts Council.

The Group Theatre's establishment in the early 1940s was due primarily to the actor-producer Harold Goldblatt's tenacity in establishing the nucleus of a professional theatre. Its greatest successes were plays written by Ulster authors about Ulster people. The theatre closed for many years and in 1978 was reopened in Bedford Street by Belfast City Council. The city council fully supports this intimate 242 seat theatre, mainly, though not exclusively, at the disposal of the many amateur dramatic societies active in the city and throughout the province. Programmes of the four theatres range across a spectrum from amateur, low cost, local productions at the Group Theatre, to the widely varied, professional, high cost, and mainly imported productions at the Grand Opera House.

Charabanc Theatre is a creative collaboration between an actors' company and a local playwright Martin Lynch; its imaginative use of Belfast working class experience and speech rhythms have been acclaimed in its productions *Lay up your ends*, *Oul delf and false teeth* and *Now you're talking*. Charabanc's reputation was underlined by appearances at the Edinburgh Festival and performances in Glasgow and in Moscow.

In 1980, playwright Brian Friel and actor Stephen Rea created the Field Day Theatre Company which is supported by the Arts Councils in Belfast and Dublin. Field Day Theatre Company aims to forge a theatre company which will rehearse in the North, open in the North, tour in the North, and then tour throughout the whole of Ireland and abroad if circumstances permit. It intends, as well, both to concentrate mainly on smaller venues where theatre is seldom seen and demonstrate that theatre can originate and flourish outside the metropolis and to perform plays of excellence in a distinctively Irish voice that will be heard throughout all of the island and, if they are overheard outside Ireland, so much the better. The first performance staged in the Guildhall, Derry, was the premiere of Brian Friel's *Translations*. An immediate success, the production went on to further acclaim throughout Ireland and then to New York and to London, where it was produced at the National Theatre. This was followed by Chekhov's *Three Sisters* in a new translation by Brian Friel and by annual productions that have included Athol Fugard's *Boesman and Lena*; Tom Paulin's *The Riot Act*, and interpretation of Sophocles' *Antigone* in the light of contemporary Northern Ireland; and *High Time* by Derek Mahon, an updating of Moliere's *The School for Husbands*. The company's most recent production was of a new play by Thomas Kilroy entitled *Double Cross*.

Writing

The considerable local poetic activity of the last twenty and more years, added to the output of novelists, short story writers and playwrights, has

Johnnie Maguire, traditional musician from County Tyrone. (Arts Council)

made an impact both inside and outside the Province. In the sixties the major poetic talents of Seamus Heaney, Michael Longley, John Montague, Derek Mahon, Seamus Deane and James Simmons, emerged to be joined in the seventies by Frank Ormsby, Ciaran Carson, Tom Paulin and Paul Muldoon and then in the eighties by Medbh McGuckian. The established literary magazines such as *The Honest Ulsterman* and *Threshold* continue to hold their own against newcomers like *The Linen Hall Review, North* and *The Belfast Review*. Similarly the Field Day pamphlets which express a "willingness to engage intellectual discussion with political realities" enrich the literary life of the Province. The engaging prose of Benedict Kiely, Michael McLaverty, Jennifer Johnston, John Morrow, Bernard MacLaverty and Brian Moore all demonstrate a flourishing literary imagination. The expanding repretoire of plays by Brian Friel, Graham Reid, Stewart Parker and Frank McGuinness have, in the past two decades, consolidated the theatrical reputation of the Province. Poets and creative writers now have the opportunity to have their work published by local publishing houses and magazines. In the past two decades Blackstaff Press, Appletree Press and Friar's Bush Press have emerged triumphant from a period which was measured elsewhere as the most difficult in the history of publishing.

In recent years many commentators have addressed themselves to the question of this literary renaissance: some attribute it to the current political unrest while others argue that it has happened in spite of politics. Whatever the cause, the Council has been actively engaged in the promotion of literature. The 1985-6 report of the Council gives an indication of its wide range of help in this area. Support was continued for the English Society at Queen's University to enable it to present a programme of readings by writers of local and international importance. Subventions were allocated to aid the publication of the work of a number of local writers. Posts of Writer-in-Residence at the two universities were part-funded by the Council. Financial assistance was given to various literary magazines in the Province which provide an important testing-ground for the novice writer as well as more established talents (Arts Council, 1985-6, 14).

Music

The Ulster Orchestra represents the major contribution to the region's musical life. Since its formation in 1966 it has grown in reputation and has won acclaim from critics and audiences for its concerts, broadcasts, records and tours. The vitality of opera has survived against all odds through its grand opera and chamber opera performances staged by the Northern Ireland Opera Trust and the Studio Opera Group. These two groups have now come together to create a new company. Musical education in schools and colleges is of a high order and the province boasts five youth orchestras, many chamber ensembles, bands and choirs. It is from this environment that famous names have emerged such as sopranos Heather Harper and Norma Burrowes, flautist James Galway and, more recently, pianist Barry Douglas and singer Angela Feeney.

Traditional music continues to flourish throughout Northern Ireland and the songs and tunes that once were sung in rural areas have come to the towns and cities. Traiditions which might have been lost are now more assured of conservation.

Belfast Festival

Since 1962, the Annual Belfast Festival at Queen's has provided two to three weeks of varied cultural events which represent all the arts and display the gifts of local artists and performers. Numerous visiting celebrities also take part in this major cultural occasion. In 1985, for example, the Moscow Radio Symphony Orchestra gave its first concert in Ireland at the Festival. The Abbey, the Royal Shakespeare Company and the National Theatre Company provided the major drama elements of the programme. The Arts Council's direct grant to this event is supplemented by the provision of concerts by the Ulster Orchestra, by performances at the Grand Opera House, and by other events under subsidy from the Council. Nevertheless, the funding of the Festival is achieved through a finely balanced budget, provided by a very large box-office income and substantial sponsorship from a wider range of the community's business and commercial interests. Important financial support also comes from the University and, of course, the University's greatest contribution is the provision of the various auditoria together with a wide range of ancillary services. The Festival is managed by the University through its Arts Centre Board and it is to Queen's University and its Festival Office that the credit must go for sustaining this remarkable annual event.

Conclusion

The position, described by John Hewitt 35 years ago, expanded and developed in the sixties: it continued to grow even more rapidly in the seventies. In all of this the Arts Council, as public patron, has played a key role. Unfortunately the eighties have brought a period of retrenchment, due to financial restraints. Hopefully, there will follow a sound consolidation of developments so far and the beginning of growth again, which will lead to greater artistic achievement and community enjoyment in the 1990s and on into the twenty-first century.

References

Arts Council of Northern Ireland, 1985-6. *Annual report*. Belfast.
Bell, S.H., Robb, N.A., and Hewitt, J. (eds), 1951. *The Arts in Ulster*. London.
Evans, D., 1985. *Images – Arts and people of Northern Ireland*. Belfast.
Longley, M., 1971. *Causeway – The Arts in Ulster*. Belfast.

ACKNOWLEDGEMENTS

Grateful acknowledgements are made to the following for permission to use material under copyright: Faber and Faber, for extract from Simon Winchester, *In holy terror*; Blackstaff Press for quote from John Hewitt, *Conacre*, and for table from Peter Roebuck (ed), *From Plantation to Partition*; Appletree Press for table from R. J. McCormack and R. D. Osborne (eds) *Religion, education and employment; Economic and Social Review* for table from vol. 7, 1; C.E.B. Brett for several quotes from *Housing a divided community*.

For permission to use their photographs we are very grateful to Christopher Hill and N. C. Mitchel. The collection of the late C.F.S. Newman, now in the Institute of Irish Studies, Q.U.B., provided many useful illustrations. The following organisations kindly allowed us to use their photographic material: The Northern Ireland Tourist Board, Belfast City Council, The Queen's University of Belfast, Arts Council of Northern Ireland, the Industrial Development Board, Pacemaker Press Int.L. Ltd, Harland and Wolff and the Northern Ireland Government Information Service.

Many thanks are due to Maura Pringle and Ian and Gill Alexander for their cartographic work. Trevor Molloy gave important assistance in the photographic field. Lorna Goldstrom and Angela White played a vital role in preparing the material for printing. Finally, special thanks are due to Gwen Buchanan who not only gave many hours of invaluable help in copy-editing and proof-reading but was responsible for organising the colour plates and writing the text for them.